Jerry Bauer

About the Author

STEVEN OZMENT is McLean Professor of Ancient and Modern History at Harvard University and the author of *The Bürgermeister's Daughter*; *Flesh and Spirit*; *Ancestors*; *Protestants*; and *The Age of Reform*, a finalist for the National Book Award and winner of the Schaff History Prize. He lives in Newburyport, Massachusetts.

STEVEN OZMENT is McLean Professor of Ancient and Modern History at Harvard University and the author of *The Bürgermeister's Daughter*, *Flesh and Spirit*, *Protestants*, and *The Age of Reform*, a finalist for the National Book Award and winner of the Schaff History Prize. He lives in Cambridge, Massachusetts.

A MIGHTY FORTRESS

A MIGHTY FORTRESS

A NEW HISTORY OF THE GERMAN PEOPLE

STEVEN OZMENT

HARPER PERENNIAL

NEW YORK • LONDON • TORONTO • SYDNEY

A hardcover edition of this book was published in 2004 by Harper-Collins Publishers.

FIRST PERENNIAL EDITION PUBLISHED 2005.

Designed by Elliott Beard

Maps by Adam G. Beaver

Library of Congress Cataloging-in-Publication Data is available upon request.

ISBN 0-06-093483-2 (pbk.)

HB 02.05.2024

To my father,
Dr. Lowell V. Ozment,
and my grandson,
William P. Greenstone

Acknowledgments

WRITING A HISTORY of the German people is a presumptuous task at best, and any who undertake it are properly forewarned and mercifully encouraged. In addition to the scholarly challenge, the modern study of Germany is riven with moral judgments, a historiography quick to typify and slow to forgive. From the beginning, I have received more warning than cheers and at least one prophecy of doom. Fortunately, what one hopes to gain exceeds what might be lost. With a history reaching back to antiquity, yet freshly reborn in the late twentieth century, the Germans have much to teach the present-day world.

In gathering the materials from which *A Mighty Fortress* has been built, I have received helpful guidance and criticism from George and Doris Finley, Victor Davis Hanson, Scott H. Hendrix, H. C. Erik Midelfort, Brennen Pursell, James Charles Roy, Laura Smoller, Frank M. Turner, and Henry A. Turner, Jr. I am especially indebted to the research assistance of Kevin Ostoyich and to the Harvard students who accompanied the book's evolution over three years in History 1302. One of those attending, Adam Beaver, drew the maps. From the beginning, Glen Hartley and Lynn Chu greased the tracks. Tim Duggan, Sue Llewellyn, and John Williams saw the manuscript through the editorial process.

Finally, Rosie and Freddie will never know how much they helped the author, but Susan will.

Contents

Maps

A MIGHTY FORTRESS

Introduction

LOOKING FOR THE GOOD GERMAN

AT A RECENT German-American social gathering, I asked a German table companion, a first-time visitor to the United States, for his impressions. "You Americans have more nice dumb people than any other country," he replied. I still regret not having delivered the perfect rejoinder, which came to me a few minutes later: 58,000,000 Americans can claim full or partial German descent.[1]

Both foreigners and Germans themselves have for centuries observed that Germans are devoted to self-discipline and good order, possess impeccable technical skills, and take pride in their history and culture—yet the same devotion, skill, and pride can border on obsession, compulsiveness, and staggering hubris. This, of course, can also be said of other lands and peoples. In the German case such stories are anecdotal manifestations of a complex and conflicted nation, which, while still a work in progress, has played a central role in European history from its inception. Although few would ever say of the Germans that they saved Western civilization, whenever that civilization has been unusually imperiled or successful, no other people have been more prominently at its center. Germans are among the most difficult Europeans to fathom and the one European people without whom the story of that civilization cannot intelligibly be told. Although often narrowly portrayed in modern historiography, the German story is Sophoclean and Shakespearean as well as Brechtian and Grassian, both a special and a universal history.

Over much of the postwar period, any general discussion of Germany has begun and ended with Hitler and the Nazi seizure of power in 1933. More recently new generations of historians have replaced the role of great men with those of greater structural forces (industrialization, economics, domestic politics), now telling a longer and more complex German story. Also mirroring this historiographical shift is a new generation of German political leaders determined to project their nation as one among others acting in tandem with the great powers of Europe and the world. The result, both historically and in the present, is the promised emergence of a normal Germany.

Despite this more optimistic direction, the legacy of the 1930s and 1940s has proved impossible to shake, its inexplicability, pain, and fascination still stopping people in their tracks, so that the history of Germany remains by and large that of Nazis and Jews. Even today a tour of German history can be a circular journey around a magnetic Nazi pole, mesmerizing the general public and distracting historians and politicians eager to move on. This enduring perspective has also turned Germany's pre-twentieth-century past into a hunting ground for fascist forerunners and defeated democratic alternatives to the absolute territorial state.

Not surprisingly, then, there is popular opinion, even within Germany, which appears to believe that Germans have always been cryptofascists, if only the surface of their history is scratched deeply enough.[2] To that false impression both academic historians and the media contribute, first by continuing to treat the two centuries between Prussia's rise to power and the defeat of the Third Reich as the history of Germany, and second, by reading that history backwards from the Nazi seizure of power in 1933. In the United States the History Channel is popularly known as the "Hitler Channel," so often are *der Führer* and the Third Reich the subjects of its programming, and not a few Americans still unthinkingly interchange Nazis and Germans. Among biographies of historical figures, Adolf Hitler still holds a lock on the most copies in print.

The study of Germany today places one at the crossroads of two contradictory approaches, each looking for precursors and precedents that brought Germany to its twentieth-century pass.[3] The first, older and waning, searches German history for shadows extending to the Third Reich and finds abnormality at seemingly every turn. The other looks instead for the dawning lights of the postwar German Federal Republic of 1949, pointing to numerous precedents and signs in the German past and present. Neither approach, however, has shown much interest in a deep German past before the modern age, to which older generations, academic and non-, had more trustingly turned for clues. Some historians even caricature the effort to examine modern Germany from the perspective of the distant past, calling it the "Tacitus hypothesis."[4] By that is meant a misguided belief that one can properly know a part of German history only as one knows the whole of it—in this case going all the way back to the first historian of Germany, the Roman Cornelius Tacitus, who lived from A.D. 55 to 120.

THE HISTORIANS

In the attempt to explain Germany's rendezvous with National Socialism, three discernible groups of historians both clash with and complement one another. They are the positivists, who believe that the facts and their meaning are self-evident; wounded émigré historians, who write about the German past with an understandable grudge; and, most recently filing in to the historiographical trenches, two generations of liberal-left social historians, a German older (the so-called critical historians) and an Anglo-American younger, who both agree and disagree. The older historians have generally construed their role as that of both physician and antiquarian, devoted not only to reconstructing the past but also to exposing and severing its dead hand from the present. Reflecting the moral imperative that inevitably accompanies the writing of modern German history, the historian's goal has been as much to liberate as to lend perspective.

In the search for culprits the usual suspects have been the most proximate—the post-nineteenth-century Prussian-German empire, with its chauvinism, militarism, and hostility toward liberal democracy, Marxism, and Christianity (especially Catholicism).[5] Farther back in time historians perceive a politically fragmented German empire evolving into a "land of obedience," in the words of Gordon A. Craig, virtually from its inception.[6] Long divided into warring territorial states and taught by a succession of Catholic, Protestant, and Pietist clergy to revere its rulers, the German heartland, in this view, was rendered immune to the Enlightenment ideas of social contract and popular sovereignty by the end of the eighteenth century. The flight to strong man rule had become second nature in the face of crisis. Between such division and passivity, the opportunities for German national unity and political democracy were lacking both early and late.

Germany's putative political and social backwardness has been further magnified by contrast with the revolutionary politics of the United States and France. Critical historians writing in the second half of the twentieth century perceived a disconnect between nineteenth-century Germany's high-profile industrial, economic, and scientific progress and its conservative political and social organization. Between 1830 and 1880 Germany became a land of railways, gaslighted cities, newspapers, and universities, the last being world leaders in the study of history, philosophy, philology, and law. Germans were even more dominant in medicine, physiology, biology, chemistry, and physics, with German scientists making seventy new medical discoveries to the rest of the world's fifty-five between 1860 and 1879.[7]

Yet, at the same time, Germans emigrated in ever-increasing numbers to the United States, South America, Canada, and Australia. Between 1850 and 1870, after a half century of reactionary politics and the failure of a native democracy movement, 1,700,000 Germans emigrated to the United States amid growing fears of social discrimination and religious persecution by their government.[8] There, as a popular German guide to America described it, the new arrivals entered a land where "fewer privileges are given to birth than to individual talent and energy, and no princes and their corrupt courts represent the so-called 'divine right of kings.'"[9]

The critical historians laid the blame for Germany's retrograde politics at the feet of a feckless German middle class. Not only had the once promising burghers failed to displace entrenched Junkers, bureaucrats, and army officers with a new democratic regime, they became progressively subject to them. The new Germany simply could not break the grip of the old. Over the course of the nineteenth century and into the twentieth, the middle class is said to have swapped its democratic enthusiasms for nationalist and imperialist ones. In doing so they joined the old elites in undermining the development of a democratic Germany on the American, British, or French model. So overpowering, in this interpretation, was the long German past that the first steps toward German political modernization had to be imposed from the outside by the more enlightened French. But for Napoleon and the French occupation of the German Rhineland in the late eighteenth and early nineteenth centuries, Germany would have remained a politically fragmented, medieval society of fixed estates.[10]

The Good Burgher

More recent historians reject such bleak and sweeping judgments of German history. Rather they point to persisting segments of an enlightened and progressive nineteenth century German civic society. Particularly contested has been the criticism of the German middle class as pushovers. In cautious, detailed studies a more complex and progressive German society has emerged, its middle class more successful than older historians had claimed, mirroring its counterparts in other European states. Although not as prominent and influential, a middle-class revolution was also occurring in Germany, elaborating individual rights—property, work, association, speech, patronage, philanthropy—and the rule of law.[11] Through the combined efforts of civil servants, entrepreneurs, and political leaders, a modern Germany was coming abreast of the old.

Despite the limited nature of this revolution and its suppression in the 1920s and 1930s, it resembled Europe's contemporary democracies. Its success suggests that the road to National Socialism was not direct and inevitable; also that the greater progress of other European states did not necessarily make them immune to what later happened in Germany, given a convergence of crises of the magnitude of those that struck there.[12] At the very least this more sympathetic reading of the German nineteenth century reveals a society more complex than the alleged "anteroom of Nazism" portrayed by other historians.[13]

Another victim of this revision has been a kindred attempt to extrapolate a special totalitarian path from Germany's geographical position as Europe's centerland, leaving it unprotected on at least two frontiers (three when Austria was removed from the states composing the German empire). Historically that geographical position made Germany both a perch and a pit, as easy to prey from as to prey on, hence, an optimal as well as a vulnerable location. Because that position was as conducive to being a raider as a victim, neither an apologetic history of geographical determinism, nor a critical one of unprovoked expansionism, does justice to the complexity of German history.[14]

Coloring History

Rescuing that more complex Germany from the gloomy moralizing of post–World War II historiography was also the task of the late German historian Thomas Nipperdey, the great critic of the critical historians. Having begun his career as a Reformation historian, he had the advantage of perspective and precedent. He also believed that reliable history must be written forward chronologically, from past to present, not from present to past, as so much postwar historiography was inclined to do. It is one thing to know the end of a story and to be moved by it to learn the whole story, and quite another to tell that story from its known outcome. "In the beginning was Napoleon," Nipperdey deadpanned in the first line of a multivolume history of Germany.[15] Modern German history began with the French defeat of Austria and Prussia in 1805–6 and occupation of the German Rhineland—not with Hitler's chancellorship, which provides few clues to what came before it. If 1933 is taken as the first page of modern German history, it will most likely be the last word on it.

No one, however, doubts that the past casts powerful shadows on the present, and more recent decades more powerful ones. The line running from imperial German elites to Field Marshal Paul von Hindenburg's presidency of the Weimar Republic is straight and clear, as are those also between Wilhelmine chauvinism and the party factionalism of the 1920s and 1930s. But fear of anarchistic and hyphenated Germans, who have a prior allegiance to a kingdom beyond the fatherland, existed among Germans since the Middle Ages. In the nineteenth and twentieth centuries Catholics loyal to Rome, revolutionary Marxists, and Jews successful beyond their numbers in the population became their modern incarnations.

Although Nipperdey appreciated the novelty of the nineteenth century, he saw no syndrome in such continuity—the history of modern Germany was not a progressive genetic disease. German fascism and National Socialism were instead "something new," neither reducible to, nor derived whole cloth from, what had preceded them. From the antiauthoritarian communal movements of the Reformation era to the short-lived democracy movement of the nineteenth century, the German past had known alternative forms of political organization. That fourteen of the twenty-five European democracies existing in 1919 had fallen by 1938 makes it clear that Germany was not the only nation to falter along the road to democracy.[16]

The larger lesson of these critiques of post–World War II historiography is twofold. Reading history from present to past is reading into it rather than learning from it. And equally distorting is the belief that history can be read as black and white. It is, as Nipperdey described, "homogenous, ambivalent [and] filled with contradictions that can never be resolved. Reality is not a system in which everything is uniformly arranged [but is] moved along by conflicts other than those a 'continuity perspective' selects—conflicts that do not fall neatly into progressive/anti-progressive, or democratic/undemocratic, categories."[17]

Despite compelling evidence of German normality in the decades before World War I, this debate, as in all things German, remains polarized. To his critics Nipperdey was no white knight dispelling a black legend, but an apologist bent on whitewashing a near century of German fascism in response to a united Germany's wish to diminish a painful part of German history. For Nipperdey critic Richard J. Evans, the pressing issue was whether a sizable segment of the German past might be "exculpated" from responsibility for the 1920s and 1930s.[18] More disturbing still was Nipperdey's acknowledgment of continuity between imperial Germany and National Socialism, yet refusal to proclaim them two peas in a pod.[19] Convinced that the color of history is a shade of gray, mixed and contradictory, Nipperdey was as loath to equate shadow with substance as he was to deny shadows. By that logic imperial Germany, the Weimar Republic, National Socialism, the Third Reich, and the present-day Federal Republic must, in the end, speak for themselves, one able neither to convict nor to exonerate another.

In siding with the critical historians, Evans, a Briton, was understandably more forgiving of those who would tar a large segment of German history with the Nazi brush than of those who would absolve any possibly complicit part. The belief that true but disproportionate measures of good and evil exist in every historical age meets a supreme test in '30s and '40s Germany. By Nipperdey's logic those decades would seem to have been as morally mixed as any others, and properly studied as such. That, however, is something many who cannot forget or forgive the horrors of those years find problematic and even blasphemous.

With many now convinced that a reading of the German past from the perspective of the 1930s is a flawed and outdated approach, a more objective and sympathetic reconstruction of that history is being written.[20] With every new generation of Germans, the tragedies of the 1930s and 1940s become, as it were, less German. Because Germany, like any other land, is the people who live and work there in any given age, Germans born after those dark decades will not readily allow their lives to be dictated by them. That accusations of whitewashing Nazism could greet Nipperdey's efforts to move this discussion forward is a reminder of the moral challenge facing anyone who would put a hand to that plow.[21]

THE POLITICIANS

At their inception in 1949, the new governments of East and West Germany had reason to put 1933 at the center of German history: Both the German Democratic Republic (GDR) and the Federal Republic of Germany (FRG) legitimated their rule by aligning themselves as closely as possible with the anti-Nazi resistance. In the GDR the Communist Party proclaimed itself the "original enemy" of National Socialism and, as such, claimed the right to continue "the legacy of the best German people." The FRG also had martyr's blood to show, which it did both to establish legitimacy and to remind Germany's conquerors, who made scant distinction between Nazis and Germans, that an alternative Germany had existed throughout Hitler's reign.[22]

Given the Allies' own political experience and low expectations of Germans, their crude notion of collective guilt was understandable and not completely misplaced. The most conspicuous act of German resistance to which the FRG appealed for its moral authority was the Stauffenberg plot to assassinate Hitler in 1944.[23] Those behind the plot were not liberal democrats. They believed no more in liberal democracy than they did in National Socialism, and understandably so given the nature of the democratic era they had lived through. These were men in the tradition of Paul von Hindenburg, the second president of the Weimar Republic, who would have let Hitler rot in obscurity in 1932 had his government been able to form a majority coalition without National Socialist support.[24] Like Hindenburg, the Stauffenberg plotters hated Hitler and the populist democracy of the late 1920s and early 1930s that brought him to power and kept him there. Had their plot succeeded, their new government would not have put a Churchill or a Roosevelt in his place, nor would it have agreed to any peace that did not return Germany to its pre–World War I borders and recognize its supreme sovereignty within Europe.[25]

That, however, is not a point stressed in the German government's official version of Germany's path over the last two centuries. Like the historians, whose occupation is looking back, the German government, mandated by the voting public to look forward, has its own German story to tell. Duty bound to move its citizens into a doable future rather than leave them stranded in an unmasterable past, the government story is one about lights rather than shadows.

The political challenge finds succinct expression in *Facts About*

Germany, the annual publication of the German government available at German embassies around the world. In addition to providing land-by-land accounts (German states are called *Länder*; singular, *Land*) of present-day Germany's economic, political, and cultural development, *Facts* provides an official abstract of two thousand years of German history.[26] In the most recent editions that history begins with a nod to the first-century Cherusci prince Arminius, better known to Germans as Hermann, whose lone German legion famously defeated three Roman ones in A.D. 9, and it ends with a sober discussion of the costs of German unification.

Keynoting that history in the 1999 anniversary edition are three excerpts taken literally from the "nines"—special years for a reunited Germany looking back at the turn of the twentieth century. The first years are those of the Frankfurt National Assembly, which proclaimed, but did not secure, democratic freedom and equality for German citizens in 1848–49. The second, 1919, saw the creation of the Weimar Republic, which, in this telling, took up where the Frankfurt assembly left off, giving women the vote for the first time and seating forty-one in the new German parliament, a still unmatched percentage.[27] Yet the Weimar Republic ended with Hitler's seizure of power by the very laws it had legislated. The final anniversary year, 1949, marks a free parliament's ratification of a new German constitution, the Basic Law, which included new safeguards against the recurrence of totalitarian rule.[28]

To these modern milestones of German democracy *Facts* adds the fall of the Berlin Wall in 1989 and the unification of the two Germanies in 1990 in further recognition of democracy's belated triumph. And taking a still longer view of German history, it notes democratic straws in the wind as far back as the seventeenth century, when the first pan-European assemblies met in the German cities of Münster and Osnabrück to negotiate the international peace that ended the Thirty Years' War.[29]

In the politicians' view, these years of "nine" attest to the dogged history of the good Germany, which has survived seemingly insurmountable challenges to become, at last, a modern liberal democracy. Like many historians the politicians also believe that their nation has been on a special historical path—an uphill battle against fascism and totalitarianism, whose defeat and rejection make clear that Germany's true political destiny was always the Federal Republic of 1949 and not the Nazi state of 1933. No longer the ugly German trapped in a circular history of promising starts and perilous stops, this good German has held his own since at least the mid–nineteenth century, keeping the flame of German unity and democracy alive.

The Tacitus Challenge

Today Germany is a unified democratic republic and a model liberal welfare state. A pacesetter in international business and trade throughout its history (one of the blessings of its geography), it has recently mastered the art of the hostile takeover.[30] Displaying its willingness to assume the responsibilities of a great power, it has joined Western states in peacekeeping missions in Bosnia and Afghanistan, while balking—as a powerful, normal nation may—at American and British action in Iraq.

Yet the past continues to haunt it. In the earliest centuries of their history, the label "barbarian" was lastingly stuck on the Germanic tribes by the Romans—this despite their comparable and even superior skills as warriors and promise as the new leaders of a post-Roman European civilization. Today Germans still must deal with opprobrious labels reminding the world of a more recent and different barbarism. From the latter neither the most sympathetic ally nor any foreign power can give safe refuge. More righteously than in earlier centuries, not a few in the outside world still wag a finger at Germans, who may understandably believe themselves to be unfairly portrayed and held back as a nation.

Like all nations that take their destiny into their own hands, a reunified Germany must also confront its history. Because that history has been alternately Western Europe's most successful and threatening, the world understandably holds its breath when Germans take counsel with themselves. Many shudder today at the expressed intent of the German chancellor to conduct the affairs of his state unsentimentally, just like any other great power in Europe. Might these be rumblings of an old German culture preparing to return to the warrior days of blood and iron? In such moments it may be consoling to remember that Germany's history has been an alternating current, not a steady stream flowing in only one direction; also that its record of civility and creativity is longer than that of its inhumanity and destructiveness.

A new guild of social historians, more hospitable to at least a segment of the modern German past, has brought a bit of balance to a postwar historiography long disposed to muckrake and accuse. In this these historians have something in common with recent German governments, which are also determined to move Germany forward as the modern nation of consequence it has been and retains a right to be. However, if there is cause to rejoice over a fuller and fairer telling of the German story, there is also reason to lament the postwar visions that continue to be projected, both in fear and in fancy, onto its future. On the one hand there remains Germany the eternal land of obedience, with its documented modern history of aggression and totalitarianism. On the other there is Germany the prostrate penitential state, an idealized egalitarian democracy with its gates thrown open to all, as portrayed by Günter Grass.[31] Each of these options projects an abject German people, on their knees either out of docility and fear of their rulers or in utopian self-sacrifice—highly unlikely future scenarios for the latter-day survivors of the twentieth century.

Over most of their history Germans have embraced ideals of order and authority without totalitarianism, and pursued freedom and equality without liberal democracy. The German difference from the American, British, and French models of society and politics does not lie in any German rejection of individual freedom in favor of absolute, or totalitarian, rule.[32] Historical experience has instead left Germans more fearful of anarchy than of tyranny, inclining them to hedge, if hedge they must, on the side of good order. This they have done in a compelling belief that it is not freedom, once attained, but discipline, carefully maintained, that keeps a people free.

For Germans the Weimar Republic and National Socialism were novel twentieth-century experiments, not familiar historic lifestyles. Emerging from the failure of its first democratic government, whose lifespan was a mere fourteen years, 1919–33, Germany's first totalitarian government endured for only twelve, 1933–45. While historians see parallels to the former in the revolution of 1848–49, and to the latter in Wilhelmine Germany, modern Germany's most prominent feature remains the novelty of democracy and totalitarianism in its historical experience.

All of which poses questions. Can a more than 2,000-year-old civilization be defined by its last 150 years? Who were the Germans before 1848 and 1933? Does the long history leading up to these disparate watershed events contribute anything to understanding them today? Accepting the "Tacitus challenge," this book attempts to survey and interpret the formative history of Germans as far back as relevant information can reasonably be found. Whatever else may be said of Germans today, they have survived their enemies and themselves, seemingly against all odds. How they have done so lies embedded in that long history.

I

FROM FIRST TRIBES TO FIRST EMPIRE

1

THE BARBARIAN COMPLEX

Roman-German Relations in Antiquity

GERMANIC TRIBES established themselves in the eastern Rhine valley by the mid–first century B.C., by which time the term "German" (*Germani*, *Germania*) was used by the Romans.[1] At this time the tribes were neither racially uniform nor transregionally united but composites, "loose and shifting amalgams of peoples," who formed no coherent Germanic front. Quickly settling, they lived within, or along the borders of, the Roman Empire by agreement with the Romans, swapping their services as soldiers, farmers, and tax collectors for land and security.[2] Of these tribes the Franks, Goths, and Lombards developed historical identities by allying with leading, or royal, families and embracing their genealogical myths.[3]

In these centuries non-Germanic tribes shared a similar barbarian experience within the Roman Empire, which casts light on the Germanic. From the start polyethnic tribes, Germanic and non-, demonstrated an ability to accommodate and incorporate the ancient Roman and Byzantine worlds. Roughly five centuries after their appearance, Romanized and Christianized Germanic tribes would raise a new, middle European empire and culture from the ashes of the old Roman one. Between the rule of the Merovingian Frank Clovis in the late fifth and early sixth centuries and that of the Saxon Conrad in the early tenth, Germanic cultures melded with Greco-Roman, Roman Christian, and Byzantine to create the Western Europe we know today.

ROMANIZING GERMANS

A trail begins in 113 B.C., when a Germanic tribe, the Cimbri, crossed the Roman frontier of Noricum, modern Austria, in a typically frustrated tribal search for food and land, and for the first time confronted and defeated a Roman army. Four years later, in 109 B.C., the same tribe, joined by another, the Teutones, appeared in southern Gaul and vanquished a major Roman army sent to turn them back. In 105 B.C. the tribes returned in still greater numbers, this time defeating two consular armies in one of ancient Rome's great military losses. By this point the Romans respected the threat of the barbarians probing their frontiers and sent a powerful new army to beat them.[4]

Among the early observers of the tribes when the migrations resumed was Julius Caesar, the recent conqueror of Gaul, who described their governance as informal and inconsistent, their society communal and egalitarian, their military tactics haphazard and "ignoble," the latter a reference to their ability to "compose" on the battlefield (that is, surprise and ambush). The tribes were ruled by "leading men" (in West German dialect, *kuning*, "leaders of the family"), whom the Romans variously called *principes*, *duces*, and *reges*. Chosen by an assembly of noble and common warriors (the tribal host), only the most outstanding men, as determined by royal birth, family service, and exceptional valor, might hold that exalted position.[5]

Insinuation and Rebellion

Over the last decades of the old millennium and the first of the new Christian Era, the Romans diminished the threat the tribes posed by brutally punishing their forays and finding ways to divide and coopt them.[6] Among the latter were simple human temptations. For stretches up to perhaps thirty miles on either side of the Roman frontier, Roman and Germanic people mixed regularly with one another.[7] Roman language, culture, and politics came to the tribes on the wheels of trading carts, as Germans exchanged cattle and slaves (the booty of battle with foreign tribes) for Roman bronzes, glassware, and furs. Before contact with the Romans, tribal leaders ruled more by persuasion than by coercion and maintained social peace by equitable divisions of land and wealth within the tribe. The new wealth gained from trade with the Romans worked to stratify tribal society, setting new rich against poor and encouraging disproportionate divisions of tribal land. Rome's autocratic government and senatorial lifestyle also impressed future tribal leaders, many of whom were educated in Rome.

Another obstructive Roman tactic was to encourage intertribal conflict, to which the tribes were already predisposed. In the eyes of their enemies, the barbarians' great strength was also a great weakness—namely, their lip-smacking taste for battle, which Tacitus, with some exaggeration, described as "a reluctance to accumulate slowly by sweat . . . what could be gotten quickly by the loss of a little blood."[8] That warrior spirit turned the tribes against one another before the Romans interfered, creating intertribal fissures for their enemies to probe. Over time, devotion to factional leaders rather than to duly elected ones, and the placement of group gain over tribal welfare, created freelancing retinues within the tribes. These were tight-knit gangs that gained superior status by raiding neighboring tribes for cattle, slaves, and other wealth-producing loot. Their victims retaliated against the tribe as a whole, adding foreign aggression to the internal disruptions caused by the retinues. Such native anarchy and tyranny also gave the Romans a foothold within the tribes, allowing them to bypass the protective order of leading men and warrior assemblies.[9]

Finally the Romans sought to have their way with the tribes by transplanting the sons of leading men to Rome, where, to their material benefit, they grew up as Romans. Such transplantation was both by invitation and by hostage taking. Selected elite barbarians were in this way Romanized, many thereafter residing in Rome for the remainder of their lives, while others returned to their homelands as assimilated servants of the Roman Empire.[10] It would be too much to call these repatriated tribesmen brainwashed, since as a rule they served the Roman Empire willingly, gaining new land and wealth for themselves while continuing to enjoy membership in the cosmopolitan Roman world. Where these pro-Roman chieftains survived their tribal enemies, they also helped make the barbarian world less threatening to Romans.[11] As a result of such tactics and measures, most barbarians, Germanic and non-, living along or within the Roman frontiers, chose service over challenge before the fourth century.

The Cherusci

The checkered history of four generations of noble Cherusci leaders illustrates both Roman success and failure at turning the barbarians against themselves. This was the tribe of military chieftain Arminius, who in his mid-twenties commanded the Germanic contingent of the imperial Roman army from A.D. 4 to 6, for which service he won laurels and Roman citizenship. In A.D. 9, Arminius led his warriors against three Roman legions then roaming the province of Germania under the command of provincial governor Publius Quinctilius Varus. Employing misdirection and ambush, what would later be called *blitzkrieg*, Arminius's legion won a never-forgotten victory in Teutoberg Forest, which ended Roman plans for further expansion of their empire east of the Rhine.[12] (His nineteenth-century monument in Hechingen-Stein is still much visited by Germans today.) Fifteen centuries later, in the age of the printing press, German humanists and nationals discovered and published Tacitus's *History of Germany* and proclaimed Arminius Germany's "liberator" and his victories the birth of German history.[13]

Why did Rome's investment in Arminius not pay off? At the time of his revolt, Cherusci tribesmen smarted under Roman taxation and justice, and, like Arminius, many saw only subservience in their future. For three generations Arminius's family seesawed between tribal and Roman loyalty yet never rebelled. Knowing of Arminius's plans in advance, his vexed father-in-law, Segestes, a lifelong servant of Rome, betrayed the rebels to the Romans on the night before the attack. Arminius's brother Flavius was equally loyal to Rome. When, in A.D. 15, the Romans sent the great army of Germanicus to punish the Cherusci, he and his federated army marched with them. Flavius's son, future Cherusci leader Italicus, Roman-born and groomed, returned to the tribe as a loyal Roman watchdog, where his autocratic rule incited a revolt that led to his banishment.

Despite similar Roman indoctrination, military success, and the highest position of trust in the Roman army, Arminius retained his tribal loyalty. Yet, in the end, he too succumbed to autocrat fever, attempting in A.D. 19 to rule the Cherusci in the Roman manner. In the name of tribal freedom, a Chatti tribal leader took up arms against him. Ultimately Arminius died at the hands of his own kinsmen, who, although prepared to fight Roman and barbarian alike, could not abide a tyrant, even a great tribal hero, within their camp.[14]

The Cherusci example makes clear that the fracturing of tribal society was not the doing of the Romans alone. For all the breathtaking brutality Romans might display, they also confronted the tribes on their borders with civility and opportunity. The tribes they infiltrated were seducible and complicit, not a few ready to act for personal gain. For this reason Tacitus, who honored the Germanic tribes by giving them a history of their own, and in some respects even held them up as a mirror to the Romans, portrayed the Germans with a mixture of praise and criticism a complex people deserves.

Commodities

In addition to their perceived racial purity, Tacitus also praised the tribes for monogamy, spousal equality in marriage, strong family ties, and a basic respect for women (one tribe, the Sitones, he asserted, treated women as the "ruling sex"). He found them loyal and honorable in both peace and war and credited them with having taught the Romans "more lessons" than any other enemy.[15] Yet Tacitus also pinpointed a major flaw in their character: a penchant for peril over peace. He found it telling that tribesmen always attended their assemblies and conducted trade and other business "fully armed," also that they trained their children thoroughly in the use of arms, the bearing of which was to the adolescent barbarian what the toga was to the adolescent Roman: a badge of manhood. The tribes' warring nature was further attested by their behavior in peacetime, when they either hunted or did nothing at all.

On the other hand Tacitus's Germans were the most guileless of contemporary people, so lacking in cunning and sophistication that they "blurted out their inmost thoughts . . . every soul [laying itself] bare." He observed the same naïveté in their hospitality, which permitted guests to request whatever they wanted from the home of a host, while the host was free in return to ask offerings of guests.[16] Although he praised the tribes, he also believed them to be inferior to the Romans. He described the Batavi, a compliant people settled within the empire whom he thought to be the bravest of them all, as "weapons and armor to be used only in war."[17] That condescending treatment of barbarians, as implements for tilling Roman fields and collecting taxes in peacetime while fighting Roman battles in time of war, was largely the barbarian experience within the empire.

If the sons of tribal leaders and other high-ranking foreigners became notable exceptions to that rule, other barbarians could look back on four centuries of discrimination, cruelty, and exploitation at Roman hands. The impoverished Frisians, for example, who came under Roman rule in the first quarter century, rebelled in A.D. 28 to protest the mounting tribute exacted from them. Having begun with animal hides, Roman demands escalated to entire herds, stretches of homeland, even wives and children.[18] Three centuries later, in 376, two hundred thousand Goths, stampeded from their eastern homelands by the Huns, arrived on Rome's Danubian frontier begging for food and land, only to discover that the conditions of settlement could still be draconian. There was now, however, one large difference: By the fourth century Rome's ability to enforce its will on the tribes had greatly diminished, making 376 a prelude to a world-changing confrontation between Romania and Barbaricum (Gothia).

BARBARIZING ROME

If during the last century of the old millennium and the first three of the new, Romans successfully intermingled with and managed Germanic tribes living on and within their borders, the fourth century saw those tribes, now joined by westward migrating Huns, Avars, Alans, and Magyars (Hungarians), challenge the Romans in similar and even more successful ways. Tribes settling along the Rhenish and Danubian frontiers still did so either by special permission, or as conquered, subject people. Their official status remained that of sojourners (*peregrini*), not citizens (*cives*), and they remained on the frontier in safety only to the extent that they became reliable Roman federates (*foederati*). Learning their military lessons well (for the most part, civil service careers were off-limits to non-Romans), assimiliated barbarians continued to earn Roman citizenship and gain other honors for their services.

Citizenship gave affiliated tribes the same legal protections and rights as native-born Italians. Yet, despite acculturation and success, Romanized barbarians, whether Africans, Germans, or Jews, could still find themselves treated as inferiors in the imperial city. That was especially true of the first generation to undergo assimilation. And while the Roman senate looked on tribal elites as occupying the same high position in native societies that senators held in Rome, there was no thought of parity between Roman and barbarian, only the recognition of a parallel aristocracy that was useful, and dangerous, to Rome.[19]

For the Romanized barbarian, life in Rome could be an ambivalent experience. While social acceptance might come after full Latin fluency and the fading of native languages and customs, the transplanted barbarian was often, in the Roman perception, a "hyphenated" Roman, and high profile success could put him in double jeopardy. There were, first, jealous rivals in Rome, who might think his ancestral, or tribal, loyalty to be greater than that to Rome, a suspicion also faced by Romanized Jews and Christians. And the Romanized barbarian also had reason to worry about his fellow tribesmen at home, who were even quicker to perceive in him a foreign lackey come to play the native despot.[20]

In the legally conformed yet still divided and culturally mixed world of Roman antiquity, barbarian-Romans were neither fish nor fowl. As barbarians they remained potential enemies of the empire, while as assimilated warriors and commanders they won Roman honors by fighting other tribes on Rome's behalf. Those living on the borders, most often without citizenship, particularly found themselves in an identity crisis. Whether an intact tribe in Germania untouched by the Romans, a federated tribe on the frontier in frequent contact with them, or an assimilated barbarian citizen pursuing a career in Rome, barbarians had reason to be wary.

Barbarians Ascendant

When Julius Caesar observed Germanic tribes in battle in the mid-first century B.C., he thought them undisciplined. But 150 years later, Tacitus cited Germanic victories over Roman legions as well as tribal rivals, describing synchronized infantry and cavalry units maneuvering in wedge-shaped formations, as naked, or lightly clad, foot soldiers ran abreast of charging horses. Between Caesar's observations in 51 B.C. and Tacitus's in A.D. 98, the Germans, instructed by the Romans, had proved to be fast learners.[21]

In the first half of the second century, a Roman army of 300,000 might still protect the fifty million people living in the Mediterranean basin.[22] Cracks, however, were opening along the Danubian and eastern frontiers where Rome met Barbaricum. By midcentury the empire's network of border forts and walls required intensive refortification. In the course of one signal year, A.D. 166, twenty-five tribes probed the Roman frontier in a foreshadowing of what the future held for the empire.[23] By the third century, Rome was becoming its own worst enemy, as internal rebellions and civil wars (235–84) forced legions to be withdrawn from an increasingly porous frontier to ensure stability at home. By the last quarter of the third century, barbarians crossed eastern Roman borders unopposed, compelling Rome to accelerate the integration of barbarian chieftains and armies into its military.[24]

During the reigns of Constantine and his successors, Franks, Alemanni, Goths, and Saxons were drafted into federated service. They replaced Roman soldiers recalled from the frontier for home defense and became part of a new mobile strike force (*comitatus*) created to confront new tribes testing the empire's perimeters.[25] Amid these changes the burning question was whether Rome's forces, in any configuration, were strong enough to deter the new barbarian armies on the eastern front. Two failed campaigns by the imperial army of the East answered that question. The first was to stop westward Persian expansion near Maranga on the Tigris, and

Barbarian Migrations into the Roman Empire, 300–500

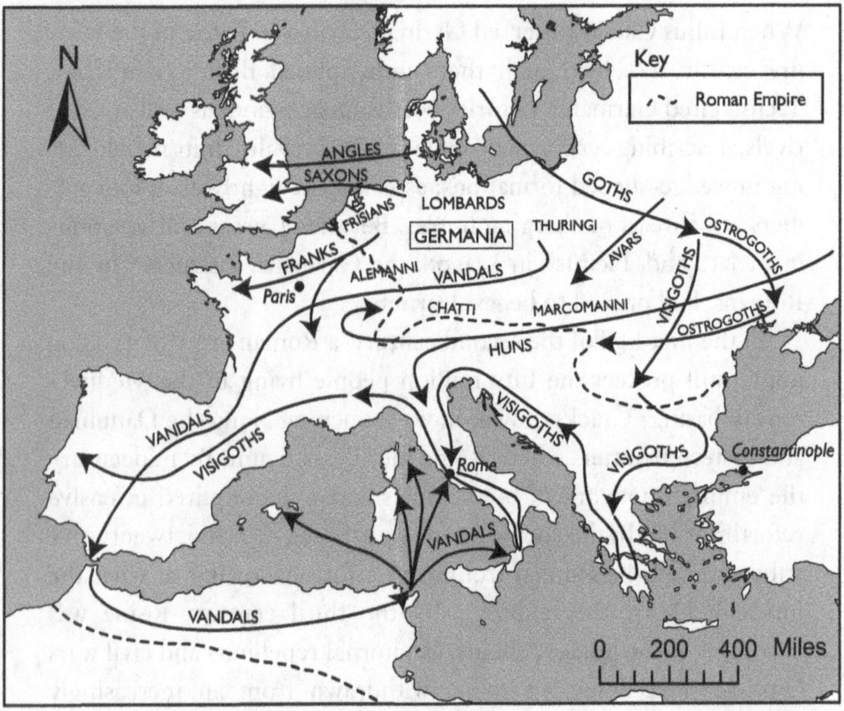

left the emperor Julian the Apostate dead on the battlefield with his defeated army. The second, and more fateful, was a preemptive strike against Visigoths (Goths who crossed the empire from east to west in the fourth century, ultimately settling in Spain) at Adrianople, northwest of present-day Istanbul.

The chain of events leading to Adrianople documents the barbarian-Roman conflict at its extreme. Led by their king Fritigern, impoverished and vulnerable Visigoths crossed the Roman frontier in 376 on the run from the Huns, who were also destined to engage the Romans. Like all foreign tribes settling legally within the empire, the Visigoths agreed to become Roman subjects and servants. They arrived, however, at a time when harried Roman armies had their fill of barbarian migrants. Coming in numbers and haste too great to allow proper processing and supervision by Roman officials, starving Goths were offered the rations of the meat of one dog for each child surrendered up to the Roman slave market.[26]

The result was a Gothic rampage, joined by other barbarians similarly settled within the empire, who, in the description of contemporary Roman historian Ammianus Marcellinus, "sprang from their cages . . . like savage beasts."[27] As the sixth-century chronicler Jordenes, who was of either Gothic or Alanic descent, remembered the event, the Goths "put an end to the[ir] famine . . . and [to] the safety of the Romans. . . . No longer as strangers and pilgrims, but as citizens and lords, [they] began to rule the inhabitants and to hold in their own right all the north country as far as the Danube."[28]

Although neither Roman nor Goth recognized it at the time, this conflict was the first step toward a barbarian reconfiguration of the late ancient world into independent tribal kingdoms, the lion's share of which would be Frankish.[29]

On a steamy August 9, 378, Emperor Valens, overly confident of his superiority, led elite Roman troops, perhaps 35,000 strong, most wearing heavy armor, against Fritigern's allied Gothic and Alanic forces, which outnumbered him an estimated threefold and employed superior battle tactics. Wounded and discovered in a hut where he had crawled to safety, the emperor was cremated in it by his captors, his ashes scattered on the battlefield, where two-thirds of his army lay dead.[30]

Two years later, in 380, and again in 382, the Visigoths, as treatied federates of Rome, returned to their southeastern Danubian homelands to create a state of their own within the empire. This allowed Rome's version of orthodox Christianity to sweep the Western Empire, as the Visigoths had been converted to Arian, or anti-Trinitarian, Christianity. Also, in the aftermath of Adrianople, the way was cleared for Germanic tribes, whose warriors now held virtually every senior military position in the Roman army,[31] to solidify their hegemony over the West.

GERMANS OVER THE TOP

Silvanus and Arbogast

In the second half of the fourth century, two Romanized Franks, each holding the highest Roman military rank of army commander, *magister militum*, usurped the thrones of the emperors they served. The first was Silvanus, military commander in Gaul during the 350s and the first Frank before Charlemagne to become emperor, albeit by forcibly removing the reigning Constantius II. The second imperial usurper, bolder still, was Arbogast, military commander in the West after 388, who, having slain the western emperor, Valentinian II, expected the eastern emperor, Theodosius the Great, to make him the new emperor in his place. Theodosius refused on the grounds that Arbogast was a Frank and a pagan. In response Arbogast's army, the true ruler in the West, recognized their commander's own pliant choice, a politically inexperienced teacher of rhetoric, as new emperor.

Both Sylvanus and Arbogast held imperial power briefly, illegally, and at the cost of their lives—Silvanus being slain by his own soldiers and Arbogast at the instruction of Theodosius. Yet their stories were cautionary for the Romans, who had not yet seen the last, or most powerful, barbarian chieftain.[32]

Stilicho and Alaric

The Romans were still strong enough to win a last victory over the tribes, briefly defeating Attila the Hun at Chalons in 451. Although modern historians do not date Rome's fall until 476, the fate of the empire had been sealed by the turn of the fourth century. Two Germans, each at the pinnacle of their respective worlds, and progressively mortal enemies, presided over the most decisive phase of that decline and fall. One was the Romanized half-Vandal Stilicho, the other the Visigoth Alaric. Stilicho commanded the Imperial Army of the West and was virtual emperor there, while Alaric's lineage reached back to the Balths (the Bold), an ancient Germanic royal family.[33]

Stilicho's father had been a Vandal cavalry officer in the Imperial Army of the East, and his mother was a native Roman. From those lowly beginnings he rose to marry the adopted niece of Emperor Theodosius. That dynastic connection enabled Stilicho to rise to the position of military commander in the West. Thereafter Theodosius made Stilicho regent for his ten-year-old son, Honorius, future emperor of the West, who would in turn draw the family circle tighter by marrying two of Stilicho's daughters.[34] Had invading Goths not spoiled their plans, Honorius's sister, Galla Placidia, betrothed to Stilicho's son, Eucherius, would have added still another dynastic link to this deeply intertwined Roman-Vandal family.[35]

By contrast Alaric the Goth had no such prestigious contemporary connections. Pursuing his destiny doggedly, he ultimately wreaked havoc on both Stilicho and Rome.[36] The two armies clashed for the first time in 392, and but for Rome's need of the Goths' federated military services, Alaric would have been summarily executed on the battlefield with his fallen army. In 394 his forces joined those of Emperor Theodosius in punishing Arbogast at the Battle of Frigid River (in what is now Slovenia). There, the famous Goth lost ten thousand men—half of his army—on the first day.[37] While Alaric expected a generalship, and his warriors land, for such sacrifice, they received only more imperial shunning.

Their disappointment erupted in another Gothic rampage that brought Stilicho and Alaric back onto the battlefield. In the intervening period Theodosius had died, and Stilicho, now regent, commanded both imperial armies, East and West, by any contemporary measure the world's most powerful man. After defeating Alaric's army again, he gave the Goths a new homeland in Macedonia in 397 and made Alaric *magister militum* of Roman Illyria. By such appeasement he hoped to retain the services of the Goths against the next barbarian wave to roll across the empire. But in typical

Roman treatment of barbarians, he denied Alaric civilian authority, preventing the establishment of a true Gothic state in any proximity to Rome.[38]

Torn between the roles of halfhearted affiliate and enraged rebel, Alaric returned to Italy in the first decade of the fifth century, drawing the hot pursuit of Stilicho's barbarian federates and suffering more costly defeats. However, after new barbarian invasions in northern Italy and Gaul threatened rebellion in Rome and the emperor's overthrow in 405–6, Alaric was called back to Italy to stay. As the price of rescuing the besieged emperor, he demanded four thousand pounds of gold, which Stilicho instructed the Roman senate to pay—a bitter pill for the senators, who thought barbarians had been paid too much for too little too long. While Alaric got what he wanted, Stilicho and his peaceably settled kin were made to pay even more for it. In 408 a Gothic rival of Alaric and recent affiliate of Emperor Honorius, Sarus, toppled and executed the half-Vandal Stilicho. The action released pent-up Roman resentment and moved the Roman senate to its own barbarous revenge: a massacre of thousands of barbarians living peacefully in Italy.[39]

In the aftermath non-Romans by the tens of thousands joined Alaric's army for the first of three marches on Rome. Blockading the city's grain imports, Alaric demanded all the city's portable wealth.[40] Between the first and second sieges in the fall of 409, it became clear that Alaric and his army wanted recognition as Rome's equal, demanding provinces of their own in Noricum, where they might try again to create a Gothic state. Having everything to lose by that concession, the emperor temporized, counting on the imperial armies to rescue him.

Unfortunately for Rome the previously resistant senate, eager to end the blockade of the city, proved more accommodating. Acceding to Alaric's demands, it recognized the prefect Attalus as new emperor in Honorius's place, a man Alaric trusted to realize his dream of Roman-Gothic reconciliation and union.[41] Elevated by the senate to commander of both imperial armies, *magister utriusque militum*, the first Germanic king to command a regular Roman army (rather than his own native host on Rome's behalf), Alaric hastily prepared for a combined Roman-Gothic invasion of Africa. These magnanimous promotions were only icebreaking decisions to be swept away on the floes of deceit. Whatever his good intentions, once in office the new emperor Attalus sided with the antibarbarian faction of the senate and blocked the joint Roman-Gothic African mission. With Sarus now attacking Alaric's army on behalf of the deposed emperor Honorius, the Gothic dream of equality with Rome disappeared forever, setting the stage for Alaric's third and most famous siege. For three days in August 410, Gothic soldiers sacked Rome and departed the city with the now sixteen-year-old Galla Placidia, reportedly carried away in the clutches of Alaric's brother-in-law, Athaulf.[42]

The Marriage of Romania and Gothia

Athaulf succeeded Alaric in 412 and led the Goths to a new homeland in the West, Narbonne, arriving there with Galla Placidia still their hostage. What a prize she was for the tribe: the granddaughter of Emperor Valentinian I, the daughter of Theodosius (the last emperor to rule over both the East and the West), and the sister of reigning western emperor Honorius. In addition she had grown up in the custody of her half-sister Serena who was Stilicho's wife. In taking her the Goths had grabbed three generations of imperial Rome. And—although unknown to them—in her they also held Rome's imperial future. Before her Gothic abduction Galla had caught the romantic and political eye of Constantius, Stilicho's successor as western military commander and future emperor.

Her value as a hostage had been clear to Athaulf since the day he snatched her. He and her brother negotiated her safe return to Rome in exchange for a federated Gothic state in Gaul and generous supplies of grain—an agreement that foundered on disruptions in the African supply lines.[43] Despite that initial failure Athaulf, reportedly smitten by her "nobility, beauty, and chaste purity," would make Galla the key to tribal peace and land.[44] On January 14, 414, she, at twenty, became his wife and queen.

Held in the home of a Roman nobleman, the wedding ceremony was a telling commentary on the centuries of barbarian-Roman conflict. It was ostentatiously Roman—the Goth Athaulf appearing in traditional Roman military dress, while the bride wore imperial robes. Among the guests was Attalus, the dethroned prefect-turned-emperor and earlier friend of the Goths, who had brokered the deal that allowed the tribe to depart Italy for Gaul in 412. He honored the newlyweds with a Roman wedding song, doing so, as it turned out, to his peril, as Constantius later took revenge on Romans who had been party to the barbarian marriage. Only the addition of a few Gothic songs at the end interrupted the ceremony's Roman theme. According to the chronicler closest to the event, the marriage caused a scare throughout the larger barbarian world, "since the empire and the Goths now seemed to be one."[45] By this ceremony Althaulf pointedly reminded the Romans and the late ancient world who he and his tribe now were.

The union was not to be blessed. A son, Theodosius, after his maternal grandfather, died shortly after birth, and unimpressed tribal rivals assassinated his father the following year. A new treaty with Rome, negotiated by Constantius, permitted the Goths to settle as Roman federates in Gaul, but not for long. Breaking the Roman connection altogether, a new tribal leader, Vallia, moved the tribe to Barcelona, where the Goths permanently settled in 415. Galla returned to Rome the following year, swapped for the now available grain and a Gothic free hand in consolidating a realm of their own at the expense of area tribes. Having earlier lusted after Galla, a woman the barbarian marriage market could not damage, Emperor Constantius took the discarded fruit of the Theodosian dynasty to be his wife. Making the most of what the fates had dealt her, Galla, in the 420s, a widowed regent for her six-year-old son Valentinian III, reigned as virtual empress of Rome.[46]

In a postscript to this story, Spanish Christian apologist Paulus Orosius, the author of a history of Christianity called *Against the Pagans*, attributed to Athaulf a comparison of Roman and Gothic cultures that was far more flattering to the Romans than to the Goths. It also attested to what was even truer: Rome's cultural triumph over the barbarians, despite its military defeat. In Orosius's construction, Athaulf aspired to make Rome a Gothic kingdom and himself a Caesar Augustus. But recalling the licentiousness of his people and their inability to obey laws—the barbarian penchant for peril observed by Tacitus—Athaulf concluded that his people could never create and maintain a republic the equal of Rome. Gothic energies were thus better turned to the "restoration and the increase of the [imperial] Roman name." If Gothia could not improve on Romania, then Gothia's course would be to revere and imitate Romania as best it could.[47] According to Orosius, Athaulf reached that conclusion under the influence of his Christian wife.

Rather than any true report of Althaulf's heart and mind, Orosius's account presents a contemporary Christian cleric's view of Romans and barbarians. After 476 the Church's bishops filled the political-administrative void in the empire's large cities, taking and exalting the Roman name as if it were their own, which indeed it now became. In late antiquity and throughout the Middle Ages, Germans and other tribal people were taught to think of the Church in Rome as Athaulf was alleged to have thought of Romania—as a civilization above all others, to be protected and obeyed by the tribes.

Fortunately for the waning Roman Empire and the emerging Christian Church, the now dominant tribes were remarkably accepting of foreign cultures. Most of the tribal kingdoms that displaced the Roman Empire sat as attentively at the feet of the Roman Church as they had at those of imperial Rome. That docility permitted the Christian Gospel, as it did also Roman language, law, and government, to coexist with Germanic and even displace the latter in a new Western European civilization.

2

FROM MEROVINGIANS TO HOHENSTAUFENS

Germanic Rule in the Middle Ages

IT WAS OF NO small consequence to the history of Europe that the "barbarians" who outlasted the Roman Empire remained receptive to its polity and culture.[1] Continuity and a plurality of cultures marked the evolution of post-Roman Europe.[2] Contrary to the old adage about the winners always writing history, the losers wrote that of the Roman-German era. By the standards of the ancient world, the Germanic tribes were magnanimous in triumph, allowing Roman language, law, government, and religion—Roman Christianity—to shape medieval Europe. From those connected civilizations sprang also the successor dynasties and societies of the second millennium.

As early as the sixth century, the emerging Western European world could be glimpsed in the names of regional tribes: Bavaria (Bavarians); Burgundy (Burgundians); England (Angles); France, Franconia (Franks, Franci); Germany (Germani, Alemanni, Teutones); Lombardy (Lombards); Saxony (Saxons); Swabia, Sweden (Suevi); and lesser regions.[3] The most historically important were the Franks, who defeated and displaced the Goths in the sixth century, the Visigoths in 507, the Ostrogoths (eastern Goths who conquered Italy in the late fifth century) in the 540s.

To create a lineage as exalted as that of the Romans, sixth century Frankish chroniclers conjured a mythical ancestry of migrant Trojan forebears. In an argument with history that has been both bloody and humorous, the French and the Germans, while attempting to distance themselves from each other, have both claimed to be the true descendants of the original Franks. In the eighteenth century a Frenchman who described the Franks as Germanic spent three months in the Bastille for insulting his ancestors.[4] In the late twentieth century, the popular French comic book *Asterix* portrayed the ancient French as pureblood Gallo-Romans, who stood tall against both Caesar's legions and netherworldish German hordes at their borders.[5] History, however, has bad news for Frenchmen and Germans. Despite efforts to separate Franci and Teutones, the two share a common Frankish barbarian past, which no amount of mythmaking can erase.

THE MEROVINGIANS

In the late fifth century a new dynasty of Franks, the Merovingians (named after their founder Merovech), began a three-century Frankish climb to the Western European hegemony they finally achieved under Charlemagne. The dynasty's base was the triangular region connecting Reims, Tournai, and Soissons, known as Belgica Secunda. From the death of the last consensus Western Roman emperor, Valentinian III, in 455, to that of the figurehead Romulus Augustulus in 476, Merovech's son Childeric effectively ruled northern Gaul. During the 260 years between Childeric's death in 481 and Charlemagne's birth in 742, Frankish kings shaped a new

Western Empire that would be recognized internationally as Rome's successor by the turn of the ninth century.[6]

Childeric's presumed son Clovis took the decisive steps after becoming king of the northern, coastal-dwelling Franks. A born Arian Christian—after the heretical Greek theologian Arius, an anti-Trinitarian—Clovis and his army converted to Roman Christianity after a victory over the Alemanni, during which he reportedly invoked the name of Jesus. Contemporary Christian bishop Gregory of Tours, chronicler of the early Franks, credited Clovis's conversion to his wife, Clotilde, the orthodox Christian daughter of a Burgundian king, who, from the birth of their first child, had badgered her husband to renounce heretical Arian Christianity.[7] On both counts, religion and marriage, precedents were set. Christian clergy and royal wives henceforth played major roles, obstructive and progressive, in Frankish society and politics.

From his base in northern Gaul, Clovis defeated the Thuringians in the east, the Alemanni in southwestern Germany, Alsace, and northern Switzerland, and the Arian Goths of southwestern Gaul. His defeat and conversion of the latter near Tours put the Merovingian dynasty in a position to conquer and unite rival Frankish tribes, a goal realized mostly by assassinating their recalcitrant kings.[8] The result was the foundation of the Frankish empire.

No barbarian's rule to date had been more Romanized than that of Clovis, who adopted the surviving elements of Roman government and chose numerous Roman advisers, lay and clerical. Although a virtual emperor, he accommodated local power and authority as no Roman emperor had done, relying on regional counts and dukes to rule the distant regions of his empire. Aware of the pope's penchant for exalting himself above the kings of men, Merovingians followed the royal Byzantine practice of restraining the clergy. A half century after Clovis's death, his grandson Chilperic complained that bishops "eyed all the king's wealth" and that the Church was more popular with townspeople than the king. Such complaints would grow in Frankish and later German history, triggering epochal German-

Roman Church-state conflicts: the investiture controversy of the eleventh century, the Reformation's national and religious protest in the sixteenth, and the pope's condemnation of modernism and the resulting "culture war" (*Kulturkampf*) in the nineteenth.[9]

The early Merovingians were the last of the Germanic tribes to serve the Romans. After the sixth-century transition of empires that brought them to power, the old Roman double standard of embracing Germans as federates and honoring them with citizenship, while inadequately compensating their valor and sacrifice, would not burden the Frankish centuries. Whereas earlier slighted chieftains and tribes had gone on rampages, usurped the imperial crown (Silvanus, Arbogast), enthroned a nonemperor of their own choosing (Attalus), and intruded themselves into the royal imperial dynasty by a coerced marriage (Athaulf), the sixth-century barbarian moved about the early medieval world as a confident equal.

Clovis's Gesture

In a consummate gesture on the heels of his victory over the Visigoths in 507, Clovis reminded Rome and Byzantium who he and his people had become. At the time Clovis fought as a client of the eastern emperor Anastasius, then at war with Italy's Ostrogoth ruler, Theodoric the Great, Clovis's brother-in-law and rival for leadership of the western barbarian kings.[10] While Clovis was en route home from this successful campaign, a letter from Anastasius reached him in Tours, conferring an imperial consulate on him—an unprecedented honor for a Merovingian Frank.

Heady with success, Clovis celebrated presumptuously. At that moment he was on the verge of ruling an empire that embraced modern France, Belgium, the Netherlands, and the future German lands east of the Elbe, with a royal residence in Paris. For the celebration of his promotion, he wore majestic purple over an imperial Byzantine military uniform, topped by a royal diadem. Thus attired he rode from the city gate to the church to shouts of "Consul and

Augustus!" tossing gold and silver to the crowd lining the way in another provocative imperial gesture. The linkage of those terms connoted a fellow emperor, something Emperor Anastasius would not have approved. Although inclined on this occasion to flaunt his consular dignity, Clovis did not again apply that exalted title to himself, his belated restraint suggesting the Franks' aplomb at the beginning of their ascendancy as the keepers of the new medieval world order.[11]

THE CAROLINGIANS

Two hundred thirty years later, the successor Carolingian dynasty took its name from Charles "the Hammer" Martel, the "mayor of the palace" in two of the three regions comprising the eighth-century kingdom of the Franks, Burgundy being the third. That title was bestowed on political and military leaders who spoke for the noble landowners. Living in an age of foreign invasion and internal collapse, Charles accomplished three feats that made possible the new empire of his grandson Charlemagne. In a week-long battle in the region between Poitiers and Tours in October 732, he stopped the Muslim invasion of Gaul through Spain, securing Western Europe's southern border. A peacemaker at home, he bent the fractious nobility to his will, becoming a kind of chancellor of the Franks. He also established an embassy in Rome, henceforth a vital link for both the Carolingians and the Church.[12]

Charlemagne

Charlemagne, who ruled the Franks for forty-three years, and was emperor of the West during fourteen of them, completed the Romanization of Frankish culture. Yet he was also the complete barbarian ruler, wearing the dress of his tribe, not that of Rome. He successfully subjected the Frankish tribes to his will, while brutally destroying rival ones. During the Saxon wars he revenged a massacre of young noble Franks by decapitating a reported four thousand Saxon prisoners in a single day.[13] His family life was also that of a tribal king, with five official wives—Frankish, Lombardian, Swabian, East Francian, and Alemannian—each taken for a political reason. One of them, the Swabian, Hildegard, he appears truly to have loved; and there were numerous concubines and illegitimate children.[14]

So tribal, yet also so cosmopolitan a king. Charlemagne's position required him to speak and write several languages. In Aachen, his native dialect of *Theodisk*, or *Deutsch*, served as a mediating language, the dialect of local dialects at the royal court. His representatives conducted business in a comparatively crude postclassical Latin, which Charlemagne spoke and helped make the diplomatic lingua franca of his kingdom. Sensitive to the threat to his native German tongue, he mandated its preservation in song and on the calendar and personally wrote a basic grammar. In addition to having a common language, the Carolingian kingdom was also a uniform trade zone with a common currency.[15]

With the intention of creating a literate court and savvy royal bureaucracy, Charlemagne built a palace school in Aachen, to which he recruited Christian scholars of reputation from England, France, and native Frankish lands, paying them with comfortable estates and open-ended academic budgets. Directed by the Anglo-Saxon Alcuin of York, the school became the center of Frankish learning and culture. Over the years, it domesticated the new empire, sowing the seeds of later, greater renaissances of ancient knowledge.

With the biblical King David as his model, Charlemagne adopted the religious-political pretensions of the Byzantine emperor. The latter's palace-church architecture became that of Aachen, a style that portrayed the ruler of a land as also its high priest, a notion destined to wreak havoc on Church-state relations in Western Europe throughout and beyond the Middle Ages.

Charlemagne also established diplomatic embassies in Jerusalem and Baghdad, extending his influence into the Middle East, whence an elephant named Abul Abbas, after the Abbasid dynasty, arrived in Aachen in October 802, a gift from Caliph Hārūm ar-Raschīd in recognition of the new western emperor.[16]

Such pretensions on Charlemagne's part attested to the quality of his rule and intended no betrayal, or challenge, of the Church's mission. That became clear in the doctrinal fight he picked with his late-eighth-century rival, Byzantine empress Irene. Because seventeen of her twenty-two-year rule were as regent for her minor son, many abroad did not show her the respect due a true empress. Yet no other ruler of the age was more determined to exercise power universally, a determination she demonstrated by imprisoning and blinding her son after he reached his majority in 797 and demanded his throne—a fate also visited on five paternal uncles, whose lineage put them in a position to challenge her rule as well. That same will displayed itself in the empress's campaign to impose Byzantine image reverence on the West, an idolatrous practice in the teaching of the Roman Church. Rushing to the Church's defense and his own self-enhancement, Charlemagne did not allow Byzantine image worship to establish itself in the West.[17]

Such service to the Church brought Charlemagne new prominence and power after rival noblemen imprisoned Pope Leo III in Rome in 799 on charges of criminality. Escaping to the safe city of Paderborn in Charlemagne's domain, the pope bestowed Roman civil authority on his protector. Thereafter king and pope became allies, the Church portraying Charlemagne as the bearer of Saint Peter's flag, imagery that prepared the way for a papal coronation as Holy Roman Emperor on Christmas Day, 800.[18]

Two days before that event, Charlemagne forced Pope Leo to undergo a public rite of purgation in Saint Peter's Church in Rome. This Germanic ceremony of reconciliation required the pope, who claimed to be subject only to God's judgment, to swear a solemn oath of innocence in the presence of his Roman accusers. By that act Leo put his past behind him, and the stained hands that would otherwise have been laid on Charlemagne were made clean again.

A weighty competition between Church and empire also began on that day. During the coronation ceremony Leo attempted to regain some of his diminished stature by rearranging the traditional order of the coronation rite. That order required the proceedings to begin with the people of Rome shouting their approval of Charlemagne, whereby their voice became the proximate medium of God's, endowing Charlemagne with the authority to rule. Pope Leo, however, invoked the assembled crowd's acclamation only after he had placed the crown on Charlemagne's head. According to the Frankish, but not the papal, records of the event, Pope Leo inadvertently gave back what he had snatched away by kneeling before Charlemagne in what the Franks interpreted to be a gesture of papal submission to the new emperor. Though subtle, such maneuvers were small steps in the direction of big trouble in Western European Church-state relations.

Charlemagne was the only Frankish king to go to Rome, and his coronation his fourth and last visit. Thereafter he bore the imperial titles of "Augustus and Emperor," while at the same time keeping his German title: "King of the Franks and the Lombards." Still believing the Western Empire to be their own, the Byzantines looked on the coronation as an outright theft of the western imperial title. In response Charlemagne made clear to them the new power of the Germanic people by having his soldiers occupy the Byzantines' main western trading post in Venice in 802. Soon thereafter eastern emperor Nicephorus I, Irene's successor, sent congratulations to the new emperor of the West.[19]

A Righteous Empire

Although Charlemagne was an all-powerful chieftain, his rule was less authoritarian than that of his imperial Roman and Byzantine counterparts. The more than one thousand laws and instructions issued during his reign were written with the counsel of a tribal assembly of nobles, ecclesiastics, and warriors. To facilitate its administration, he divided the empire into "counties" ruled in the king's name by "counts," who were local nobility. Charlemagne paid them with grants of land usurped from a Church that would not forget it.

The counts exercised their authority through a local court called the *mallus*, derived from the German word for a judicial assembly. There plantiffs and defendants made their case, and verdicts were rendered. Carefully measured punitive fines, or *wergild*, were levied when the evidence permitted a clear judgment. Where such evidence was lacking, the court might arrange an ordeal, allowing all-knowing God to decide guilt or innocence. The preferred test was the ability of a wound, inflicted by boiling water or fire, to heal in a timely fashion, proving the accused innocent when it did. Although extreme, the ordeal was a principled effort to render justice and, as such, expressed the Carolingian wish to be a righteous and enlightened society.

Also to that end, Charlemagne created a special corps of imperial envoys, *missi dominici*, and legal experts, *scabini*, to oversee the local courts. The former were chosen from trusted, leading families close to the throne, who regularly visited the courts of the empire to admonish the counts "to settle fully, equitably, and justly the claims for justice presented by churches, widows, orphans, and all others without fraud, undue cost, or excessive delay."[20]

Royal government by counts and envoys could, however, be only as strong as those who gave the orders and obeyed them, and the royal emissaries appear rarely to have reported misconduct.[21] With the passage of years, the emperor's land grants became hereditary, piling new royal lands and powers onto those the counts already possessed—enrichment more conducive to local self-aggrandizement than to high standards of royal justice.

Family Feuds and Frankish Division

Over the ninth century, Frankish inheritance law combined with fluid family numbers and dynamics to create the geographical and political landscape of modern Europe. The royal Frankish custom of giving equivalent or substantial legacies to each male heir was the main structural force. Based in the moral and religious belief that parents should treat their children evenhandedly, Frankish partible inheritance remained prominent in German, especially Protestant, regions down to the seventeenth century.[22] While the practice promised greater political unity, a kingdom divided, and often redividing, also invited predators. With the increase of such division, the Franks became their own worst enemies.

The Merovingians set the precedent for fragmenting empire, yet without the terrible consequences. Clovis's four surviving sons inherited equal shares of their father's kingdom. At the death of the youngest, Chlothar, the kingdom briefly reunited, but only because his three brothers predeceased him. Following his father's example, Chlothar gave equal portions to his four sons, a second quartering of royal Frankish lands within a half century. Further complicating the situation was the fact that Clovis and Chlothar had four surviving sons from two different marriages, successive familial tinderboxes of self-interested mothers and competing half-brothers. In Clovis's case there was an eldest son by a first wife and three younger ones by a second, while with Chlothar the numbers were reversed. Neither queen mother wanted her son(s) to receive a lesser inheritance than their royal half-brother(s), because as children fared, so fared their mothers. And once in their majority, the children, too, were prepared to take up arms in defense of their fair share. These circumstances ensured Frankish queen mothers and royal sons a powerful voice in matters of inheritance and state.[23]

However, due largely to the higher mortality of siblings, royal Merovingian families escaped the fraticidal jealousy, fragmentation of empire, and vulnerability to foreign invasion that awaited the

Carolingians. Early in his reign Charlemagne's sole surviving son and successor, Louis the Pious, foresaw the danger and attempted to preempt it by replacing partible inheritance with a version of primogeniture—taken from a plan his father had drawn up when he had contemplated the consequences of dying with multiple, warring heirs.[24]

By imperial *Ordinatio* in 817, Louis made twenty-three-year-old Lothar, his eldest son by his second wife, Ermengard, coruler and sole heir to the undivided Frankish heartlands. Younger brothers Pippin and Louis received the lesser inheritances of Aquitaine and Bavaria respectively, which also disappointed other powerful people, whose interests were better served by partible inheritance and royal succession.[25] Still, Louis's decree might have survived the opposition and secured a foundation for Frankish unity and early nationhood, had it not been for his conflicted marital and familial life.

The most immediate enemy of the decree was third wife, Judith, whom Louis had married in 819. The daughter of Count Welf, lord of domains in Bavaria and Alemannia and a useful ally for the Franks' eastern military campaigns, she was by contemporary accounts a younger woman of "fabled beauty and intelligence."[26] She gained regal power to match after delivering Louis's fourth son in June 823, the future Charles the Bald, whose arrival focused the intimacies and fears that bound the two royal broods together and threatened their mutual destruction.[27]

Knowing his stepmother to be pregnant again (Judith had earlier given birth to a daughter), Lothar acted posthaste to secure his succession to the throne in accordance with his father's decree. On Easter Day, 823, Pope Paschal crowned him coemperor. Three months later, at his father's instruction, he lifted his stepmother's newborn son from the baptismal waters in the royal church in Aachen, thereby becoming his half-brother's godfather. The incongruity of the spectacle could not have been lost on Lothar and Judith, as each contemplated at the altar the challenge posed to the new order of inheritance by the babe in arms. Lothar had a kingdom to lose, or to see weakened, and Judith a husband very likely to predecease her to the mercy of her stepsons.[28]

That her own son should receive a comparative sop as an inheritance was unthinkable to the empress, who, within a decade, would demand the equal division of the Frankish heartlands between her son and Lothar. The other self-interested parties, local and foreign, joined her effort to reinstate partible inheritance. The divided brothers of the second marriage harbored fears that Judith, ever bewitching to their father, would gain advantage over them as well. The emperor startled them at an assembly in Worms in 829 by creating a new kingdom for their half-brother on his sixth birthday, one that included Alsace, Chur, the duchy of Alemannia, and a slice of Burgundy previously belonging to Lothar. He then stampeded the three older brothers by abruptly sending Lothar away on a mission to Italy.[29]

The result was a revolt against their father in 830, which ended in the house arrest of the emperor and young Charles, and Judith's removal to an Aquitainian convent on charges of adultery and witchcraft. Although Louis restored partible royal inheritance, this shakeup of the tenuous Carolingian political order was too bold to succeed even in the chaotic ninth century. By 832 the partisans of primogeniture, with papal support, had reinstated it. The counterrebellion, however, proved even more disruptive of the traditional order than Judith's coup, and the three brothers now forced their father to renounce his crown in Lothar's favor. The balance of power reversed itself still again in 835, allowing the dethroned emperor to rejoin his wife and receive his crown again in the city of Metz.[30]

At the end of a long, conflicted story, the Frankish tradition of partible inheritance prevailed over the innovation of primogeniture, leaving the Carolingian empire geographically and politically in sight of its permanent division. After Louis's death in 840, Lothar, Louis, and Charles (Pippin having since died), battled and bickered for another three years before dividing their father's empire equally among themselves. With only small exaggeration the Treaty of

The Frankish Empire and Its Divisions, 814–843

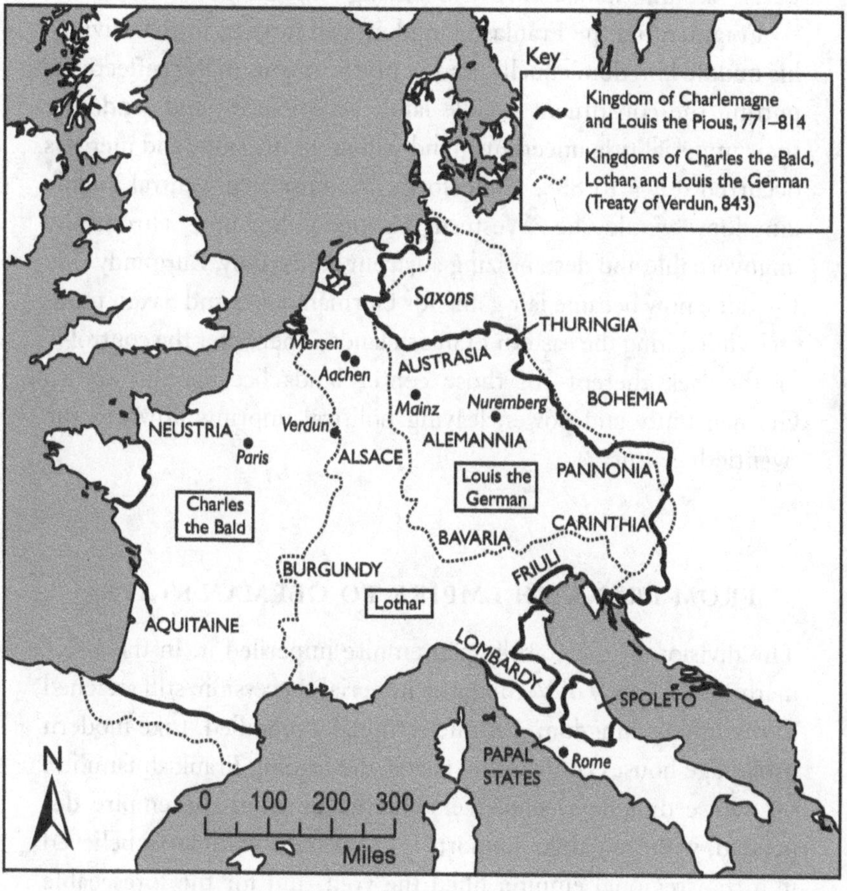

Verdun in 843 has been called "the 'birth certificate' of modern Europe."[31] By it Lothar reclaimed the imperial title and a middle kingdom centered around the ancient capital of Aachen and embracing what are roughly modern Holland, Belgium, Switzerland, Alsace-Lorraine, and Italy. To Louis of Bavaria, later to be known as Louis the German, went the eastern Frankish kingdom, or roughly modern Germany. And Charles, whose birth had triggered the epochal Frankish family feud, ruled the empire's vast western kingdom, roughly modern France, with a royal residence in Paris—an inheritance worthy of a living empress mother's son.[32]

Fragmenting the Frankish kingdom still further, Lothar divided his middle kingdom equally among his three sons in 855, effectively putting the constituent middle lands up for grabs and rendering their imperial title uncertain—and still more divisions and mergers occurred down to 888. Henceforth, the unsettled, central middle kingdom would be Western Europe's hotspot, chronically ungovernable and destabilizing adjacent lands. Italy, Burgundy, and Lorraine now became fair game for German dukes and Saxon monarchs inhabiting the eastern Frankish lands. Thereafter the control—or the lack thereof—of those center lands became the key to German unity and power, leaving political imprints down to the twentieth century.[33]

FROM FRANKISH EMPIRE TO GERMAN STATES

The division of the Carolingian empire imperiled it. In the aftermath of the Treaty of Verdun, the imperial succession, still attached to the middle kingdom, became terminally muddled. Like modern brokerage houses confronting chaos, the leading Frankish families, on whose diplomacy and oversight the unity of the empire depended, withdrew their support. Local counts, who never believed in a transregional empire, filled the void, and for the foreseeable future, ruled their lands as they had always preferred, with abandon and impunity. Local rule by the nearest and the fittest, those able to save one from pillage and rapine, dominated the political landscape during the dark age between the Treaty of Verdun and the rise of a new Saxon dynasty. Even if the royal family had been less self-destructive, and the geographic and cultural divisions of the Carolingian kingdom less extreme, the new state of affairs was probably inescapable. New invasions of Vikings and Danes from the north, Magyars from the east, and Saracens (Muslims) from the south would have made the second half of the ninth century no less a wrecking of empire.

Where were the tribes to go from there? In the eastern Frankish kingdom, five loosely organized duchies (Franconia, Saxony, Thuringia, Swabia, and Bavaria), each with its own language, law, and culture, built themselves up from Carolingian remains into hierarchically structured principalities. These lands were thenceforth the foundation stones of a fragmented and competitive medieval German realm. This smaller, familiar Germany began in the early tenth century when the Franconian duke Conrad succeeded the last blooded eastern Carolingian ruler as King Conrad I. Reflecting a still-ambitious reading of its history, the titles of "Roman king" and "Roman Empire" replaced those of "Frankish king" and "Frankish empire" over the eleventh century, as royal power passed from Frank to Saxon in 919, and the first German Reich was born. By the thirteenth century, the lands of the old Frankish middle and eastern kingdoms made up the "Holy Roman Empire," which by the end of the fifteenth century would be known as the "Holy Roman Empire of the *German* Nation" in recognition of the new transregional German identity and supremacy.[34]

The Rise of the Saxon Dynasty

The east Frankish dukes chose the Franconian Conrad to succeed the last Carolingian because they believed him to be the best prepared to meet the life-and-death challenges of the waning empire. When, however, Conrad failed to defeat the Magyars and, conniving with the Church, tried to impose his rule over eastern Frankish lands, the large duchies turned on him. Still, the east Frankish dukes had brought into existence a floating claim to German imperial lordship. On his deathbed Conrad transferred that claim to the Saxon Henry I, "the Fowler," who thereupon opened a new era of German unity and power.

At a public ceremony of his own creation, Henry took the royal

Frankish colors in hand and proclaimed himself an imperial ruler in the line of Clovis and Charlemagne. Therein lay a bold message for the German duchies and the Church in Rome: The duke of Saxony was the German monarch not by ducal election or papal coronation, but by the unbroken transfer of royal power from ancient kings to medieval ones. Henry, in other words, claimed to hold royal authority directly from God—something future German kings like those of other lands and emperors, would continue to do into modern times.[35]

Throughout the remainder of the tenth century and into the eleventh, eastern dukes and lesser authorities repeatedly tested the Saxon monarch's mettle. Henry's son and successor, Otto I, met those challenges as his father had done, by invoking the traditional bonds of lord and vassal—an overlord's only peaceful way to gain respect from his rivals in the tenth century. By virtue of their own royal estates, loyal local counts, and invested clerical administrators, the Saxon monarchs presented a commanding military, propertied, and religious presence among the German duchies. The Saxon king also succeeded in war where the Franconian Conrad had failed, twice defeating the Magyars in victories that secured eastern borders and opened new lands for Saxon expansion.[36]

Securing the new Saxon-led empire consumed Otto's reign, and the lands of the old Frankish middle kingdom, extending from Friesland to Italy on Germany's western flank, were the key to success. Divided and subdivided throughout the ninth century, these lands were ripe for the taking. Since Italy was the powerful tail of this geographical beast, it became the target of Saxon stabilization efforts. For Otto wrestling Italy down meant not only the imperial crown but the ability to secure the Saxon homeland as well.

Having seized the claim to the Lombard-Italian crown by conquest in 937–38, Otto invaded Italy in midcentury to secure it. His success was impressive and included a new Italian wife. However, it came at the threatened loss of his German kingdom, as enemies at home plotted with those abroad (including, increasingly, the pope) to defeat a chronically absent overlord. It was, however, a risk Otto and future imperial German rulers were willing to take to secure their claimed Italian lands and titles. But with Otto encamped in Italy, Franconian and Swabian dukes rebelled against Saxon rule, igniting a German civil war that Otto was forced to return home and quell.

A decade would pass before Otto took his army back to Italy and asserted imperial rule. When he did so in 961, it was to rescue a pope besieged by mutual Italian enemies, including some who had plotted the ducal rebellion against Otto in Germany. His hide saved, a grateful Pope John XII crowned Otto Holy Roman Emperor a year later. Because that coronation gave Otto undisputed title to the lands of the Frankish middle kingdom (Burgundy and Italy, to which Lorraine was added), it put the strategic goal of the Italian campaign within reach—namely, calm on Germany's western front. That peace, in turn, made Otto the unquestioned master of the eastern German kingdom. Returning home with the imperial crown, he never again marched his army back into Italy.[37]

At War with the Church: The Salian Dynasty

In 1024 a new line of Salian Franks succeeded the strong Saxon dynasty.[38] By then the counts, high clergy, and royal family members who made up the Saxon bureaucracy were entrenched and self-serving, much as had happened in the later decades of the Carolingians. Hoping to create a more reliable administration, Salian kings turned to the nonnoble, nonclerical servant class of *ministeriales*. These disciplined and able men possessed neither land nor power, yet now were given both as retrievable, lifetime holdings. The conditions of their tenure approximated those of a vassal, however without the personal freedom and contractual guarantees of vassalage, a deficit that would sour the Salian experiment in the end.[39]

The scheme also did not endear the new dynasty to those the *ministeriales* displaced. One class of diminished royal bureaucrat in particular had a great deal to lose: the high Christian clergy. Under Kings Henry III and Henry IV, crown lands that had become virtual possessions of the Church were reclaimed and awarded to the *ministeriales*. Because the Church still harbored a centuries-old grudge against earlier Frankish usurpation of lands it deemed its own, the Salian reclamation rubbed salt into old wounds.[40]

Other free groups also resisted the new Salian approach: freemen farmers, small noble estate owners, and, most ominously, the aristocratic princes to whom Germany's future belonged. Early in the eleventh century, the princes determined that the king and his new servant class would not build a nation at their expense. To that end they joined forces with the Church in a clever obstruction: They became independent advocates, that is, founders and protectors, of hundreds of new Christian monastic estates.[41] These jointly created domains legally belonged to the Church and, as such, were beyond the king's reach. By this opportunistic alliance, the princes and the pope increased their holdings and power with impunity, and by the mid–fourteenth century soundly defeated royal efforts at national unification.

Since Merovingian times, the alliance of king and Church had served both sides well, bringing new lands and royal protection to the Church and providing the crown with a highly competent and seemingly noncompetitive administration of the royal estates. Dangers to both sides lurked, however, in this pragmatic cooperation. The spiritual status bestowed on a king by papal coronation gave him a new dignity—now a priest as well as a king (*rex et sacerdos*)—grandeur that might tempt a basking king to imagine himself the pope's equal or superior. A more immediate regal action was to treat royally endowed bishoprics and abbeys as departments of state, diminishing their independence under the aegis of Rome.

On the other hand an inflated pope, having divinely sanctioned kings, might think secular rulers only empty robes without his blessing. In such ways medieval Church and state positioned themselves to raise deeply critical questions about, and to make great demands on, each other. Between the late eleventh and late thirteenth centuries, both sides would do so to increasingly destructive effect within the German empire.

The alliance breaker was a royal ceremony in which the king presented the symbols of Church office (a bishop's ring and staff) to the clergy on whom he also bestowed lands and the power of royal office. Over the first quarter of the eleventh century, royal investiture of high clergy became a routine practice. Henry II personally invested forty-nine of the fifty bishops appointed during his reign, and he also instructed them collectively in their duties at church synods he convened and chaired. The clergy became partners in military conquest as well, trailing royal armies on their eastward march through Slavic lands, planting new churches as they went and creating new mission districts for their ministry to the conquered heathen. That the king supported his army and court with taxes levied on clerical estates only underscored the royal blasphemy in the eyes of religious reformers.[42]

Pope Gregory VII threw down the gauntlet in February 1075, by condemning lay investiture of clergy as the sin of simony (the selling of spiritual things). Being then in a life-or-death campaign against the Saxons, King Henry IV took little notice of the papal challenge. Yet, by that action, the pope lit a fire that would consume the medieval alliance between Church and state, deepening Germany's political divisions at a time when they might have been overcome.

Behind the papal challenge lay both true presumption on the part of German kings and the vaulting ideals of a reform movement based in the Benedictine monastery of Cluny, in east-central France. The religious there wanted to free the clergy from kings, specifically from royal investiture in their clerical offices. For Henry IV the consequences were dire. The inability to appoint loyal clergy to royal offices seemed a death knell for any reliable and efficient governance of his kingdom. Where the Church's reformers saw a clear-cut matter of religious principle, the king saw only power-grabbing and church-sponsored anarchy.[43]

By December, Gregory pointedly reminded Henry that kings were Christian laymen subject to the pope's decrees in matters of religious doctrine. That ultimatum could not have come at a worse time. Having recently defeated the last Saxon duchy, Henry was then moving to subject all German lands to his will. Exuberant over the prospect of a unified Germany, he dismissed Gregory's threat and instructed his council of bishops to denounce him as a false pope.

Unfortunately for the incipient German nation, Gregory was more determined to secure his kingdom against the state than Henry was his against the Church. Grasping the powerful weaponry of papal slander and delegitimation, Gregory excommunicated Henry and put his lands under interdict. That freed the king's subjects from obedience to his rule, at least in the eyes of God, a virtual sanction of rebellion and anarchy for any who wished to defy the king. Again Henry responded with his own, lesser spiritual artillery, now directing an assembly of his loyal German bishops to excommunicate Gregory. In an age of belief, that was a vain action, and Henry's only exit from a threatened civil war was the pope's absolution and lifting of the interdict. So the king bit his tongue and repented on his knees in the snow outside the pope's winter quarters in Canossa, a spectacle German rulers down to Bismarck remembered in their dealings with the Church.[44]

Although Henry got his absolution, the damage to king and empire had been done. In the aftermath the important events surrounding the German monarchy only called attention to its diminishment. Rejecting Henry's royal authority, the German princes elected their own counterking. Gregory excommunicated Henry a second time, and Henry's bishops responded by electing a counterpope. Each new escalation brought diminishing returns, and the conflict became tragicomic. Three decades of such on-and-off civil war ended what political unity had been gained over a century of aggressive Saxon and Salian rule.[45]

Henry IV died in 1106 and the quarter-century rule of his successor, Henry V, to all intents and purposes saved the German crown by forfeiting it. He took away the edge the pope had gained over his predecessor by his own alliance with the princes, giving them that edge himself and becoming their passive voice. Joining those he could not defeat, Henry V united Germany in the only way then possible—under the aegis of the princes. Showcasing the triumph of aristocratic over monarchical Germany, an assembly of princes composed the peace terms Henry signed in Worms in 1122, ending the royal disaster that was the investiture struggle. The king renounced the investiture of bishops with ring and staff, while remaining free to confer property, land, and titles on them. In the short term the controversy was a loss of sovereign control and princely allegiance for the king, while the pope gained in reputation and clerical loyalty.[46]

MONARCHY'S LAST HURRAH: THE HOHENSTAUFEN DYNASTY

Papal aggression and civil war marked the last quarter of the eleventh century and first of the twelfth. Over those fifty years, Germany was transformed into a patchwork of sovereign princely states.[47] The result left Germans distrustful of both popes and princes and favorably disposed to the restoration of a strong new monarchy.

Frederick I Barbarossa

A new dynasty, the Hohenstaufen, born of the marriage of Henry IV's daughter Agnes and Frederick of Hohenstaufen, and destined to rule for a century (1138–1254), became medieval Germany's last best chance to create a unified nation. It was this pair's grandson, Frederick I Barbarossa, who made the new royal case against papal claims to power over secular rulers. In his provocative *Papal Dicta* of

1075, Pope Gregory VII had instructed kings and princes to be prepared to kiss the feet of popes, while in the mid–twelfth century Pope Adrian IV described Frederick I's crown and empire as royal "benefits" courtesy of the papacy.[48] Like Henry I before him, and German monarchs as late as the nineteenth century, Frederick I claimed to hold his crown directly from God, a point driven home by the addition of the adjective "holy" to it.[49] Here Frederick set a precedent for royal dynasties in England, France, and Spain during their own, more successful confrontations with post-Gregorian papal theocrats.

Lacking the resources to enforce his will in his German lands, Frederick, like the Saxon Otto before him, sought needed assets in the old Frankish middle kingdom. Taking Burgundy and Provence peaceably by marriage, he proceeded to make Italy the fulcrum of his new empire. Before he could exploit the political and material resources of its crown, he had first to pacify the German princes at home, which he did by taking a page from Henry V's book: He gave them a free hand in their own lands and trusted their fidelity to their feudal oaths to maintain the peace. In doing so he winked at recent history, which taught that such license only weakened the bonds between lords and vassals.[50]

The German homeland thus secured, Frederick marched his army to Italy for the first of five military campaigns there over two decades. Successful against a papal adversary, he received an expected coronation in 1155, an important step in legitimizing his restoration of empire. In the long run, Milanese resistance scuttled his Italian mission by inspiring the formation of the Lombard League in 1167, a union of north Italian communes determined to expel the now unwanted Germans. A near decade of intermittent warfare with anti-imperial forces ended in abject defeat at Legnano in 1176, often seen as the end of German dreams of empire.

However, to Frederick's undeserved good fortune, the final peace terms left him a foothold in central Italy. Given Frederick's utter failure to accomplish his original goals, this recovery seemed an act of divine providence and gave rise to his reputation as the prototypical, or good and invincible, German ruler. After his death in 1190 while on the Third Crusade, he became the namesake of a mythical, future Frederick, whom Germans popularly believed would one day return in righteous vengeance to prepare the way for the Christian millennium. Ironically contemporaries extended that prophecy to the last Hohenstaufen ruler, his grandson Frederick II, arguably the least German of all the Holy Roman Emperors and by far the most neglectful of the German kingdom.[51]

During Frederick's frequent long absences, the German princes ruthlessly secured their homelands. The most ambitious of them, the Saxon duke Henry the Lion, extended his eastern borders into Slavic lands, while establishing a dynastic connection with English king Henry II by marriage to his daughter. In the late 1160s he challenged Frederick's rule. Among the causes of the imperial army's humiliation at Legnano had been Henry the Lion's refusal to send promised reinforcements, a breach of vassalage that made him an outlaw within the empire and an eventual exile to England.[52]

That the princes did not rend Germany completely asunder in Frederick's absence seems in retrospect as great a miracle as his recovery from utter defeat. The same may be said of his success in keeping his crown intact and preserving royal succession to it. However, the German princes, more powerful than ever after Legnano, could not be indefinitely contained, and other imperial enemies now surfaced boldly in Rome and England.

The Sicilian Emperor

Inheriting this dire situation, Frederick's son and successor, Henry VI, did much in his short reign to make matters worse. Like his father, he succumbed to the siren call of foreign empire, now from the kingdom of Sicily, whose crown he had gained by marriage to the Sicilian princess Constance. Like his father's invasion of Lombardy, Henry's hold on Sicily threatened the pope, on whose domains the Hohenstaufen shadow was now cast from both north and south. Henry nonetheless succeeded in gaining both the pope's and the German princes' recognition of his Sicilian-born son Frederick's succession to the imperial crown. His success in doing so was not, however, a good omen, as Henry died the year after, in 1197, and the queen mother the year after that, leaving the four-year-old heir to the kingdom of Sicily and the Holy Roman Empire at the mercy of highly partisan strangers.

Before her death the queen mother had made Pope Innocent III toddler Frederick's guardian and Sicily's regent until the boy came of age. Meanwhile, in Germany, the princes turned to Henry VI's brother, Philip of Swabia, for an interim imperial guardian and regent. Many years stood between those agreements and young Frederick's majority. While key authorities acknowledged the boy to be his parents' heir, none had signed off in stone on any hereditary Hohenstaufen claim to either the imperial, or the Sicilian, throne. Meanwhile there was much room for maneuver and strife over who would rule Germany and Sicily in the boy's place during the intervening years.[53]

As young Frederick's guardian, Pope Innocent never doubted that the crown of the Holy Roman Empire was his to bestow. From the start his primary goal had been to rid Sicily of the Hohenstaufens and their notion of the divine right of kings. Joined by two equally self-interested great powers, England and France, Innocent plotted to take advantage of the murky German situation. Assisted by English king Richard I, "Coeur de Lion," he helped maneuver a well-connected anti-Hohenstaufen rival onto the imperial throne: Prince Otto IV of Brunswick of the Welf dynasty, King Richard's nephew and the youngest son of old Hohenstaufen foe, Henry the Lion. After Otto's coronation in Aachen in July 1198, French king Philip Augustus rushed to the side of the Hohenstaufens to counter the new English advantage. With that action began recurrent foreign intervention in internal German affairs, especially by the French.

The new Welf emperor now served the papacy's purposes in the heart of Germany, for which Pope Innocent rewarded him with a papal coronation in Rome. Yet before a year had passed that crown was blackened by a papal excommunication. In the months after his coronation, Otto had committed the unforgivable sin of the Hohenstaufens by marching an imperial army into southern Italy and reincorporating it into the German empire, an action the pope had hoped to prevent by crowning him emperor.[54] After such betrayal it was time to end the Welf interregnum, and Pope Innocent had at hand the very person to do so: young Frederick of Hohenstaufen, who had been raised a Sicilian-Italian and was now of age and ready to claim his German crown.

That happened in Mainz in December 1212, to all appearances a restoration of the Hohenstaufen line of German kings, broken fifteen years earlier by their Welf rivals. The royal connection was not effectively repaired, however, until the French defeated English and Welf armies on the battlefield of Bouvines in July 1214. From the site, King Philip Augustus sent new emperor Frederick the fallen German imperial eagle, a symbol of Welf defeat and Hohenstaufen restoration. The following year Frederick was crowned a second time, in Aachen, now unquestionably the German king and emperor.[55] The big question for the Germans was whether this twenty-one-year-old grandson of Frederick I was indeed his grandfather's heir, that is, a German warrior against all odds. Or had Pope Innocent groomed the boy to be the perfect German nemesis?

During Frederick's reign the Hohenstaufens' Italian foreign policy took its full toll on imperial Germany. Despite his German lineage, the new emperor had grown up in Sicily, from which vantage point Germany seemed a forbidden land. He had also come to power by the connivance of the age's strongest pope, Innocent III, and king, Philip Augustus. That Frederick was ill disposed toward his German kingdom was hardly surprising. Whereas his predecessors had pursued their Italian claims to ensure their German empire, he exploited his German base to strengthen his Silician kingdom and fulfill his ambitions in Italy. Before he abandoned

Germany the princes there gave him the two things he needed to remain a contender in Italy: the imperial title and material support. He spent only nine of thirty-seven years as emperor on German soil, six of those before he turned twenty-five. [56]

Taking to new heights the Hohenstaufen habit of buying off the German princes with open-ended political power, Frederick made the bestowal of the imperial title and its encumbrances a very good barter for them. And he treated the German church with similar abandon, allowing the clergy to govern their lands by and large as they pleased. In 1232, in what has been called "a *Magna Carta* of princely liberties," the German princes became sole arbiters within the courts of their lands.[57] This was a far cry from the days of Charlemagne's *missi dominici* and even lesser breeds of royal watchdogs, who had previously traveled, or been stationed around, the empire on the emperor's behalf.

In the end, such carte blanche governance undermined both his German base and his Italian plans. He made himself strong in Italy by making himself weak in Germany, and his new Italian strength, in turn, drew his Italian enemies closer together against him. For a talented and powerful succession of thirteenth-century popes, Hohenstaufen claims to Lombardy and Sicily had been the front and back doors to an unacceptable imperial rule, both banging directly on Rome. Having watched three generations of Hohenstaufens progressively extend imperial power the full length of the boot, from Lombardy to Sicily, Frederick's enemies, led by the pope, were determined to end the German presence at any cost.

In the cycle of political creation and destruction, the Hohenstaufen emperors, none more than Frederick, owed their existence, improbably, to the approval of the German princes and the Italian pope. In turn the Hohenstaufens' strategic goal of strengthening themselves in Germany by gaining titles and assets in Italy made the princes and the pope far stronger in Germany than either could ever have been alone—the princes empowered by royal neglect, the pope by royal confrontation. Repeatedly the princes and the pope found their interests best served by alliance against the German dynasty each had done so much to create.

With Frederick still claiming imperial rule over Lombardy and Sicily, the Lombard League, which had earlier foiled his grandfather's attempts at occupation, declared war on him in the 1230s. The pope entered the fray by buying the services of the German princes, who were equally expert at playing pope and emperor against each other. Between 1227 and 1250 popes excommunicated Frederick four times for acts of disobedience and aggression against the Church. During these decades foreign armies and willing native sons transformed individual German lands into mighty states, leaving Germany fragmented and decentralized down to the nineteenth century.[58] In 1257 the princes, meeting as an informal electoral college, chose Germany's royal overlord and forbade him any right of hereditary succession. A century later, in 1356, that same college, with even greater powers of election and political management, was recognized in imperial law.[59] For the next six centuries, the princely territorial state would be supreme in Germany.

II

THE HOLY ROMAN EMPIRE OF THE GERMAN NATION

3

MAN AND GOD

Germany in the Renaissance and Reformation

IN THE EARLY sixteenth century Martin Luther and his followers defended the right of German Christians to worship in ways other than those sanctioned by the pope in Rome. In doing so they reminded Germans of two older and still continuing conflicts. The first dated back almost three centuries and pitted the German princes against their political overlord, the Holy Roman Emperor. The second, emerging in the fifteenth century, set those same princes against lesser, but also independent, political entities—knights, imperial and territorial cities, and countless rural villages in between. In both conflicts the princes were spectacular winners.

In their contest with the emperor, the rulers of the larger states reached a favorable standoff in 1356, when Czech emperor Charles IV conceded German strength and imperial weakness by affixing his golden seal to a new German constitution. Known as the Golden Bull, it gave the princes what they had wanted since the demise of the Hohenstaufen empire: semiregal rights within their respective lands. Thenceforth seven German princes, four secular and three ecclesiastical, elected the emperor on terms they negotiated—and without the involvement of the pope.[1]

In the century and a half between the Golden Bull and the Protestant Reformation, the German princes showed little interest in national unity. Rather, they used their new political clout to make their own states stronger, subjecting the lesser nobility, townspeople, and peasants to princely law and culture. Not coincidentally that political conflict reached its crisis point at the same time the Protestant Reformation was emerging.

Religious reform found a welcoming home in the newly beseiged German cities and towns. Perhaps three thousand existed in the late fifteenth century, the vast majority small (two hundred had populations of more than one thousand, only a few twenty thousand or more). Sixty-five were free imperial cities, owing allegiance to the Holy Roman Emperor rather than to more immediate territorial powers. But whether imperial or territorial, all had fixed obligations to their respective rulers based on founding charters or special contractual agreements. Wittenberg, the birthplace of the Reformation, for example, was the main residence of the electoral prince of Saxony, who, as its overlord, was owed hospitality (lodging and board), taxes, and conscripts for his army.

During the course of the sixteenth century, fifty of Germany's sixty-five imperial cities adopted the Reformation, and more than half did so permanently. In territorial cities and towns minority Protestants might coexist side by side with majority Catholics, while a smaller number suppressed the Reformation altogether after a brief stint. Many more, especially those with populations above one thousand, embraced the Reformation for the long term.[2]

Local grievances against the Roman Church and a desire for communal sovereignty attracted urban populations to Protestant reforms. Viewing themselves as oases of republican government within a desert of autocratic rule, self-governing townspeople believed themselves to be morally superior to the landed nobility and royalty. They had gotten where they were not by birth, fortune, or military force, but by native ingenuity and the skills they acquired through productive work.[3] Urban chroniclers expressed the cities' self-esteem by beginning their histories with Adam and Eve. Belief in specialness intensified in the free imperial cities, each a self-conscious part of a transregional and transhistorical empire, whose universality was palpable in the imperial traffic and residences along its streets. Given such self-importance, the native spokesmen for late medieval cities assailed threatening princes and peasants with the same epithets the clergy used ("Turks" and "Hussites") to indict spiritual predators.[4]

Self-portrayed as the hub of the universe, whose air set one free, the sixteenth-century city was a place of heightened security and opportunity. Yet its councils and magistrates also acted as oligarchs and sovereigns, as *Oberen* and *Herren*. And to noblemen and peasants living outside city walls, no political entity in the late medieval world was more egotistical than the city that thought itself a world.[5]

The noble lords and princes dismissed the cities' vaunted constitutions as legal instruments tailored to local power. To the extent that every city and village could act as its own supreme court, royal lawyers reasoned, there would be no equal justice across a land. When, in the fifteenth century, princes overrode local laws with new territorial codes, they did so in the name of fairness, presenting themselves as the advocates of one law for all. For the subdued, such arguments were mere pretexts for naked aggression, what Gerald Strauss has called "creeping death by state regulation."[6] The new codes began to be implemented in earnest in 1495, after the new imperial supreme court (*Reichskammergericht*) made Roman law the guideline for all secular courts of the empire. In Roman law the highest authority within a land became the supreme authority over it, which is why Roman law became the legal tool for centralizing European regimes. The decades of Renaissance and Reformation in Germany were also those in which this embittering political and legal conflict occurred.

The late medieval German city was a mix of opposites, and in this respect, too, what an older historiography called the "protoplasm" of the modern German state.[7] On the one side was vexing *Verordnungsfreudigkeit*, the need to put everyone unambiguously in his place down to the clothes one might wear, the sections of town one might inhabit, and even the words one might properly speak—all reflections of a society more fearful of anarchy than of tyranny. On the other side were consoling security and freedom, which in late medieval and early modern Germany meant physical safety and material prosperity. When, in 1520, Martin Luther famously defined the "freedom of the Christian" in a treatise of the same title, he did not talk about "one person, one belief," or any right to worship as one pleased. He instead described a condition in which one might live as both "a lord over all and a servant to all." By that he meant a life beyond the spiritual fray, safe from sin, death, and devil, internally secure enough to act confidently on both one's own and one's neighbors' behalf. Here was a spiritual and moral parallel to the freedom and security urban populations sought in their cities, and that those fleeing persecution and joblessness in the countryside hoped to gain there as well.

As territorial and urban governments tightened their hold in the late fifteenth and early sixteenth centuries, besieged cities, towns, and villages saw an ally in the Lutheran revolt. The latter's call for biblically informed, self-regulating Christian communities, free of foreign papal influence and exploitation, seemed to many across the social spectrum a precise spiritual counterpart to the civil struggle to maintain local republican institutions in the face of overreaching urban oligarchs and territorial princes. Luther even spoke of the church as a *Gemeinde*, a neighborly community of fellow believers, who were spiritual equals and took moral responsibility for one another's welfare—not a Church pyramiding from lowly laity through the clergy and the pope to the saints in heaven.[8]

German cities were not the only contemporary societies to perceive an affinity with the Protestant Reformation and to embrace it for purposes other than those foremost in the reformers' minds. Some imperial knights saw an ally in the Reformation, as did the common man in the countryside.[9] Across the confessional divide, it is a telling commentary on the reformers' priorities that they aided and abetted the causes of the cities, the countryside, and the princes indiscriminately, both biting and kissing the political hands that fed them in all three venues. They did so because everything they wanted to accomplish rested on the survival and success of their respective ecclesiastical institutions.

THE FIRST PROTESTANT PRINCE

No one person had more to do with the Reformation's survival and success than Saxon elector Frederick the Wise. His defense of Luther after 1517 allowed the Reformation to merge with a German national movement that preceded and embraced it. The result was a more self-aware and culturally unified Germany, in spite of the new confessional divisions the Reformation created. Why did this most devout of German Catholic princes become a young heretic's protector?

Frederick's court chaplain and cabinet secretary, Georg Spalatin, created the vital link between the two. Before joining the Wittenberg court in 1509, he had studied law and theology at the universities of Erfurt and Nuremberg—the former home of the religious order of Observant Augustinians Luther joined in 1505, the latter that of leading humanists. In 1511 Spalatin was instrumental in bringing Luther to Wittenberg, and he also played a key role in making Willibald Pirckheimer's Nuremberg humanist circle the Reformation's first publicists. In Spalatin, Germany's native religious and educational reform movements found an influential friend at the pinnacle of Saxon government, willing and able to facilitate their national merger.

Like other great princes of German history, Frederick was both a man of his time and of the future. Visitors and guests hunted with him in the rich game preserves surrounding his favorite retreat at Castle Lochau, where incredible numbers of game and fowl were bagged (208 bears, 200 lynxes, and even larger numbers of wolves, boar, deer, and fowl reported by a single hunter in one autumnal hunting season).[10] The same visitors also jousted with the elector on the tournament fields of Wittenberg, scenes immortalized by court painter Lucas Cranach (and, later, Pablo Picasso, who redrew Cranach's sketches during his own transition to cubism).[11] After sport, there were lectures and sermons in the new university, founded at the turn of the century, and in the refurbished castle church.

As one of the first German princes to be liberally educated, Frederick knew enough Latin to translate a classical text and collect bons mots from Seneca, Terence, Cicero, and Cato. The humanist influence on his upbringing could be seen in Cranach's wall decorations in Wittenberg castle, wherein Perseus freed Andromeda from a sea monster, the Hesperides watched over a garden of golden apples, and the Argonauts searched for the Golden Fleece.[12] At twenty-two the newly crowned Frederick lobbied the imperial coronation of Germany's first poet laureate, the rakish Conrad Celtis, a great fan of Roman historian Tacitus and leader of a cultural campaign to bring Apollo to Germany. Frederick corresponded with Desiderius Erasmus and his Italian publisher, Aldus Manutius, also Germany's leading Christian Hebraist, Johannes Reuchlin, whom he protected from Dominican zealots intent on destroying Jewish writings and punishing their Christian friends. Dürer was on Frederick's payroll as early as 1489 and twice painted his portrait, the first time with Celtis and later, in a commissioned altarpiece, as one of the three kings who greeted Jesus on his birthday. At the annual Leipzig fair, Wittenberg was the reputed best buyer, and modern art historians refer to Frederick's collection as the "Wittenberg canvas Renaissance."[13]

The Believer

Traditional religious piety was an equally great princely passion, and a vital point of contact with Luther. Several times a pilgrim, including a journey to Jerusalem in 1493, Frederick revered Saint Anne, the patron saint of travelers in distress, whose invocation, "Help me St. Anne," he had imprinted on Saxon coinage.[14] During his Jerusalem pilgrimage Frederick collected numerous relics, the beginning of what became northern Europe's largest relic collection, which included an arm bone from his namesake, Saint Frederick, a gift from the bishop of Utrecht. Late in the second decade of the sixteenth century, the collection peaked at more than nineteen thousand pieces arranged in ten galleries in the castle church, which, when properly toured and revered, promised pilgrims 1,902,202 years of absolution for unrepented sins, time that would otherwise be spent in the purifying fires of purgatory.[15]

Luther hated the great relic collection and the even greater indulgence it promised. He waited to post his famous Ninety-five Theses until Frederick had departed Wittenberg for the 1517 autumn hunt in Lochau, and then did so on the day of the collection's highest veneration (All Saints'). When, however, the crafty indulgence peddler John Tetzel, on the instructions of the archbishop of Mainz, began selling the famous indulgence for the rebuilding of Saint Peter's in Rome on the borders of electoral Saxony, Frederick was as offended as Luther—albeit over the political intrusion rather than any religious impropriety. In 1518, after the Church moved against Luther, Frederick stopped the indulgence traffic in his lands, as the action was also a challenge to his authority. In the same year he saved Luther from deportation to Rome and a likely death.[16]

Ruler

A lifelong bachelor, Frederick was called "Wise" because of his ability to keep the peace. Before astutely managing the Luther affair, he had survived the challenge of competitive peers, among them Archbishop Albrecht of Mainz. Fatalistic by the end of his reign (1525), Frederick had a reputation as a "man of the middle," which was reflected in his personal mottos: To the Best of My Ability and Always Forward Slowly.[17] Spalatin, who was also Frederick's biographer, believed the elector's mettle had best been proven during two great challenges of his reign: the honest brokering of the election of Charles I of Spain as Emperor Charles V in 1519, and his equally deft handling of the Protestant revolt in the early 1520s.

In the imperial election two other rulers competed with Charles for the imperial crown: Henry VIII of England and Francis I of France, and everyone knew that Frederick's vote would be the most decisive. The king of England was the first to offer a bribe, which, if Spalatin may be believed, Frederick ignored.[18] In this competition the nineteen-year-old king of Spain had all the advantages. The grandson of deceased emperor Maxmilian, he was heir to both the crown of Spain and kingdoms reaching from Sicily to Austria. Pope Leo X feared the emergence of a new Spanish-German monarchy greater than the empire of Charlemagne, and initially joined others in backing the king of France, whose assets, however, paled by comparison.

Taking their best shot at Charles, the papacy, the French, and the Swiss turned to Germany's favorite son, Frederick. Papal legate Cardinal Cajetan, who had recently grilled Luther in Augsburg, unveiled that option to the fifty-six-year-old elector. The notion had also crossed Frederick's mind, only to fade before two sobering facts: his lack of the resources to rule an empire, and the likelihood of a losing war with Charles and the dissolution of the German electoral college, should he try.

Under no conditions could the electoral college be lost by the

Germans. Its power gave Germany gravitas in the European world, enabling the princes to wring huge financial and political concessions from imperial candidates. Indeed, that election was an occasion on which Germans might welcome foreigners out to take advantage of them. The electoral college also gave Germans their best hope for functional unity and a pragmatic peace, if not early nationhood.

According to Spalatin, Frederick arrived in Frankfurt to find three of his fellow electors prepared to vote for him. If Frederick merely cast his own vote (in the election of the emperor, the minority capitulated to the majority, which reported a unanimous vote), he would enable a German seizure of the imperial crown. The seven electors, dressed in ermine-lined red mantles and berets, voted on June 27, 1519. As Spalatin told it, Frederick joined three other electors in voting for himself, thus becoming the Holy Roman Emperor—but only for three hours and within the closed chambers of the electors! Before reporting out a unanimous vote for Charles, Frederick explained to his fellow electors why even the strongest German prince could not be emperor and redirected his own vote and theirs to the king of Spain.

Because no public record of these events exists (there are only Spalatin's admiring biography and the rumors emanating from Frederick's circle), the story remains the stuff of legend, and very flattering to Frederick. Taking it for fact, some historians see in his presumed capitulation another twist of fate in the snakebitten history of Germany. If the Saxon elector could have ruled successfully as Holy Roman Emperor in 1519, the smaller German empire of 1871 might have become reality three centuries earlier.[19]

After the election the Saxon princes suffered an indignity at the hands of the Spanish. In an evident gesture of gratitude for Frederick's support, the new emperor proposed a marriage between Frederick's nephew and godson, future Saxon elector John Frederick, and Charles's sister Catherine. The Wittenberg court received the formal commitment letter in 1521. Neither Frederick nor young

John Frederick's father, Prince John, had been inclined to pursue the marriage, which, portended more Spanish Hapsburg meddling in Saxon politics. However, a Spanish Hapsburg proposal of marriage could not lightly be refused.

In the end the protestations of the Spanish queen mother, who did not want her daughter to leave her side—certainly not for a distant German prince—saved the Saxons from the match. Still, the Germans had been insulted by the rude turn of events, which gave the Saxon princes a new grudge to nurse, one that would cost the Spanish emperor dearly when the Protestant Reformation erupted in Saxony.[20]

A desire to keep Spanish Hapsburg might and Roman papal influence as benign as possible within Germany lay behind Frederick's defense of Luther. Beyond traditional piety and the need to protect his subjects, there was Luther's popularity to consider. Should the emperor and the pope succeed in executing the superstar of Wittenberg University, Frederick's authority and the peace of his land would suffer along with Luther. When, in April 1521, Luther, a condemned heretic, was summoned to the Diet of Worms to answer for his teachings, the elector of Saxony attended that meeting also, as a guardian angel.[21]

Anticipating Luther's condemnation at Worms and the political fallout in Saxony, Frederick acted to save Luther's life by placing him in protective custody at Wartburg Castle. There, hidden from his enemies for a year, Luther translated the New Testament into German and plotted the Reformation by mail. At the conclusion of the Diet, the vast majority of German lands and cities joined electoral Saxony in refusing to sign off on its proceedings and to publish Luther's condemnation in their lands.

Although Frederick had sufficient political reason for standing by Luther, the evolution of his religious piety in response to Luther's teachings cannot be discounted. In 1522 he acronymically displayed a new motto on the sleeves of his winter clothes: The Word of God Is Eternal (*VDMIA—Verbum Dei Manet in Aeter-*

num).[22] By that year Frederick knew Luther's teachings well enough to ponder them on their merits and to judge them as that Word. He had also long recognized Luther's right, by power of his doctor's beret, to teach Holy Scripture and test the truth of traditional Church doctrine. Even before Luther had come on the scene, Spalatin reported Frederick's "great displeasure and wonder" at the disrespect shown God's Word, insisting that "matters of faith should be as clear as an eye," by which he meant biblically transparent and pure. Reluctant to preempt impending religious violence, Frederick declared himself ready to lead a hermit's life rather than unwittingly challenge God's will in history. Such personal piety led him in 1523 to impede early action against Thomas Müntzer, who later led a peasants' revolt. Ten months before that revolt, in July 1524, Frederick gave the then incendiary preacher an audience with the Saxon princes, allowing him to make the case for a radical egalitarian reconstruction of society in place of Luther's moderate program of reform.[23] When, in the spring of 1525, peasant armies mustered against him, Frederick, professing his belief that divine providence overrode the will of princes, vowed to accept peasant dominion over his land if it proved to be God's will.[24]

Last Words

Between spring 1524 and spring 1525, Frederick retreated from public life to Castle Lochau. On the day before he died, Spalatin, by then his constant companion, recalled the famous prince sitting on a stool fitted with wheels so that he could roll around the residence. His brother, John, visited him daily in full armor, as he waited to engage a forming thirty-two-thousand-man peasant army. Near the end Frederick sent for Luther, who was then traveling in Thuringia and could not come to his bedside.[25] After taking down his last will and testament, Spalatin asked his prince if he was "burdened," to which Frederick replied, "Only by pain."

Those were Frederick's last recorded words. After receiving the

Eucharist in the new Lutheran manner, with both bread and wine, apparently for the first time, he died in his sleep on May 5. Ten days later Saxon and Hessian forces slaughtered the peasant army at Frankenhausen. Among Frederick's final requests had been that the triumphant princes "be merciful to the peasants" and not burden them with long, harsh monetary penalties. Had he lived, Spalatin believed he would "certainly have given [them] some relief." Frederick likely made that request with a stinging pamphlet of Luther's in mind. A few months earlier, Luther had blamed the peasants' uprising on the tyranny of the princes, calling the revolt and its anarchy a just divine punishment for their tyranny. In contrast to the elector, Luther the cleric and the miner's son called for the "merciless punishment" of the peasants in the aftermath of their revolt, a judgment he based on both Scripture and Saxon law.[26]

Embalmed and placed in a coffin preserved with tar, Frederick's body was delivered to the castle church in Wittenberg five days after his death. At the service Luther's colleague, Wittenberg humanist and professor of Greek, Philipp Melanchthon, read a Latin tribute, followed by one in German by Luther, a consoling sermon on Saint Paul's Epistle to the Thessalonians.[27] At the burial the next day, Luther preached still another sermon, thus twice having the last word over the body of the patron and protector with whom he had never had a live exchange in life, all communication between them having gone through Spalatin.

A GERMAN REVOLT

In much modern scholarship and punditry, Martin Luther has become the man who put miters on princes. He is also said to have been obsessed with the devil, the imminent coming of Christ, and a Reformation that could occur only at the end of time—a man and a movement detached from society and politics. Those same preoccupations are alleged to have turned him against the progressive antiauthoritarian movements of the age: the burgher-artisan protests in the cities, the peasants' revolt in the countryside, and new separatist religious groups—all promising medieval Germany a modern escape from its benighted politics and morals.

Contemporaries knew a very different man and Reformation. During his formative years, from 1518 to 1528, Luther was as devoted to German nationalism and civic reform as he was to the restoration of biblical Christianity. When, in 1520, he appeared on the European stage for the first time as a graphic image, Nuremberg humanists and the Wittenberg court were behind it. Luther and Dürer, who signed his paintings "Albrecht Dürer, German," were never to meet.[28] They touched one another only with their works and through mutual friends in Wittenberg and Nuremberg.

Through the mediation of Spalatin, Luther's early writings circulated widely among German intellectuals. Dürer had early access to them as a charter member of Pirckheimer's dinner group, known after 1517 as the Staupitz Society after Luther's mentor Johannes von Staupitz.[29] In a joint effort to educate Germans and bolster German standing in the outside world, particularly among the Italians and the French, the members of the group devoted themselves to the recovery, preservation, and export of German history and culture. A select gathering of Nuremberg scholars, lawyers, merchants, and politicians influential beyond the city, the group met regularly to discuss pressing issues of the day.[30]

Dürer was among the first Germans to read Luther's Ninety-five Theses in the 1519 German translation of group member Kaspar Nützel—sponsorship that put Luther's protest directly into the service of the German national movement. In March 1518 Luther sent Dürer a letter of thanks, possibly for a print of a recent drawing of Christ's Passion, both conveyed by Spalatin. Two years later Dürer wrote Spalatin to thank Frederick the Wise for "a little book of Luther's," possibly one of the Reformation tracts of 1520, which presented his teachings and reforms to a popular audience. As Luther was now a controversial national figure, Dürer also begged

Spalatin to take steps to ensure the safety of "this Christian man who has helped me out of great distress." The latter referred to the depression and melancholy that had beset him in 1514–15 after his mother's "hard death" and, less traumatically, a thankless, payless year in the employ of Emperor Maximilian I. Saluting Luther, Dürer expressed a wish to immortalize him in a work of art.[31]

With that letter Dürer sent three copies of his recent etching of Frederick's old adversary, the new cardinal, Albrecht of Mainz, apparently as an example of how he would memorialize Luther, given the chance. Albrecht was another Dürer patron, then best known in Saxony as the highest-ranking German church official behind the Saint Peter's indulgence. Wishing to go ahead with an official court portrait of Luther, Spalatin passed a copy of Dürer's Albrecht on to Wittenberg court painter Cranach.

To prepare the court-requested etching of Luther "in the Dürer style," Cranach first copied Dürer's Albrecht—however, not with any intention to flatter either the cardinal or his painterly rival. He portrayed the cardinal as a pudgy, apathetic youth with little resemblance to Dürer's mature and confident prince of the Church. By contrast Cranach's Luther was a muscular, righteous monk with a large chip on his shoulder.[32] The jarring juxtaposition of images suggests that Cranach's competition with Dürer, friendship with Luther (his daughter's godfather in 1520), and remembrance of Albrecht's role in the indulgence controversy had created their own personal acids.[33] That Cranach refurbished the cardinal's residence in Halle three years later—a commission undertaken at the same time he was drawing cartoons of the pope for the Reformation—makes clear that ideology did not trump patronage among the age's artists.[34]

This early conjunction of Saxon art, politics, and religion around the persons of Spalatin, Dürer, Luther, Cranach, and Frederick the Wise began the torrent of organized religious dissent that became the German Reformation. The two movements, the new religious and the older political, spoke with one voice at the Diet of Worms in April 1521. There, the German estates, none of which was yet Protestant, presented Emperor Charles V with 102 "oppressive burdens and abuses imposed upon, and committed against, the German empire by the Holy See of Rome"—a national laundry list of political, economic, ecclesiastical, and spiritual complaints, echoing many of Luther's.[35]

This was not, however, the moment for German grievances to roll themselves up into a juggernaut. The success of national reforms would be commensurate with the reformers' tact and discipline—which brings us back to Cranach's provocative etching of Luther. Having commissioned it, the electoral Saxon court now deemed it too incendiary for the times and instructed Cranach to personify a less angry Germany in a new etching of Luther.[36] The result was a Luther placed within a traditional saint's niche, with an open Bible in hand, a reformer apparently ready to listen and ponder, perhaps even to doubt and heed—a Luther the princes could work with.[37]

The Cranach workshop, with others, created multiple propagandistic images of Luther for groups the court and the reformers wished to win over. Luther freely cooperated in the venture, allowing his physical image to be portrayed as the politicians wished, so long as accompanying biblical verses and evangelical captions gave prominence to his spiritual message.[38] For patricians and well-to-do burghers, Luther appeared as the bearded Junker Jörg, the translator of the New Testament into German. For the intellectuals there was the learned professor in a ballooning doctor's beret. For the learned and simple alike, Hans Holbein depicted Luther as the German Hercules, proceeding to club to death the Dominican inquisitor of Cologne, Jakob Hochstraten, and add his body to a great pile of slain generals in the pope's scholastic army of occupation, from Aristotle to John Duns Scotus. Finally, for all Germans ready to expunge predatory foreigners from German soil, Luther,

Bible in hand, was portrayed side by side with the Franconian leader of knightly resistance, Ulrich von Hutten, sword in hand, under a banner that read "Christian Liberty."[39]

The contributors to the Reformation's propaganda and success—the humanists, the Saxon court, the reformers, and the artists who served all three—recognized the degrading effects of papal power on German politics and the cure of souls: what the politicians called Rome's "burdens and abuses" and the religious reformers its "lies and fabrications." German lawyers, humanists, and theologians all searched the German past for traditions and examples to set against foreign critics, mainly Roman, in a reaffirmation of German sovereignty and cultural equality.[40]

While still an obscure figure, Luther became part of that search, one small contribution to which was an anonymous mystical work he discovered, edited, and published under the title *A German Theology*. In the preface to the complete edition, he praised it as having "led the German people to God where books in Latin, Greek, and Hebrew had not"—proof, he further claimed, of the superiority of German theologians over Roman, Greek, and Jewish. He pointedly cautioned ill-intentioned foreigners not to mistake the simplicity of Germans for weakness.[41] This pamphlet was another native root for Germans to cling to and a reminder of a still unhealed, historically wounded German pride. Its publication was an early step toward the integration of the new religious protest against Rome with those of an older national movement, then also recovering German history and culture.

THE NEW THEOLOGY

A Christian is a perfectly free lord of all, subject to none.
A Christian is a perfectly dutiful servant of all, subject to all.

—MARTIN LUTHER, 1521[42]

Memorable expressions of self-transcendence and self-abasement fill German art and literature, philosophy and theology, and political tracts and speeches. At one end of the spectrum is the sweet nihilism of the medieval mystics, who wanted to lose themselves altogether in the being of God "like a drop of water in a vat of wine," becoming "One Single One."[43] At the other are the modern supermen, who would individually overcome an imperfect world or collectively transform it into a thousand-year Reich. The medieval Church made heretics of the former, while the present-day world continues to pick up the pieces of the latter's fabled utopias.

Man in His Own Image

The thinkers of the German Renaissance and Reformation, both Catholic and Protestant, pondered the predicaments of soul and society more deeply than those of any other German century prior to the nineteenth, when such matters again came under scrutiny to revolutionary effect. In the sixteenth century the result was a portrayal of human nature and destiny that would remain at the center of German Protestant thought and culture for three centuries. The age's most famous painter, Dürer, and theologian, Luther, produced the most memorable expressions.

Dürer's immediate world was personally bounded by the fathers of German humanism (Rudolf Agricola) and German Protestantism (Luther), whose careers bookended Dürer's own. Among German Renaissance artists, Dürer drew more self-portraits than any other, and at the turn of the fifteenth century, he painted two, one in 1500, another in 1502–3, that pointed the way to the religious transition that was the German Reformation.

In the first of these portraits, Jesus Christ is given Dürer's face in what modern art critics have called "a Copernican revolution of the Christ image," precociously marking the birth of modern art and self-perception.[44] Behind and accompanying this famous incarnation were many eloquent humanistic orations on the dignity of man, a literary and painterly tradition brought to a crescendo by Dürer's 1500 self-portrait.

In the self-portrait of 1502–3, by contrast, Dürer presented a mirror image of himself as he recovered from plague, tapping still another medieval genre—Christ the Man of Sorrows—as he now portrayed himself in all his human impermanence and ugliness. Far from the Christ-bearing Dürer of 1500, the artist appears as a dark nude, man alone facing imminent death with no pretension to strength, beauty, or genius, protected only by his foreskin.[45]

While models of both portraits thematically preexisted Dürer's, Luther's dialectical theology of exaltation and abasement waited just over the horizon and would give them an interpretation that drew Dürer into the Reformation and put Luther prominently on the German stage.

The New German Christian

Five years to the month after receiving his doctorate, in October 1517, Luther sweepingly condemned traditional Aristotelian-based theology, with its focus on good works and self-justification.[46] The Church on whose doors legend has him posting his famous theses adjoined Elector Frederick's castle. There university classes in law were taught, and its second floor housed the university library, fitting symbols of the intertwined educational, political, and religious movements of the times.[47]

Luther based his protest on a claimed recovery of the true biblical account of who man is and how he is saved, primary lessons he believed medieval Christianity had lost or perverted. A similar deconstruction of Christianity would not be seen again until the late eighteenth and nineteenth centuries, when a remarkable succession of Protestant academics, beginning with Immanuel Kant and peaking in Friedrich Nietzsche, subjected Christianity to a similar searching critique. In the sixteenth century Luther's theology was as strong a challenge to the medieval religious universe as the later "death of God" philosophy would be to the reformed Judeo-Christian tradition in the modern world. In addition to creating rival Western Christian confessions, Luther's writings united Germans against the Roman papacy and strengthened German territorial sovereignty along lines championed by the national cultural movement.

Both Luther's theology and that of the Roman Church he attacked directed Christians to the biblical promise of salvation, which the incarnation and crucifixion of Christ secured—saving events that lived on in the preaching and sacraments of both churches. Their ways parted, however, when the two confessions looked to the future, where a risen Christ waited in judgment. How one prepared for and survived that future encounter lay at the heart of the division of German and European Christendom during and after the sixteenth century. Looking forward, the Catholic pilgrim traveled a road from mercy to judgment, comforted by the sure promise of Christ the Savior, yet still facing the scrutiny of Christ the Judge. Medieval theology taught the laity to resolve that conflict by penance, absolution, and good works. And by the fifteenth century, indulgences were readily available to those who still had doubts.

For Luther such notions were abominations traceable to legalistic and ritualistic Judaism, which he believed had undermined prophetic and Psalmic Judaism in antiquity and, through the medieval Church, subsequently corrupted biblical Christianity as well. In Protestant theology, the only righteousness that assured survival on Judgment Day was that of the incarnate, crucified, resurrected, and enthroned Son of God, whom faith alone grasped. The Lutheran formula thus directly repudiated the composite medieval formula of faith enriched by love, or good works. Luther compared the all-satisfying moment of faith to the "happy exchange" of a bridegroom and his bride:

> As Christ and the soul become one flesh [Eph. 5:31–32] . . . it follows that everything [each has] is [thereafter] held in common, the good as well as the evil. The believing soul can boast of and glory in whatever Christ has [grace, life, and salvation], as though it were its own, and whatever the soul has [sin, death, and damnation] Christ claims as his own.[48]

For the contemporary guild theologians, the attribution of saving power to faith alone was the height of ignorance and blasphemy. In 1526 Jacob Hochstraten, the Dominican inquisitor of Cologne, distilled the essence of traditional Catholic teaching on the subject in a ridicule of Luther's "happy exchange":

> [Luther] lists no preconditions for the spiritual marriage of the soul with Christ except only that we believe Christ . . . and trust that He will bestow all [that He promises]. Not a single word is said about the mutual love by which the soul loves Christ. . . . Nor do we hear anything about the other divine commandments, to the keeper of which eternal life is both promised and owed.
>
> What else do those who boast of such a base spectacle do than make of the soul . . . a prostitute and an adulteress, who knowingly and wittingly connives to deceive her husband [Christ] and, daily committing fornication upon fornication and adultery upon adultery, makes the most chaste of men a pimp? As if Christ does not take the trouble . . . to choose . . . a pure and honorable lover! As if Christ requires from her only belief and trust and has no interest in her righteousness and the other virtues! As if a certain mingling of righteousness with iniquity and of Christ with Belial were possible![49]

Luther's marriage of faith was neither a medieval mystical union nor any misreading of faith's traditional role. By comparison with medieval theology, he radically reformulated the definition of a "saved" person this side of eternity. Instead of becoming intrinsically like Christ, the good Christian had rather to recognize and accept his abiding dissimilarity from him, this side of eternity. Yet, in Luther's new definition of the "perfect mortal," God and man were as fully reconciled with each other as they would be in eternity—and without any blasphemous diminution of God, or exaltation of man in the process. Here, precisely as Hochstraten had scolded, there was a "certain mingling of righteousness with iniquity," yet not such as to make Christ an incautious pimp, or the soul a wanton whore. In the German Protestant tradition the believer was righteous and sinful simultaneously, *simul iustus et peccator*—righteous by his union with Christ in faith and sinful by his irradicable finitude and fallen humanity.

This dialectical theology was of one piece with Dürer's juxtaposed portraits of himself as the risen Christ and the death-afflicted man of sorrows. The good news of the Christian Gospel, according to Luther, was that a person is not required to be internally "like" God to be one with him. In the "happy exchange" that repeats itself in lifelong moments of faith, the believer gained the clarity and certainty that God was no fiction and his biblical promise, "all who believe will be saved," no lie.

With that bright spiritual insight came also the dark awareness that the soul, in itself, alone and apart from its divine Bridegroom, remained a hapless creature, capable neither of fulfilling the Law in this life nor of surviving the judgment of God in the next. In Luther's view the German Christian, unlike the Roman, did not see his life on a spiritual continuum from diminishing sinfulness to increasing righteousness. His soul spanned two poles and he led a double life—hopeless and mad in the life he alone could sustain on earth, yet eternally secure in the heights to which his faith momentarily lifted him. German Christians who attained such self-understanding, whether through a traditional confession or in some secular experience, gained a sense of permanent opportunity. Although a Lutheran formulation, uncountable strains of previous religious experience and insight had been packed into it. Here, in a word, was a theology for a people always starting and stopping in their history, the ultimate pulling-oneself-up-by-one's-bootstraps philosophy, which allowed neither self-contentment nor self-despair. Here was also the cautionary lesson that Johann Wolfgang von Goethe would later modernize in his retelling of the sixteenth-century German story of Dr. Faustus.[50]

A NEW CIVIC SOCIETY

The new theology critically reassessed not only the problems threatening the soul, but also those facing society at large. In the Lutheran version, Christians, who were "lords over all" in conscience and soul, had a duty to be "servants to all" in their bodily lives and secular vocations. Also pushing the political, social, and domestic extension of the Reformation were the dissent within Lutheran clerical ranks and the demands of peasants and artisans in the name of Christianity and the Reformation.

Given the ink modern scholars have spent to portray Luther's political and social thought as enabling the triumph of the absolute German territorial state, a Lutheran civic society may seem an oxymoron. However, the religious reformers embraced not only the German national movement but also the goal of a just and fair society for all Germans. Before Luther's reforms had changed the ecclesiastical laws of a single town or village, he had published major treatises on political philosophy, poor relief, marriage and family, Jewish-Christian relations, and educational reform.

On two points the competing reformers of the age agreed: Winning meant securing reform in law and institutions, and the most effective way of doing that was to coopt established power. The

Lutherans accordingly portrayed separatism and revolution as a shirking of Christian moral and civic duty—society's abandonment and destruction rather than its internal reform. Both Thomas Müntzer, who led a peasant's revolt, and radical Dutch and German Anabaptists, who created a reign of terror in the city of Münster, understood that well—the former pitching the peaceful adoption of his reforms to the Saxon princes, while the latter came to power by legal means.[51]

For the age, the cumulative effects of the reforms pursued in politics, social welfare, domestic life, and education were as consequential as those sought in Church and religion. In the struggle for just laws and honest institutions, God and the devil competed both for individual souls and earthly rule. Luther envisioned two coeval authorities ordained by God to govern the secular and ecclesiastical spheres of life—the princes and lords to oversee body and property, the pastors and priests to safeguard consciences and souls.

For Luther the German problem of the sixteenth century was the devil's success in tempting both rulers and clergy, subjects and laity, to sell their souls and shirk their moral and spiritual duties. The politicians did so by permitting injustice and obstructing the Gospel; the ecclesiasts by false assurances of salvation and improper secular ambition; and the general run of humankind by allowing itself to be so easily fooled and cowed by both. In addition to a foreign, predatory papacy, two other enemies were seen to threaten civic society in the early decades of the Reformation: Catholic rulers who suppressed Protestant religious reforms, and renegade Protestant gospelers and revolutionaries, who urged the common man to take up arms for alleged Christian rights.

In pursuit of his goals Luther, too, fatefully blurred the lines of authority and power he himself had drawn. He did so, first, by inviting the Christian nobility of the German nation, as Christian laity, to take up his cause against an intractable Church. In 1523 he commended the example of a lay congregation in the German town of Leisnig for replacing its Catholic priest with a Lutheran pastor of its own choice, praising its action as an appropriate rejection of false "human law, principle, tradition, custom, and habit."[52] If this was a new ecclesiology, it was also a timely rationalization.

Again, in 1528, after Saxon visitations discovered spotty religious knowledge and scant moral improvement among the laity in the country parishes, Luther exhorted the German princes, again as lay Christians, to become "emergency bishops." In that capacity they were to provide the fledgling Protestant churches with the administration, authority, and force required for their proper maintenance and discipline.[53] Despite qualifying clauses, which stressed the princes' lay status and the exceptional nature of their new powers, that concession set an ominous German precedent.

When, in 1523, princes began persecuting Protestants, Luther attempted in vain to put the genie back into the bottle, lecturing them on "what they might *not* do."[54] By 1528 German rulers never again—if ever they had—confined their rule solely to body and property. Luther's weaving together of temporal and spiritual power enabled the new church to survive its infancy and pursue its mission in relative safety. It became a more cooperative state church, empowered and eager to mix large doses of religion into civic life through the new schools, welfare system, and domestic arrangements it helped create.

Schools and Universities

The first transregional unification of the German people was linguistic and cultural, centered around Luther's vernacular sermons, pamphlets, Bible, hymns, and catechisms. Few contemporary Germans were as qualified to oversee the reform of Germany's schools and universities as he. Between 1520 and 1546 one-third of all German-language publications were original or reprint copies of Luther's works. He wrote and spoke a simple, lucid, rhythmic German, which still today sets his writings apart from "the awful

German language," whose fragmented, multisubject sentences go ever so slowly in search of their verbs.[55] He claimed that language also to be that of the Saxon court, imitated by "all the princes and kings of Germany," thus allowing him to speak to a nation.[56] That dialect was also an early form of the pan-German language we know today as High German, evolved from composite East Middle and Low German dialects. Luther enriched it with words and phrases of colleagues and students from other German regions—also those of his West Saxon wife, Katherine von Bora, whose fluency he praised above his own.[57]

In 1524 Luther appealed to magistrates and councilmen across Germany to fund public schools for all boys and girls. With the stated goal of creating "men able to rule over land and people, and women able to manage households and train children and servants aright," the new schools provided both new religious and secular education.[58] Boys received up to two hours a day of formal study and girls at least an hour, the remainder of their day devoted to parentally determined domestic work at home or apprenticeship in a trade.[59]

Trusting neither the common man, who was deemed incapable of what was required, nor the princes, who were accused of being addicted to play, the reformers looked to city governments to provide skilled schoolmasters and -mistresses able to teach children languages, history, and the arts "with pleasure and in play." Recalling his own school days as a hell and purgatory, with frequent "flogging, trembling, anguish, and misery," Luther proposed a global education for German children who now lived in a new world—an education that could put before them, "as in a mirror, the character, life, counsels, and purposes . . . of the whole world, [from which they might] draw the proper inferences and . . . take their own place in the stream of human events."[60]

Another goal of educational reform was to get the German story straight. Due to the lack of properly trained historians, Luther believed, little was known of the history of the Germans, leaving people in other lands to imagine them to be "beasts, who know only how to fight, gorge, and guzzle."[61]

When, in the late 1520s, these ambitious efforts to reeducate the countryside seemed to be a total failure, previously progressive educators reached for the rigor of the old system. The disappointment was apparent in Luther's reaction to the visitation reports, moving him to describe countryside pastors as better fitted to "herd swine and keep dogs than to watch over Christian souls," who seemed to think the new Gospel a message of "carnal liberty."[62]

The solution was the vernacular catechism, which addressed religious education within the friendlier confines of the family circle as well as the churches. With versions for both children and adults, daily recitations of the Ten Commandments, the Apostles' Creed, and the Lord's Prayer would now bring German souls the enlightenment and protection pastors had failed to deliver.[63]

It would be wrong to think that the appearance of catechetical drills at home and the return of Aristotle to the lecture halls ended the pursuit of a better education. The happy exchange of faith did not become a hard bargain overnight. Nor with the passage of centuries did the new Protestant establishment surrender its high scholarly standards or return to the scholastic commentaries it had earlier rejected. Over the centuries the pervasiveness of Lutheran and Catholic theology in gymnasiums and universities infused German public education with religious knowledge,[64] which in turn exacerbated confessional divisions. Yet that same knowledge also made the Germans Europe's most theologically literate people and facilitated both confessions' cooperation with the state.

Some have argued that the Reformation left the majority of Germans in both a religious-secular and medieval-modern time warp, always "questioning and doubting, probing and searching, without fences and security."[65] That had also been the reformers' critique of the medieval cure of souls and justification for their reforms. Germans who knowingly turned Protestant in the sixteenth century did so in the principled belief that many traditional spiritual reliefs were bogus, and hence of little use to a devout soul. By comparison, Luther's happy exchange of faith, even in the new disciplinary form of the Lutheran catechism, seemed to Protestants a more credible spiritual transaction.

Poor Relief

At the turn of the fifteenth century, two-thirds of the Saxon population lived in the countryside, and, much as today, the poor gravitated toward the cities where opportunities to work and beg were greater.[66] As with most medieval social and domestic legislation, traditional care of the poor had a religious inspiration. Hand-to-hand, eye-to-eye almsgiving had been the original biblical model for the penitential Christian, and those extending such personal charity could expect a share of God's blessing on the poor in return. For centuries that belief moved devout Christians to endow clothing, housing, and schooling for the poor as well.

By contrast the new Lutheran church looked on charitable acts as a moral and civic duty, not a spiritual one, and believed that—while pleasing to God—they saved no one. Good works belonged to the recipient, not to the giver, whom God saved for his own merciful reasons, irrespective of his deeds. Such argument helped clear the path to a rationalized system of poor relief, expanding its scope and putting it on a surer economic basis, something desired by both confessions. The result was a landmark shifting of responsibility for the poor from the clergy and the Church to society at large through local and territorial governments.

Lutherans helped create model welfare ordinances that distinguished the worthy native poor from foreign, able-bodied beggars, including itinerant friars, who were turned away from the city gates.[67] The guiding principle behind such discrimination was an early version of the formula later adopted by the Diet of Augsburg to resolve the age's religious divisions by allowing the ruler of a land to choose its official religion ("his realm, his religion"). In the welfare version the ruler of a land became responsible for the poor within it ("his realm, his poor"), bound by his oath of office to allow neither the poor of his land to burden that of another, nor alien poor to take from his.

In dispensing charity, both handouts and loans, the recipient's rehabilitation counted most, welfare being looked on as a means to recovery, not a permanent dole. The Wittenberg Ordinance, influenced by Luther and his colleagues, provided for a carefully guarded "common chest," or locked box for the poor. Applicants had to meet community standards of virtue (past behavior and present attitude were scrutinized), and, once back on their feet, repay what they had received. Struggling workers and artisans could apply for low-interest loans, and subsidies existed for training the children of the poor.

Funding initially came from secularized church properties and the confiscated endowments of closed cloisters and chapters. Anticipating the diversion of such funds to other purposes, or their eventual drying up, the ordinance looked to graduated taxes on clergy and citizens as the best way to keep the chest full. Through the efforts of Wittenberg pastor Johannes Bugenhagen, the early Lutheran welfare ordinances found imitators throughout north Germany and in Scandinavia by midcentury.

Marriage and Domestic Life

When in the late fifteenth and sixteenth centuries, Europeans made the transition from a society of predominantly single people to one in which marriage became the dominant lifestyle, the Lutheran family provided an attractive model within and beyond Protestant lands.[68] Motivated also by a personal desire for clerical marriage, the religious reformers recast marriage from an exclusively religious sacrament to a social contract sanctioned primarily by the state, effectively creating marriage as we know it today.[69] As with other civic reforms, the reframing of marriage was part of a larger protest against medieval Church and society.

In 1520 Luther scorned the canonists who wrote the unbiblical marriage laws of the medieval Church as "merchants selling vulvas and genitals," condemning their new laws as only "snares for taking money," a reference to the payments required by church authorities to dispense impediments to claimed illicit marriages.[70] During the Middle Ages the Church inflated the biblical prohibitions of marriage to the fourth degree of affinity and consanguinity, or as far as third cousins. Even godparentage and adoption created forbidden lines of marriage. And the Church recognized interfaith marriages only if the non-Christian spouse agreed to convert.

The Reformation, by contrast, restored the biblical first degree of affinity and second of consanguinity, allowing unions with cousins by marriage beyond the first degree and with blood relations beyond the second. Calling numerous canonical impediments to marriage fabrications, Luther condemned them all as bluntly he did the notion that a Christian could not marry a non-Christian: "Just as I may eat, drink, sleep, walk, ride with, buy from, and speak with a heathen, Jew, Turk, or heretic, so I may marry him [or her]."[71]

The reformers also treated certain restrictions on the annulment of failed or unwanted marriages as unbiblical. Over the course of the sixteenth century, they recognized several acceptable grounds for ending a marriage: adultery, impotence (sexual incapacity), polygamy or deception (a concealed first marriage), prolonged desertion, and grave incompatibility. Unlike the medieval Church, which permitted only separation from bed and table and not the dissolution of a marriage, the Reformation sanctioned modern divorce and remarriage for those willing and able to see it through, whose numbers however remained quite small until the nineteenth century. In his definition of a "fully confirmed" marriage, Strasbourg reformer Martin Bucer, the most liberal on the subject, included an "assent of hearts" and "plenty of carnal intercourse." Here, the

Reformation anticipated John Milton's defense of the absence of "true companionship" as a proper ground for divorce—what today are called "irreconcilable differences."[72]

THE REFORMATION AND THE JEWS

In 1523 Luther surprised his contemporaries by writing a friendly overture to German Jews. The immediate occasion was a refutation of Hapsburg archduke Ferdinand's slander of him as one who, like the Jews, believed Jesus's mother was no virgin. Luther seized on the accusation to extend his religious and civic reforms. By pointing out what the New Testament clearly taught, that Jesus was a Jew born of a virgin, he both defended himself against the archduke and curried favor with German Jews, who welcomed the security and opportunity his kindness extended. The result of gentler Christian treatment, he expected, would be the assimilation of Jews into Christian society and the eventual conversion of "some," perhaps "many," to Christianity.[73]

By the 1530s the Reformation's vision of a culturally and religiously united Germany with magnanimous rulers, justly treated peasants, and assimilated, even baptized, Jews was gone, the casualty of peasant revolts, religious division, and unrealistic expectations. Like his mid-1520s pamphlets against peasants, Luther's writings against the Jews in the late 1530s and early 1540s measured the great distance from the original plan. Having implored Christians in 1523 to pursue the conversion of the Jews with honey rather than vinegar, fifteen years passed before he again publicly addressed the subject of Christian-Jewish relations. With no progress on the immediate home front, reports of Christian casualties abroad moved him to take a harsh stance. In Bohemia and Moravia, he was told, Jews proselytized among Christians, some of whom denied that Jesus was the Messiah, embraced the Jewish law, observed the Jewish Sabbath, and even circumcised themselves.[74] Instead of winning Jews to Christianity, Luther now found reason to fear that his earlier kindness had allowed the Jews to steal a march on Christians. Thereafter he viewed German Jews as another in a long history of foreign German predators, no longer the kindred subjects and promising converts he had recommended to fellow Christians in 1523.

The very first line of his longest and harshest tract, entitled *On the Jews and Their Lies*, cited Jewish attempts "to lure to themselves even us [Christians]."[75] He reports two face-to-face meetings with Jews in Wittenberg, one of which brought three rabbis to his door in the hope of "finding a new Jew in me," as they had heard that Luther was then studying the Hebrew scriptures.[76] Had the year been 1523, when the Reformation was taking wing, and not 1543, when he believed his reform had peaked and he was counting its disappointments, his German-Christian conscience might not have been provoked so.

The specter of German Jews successfully playing the tempter stirred German memory and suspicion. For a Luther now at the end of his career, there could not have been a more brazen slap in the face than a Jewish attempt to convert him. Both German history and Christian theology fueled the reformer's great presumption in this matter. As a Christian theologian he believed that the destruction of Jerusalem by the Romans in A.D. 70 had been God's passing of the torch from Jews to Christians, thenceforth the "true Israelites." For Luther the German, the insulting, coopting, and bullying of Germans by clever foreign peoples was an older and more upsetting story, reaching back to Roman times, and recently refreshed by his own career struggles against papal Rome in the German Christian world. To document his accusation that the Jews had become another "arrogant, vengeful, foreign presence" in Germany, he drew parallels between Jewish disrespect for Jesus ("a hanged highwayman") and the Virgin Mary ("no virgin") and papal ridicule of himself (a "changeling") and his mother (a "whore and bathhouse attendant"). The Jews, he now believed, had proved themselves to be Korahites (after Korah, an unsuccessful leader of a dissident rebellion against Moses) and were no longer true Israelites or true Germans.[77]

Luther found it revealing that Jews reviled Gentiles as *Goyim*, which, he pointed out, was no unbiased description of Gentiles, but a deliberate slander, meaning

> poor muck-worms, maggots, stench, and filth . . . dirt and nothing . . . benighted heathen . . . a stupid [people] slow to learn. . . . The Jews boast that they are the . . . only noble people on earth . . . in comparison with [whom] we Gentiles are not human, [because] we are not of [their] high and noble blood, lineage, birth, and descent.[78]

In ritual prayers Jewish men thanked God that they had been born Israelites and not *Goyim*, human beings rather than animals or slaves, and males instead females—for non-Jews, a disparaging set of parallels. In such pride and prejudice, Luther heard the boasting of the Greeks (he mentions Plato) and the Italians over their not having been born "barbarians" like the Germans. Greeks, Romans, Byzantines, papists, and, now, in this succession of great cultures, minority German Jews "imagine all the other people in the world [to be] mere ducks or mice by comparison." The rabbis with their Talmud were no different from the popes with their decretals (decrees), and sectarian Protestants with their Gospel excerpts—all presumptuous religious elites wanting to be "our masters within our own land."[79]

The convergence of historically wounded German pride with overweening Christian confidence in the history of salvation created Luther's late writings against the Jews. The one was the fruit of centuries of perceived German diminution to an inferior people, the other that of almost as old an exercise of Christian hubris. "This," Luther concluded,

> is the bone of contention [and] the source of trouble between Christian and Jew. The Jews do not want [and] cannot endure that

> we Gentiles . . . whom they incessantly mock, curse, damn, defame, and revile . . . should be their equal before God, and that the Messiah should be our comfort and joy as well as theirs.[80]

In the end Luther wanted the German princes to repay Jewish betrayal with "rough mercy," an oxymoron meaning their forced recognition that Jesus was the Messiah. Failing that, he wanted them exiled to a land of their own, where they might practice their minority religion without proselytizing or ridiculing the souls of Christians. To that end he recommended burning the synagogues, schools, and houses of nonconverting Jews; confiscating Talmudic writings and banning rabbinical teaching; denying safe-conduct; prohibiting usury and giving existing moneys gained thereby to Jewish converts to Christianity; and, finally, forced labor—"putting a flail, an ax, a hoe, a spade, a distaff, or spindle [in the hands of] the idle holy people." If such measures did not produce Christian conversions, German rulers were then advised to end Germany's exceptional tolerance by "emulating the common sense of France, Spain, and Bohemia [which had already] ejected them forever."[81]

Luther's disappointment in German Jews was more than matched by theirs in him. Josel of Rosheim, the spokesman for German Jews in the Holy Roman Empire, declared such words by a Christian scholar to be unprecedented and hardly to have been expected from the author of *Jesus Christ Was Born a Jew*. German Jews then also had a powerful, self-interested ally in the emperor, who relied heavily on their fiscal resources. Even more helpful to them at the time, and also to the Reformation over time, was the small impact Luther's harsh words made on his contemporaries. In electoral Saxony a lapsed decree of 1536 that had denied residence and safe-conduct to nonconverting Jews was revived. Martin Bucer prepared a harsh new Jewish ordinance for the land of Hesse, intended to restrict Hessian Jews to lowly jobs. However, in implementing it, Landgrave Philip limited the enforced measures to restrictions on Jewish interest charges, prohibition of new synagogues and Jewish proselytizing, and Jewish attendance at consciousness-raising sermons. Nowhere did any prince burn synagogues, raze Jewish houses, or seize Jewish books, per Luther's recommendation.[82]

Luther's anti-Jewish tracts lived on in the complete editions of his works, but did not as a rule find their way into Lutheran confessions, catechisms, and hymns. One of the few exceptions was a novel listing of the Jews in the Lutheran Formula of Concord. There Jews appeared as the last in a line of heretics specific to the rise of Protestantism, as if nonconverting Jews were another abberrant offshoot of Lutheranism: "Sacramentalists [Zwinglians], Calvinists, Enthusiasts [Anabaptists], Epicurians [Spiritualists], and Jews."[83]

In 1523 Luther had opened the door to culturally non-German Germans, only to slam it shut two decades later. Far more influential in the German Lutheran world were the many reformers, including his Wittenberg colleague Justus Jonas and the Lower Saxon reformer Urbanus Rhegius, who, together with most of the political leadership of Protestantism, were prepared to wait indefinitely on the conversion of the Jews and rejected intimidation and coercion.[84]

Before National Socialism no direct link between Christian anti-Judaism and modern racial anti-Semitism existed in a German government program of Jewish extermination. Nor did Luther ever espouse any Manichaean dualism of the "first" and the "last" man, the waxing Aryan and the waning Jew of nineteenth-century German and other intellectuals. For him, it was the fledgling evangelical church, not German Jewry, whose future lay in the balance in the sixteenth century. Although suspecting converted Jews to be disingenuous Christians, it was attitude and will, not blood or race, that made the difference.[85] Even at the heights to which Luther carried Christian anti-Judaism, and against the background of late medieval Christian persecution and pogroms, Luther's was never the racial anti-Semitism of the National Socialists, a term coined not in the late 1530s and 1540s but in 1879.[86] Had Luther had his way, nonconforming Jews would have been exiled by contemporary governments in the same way "stubborn" Anabaptists and other sectarian dissenters to Protestant and Catholic Christianity were exiled. Also, Judaism never became a capital crime in German or imperial law, as happened with Anabaptism in 1529.

Still, Nazis later matter-of-factly conscripted Luther's writings into the Holocaust. As with earlier anti-Semites, they were shown that road not by Luther, but by Jewish converts to Christianity, whose exposés and assaults on their own faith had been assembled by the German Calvinist Andreas Eisenmenger and published in 1711. Entitled *Judaism Unmasked*, this infamous collection of diatribes by Christianized Jews has been called the nineteenth-century anti-Semite's "literary munitions arsenal."[87] Nowhere in its more than two thousand pages is the name of Martin Luther so much as mentioned.

Today few scholars examine Luther's late writings against the Jews with any hope of finding a qualifying biographical or historical context that might place the theologian and his reform in a less damning light. Rather, appeals have been made to his old age, health, and disappointment over his reform, which was then rapidly losing ground not only to Protestant and Catholic rivals, but, Luther sincerely believed, to opportunistic Jews as well. Another popular explanation has been an alleged obsession with the imminent second coming of Christ, a definitive signal of which was the conversion of the Jews or their removal from the company of Christians.[88]

The truest explanation here is probably the most historical and best documented. From his earliest writings, Luther targeted legalistic Judaism as the corruption of prophetic Judaism and early Christianity, turning original religions of faith and hope into those of ritual observance and good works. By the 1530s he feared a similar fate was befalling his own reform. Because his anti-Judaism was intertwined with a reading of the German past as a history of foreign predation, Luther, without any sense of disproportion, could place contemporary Jews in a long succession of peoples and nations who had put Germans down. That combination of history and theology also made his anti-Jewish writings especially vulnerable to cooptation by the anti-Semites of the nineteenth and twentieth centuries.[89]

THE REFORMATION IN MODERN CRITICISM

From Luther's contemporary rival Thomas Müntzer to the dean of American German historians, Gordon A. Craig, the big story of the German Reformation has been the "unhindered expansion" of the absolute German territorial state.[90] A similar conclusion has been drawn from the Reformation's perceived effects on family life—the new Lutheran family being held up as "the prototype of the unconditionally patriarchal and authoritarian household."[91] Yet, at its inception, the Reformation promised pathbreaking relationships between lords and subjects, Jews and Christians, and men and women. The new theology proclaimed the spiritual equality and freedom of all Christians regardless of social estate, juxtaposed honest peasants to greedy landlords and corrupt clergy, scolded Christians for bullying Jews, and defended a model of marriage based on spousal sharing of domestic authority. Yet, when peasants threatened violence, Luther's response to their leaders was harsh ("suffering suffering, cross cross"), and after they revolted in Saxony and Hesse, looting, burning, and killing their lords, his counsel to the latter was equally pitiless ("smite, slay, stab").[92] On both occasions he spoke for established Germany.

Such responses have moved modern scholars and pundits to wonder aloud whether the men behind the Reformation sowed a bitter social and political harvest for later German generations. Having failed to win the masses by direct appeal, the Reformation is said to have undermined alternative quasi-democratic, communal self-government by embracing the authoritarian territorial state, thereby putting early German nationhood and parliamentary government permanently out of reach.[93] This interpretation of the Reformation as an initially progressive, yet in the end (1525) easily coopted bourgeois movement, mirrors the interpretation of Germany's evolution over the nineteenth century by modern German historians, who also perceive the betrayal of a budding democracy by a weak-kneed middle class.[94]

In weighing the Reformation, modern critics have especially scrutinized the character and work of the still famous contemporaries at its center. Lucas Cranach was sixteenth-century Germany's second most famous painter, a close friend of Luther, a two-term Wittenberg *Bürgermeister*, and one of the city's richest men at his death. Unfortunately for his reputation among modern historians, who detect a sympathetic social commentary in his early art, Cranach lived eighty-one years, long enough to leave a canvas trail that told a different story. Running a gamut from evangelical protests on behalf of the poor to titillating nudes for the bourgeoisie and flattering portraits of the political and commercial elite, Cranach's biography and repertoire are also read as a metaphor for the Reformation's promise and failure.[95]

Dürer's painterly services also straddled the age's political and social fences, and his wealth at his death was even greater than Cranach's. Yet, because he died so much earlier than Luther and Cranach, Dürer did not have to take stands on the unforgiving confessional and political conflicts of later decades. His more positive modern reputation, like that of the early Cranach, also owes something to Friedrich Engels and nineteenth-century Marxists, who placed him quickly in the pantheon of premodern proletarian heroes. Among the graduates of the Dürer workshop were three students who came to be known as the "godless painters" of Nuremberg.[96] Arrested and interrogated after the Peasants' Revolt for urging workers to strike for higher wages, the three expressed doubts about the powers of God and of the magistrates of Nuremberg—activities and perspectives then associated with the teaching of the revolutionary Thomas Müntzer. Dürer's sculptor also landed in jail for his support of the Peasants' Revolt.[97]

A more direct link to possible radical sentiments on Dürer's part is a drawing made in 1525, after the princes crushed peasant rebels in Franconia. Appearing in a study of perspective in art, it depicts a possible monument to the revolt, in which a peasant sits atop a chicken coop, a sword thrust prominently into his back, the classic iconography of betrayal, with the accompanying caption: "He who wants to commemorate his victory over the rebellious peasants might use to that end a structure such as I portray here."[98]

Was the drawing an expression of sympathy for the peasants' cause or a repudiation of it? Although modern scholars argue both sides, the more correct interpretation may lie in between. The monument appears to lament the harm brought about by princes and peasants alike, suggesting a graphic parallel to Luther's own pre-revolt plague on both houses, and post-revolt description of robbing and murdering peasants as "mad dogs." At the time of its drawing, Dürer's peers, friends, and associates strongly condemned the rebellion, and his own professional and personal activities during the conflict suggest that he did so as well. While Hessian and Saxon soldiers massacred peasants, Dürer painted portraits of the Fuggers, contemporary banking magnates, and the wife and sister of Margrave Casimir of Brandenburg-Ansbach, a brutal slayer of rebellious peasants who also blinded Anabaptists before exiling them from his land.[99]

Dürer's professional association with Nuremberg's godless painters of course no more means that he shared their atheism and rebellion than his associations with political and social elites mean that he could not sympathize with the peasants' plight. Luther, too, championed justice for the peasants before their attacks on their landlords and mercy for them after they were crushed by the princes.[100] By this measure Luther might have joined Dürer in the Marxist pantheon, although neither he nor Dürer, by any contemporary measure, would have wanted to be enthroned there.

Four hundred years after Dürer's death, the National Socialists involuntarily conscripted him and Cranach into their propaganda. In 1943 Dürer's 1500 *Self-Portrait* even adorned the cover of the National Socialist magazine, *People and Race*, and Hitler publicly praised Dürer and Nuremberg as the "most German" of artists and cities. When the National Socialists cleansed German museums of "degenerate" modern art in the 1930s, the works of Cranach and Dürer were prominent among those that took its place.[101]

As with his early and late writings against the Jews, Luther's condemnation of the Peasants' Revolt is what his strongest critics today remember most about him.[102] In the early 1520s Protestant pamphleteers promised both burghers in the cities and peasants on the land a new spiritual egalitarianism (the "freedom of the Christian," the "priesthood of all believers") in place of the Church's hierarchical cure of souls. Like the Jews in 1523, the common man, too, heard in the Reformation a timely political message of autonomy and social cohesion. Backing up those overtures were Luther's denunciations of the tyranny of princes and lords and the sheepishness of their subjects:

> "Our rulers [are] mad; they actually think they can do whatever they please and order their subjects to follow them in it, while their subjects, in turn, make the mistake of believing that they must obey whatever their rulers command."[103]

Such sympathy for the peasants notwithstanding, he believed that the disputed issues of body and property were matters for the secular courts and not to be freelanced by gospelers and revolutionaries. Thus the bracing counsel:

> Peasants should fight as a people who will not and ought not endure wrong or evil according to the teaching of nature. [Your grievances regarding] game, birds, fish, wood [and] forests [and the unfair levying of] services, tithes, imposts, excises, and death

> taxes [are matters for] lawyers . . . and do not concern a Christian. . . . [You must] let the name of Christian go and act . . . as men and women who want their human and natural rights.[104]

That was a proper instruction for a society based on the rule of law, but bitter counsel for the peasants. When peasant leaders subsequently jeopardized the Reformation by tying its religious teachings to sociopolitical revolution, they forfeited any possible chance of holding Luther's support. On the eve of the revolt, Luther, speaking for his society, denounced peasant refusal to pay small tithes as "theft and highway robbery" and scorned peasant appeals to Christ for release from serfdom as "carnalizing" Christian freedom. The classless, godless society envisioned by peasant revolutionaries was not the cohesive civic society the Reformation wanted to build. "Unless there is an inequality of persons, some free, some bound, some lords, some subjects," he lectured, a society cannot survive. But neither could Luther find anything Christian on the princes' side. More than anything else, their repression and tyranny had occasioned the great rebellion and anarchy. His last word to both sides was a plea he knew to be in vain: "[Please] be advised and attack [your differences] with justice, not with force or strife, and do not start an endless bloodshed in Germany."[105]

After peasants attacked their landlords in Swabia, Franconia, and Thuringia, Luther—confronted by the specter of a full-scale revolution—exhorted the princes to kill the rebels pitilessly.[106]

If, as many argue, his political philosophy raised the German state to new political authority and power after 1525, it was only the latest in a long series of lifts. Had such enhancement been the only thing the Reformation had to offer the princes, its appeal to them would have been small. The German state had grown impressively on its own throughout the late Middle Ages. By the late thirteenth and fourteenth centuries, the princes had become supreme rulers within their lands and were collectively so within the empire by the late fifteenth.[107] Long before there was a Reformation to assist them, they had reformed local churches and cloisters at their own initiative, punishing clerical abuses and assisting the cure of souls. What the German states gained most from the Reformation was the opportunity to establish an independent German culture and break with the pope in Rome, who, by 1519, had become a more disruptive foreign force in Germany than the still useful and respected Hapsburg emperor.

The defense of Protestant religious freedom gave rise to an interterritorial military alliance, the Schmaldkaldic League, and a political-religious war with Emperor Charles V. The war's resolution established German religious pluralism and the confessional division of Western Christendom. After 1555 rulers in lands with mixed religious confessions designated the official religion. In some places old Catholic and new Lutheran communions learned to coexist.[108] Where dissenters found the public worship of their faith forbidden, they might emigrate to a land where it was legal, travel on feast days to neighboring areas where their faith was practiced, hire a visiting priest or pastor to perform desired services on the border of a territory or city, and/or practice their faith quietly in the privacy of their own homes.

The Lutheran embrace of the German territorial state not only enhanced its sovereignty, it also endowed it with an ethical and cultural mission over which the new clergy and duly appointed lower magistrates were duty-bound to stand a vigilant watch.[109] That watch evolved into a principled doctrine of resistance to tyrants among Lutherans facing imperial and papal armies in the mid-1540s, and among French and Netherlands Calvinists fighting similar religious wars in the second half of the century. When in the wake of the Saint Bartholomew's Day Massacre in 1572, John Calvin's successor, Theodore Beza, published his defense of the right of lower magistrates to overthrow tyrants, including princes, kings, and emperors, his work appeared as an anonymous tract published in the Lutheran city of Magdeburg, the fabled center of German resistance to imperial occupation and tyranny.[110]

4

EUROPE'S STOMPING GROUND

Germany During the Thirty Years' War

THE THIRTY YEARS' WAR has been called "the trauma of the Germans" before the world wars of the twentieth century.[1] For the first time in their history, Germans found themselves in a catastrophic conflict that was both international and interminable. Through thirty years of alternating hot and cold war, Germany became an involuntary battlefield on which militarily superior nations settled their conflicts and increased their assets. Although German princes started it all, once the war had begun neither the German people, who endured most of its pain and sacrifice, nor their leaders, who made overtures to foreign powers, controlled either the war's development or the terms on which it finally ended.

Loose Ends

The root cause of the war was a century of imperial Austrian determination to keep a key electoral state, Bohemia, within the Hapsburg orbit, while reversing galloping Protestant gains there. Since 1438 the Holy Roman Emperor, Germany's overlord, had been a Hapsburg. By the founding decree of the German electoral college in 1356, the seven German electors set the terms of each new emperor's rule before electing him unanimously. Once the crown was on a new emperor's head, however, he quickly developed a mind of his own—something that was never truer than in the seventeenth century.

The key players in the war's outbreak provocatively mixed religion and politics. The first was Archduke Ferdinand of Styria, a province in southern Austria, later to become Emperor Ferdinand II. Between 1598 and 1600 he expelled Protestants massively from his land, among them astronomer Johannes Kepler, soon to discover the laws of planetary motion and join the court of Ferdinand's cousin, Emperor Rudolf II, the age's enlightened patron of culture and science. The other key player, or, more accurately, playground, at the war's onset was the kingdom of Bohemia, a land of fervent religious liberty situated on Austria's northern frontier. There, in 1575, native Hussites and Lutherans had merged around a new Protestant confession, the Bohemian Confession.

Catholicism strengthened over the first decade of the seventeenth century after Hungary and Transylvania (modern western Romania) were forcibly reconverted in 1602. To East European Protestants, the Austrian Hapsburg threat had become increasingly dire. Fearing they might be next, the Bohemians asked the emperor for reassurance, which he gave them in the form of a letter of majesty. Emperor Rudolf's brother, future emperor Matthias, added his weight to the letter by accepting it as a condition of his succession to the royal Bohemian crown. That promise, however, proved false; no sooner did he become king of the Bohemians than he revoked their religious liberty.[2]

Protestant efforts to deflect such bullying by so powerful a sovereign, and one within the larger German family as well, were hamstrung by geographic and political divisions. With its population approaching twenty million, the empire contained 2,500 independent political entities, depending on how far down the political scale, from electoral prince to lowly *Schenk* (a noble servant to higher royalty), one counted. Well before the turn of the sixteenth century, the institutions created in the fifteenth to ensure the peace and security of the empire—the imperial diet, the imperial supreme court, and the interterritorial defensive blocs known as "the circles"—had been undermined by the growth of territorial state sovereignty, imperial retaliation, and new religious divisions.[3]

In the mid–sixteenth century, new measures had been taken to prevent interminable warfare based on confessional differences. Together with a pragmatic endorsement of princely sovereignty over religious conflict, giving the ruler of a land the right to determine its official religion, the imperial Diet of Augsburg also embraced an "ecclesiastical reservation" agreed to in a previous treaty at Passau in 1552. That clause prohibited any archbishop, bishop, or abbot who turned Protestant after 1552 from taking his church office and property with him into the Protestant camp. High Catholic clergy who converted to Protestantism had instead to forfeit their ecclesiastical dignity and possessions to a proper Catholic successor. The intention was to prevent the secularization of ecclesiastical principalities from within at a time when the insurgent confession was strong enough to take advantage.

To encourage Protestant restraint at the time, the then king of Bohemia and Hungary and soon-to-be emperor Ferdinand I privately agreed with Protestants to allow any city converted to Protestantism by 1552 to remain such. This declaration did not, however, become part of the Diet of Augsburg's rulings in 1555. Nor did those rulings make any provisions for new Protestant and Catholic congregations that came after, another loose end soon to be flapping around.[4] For their part Protestants continued to invoke Ferdinand's declaration to justify the replacement of Catholic priests with Protestant pastors in the territories they controlled.

Neither Augsburg's "reservation" nor Ferdinand's "declaration," the one favoring Catholics, the other Protestants, was absolutely definitive. Thus these exceptional clauses gave both sides a basis for conflict over the date and conditions under which a land or a city might legally be Protestantized or returned to the Catholic fold. Before the seventeenth century the issue did not get out of control. During the 1560s and 1570s, German Protestants resolved any confusion they may have had by simply installing their own clergy in vacant offices, something Luther had encouraged local evangelical congregations to do as early as 1523.[5] That practice continued for thirty years before Catholics drew a line in the sand in Cologne in the mid-1580s. There a converted archbishop, who clung to his church office after turning Protestant, was deposed by the pope and replaced (amid sword-rattling) by a loyal Catholic bishop, thus ending the Protestant theft of Catholic property.[6] The successful reclamation encouraged Catholic rescue, short of war, of other previously Protestantized Catholic bishoprics in Westphalia.

By century's end a new element was injected into the poisoned atmosphere: forcible re-Catholicization of Protestant cities by imperial soldiers. The first to go, in 1598, was the northwestern city of Aachen, Protestant since the early 1580s. Nine years later the religiously mixed imperial city of Donauwörth was coerced back into the Catholic fold after Lutherans gained control of the city council. The point of no return between the two confessions came a year later, when the Diet of Regensburg, dominated by Catholic princes, demanded the return of *all* Church lands, properties, and offices Protestantized after 1552. Promptly marching out of the proceedings, the minority Protestant delegation did not attend another imperial diet for forty years.

Rival military leagues quickly formed: the Protestant Union, led by the Lutheran-turned-Calvinist Christian of Anhalt, governor of the Upper Palatinate, and the Catholic League, led by the duke of Bavaria. No sooner were these leagues in place than each began recruiting European allies. The union turned to England, the Netherlands, and Denmark, while the Catholic League received immediate support from only one of its own, Archduke Leopold of Upper Austria.[7]

The Outbreak of War

In 1618 Czech and German noblemen led a revolt against the new Bohemian king, Archduke Ferdinand of Styria. With Spanish backing, the Jesuit-educated Ferdinand had taken the crown of Bohemia the previous year, and would soon succeed his childless cousin Matthias as Holy Roman Emperor. Thereupon the defiant Bohemians chose the Calvinist elector Palatine, Frederick V, to succeed him as their king, thus inviting war. Foreseeing the disruption that election promised within the international order, Frederick's prudent father-in-law, King James I of England (Frederick had married his daughter Elisabeth in 1614), counseled his son-in-law to forgo that kingship.[8] Although having sought his father-in-law's advice, Frederick was neither patient enough to hear him out nor docile enough to heed what he said.

Although the war began badly for the emperor, the German Protestants were no match for the imperial army. Confronted by superior military leadership in a succession of imperial commanders—Johann Tserclaes, count of Tilly, Gonzalo Fernández de Córdoba, Elector Maximilian of Bavaria, and Albrecht of Wallenstein—Protestant armies did not celebrate a decisive victory until 1631. So one-sided was the first great battle of the war, at White Mountain on the outskirts of Prague in 1620, that the emperor regained Bohemia and extended his sovereignty over the Palatinate as well. In the wake of such a defeat, the divided German princes could not present a unified front. Had the strongest among them, the Lutherans of Saxony, been willing to join with the Palatine Calvinists against the emperor, the outcome might have been different. But they hated their Protestant rivals too much, and the war in Bohemia did not then threaten them. Their history and religion also disposed them to obey imperial authority. Between 1619 and

The Religious Allegiance in German Lands
on the Eve of the Thirty Years' War, 1618

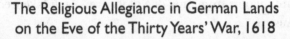

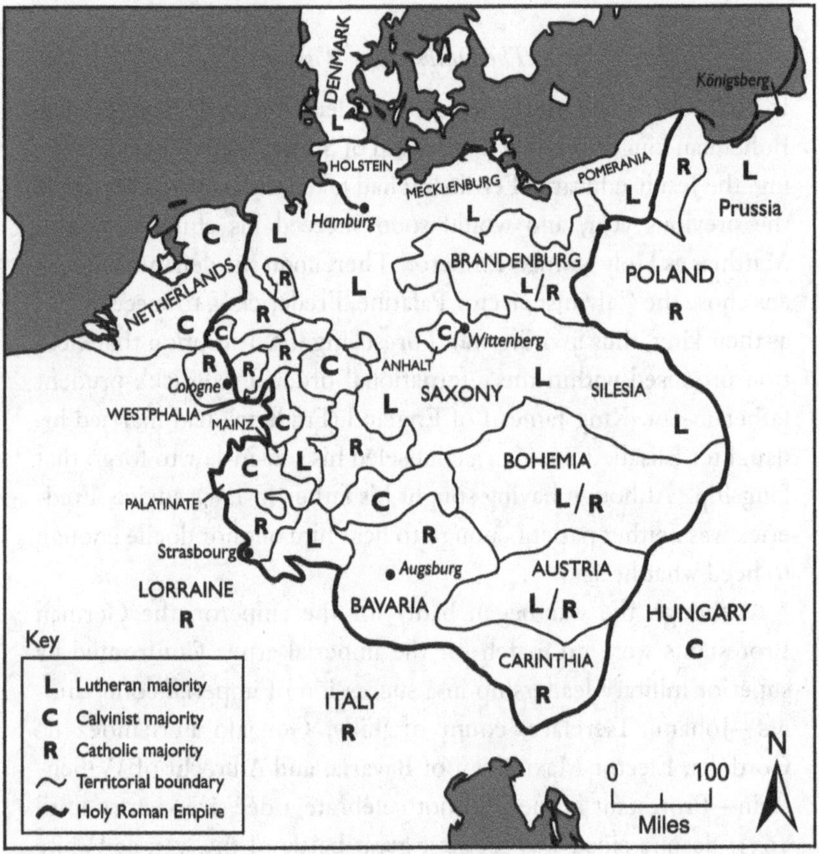

1620 they actually fought for the emperor in Lusatia and Silesia in the hope of gaining significant spoils there.

Despite humiliating defeat and unreliable allies, dethroned Elector Palatine and Bohemian King Frederick soldiered on, claiming both imperial law and religious truth, in that order, to be on his side.[9] In addition to his royal English father-in-law, his uncle was the king of Denmark, which gave him reason still to hope for abundant aid. Such assistance proved to be roundabout, however, coming only in dollops in the first years, as the English king wanted the conflict resolved diplomatically. And while the Palatine Germans and their putative allies dithered, the Austrian emperor secured his gains in ways most painful to them. Honoring his great warlord, Maximilian of Bavaria, who had prevailed in Bohemia and the Palatinate, Ferdinand designated him, quite illegally, elector Palatine in Frederick's place.[10]

Although the Spaniards had both dynastic and treaty reasons for getting involved in the dispute in the empire, they initially backed into it. In the early 1620s the king of England had sought a Spanish marriage for his son and future successor Charles, through which instrument he planned also to gain a diplomatic solution for his hapless son-in-law in the Palatinate. In 1623 the English delegation, including Charles, arrived in Spain to negotiate the marriage contract and pursue the issue of the Palatinate. However, before that could be done, the twenty-three-year-old heir to the English throne was made an offer he could only refuse, namely, the hand of a princess in exchange for his—and implicitly the future elector Palatine's—conversion to Catholicism. Thanks to Spanish arrogance, the English mission to Spain ended up helping Frederick, for the English thereafter made common cause with Hapsburg enemy France. A royal marriage between Charles and the sister of French king Louis XIII sealed the new English-French alliance and promised the assistance Frederick needed to recover his Palatine estates.

But again, as from the blue, religion muddled politics. The new French minister, Cardinal Richelieu, hastened to point out to the king of France the difficulties his Catholic land would face in the international Catholic world, should it press the German Protestant cause in the Palatinate. After sending initial, covert financial aid to the German Protestants, the first of many baited hooks cast by Cardinal Richelieu into troubled German waters, he sent the French army on exercises in southeastern Switzerland and Italy—about as far away from the war in the Palatinate as it might go.[11]

Danes

To the good fortune of German Protestants, the Danes recognized that a defeated and imperially occupied northern Germany would be an ideal staging area for their own imperial defeat and occupation. That concern was also shared by the Swedes, who then competed with the Danes for control of the Baltic and Germany's seaward ports. As the duke of Holstein, Danish king Christian IV already held title to territory at the top of the empire's Lower Saxon Circle.[12] England and the Netherlands, the two great powers sympathetic to the German Protestant cause, believed that foothold tapped the Danes to thwart further imperial expansion northward.

Twice the Danes invaded northern Germany to that end only to be defeated by Emperor Ferdinand's armies, abjectly so at the battle of Lutter-am-Barenberg in Brunswick in 1626. With that defeat the occupation of Denmark, which the Danes had entered the empire to prevent, seemed a certainty—and the Danes were not the only ones with trembling hearts. After Tilly's victory at Lutter, the army of imperial generalissimo Albrecht of Wallenstein took possession of Mecklenburg and Pomerania en route to Holstein. At that turn of events, the elector Palatine's potential European allies put their fingers to the wind and got well out of the emperor's way. The French now joined the Spaniards against the English, while the Swedes turned on the Poles.

Such breakneck imperial expansion threatened not only Scandinavia but the European balance of power as well, and the great powers could not allow it to run its course. In a weak effort to recreate the 1625 status quo ante, England, the Netherlands, and Sweden restored King Christian's lost Danish territories in 1629.[13] However, it was a restoration to oblivion, as the Danes were out of the empire for the foreseeable future, and German Protestants would have to find allies elsewhere.

Hapsburg behavior in the wake of victory accelerated that search. After White Mountain, the Hapsburgs scared all of Europe by their relentless re-Catholicization of their eastern lands—a perceived abuse of power and law that did not stop in Bohemia. Disposing of clergy and church property as if he were pope, Ferdinand II had raised the specter of caesaropapism, a display of totalitarian power as disturbing to Catholic lands as to Protestant ones. Between 1625 and 1628 imperial Bavarian and Austrian armies punished the Protestant Rhineland with blockades and densely quartered soldiers. In Protestant Bohemia and the Palatinate, properties were confiscated, leaders expelled, and laity forced, as if children, to sit at the feet of imported Italian missionaries.[14]

Between Danish withdrawal and the irresolution of north German Protestants, the emperor made the most of his opportunity to turn the confessional clock back seventy-seven years. In his most forceful statement yet, the Edict of Restitution in 1629, he again invoked the Peace of Passau's cut-off date, 1552, for Protestant conversions of Catholic lands, and decreed what Catholics had been demanding since 1608: the return to Catholic jurisdiction of all lands seized by Protestants after that original date. This put at risk the bishoprics of Lower Saxony and Westphalia, along with hundreds of lesser Protestant establishments.[15] Despite the deep roots of Protestantism in these regions, the threat of such confessional reversal was real and might have occurred, had it not been for the military might of the Lutheran Swedes.

For the German Protestant world, the Edict of Restitution came at a particularly sensitive time. As no imperial diet had been held since the formation of the confessional leagues in 1608, the Germans had not aired their grievances before the empire's highest forum for more than two decades. That situation changed in July 1630, when the electoral princes succeeded in working their will on the emperor at Regensburg in one of the few electoral gatherings since 1608. There the Germans had their hearing and won the retirement, to Bohemia, of the hated Wallenstein, a small comfort that would not last.

Viewing Wallenstein as the only principal with might and will sufficient to unify Germany, some historians have deemed his withdrawal devastating to the imperial side. Yet, had the emperor implemented his edict by superior force of arms without any realpolitical compromise with German Protestants, would any resulting unity have lasted for long?[16] In 1629, a return to the status quo of 1552 was laughable. For an imperial solution to have worked at this stage, the terms of union would have to have conceded a degree of religious freedom. In demanding Wallenstein's removal, the Protestant electors had accurately identified the true obstacle to peace.

The Swedes

In 1630, after the Danes' defeat and imperial re-Catholicization, the Lutheran Swedes descended upon the battered German Protestant world, coaxed on by the Catholic French and Bavarians, neither of whom wanted the Catholic emperor to become all-powerful there. Like the Danes, the Swedes marched into Germany only secondarily to help fellow Protestants. Mobilized by brutal Hapsburg expansion to the shores of the Baltic under Wallenstein, and wary of northern Polish aggression as well, the Swedes' goal was to make northern Germany a reliable buffer between Scandinavia and imperial Austrian Germany. In this they courted the assistance of the two north German titans, Lutheran Saxony and Calvinist Brandenburg, which had only belatedly appreciated the jeopardy the emperor's generals put them in. But these great states also did not want the Swedish Lutheran king, Gustavus Adolphus, to challenge their sovereignty.[17]

Perceiving the Germans' exasperation, Ferdinand dangled an amended Edict of Restitution before the electors he had earlier stroked at Regensburg, promising them a new meeting on the subject before the year was out. The intent of that promise was to prevent any precipitous action on their part, particularly the creation of a Franco-German alliance. The north Germans, however, were at last done with playing the mouse to the imperial cat. In March 1631, a Protestant assembly in Leipzig received the theologians' blessing to resist the edict by force of arms. By so acting, they made it clear that the Protestant princes of the 1630s obeyed higher imperial authority no more blindly than had the Lutheran princes who created the Schmalkaldic League in the 1530s. The resulting Leipzig Manifesto in April 1631 mustered a forty-thousand-man Protestant army pledged to defend the imperial constitution—which the emperor's Edict had transgressed—and German Protestant liberties.[18]

Thus did the north German princes put their enemies on notice, both Emperor Ferdinand, who intended militarily to conquer and religiously to conform, and King Gustavus Adolphus, who sought no less perilously to restore the German estates under a new foreign rule. Meanwhile the French, plotting opportunistically against all sides, hoped to see a Catholic restoration of the German estates powerful enough to counter any restoration of the conquered Protestant states, while at the same time tossing out the Hapsburgs. To that end, the French entered a nonaggression pact with the Bavarians. Properly supported, either of these new confessional leagues, the Leipzig Protestants or the French-Bavarian Catholics, might have resolved matters once and for all, had the Swedes not held military superiority and been determined to pacify northern Germany on their own terms.

Swedish occupation of northern Germany promised to put another anti-Hapsburg force on the Continent, one the French believed would never ally with north German princes against them. As they had done with the Bavarians, the French offered the Swedes five years of subsidies to pursue a complementary foreign policy in Germany. However, as happens in the fog of war, the Swedes and the Germans (minus the Bavarians) found themselves in each other's arms after the imperial army, under General Tilly, razed the city of Magdeburg, then the Swedes' only committed German ally, in May 1631. That massacre of twenty thousand inhabitants became one of the most publicized atrocities of the war, and drove Saxony and Brandenburg into an unexpected military alliance with Sweden.[19]

Four months later, in September 1631, the new Protestant alliance, with superior numbers, tactics, and motivation, produced the first Protestant victory of the war at Breitenfeld. There imperial forces lost two of every three soldiers, carnage proportional to that suffered by Protestants at Magdeburg. By May 1632, Tilly was dead, and the armies of Gustavus Adolphus, accompanied by Palatine elector Frederick, marched together into Munich.[20] By successfully positioning itself in Germany, Sweden had thwarted imperial domination of the Baltic and realized the original goal of its continental mission.

Last Battles

During the Swedish reversals of his fortunes, the emperor had not slept. In the spring of 1632 he called the invincible Wallenstein out of retirement and equipped him with a new imperial army. True to his billing, Wallenstein impressively overran Saxony by early November—only then to be surprised two weeks later by the Swedes when he prematurely sent his soldiers into winter quarters. The ensuing Battle of Lützen, in November 1632, left Gustavus Adolphus dead on the battlefield and a defeated Wallenstein in flight back to Bohemia. Yet in this war that would not end, the opposing armies soon had new recruits and resumed hostilities. Wallenstein was again back in harness, commanding an imperial army, now for the last time. His power had become such that he was a threat to his keeper. Discovering evidence of a plot against his authority in January 1634, the emperor had his great general assassinated a month later.[21]

Between 1633 and 1634 the Swedes dug in in Pomerania and Prussia, making Catholic Mainz the hub of their west German operations. Lying directly in the path of the war, the besieged city lost

25 percent of its dwellings, 40 percent of its population, and 60 percent of its wealth—typical devastation for a German city by this point in the war.[22] Although formally allied with the Swedes since 1632, the elector of Brandenburg contemplated an unholy alliance with the emperor to remove them, so great had north German resentment of the Swedish occupation become. That prospect vanished overnight, however, after the imperial Hapsburg army demolished the Swedes and their Saxon allies in Nördlingen in September 1634, a massacre of twelve thousand Protestants. Happily for the north Germans, the spent Swedes began their withdrawal home in November.

With the Lutheran Swedes gone, only Catholic lands were strong enough to save the north Germans and the Protestant cause from the emperor; yet, after Nördlingen, those Catholics could not be the imperial Austrian Hapsburgs. North German Protestants again turned to traditional Hapsburg enemy France, a desperate step backward that both sides knew could not long continue. Fortunately it did not have to, as the specter of that new alliance brought the emperor to the negotiating table. By May 1635 the electors of Saxony and Brandenburg had signed the Peace of Prague with the emperor, the three disparate German powers now agreeing to keep predatory foreigners out of German lands. The final peace terms prohibited the princes from entering foreign alliances, proposed a jointly provisioned standing German army under imperial command, ordered German principals (with the exceptions of Bohemia and the Palatinate) to return to the status quo of 1618, suspended the Edict of Restitution, and moved the date for legitimating Germany's religious divisions up a realistic seventy-five years, from 1552 to 1627.[23]

Although the Peace of Prague has been called a victory of pragmatism over religion, it was in fact a triumph of both, and owed at least as much to physical exhaustion and the inertia of history.[24] Since the thirteenth century, the emperor and the German princes had alternately fought to the death and joined hands freely within a loosely bound empire. In the ongoing crisis of the seventeenth century, the Peace of Prague became another contorted German balancing act.

Peace

The Thirty Years' War began out of German fear of a native emperor—Ferdinand II—and it ended in German revulsion from foreign allies—Sweden and France—the Germans themselves had invited into their lands to oppose him. The Peace of Prague and the death of Ferdinand II in 1637 exorcised the first, while the second never completely disappeared. That was because Sweden and France had too much invested in the German empire simply to vanish from the scene after an internal German peace. For the Scandinavians the imperial-Protestant Peace of Prague revived the original threat of northern invasion and occupation that had brought Danish and Swedish armies into Germany. Any lasting postwar treaty would have to compensate their sacrifices and guarantee their future security. Nor were the French going away without secure staging areas in and around the empire that would allow them easy reentry in the event of any future imperial or German state aggression.

In 1641 the cities of Münster and Osnabrück became the twin sites for imperial negotiations on the Germans' behalf with France and Sweden respectively. There, over the course of six years, diplomats representing the three parties forged the final peace terms. A cessation of hostilities in northern Germany did not, however, accompany the peace talks. Yet even the most determined warriors now had to weigh the political and economic costs of continuing the conflict—for the Hapsburg emperor, an irreparable empire, for the French king, civil war at home. Within Germany the war's alternating tyranny and anarchy had deposited a huge residue of destruction and fear that would take decades, even centuries, to remove. In some areas hundreds of villages and urban households appear simply to have vanished, others to have suffered scarcely any hardship at all. The greatest devastation occurred in the Palatinate, Mecklenburg, Pomerania, Brandenburg, and Württemberg. An exact accounting of the total loss of life due to killing, malnutrition, and disease has not been easy to make. That is because local officials, in the hope of gaining maximum tax relief and the fullest possible government assistance for the reconstruction of their village, city, or region, inflated reports of the dead and missing in the aftermath of war. Modern estimates range from as low as 15 to 20 percent and as high as 30 to 40 percent of a total population of perhaps eighteen million.[25]

The final, unified Treaty of Westphalia in 1648 gave the Swedes parts of Pomerania with its coveted Baltic ports, two bishoprics, and five thousand talers—a gross reduction of the original demands for all of Pomerania, parts of Mecklenburg, and thirty thousand talers. The French got the strategic footholds they desired within and around the empire: three neighboring bishoprics, two bridgeheads over the Rhine, and, best of all, Alsace and Lorraine.[26] All became staging areas for the French in later Franco-German conflicts, while for the Germans their loss was a reason for starting those conflicts.

Within the empire the Peace of Westphalia recognized the German princes as sovereigns within their lands, and, as such, free to enter foreign alliances so long as the latter did not threaten the emperor. In turn the emperor's historical role as overlord of all who lived within the empire was merely reaffirmed, along with his regal powers to charter universities and grant titles of nobility.[27] Westphalia resolved the hot issues of minority religious freedom and the restoration of secularized Catholic lands by pushing the date set by the Peace of Prague for a valid Protestant conversion back another three years, to January 1, 1624. Where minority religious worship had existed before that date it legally continued, and land and property under Catholic jurisdiction on or after it remained such as well. Finally Westphalia made Calvinism the third legal religion within the empire, while continuing the ban on Anabaptism and kindred sects.

Religiously the treaty increased acceptance of confessional difference and reduced confessionally driven politics. In the late seventeenth century the elector of Lutheran Saxony could convert to Catholicism and still lead the official state delegation at the imperial diet.[28]

After 1648 the shadows of foreign wings hung heavier than ever over Germans, there now by an international treaty guaranteed by

Germany at the End of the Thirty Years' War, 1648

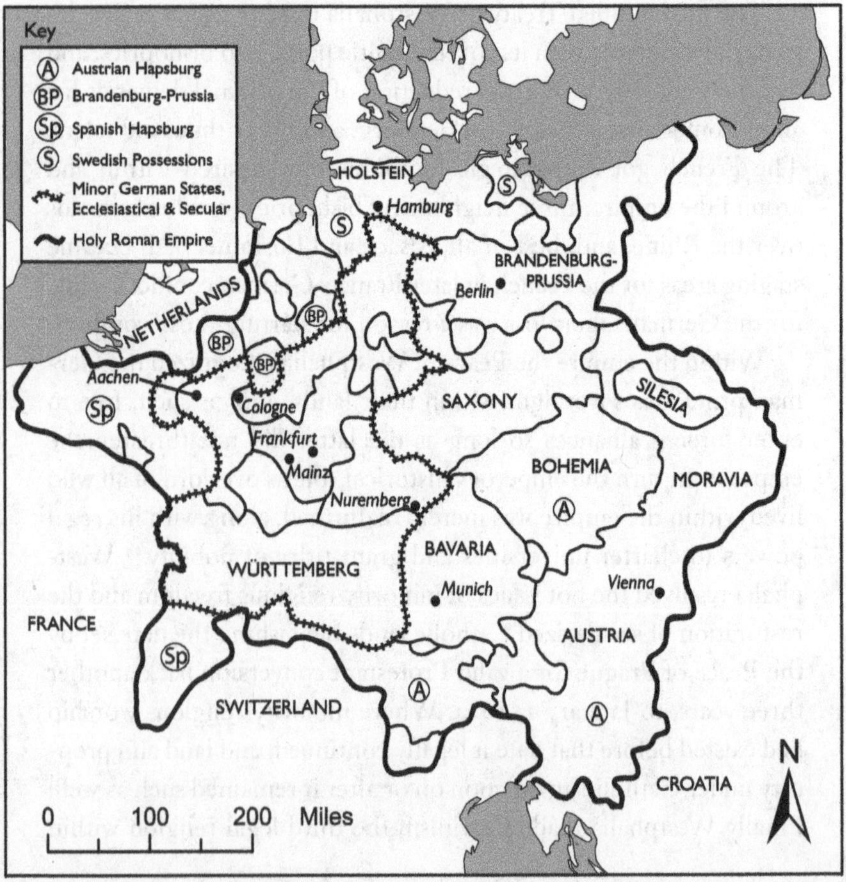

the armies of France and Sweden. The German princes emerged from the war both more powerful and politically divided, while the emperor had been reduced to the status of roughly a great German prince. Thenceforth legal warfare would precede war with arms, as greater Germany had become, through the war, a land of international law and foreign self-interest.[29] In the end the Germans found themselves again in a cage, and with reason to be resentful and jumpy. Their future freedom from foreign intervention depended on nothing so much as their internal discipline. Germany would be safe from Europe's great powers to the extent that its houses remained in order—that is, unprovocative but able to counter provocation.

5

ENEMY MINE

Absolutism and the Rise of Prussia

A CROSSROADS OF INTERNATIONAL TRADE since the Middle Ages and a battlefield for Europe's great powers during the seventeenth century, Germany became a land of absolute states in the eighteenth. That was because sovereign German states, newly empowered by the Peace of Westphalia, spun still farther away from their historically unifying Hapsburg imperial hub. Historians call this development *Kleinstaaterei*, "small stateship," but in German history the consequences of increased state power and competition were never small. Austria, Bavaria, Brandenburg-Prussia, Saxony, and Württemberg became internally centralized powers with their own professional armies, state bureaucracies, foreign alliances, international courts, baroque palaces, and pretensions to be—and even to speak—French.[1]

Having presided over a movable hierarchy of German princes and cities for three centuries, the emperor found himself after 1648 negotiating with the ambassadors of virtually equal, and, in Prussia's case, soon-to-be superior German states. The Peace of Westphalia did little more than remind the states of their historical relationship to the emperor, leaving each to negotiate the specifics more or less at will, if at all. The more powerful states dealt with the emperor as if he were another foreign power.[2]

Against this background contemporary jurist Samuel Pufendorf, coiner of the phrase "the Thirty Years' War," described the political structure of the empire in 1667 as a political and constitutional "monstrosity": one part monarchical—the emperor, the empire—the other confederational—the princes, the states—yet, after 1648, constitutionally arranged to allow an escalation of parochial, princely rule.[3] Underscoring the ill intentions of the European powers who created this situation, an imperial councilman, writing in a similar vein, lamented the Peace of Westphalia for having made Germans "booty for [their] neighbors, the butt of their ridicule, [a people] divided . . . and weakened by . . . partition, [now] strong enough to harm themselves, [yet] powerless to save [them]selves."[4]

Although the war and the peace had weakened traditional restraints, the age of absolutism would not be wall to wall. In many states and cities, political checks and balances still existed, and lawyers were never busier. The privileged estates—nobility, clergy, and commons—of the Duchy of Württemberg, for example, maintained a functioning parliament into the nineteenth century.[5] Still, division increased the vulnerability of the old German empire. In the late seventeenth century, merchant barges navigating the Rhine to the North Sea paid tolls at some principality's border on average every six miles.[6] And as the French demonstrated by seizing much of Alsace and the Palatinate in the 1680s and 1690s, poaching on post-1648 Germany posed small challenge or risk.

Rather than retrieving and repairing lost imperial lands and unity, the empire's Austrian Hapsburg overlords saw its foundations shaken to the core by new foreign and native powers. In the second half of the century, Leopold I fought costly wars with France and watched the Ottoman Turks panic Austria, including his residence,

Vienna, which he fled with his family in July 1683.[7] During the reign of Emperor Charles VI in the early eighteenth century, the Hapsburgs had to secure their intact lands and claims to lost German possessions by rewriting the law of imperial succession. Having lost all of his sons in infancy, Charles enabled his eldest daughter, Maria Theresa, to succeed him as empress in 1740 by a controversial document appropriately named "Pragmatic Sanction."[8] Over these same years the Austrians also watched, with little ability to alter or control, the buildup of the Prussian army in the north, soon to become their nemesis and the German empire's new overlord.

Losing its grip, if not influence, on the changing German empire, Austria built up its immediate empire, of which Hungary and Bohemia were the other major lands, doing so at the expense of the Ottomans. By mid-century the decades of even titular imperial sovereignty over the German empire were numbered. Having held its fratricidal impulses in check for almost three centuries, the Hapsburgs would now be picked apart by them. Over the eighteenth century, German unification ceased to be the task of the Hapsburg emperor and became that of the strongest German prince. In the eighteenth century and for a very long time to come, that prince, would be Prussian.

Brandenburg-Prussia

In 1700 sprawling, Catholic, Hapsburg Austria, nine million strong, was still the seat of the Holy Roman Empire of the German Nation. By comparison Prussia was a land of only three million, and ten European states had greater landmass. Yet, by the mid-eighteenth century, Protestant Hohenzollern Prussia fielded Europe's third strongest army and had Austria in its sights. Before the two clashed, the northern Sparta annexed and unified its more immediate neighbors. Link by link, for more than a century, the modern Prussian state gradually formed, its geographical diversity matched by the sociopolitical-cultural variety of its constituent

The Expansion of Brandenburg-Prussia, 1648–1786

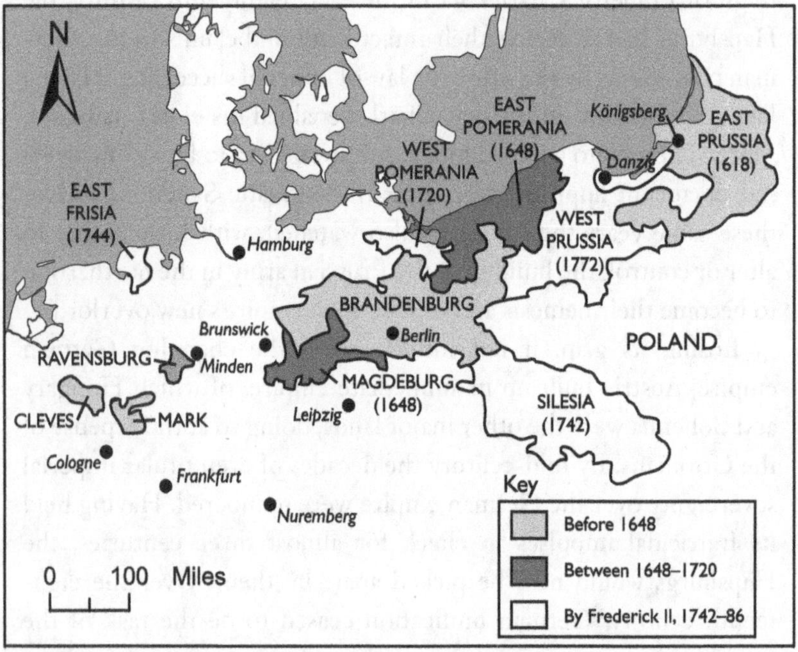

lands. The Treaty of Westphalia had started the process by adding East Pomerania, Magdeburg, Minden, and the Rhineland provinces to Prussia's two large territorial anchors: the far eastern frontier of East Prussia, settled by the Teutonic knights, and the large, central electoral state of Brandenburg.

The key to Prussian success lay in a dynasty of kings who lived long lives and had a rare ability both to conquer and to build. Frederick William, known as "the Great Elector," laid the economic and military foundations by successfully bending the nobility to his rule.[9] His son and successor, Frederick I, became strong enough to crown himself "King in Prussia" in 1701 and leap onto the European stage. No longer a subject state of the Baltic powers, Prussia now became the kingdom of the Hohenzollerns with its own hereditary crown, and would remain such for the next two centuries. Frederick also set Prussian expansion in motion by challenging Austria. Thus began the rivalry that would shift German imperial power from Hapsburg to Hohenzollern and dissolve the Austrian-based Holy Roman Empire in 1806, leaving Austria with only the title.

Frederick was a grand patron of the arts and of education, turning his Berlin palace into a baroque showplace and founding Germany's premier eighteenth-century university, Halle in Saxony. His son and successor, Frederick William I, reasserted the dynasty's reserved Calvinist heritage by replacing his father's opulent court with one that observed the Prussian virtues of discipline and obedience. Those were also the pillars of the military, whose ranks Frederick William doubled, exalting military service to a citizen's supreme self-sacrifice. Although that great army added West Pomerania to Prussian lands in 1720, it spent far more time goose-stepping in parades than marching over foreign enemies.

That changed under Frederick William's son, Frederick II, "the Great," who ruled from 1740 to 1786. Inheriting a disproportionately large army of eighty thousand, to which eighty percent of state revenues were devoted in the year of his ascension, the new king more than doubled its size and employed one-sixth of the Prussian population in military-related services.[10] In addition, he successfully pursued two other major initiatives of his father: the opening of the civil service to the middle classes and the codification of Prussian law.[11]

Pietism and Politics

In 1711 the Calvinist Frederick William I converted to Pietism, a reform movement within and, critics believed, against the established Protestant confessions, centered at Halle. Emerging in the aftermath of the Thirty Years' War, Pietism promised to accomplish what its adherents believed state authority and orthodox Protestantism, Lutheran and Calvinist, could never do: reconstruct Germany spiritually, morally, and socially. In a society of rigid class divisions, formulaic religions, and iron rule, Pietism's promise caught the imagination of many.

Enlightened and open to the secular world, Pietists funneled religion directly into the service of society and state. In sanctioning the movement, Frederick William opened the doors of government, the military, hospitals, and schools to Halle's graduates, who became administrators, chaplains, and teachers in disproportionate numbers. This top down integration of new religion and old politics proved fruitful to both sides, increasing church-state cooperation and gently pushing religious and social reform forward.[12] In addition to its university, Halle's educational system included schools for girls, orphans, and the poor, a Latin boarding school for upper class boys, and a famous seminary.

Three leading Lutheran lights led the way: Johann Arndt, the author of a mystically tinged devotional book, *True Christianity*; Philip Jakob Spener, author of the other Pietist classic, *Pia Desideria*; and August Hermann Francke, a successful businessman and professor of Oriental languages and theology, who succeeded Spener as leader of the movement. Hohenzollern kings saw in Pietism a superior preparation for their citizens and subjects, and encouraged the dissemination of its educational philosophy across Prussia. Not only did it satisfy heartfelt religious yearnings and instill moral principles, it also subjected students to a practical education, requiring the study of law and rhetoric, mastery of modern as well as ancient languages, and acquaintance with real-world trades—the latter a pragmatic-technical supplement to traditional academic learning.[13] In these various ways the Pietist challenge to orthodoxy extended and deepened the Reformation's effort to foster a civic society based on lay initiative and principled cooperation between Church and state.

Though generously patronized by Hohenzollern kings, Pietism was not so popular among the established clergy, who doubted its orthodoxy and feared its influence on liberal clergy, a fear evident in the epithets hurled at Spener by his critics: Quaker, Rosicrucian, chiliast (millenarian), and fanatic.[14] The alliance with secular authority drew Pietists deeper into politics, where they had to rely on the moral restraints attached to the office of the prince by the

Reformation and Counter-Reformation to ensure a proper separation of Church and state. Those restraints portrayed the prince as a lay Christian steward of a public trust, whose civic-political goals the Church might share and assist without jeopardizing its spiritual mission. Each side had much to gain from their cooperation, but also much to lose by either's overreaching.[15]

Hohenzollern influence over Pietist clergy and churches occasioned charges of compromising with the world. Francke was said to have straddled, impossibly and thus hypocritically, the line between Church and state, hobnobbing one day with autocratic kings, while trying to help orphans in the street on the next.[16] Critics also believed that the perfectionist strain in Pietism made it vulnerable to cooptation by the Enlightenment. "We are under an obligation to achieve some degree of perfection," Spener liked to write, by which he meant a perceived moral duty to be guided by the Holy Spirit in one's moral actions. Here, he anticipated Immanuel Kant's secular notion of a categorical imperative in conscience, demanding a universally applicable response to moral challenge.[17] In Francke's straddling one may, however, discern the dialectical rather than the ugly German—one who believed, as his church taught, that man must live, at one and the same time, in parallel religious and secular universes.

An Enlightened King

After 1740 the military ventures and civic reforms of Frederick the Great completed Prussia's transformation into Germany's premier state and one of Europe's great powers. The formative years did not suggest such a triumphant outcome, and but for history's hidden hand, he might be known today as Frederick the Small. That is because he grew up in a conflicted royal family whose passions and divisions threatened to cripple, and even to end, his life. His mother and grandmother were Hanoverian princesses, whose brothers became English kings, a lineage offering important venues for acquiring influence at home and abroad. Frederick's exuberant mother was not at ease in the dour, masculine world of her husband, nor did she allow the Prussian virtues to smother her children. She wanted royal English marriages for her eldest daughter and eldest son—the Prince of Wales for Wilhelmina and the Princess Royal for Frederick. By contrast their father was determined to keep the dynasty all German and on good terms with the Hapsburgs, then reassessing their alliance with Britain.[18]

In the parental battle for the children's hearts and minds, Frederick William could be his own worst enemy, supremely capable of alienating his offspring without the intervention of a conniving mother. He worried that the queen's indulgent child rearing was "effeminizing" his son and successor and thus imperiling a Prussian kingdom whose neighbors, as the king told the boy when he was twelve, wanted only "to blow us out of the water." Both as a father and a king, Frederick William expressed the most ancient of German fears when he observed geopolitical maneuverings by England and France: "I will put pistols in the cradles of my children, so that they can help keep foreigners out of Germany!"[19] He directed Frederick early to the art of making war by putting him in the hands of Huguenot soldiers, who tutored him throughout childhood and adolescence in math, economics, fortification, Prussian law, and modern history. At his mother's insistence he was given his own private library of several thousand books, which allowed him in his teens to read the leading French, English, and German writers.[20]

While fearing the queen's influence on his son, the specter of his being won over by royal enemies at court worried the king more. Further complicating the relationship was young Frederick's resistance to his father's plans to marry him to the princess of Braunschweig-Bevern, Elisabeth Christiana. Should he take a wife at all, Frederick wanted her to be his English cousin, to which end he attempted three times to flee to England in the years he was entering his majority and able to claim a crown.[21]

Another factor alienating father and son was Frederick's apparent blossoming homo- or bisexuality—a disputed subject for historians, many of whom acknowledge only a "generally abstemious" nature, particularly with regard to the woman who became his wife.[22] Yet evidence exists, and the consequences are sufficiently germane to the story to forbid dismissing the subject as mere venomous French gossip. Manifestations of sexual attraction to males may have been what his father meant by the boy's "effeminacy," perhaps evoked in the intimate company of his male military tutors, at least one of whom was reputedly homosexual.[23]

A key piece of evidence is Frederick's intimate friendship in 1729–30 with a police officer eight years his senior, Hans Hermann von Katte, who reportedly carried on with Frederick "as a lover with a mistress."[24] Katte accompanied the future king on his third failed attempt to join his royal relatives in England. After they were arrested together and discovered to have plotted their flight with the British ambassador, the king greeted his returned son with a cane across his nose. Then a lieutenant colonel in the Prussian army, Frederick could have been tried for desertion and treason, and the possibility of his execution rallied the princes of Europe behind him. In the unruly eighteenth century, any currency given to the execution of kings, especially a future king by his father and predecessor, did not serve the interests of royalty anywhere.

Although pardoned in the end by his father, Frederick was put under arrest, in Fortress Küstrin on the Oder, for almost two and a half years, from 1730 to 1732, his only companions a Bible and a copy of Johann Arndt's *True Christianity*. There he followed a punishing regimen intended to transform him into a regal Hohenzollern. Because his mother and sister had been party to his flight to England (the king in the aftermath also greeted Wilhelmina with a beating), they were forbidden direct contact with him for a year. He could however, receive their letters, if written in German and not treasonous foreign languages. The cruelest blow of his confinement came early, when his father had Katte beheaded in Küstrin's prison yard, forcing Frederick to watch every moment of it from his prison window.[25]

By the end of his confinement, Frederick had been reduced to compliance with his father's will, at least outwardly. In February 1732, amid protests of having no feelings for the opposite sex, he married the princess of Braunschweig-Bevern, a union reportedly without sexual relations and certainly without offspring.[26] By the mid-1730s the royal couple were at home in Rheinsberg, a specially prepared French-style castle forty miles northwest of Berlin. In the intervening years Frederick had his first taste of battle, fighting with Austro-Russian forces against the French in the War of the Polish Succession, from 1733 to 1735, gaining a valuable firsthand look at the military tactics of Prussia's future enemies.[27]

Frederick's days alternated between letters and war, as books and argument competed with strategic planning and battle for his undivided attention. No sooner did he become king than he created the Academy of the Arts and Sciences in Berlin. Directed by a distinguished French mathematician, Pierre Louis Moreau de Maupertuis, the academy recruited the best available European talent to form a learned circle around the king.[28]

Frederick ran his government from both the refurbished Charlottenburg Palace outside Berlin and a specially built retreat in Potsdam, Sanssouci, the gathering place for the intellectuals he fancied most, who were mostly French. Among the visitors after mid-century were the age's most famous philosopher, Voltaire, and Jean le Rond d'Alembert, coeditor of the seventeen-volume French *Encyclopédie*, a convoluted roadmap through enlightened French philosophy, politics, and religion.

Both at work and at play, the king and his associates spoke French. Although the latter part of his reign was accompanied by an early German Enlightenment, and a pan-German literature—Goethe, Schiller, Lessing—and music—Bach, Handel, Haydn, Mozart, Beethoven—began to blossom, Frederick spurned his native German as a "barbaric tongue" whose literary time had not yet come.[29] In 1780 he caused not a little resentment by publicly criticizing the German language. Even for an age generally infatuated with all things French, he was something of a spectacle. Here was a German king, deemed the greatest of all by his contemporaries, who read French so much more easily than he did German that he ordered challenging German books he wanted to read to be translated first into French—an irony he compounded by his espousal of a belief that only 1.25 percent of Frenchmen possessed any power of intellect.[30]

Frederick's own literary legacy included poetry, political and military tracts, philosophical treatises, and a huge correspondence with the age's leading intellectuals. He embraced trendy Freemasonry and Pietism, whose universalism and perfectionism reflected his own high-minded ambitions. A first philosophical work, rejecting Machiavelli's politics, *L'Antimachiavel*, praised kings who served and sacrificed for their subjects over those who deceived and manipulated them.[31] Such youthful idealism would not survive the Silesian wars, on whose battlefields Frederick discovered that even good princes at times must be Machiavellian. His mirror for princes did attest, however, to the persistence into the eighteenth century of high German political ideals dating back centuries.[32]

The Philosopher-King

That so earnest and idealistic a king could pursue someone as equivocal and cynical as Voltaire was poetically just, if not quite Machiavellian. Though jarring, the king's two passions, the life of the mind and the death of his enemies, seamlessly fitted the man and his times. Voltaire served his purposes by exporting his reputation as a philosopher-king throughout Europe, while Frederick, in return, offered himself to Voltaire as a ruler eager to be enlightened by the French.

Even before he became king, Frederick, at twenty-four, had written to Voltaire in the hope of bringing him to Berlin as his tutor. Intermittently over forty-two years Voltaire exploited the king's infatuation, as quick to ridicule, slander, deceive, and spy on the younger man as to share his knowledge and venomous gossip. But if, in Samuel Johnson's description, Frederick was "Voltaire's footboy," he was also one who knew how to kick back.[33]

The two met for the first time in Cleves in 1740 and thereafter developed an intense intellectual and personal relationship. When Voltaire visited Berlin for the first time in 1743, the two traveled together to Bayreuth, in Franconia. Those were the years in which Frederick's army was invading Silesia, moving Voltaire to question the propriety of a philosopher-king's waging an aggressive war. In Berlin, Voltaire found less high-minded reasons to be irked, and he behaved badly among the royal family, making apparently successful advances to Frederick's sister Ulrica under her brother's nose. The visit started a nasty exchange of insults and ridicule, with Voltaire openly alleging the king's homosexuality, while Frederick, more circumspectly, bemoaned Voltaire's disloyalty in his poems.[34]

The relationship deteriorated further during Voltaire's visits to Berlin and Potsdam in the early 1750s. Intellectually neither questioned the superiority of French language and culture to German, and Frederick was prepared to surrender to the Italians as well. Yet while the king might self-effacingly acknowledge German backwardness, it was unpardonable of Voltaire, on whose magnanimity their friendship also depended, to gloat over the national cultural divide. Frederick's prose may not have been as good as his poetry, but when Voltaire turned his wit on either, both came up wanting—and ridiculing the king's poetry was only the start. Although he had enjoyed Sanssouci's hospitality, Voltaire continued to serve up Frederick's prized circle of intellectuals to gossipy literati as "the Seven Sages of Greece in a brothel."[35]

While at Sanssouci, Voltaire also embarrassed Frederick by getting caught in illegal currency speculation, aided by a Jewish middle man. The spectacle, with anti-Jewish overtones, tried the king's patience and he banished his famous guest to Berlin in early 1751. There a humiliated and outraged Voltaire portrayed Frederick's beloved retreat as a homosexual circus, moving the once-fawning king to discern, perhaps deeply for the first time, the true size of the great Frenchman's cloven feet. As early as 1749, while wooing him to Berlin, Frederick had described Voltaire as both a despicable coward and an admirable genius.[36]

Upon departing Sanssouci, Voltaire took with him honorific gifts from the king and a collection of his poems, the latter on condition that they not be taken out of the country. Frederick worried that his poems might fall into the wrong hands—apparently his father had successfully instilled in him the pitfalls of perceived unkingly effeminacy. In two retaliatory acts, one private and one for all the world to see, Frederick made clear his personal unhappiness. He redecorated Voltaire's room at Sanssouci with animals symbolic of human moral failings (monkeys, peacocks, snakes, and toads), and, doubting the return of his poems, he issued an order for his arrest in flight. The latter occurred in Frankfurt in May 1753, where a frightened and livid Voltaire was placed under house arrest.[37] Thus did the philosopher-king remind the king of the philosophers who the Prussian king was—a lesson for which Voltaire again made him pay in the gossipy salons of Paris and London.

The Silesian Wars

In 1740 Frederick and Maria Theresa, he twenty-eight and unquestionably king, she twenty-three and a most disputed empress-to-be, ascended their respective Prussian and Austro-Hapsburg thrones. Soon thereafter Frederick's army invaded Silesia, then part of the Austrian empire, defying the empress's pragmatically sanctioned imperial succession.[38] Thus began the first of three staggered and increasingly bloody Austro-Prussian wars over this largely German Protestant land. While most of the fighting was confined to Silesia, blood was splashed on Saxony, Mecklenburg, Poland, Bohemia, and Moravia as well, making the Silesian wars a European event.

The initial seizures occurred in the German "smart war" fashion, with concentrated Prussian forces targeting a segment of the enemy's line—a scattering tactic that dated back to the Germanic tribes.[39] Frederick employed it against the Austrians at Mollwitz in 1741, his first major battle, which is remembered less for the king's military expertise than for putting the two great German states on a competitive course that would end in Königgrätz (now Hradec Kralove, Czech Republic) 125 years later. In a novice's mistake, Frederick misdeployed his troops and lost command, which Major General Kurt von Schwerin assumed, saving the day and becoming the battle's hero. With his soldiers posting proclamations of religious freedom on church doors, the titular Calvinist monarch, who looked forward to a postreligious age, promised equal protection to Silesian Catholics and Protestants.

At Chotusitz in 1742, Frederick, fighting with French, Bavarian, and Saxon allies, again lost control of the battlefield, yet still defeated the Austrians a second time, giving him virtual control of Silesia. After the victory he took the title "King *of* Prussia," which replaced his father's lesser rule as "King *in* Prussia." Subsequent victories at Hohenfriedberg and Soor, during the shorter, second Silesian war, brought the king home to shouts of "Frederick the Great." After five years of on-and-off fighting, Prussia's landmass had been increased by half and its revenues by a third.[40] The great powers of Europe now had a new member state in their ranks.

The years of war drained Prussia's treasury, which Frederick replenished by plundering newly annexed lands and raising taxes on older. That a toll had also been taken on the king became clear in a new introduction to his earlier treatise on Machiavelli. He now maintained that no sacrifice a ruler might ask of his people could be worse than defeat at the hands of their enemies, an acknowledgment of the high military and civilian price paid for victory in Silesia. By 1745 the seasoned king believed with Machiavelli that a successful ruler had first and foremost to win.

Eighteenth-century rulers practiced realpolitik unsentimentally, yet it is difficult to find a German prince or king before the twentieth century who considered his rule an altogether arbitrary, mundane, and cynical business. Although thoroughly chastened by war, Frederick's vision of a good and just society remained as bright in 1746 as it had been in 1739, moving him still to write:

> A prince is the first servant . . . of the state [whose duty it is] to reward service and merit, establish some . . . balance between rich and poor, relieve the unfortunate in every walk of life, [and] breed magnificence in every limb of the body of the state.[41]

Royal idealism and sanity met their supreme tests, however, during the third and final Silesian war, the so-called Seven Years' War of 1756–63. A monotonous succession of sixteen large battles, it saw staggering defeats, Pyrrhic victories, and a few miraculous escapes or triumphs. Half of those battles Prussia won, but with heavy loss of life in almost every one. In this final round of conquest, Prussia, with British support, confronted a seemingly overwhelming coalition of Austria, France, and Russia determined to return Silesia to the Hapsburg empire and reverse Prussian expansion elsewhere. Finding his state vulnerable to serious attack from three points of the compass, Frederick, perhaps rephrasing words his father had drummed into him in his youth, expressed a dread feeling of being "surrounded by . . . rogues."[42] During the course of the new war, the Russians twice occupied Berlin and, together with the Swedes, Pomerania and Neumark as well, while the French took Minden and Cleves and the Austrians reoccupied Silesia.

Taking a leaf from the first Silesian war, Frederick strategically countered the coalition against him by making Saxony a buffer and staging area. Within a year, the battle of Kolin in 1757 gave Prussia its first and, in percentage of soldiers lost, greatest defeat of all the Silesian wars: 9,428 men, 281 officers, twenty-two regimental colors, and forty-five cannon.[43] In the same year Prussian armies, although outnumbered two to one at Rossbach and six to four at Leuthen, were victorious. Contemporaries believed Rossbach to be Prussia's greatest victory ever, while not a single Austrian escaped death, or capture, at Leuthen. A Pyrrhic victory at Zorndorf left eighteen thousand Russians and thirteen thousand Prussians dead on the battlefield, quickly to be followed by three staggering defeats between 1758 and 1759: Hochkirch, where a third of Frederick's army lay dead; Kunersdorf, from whose battlefield only an estimated 3,000 of an original 48,000 walked away; and Maxim, whose loss of life was exceeded only by Kolin. This lowest point to date in German military history would later be invoked by Adolf Hitler, when the Third Reich faced utter military defeat in 1945. Waving newspaper clippings of the death of Franklin Roosevelt at his skeleton staff, the führer proclaimed the American president's death a portent of the repetition of "the miracle of the House of Brandenburg" in 1763—a year of changing alliances that brought Frederick complete victory.[44]

In addition to tens of thousands of military deaths, the Silesian wars killed half a million civilians, or one-tenth of Prussia's prewar population. By war's end in 1763, a quarter of the population was destitute and scavenging, a wreckage so shocking that Frederick imprisoned the bureaucrat who led the team that totaled the damage.[45]

A Modern State

Looking forward, that spillage of blood and wasting of treasure were not in vain. Prussia had become and would remain a major European power. As in the beginning of his reign, Frederick's response to challenge was always to build and rebuild, which his government began doing within months of the war's conclusion. His rule has been called "enlightened" absolutism because it was both hierarchical and strong-armed, yet optimistic and progressive for the times. During his forty-six-year reign, he created special government agencies for strategic economic development, an initiative that helped make Berlin an enduring European cultural capital. The king also permitted sufficient freedom of the press to earn him the posthumous title of "prophet of unlimited freedom of the press."[46]

Also greatly advanced was the codification of Prussian law, a project begun in earnest in 1780 and completed, after Frederick's death, in 1793–94—the same years in which the French presented Europe with new rounds of anarchy, de-Christianization, regicide, and a civil war known as "the Terror." Chastened by the rapid degeneration of the French Revolution, whose promises were not kept, the German lawmakers responsible for the final version of the Prussian General Code, *Allgemeine Landrecht*, published in 1794, made it a more conservative body of law than observers previously had been led to expect. Still, by the standards of the age, it was progressive. It allowed only a fraction of the capital executions for political reasons common in other states, while forbidding judicial torture, arbitrary arrest, and execution for petty crimes, all of which continued to exist in thoroughly modern France.

Frederick's civil reforms targeted the social problems of contemporary family life, particularly out-of-wedlock births and the care of orphans.[47] Education became compulsory for all, and the king urged religious pluralism and toleration upon the Christian confessions. So far did a new middle class and civil society advance by the end of Frederick's reign that German intellectuals could look on the revolutions in America and France as belated efforts to catch up with Prussia and Austria![48]

Despite the king's reforms, his domestic agenda was not, in the end, as thorough and disciplined as his war making. The upper classes continued to be favored in civil service appointments. And although the king abolished serfdom on his royal domains, he did not challenge its continuation on the estates of the landed nobility—an inconsistent concession, evidently to reward the latter's vital support and service during the war years. Frederick's treatment of Prussian Jews also remained static. Believing that Jewish merchants had an unfair advantage over Christian in the large cities, the areligious king, who tolerated Catholics and Protestants and demanded their acceptance of one another, dispersed large numbers of Jews from Prussia's cities to the borderlands.[49]

The Absolute Musician

Frederick's most recent biographer describes him as a ruler torn between contradictory principles: devoted, on the one hand, to monarchical autocracy and, on the other, to the rights and dignity of the individual. A lifelong admirer of John Locke and the evolving American democracy, the king granted the United States the eighteenth-century equivalent of most favored nation status in one of his last official acts.[50]

The conflict in Frederick between autocracy and liberalism reflected the evolving politics of the century. By comparison with the American, French, and British systems of government, Frederick's addressed its choices more conservatively, embracing an older German notion of balanced rule, in which authority and order were viewed as complementary to, and protective of, freedom and equality. A ruler held authority over individuals not because he was supreme or absolute in himself, but because he represented and enforced the order that made possible individual freedoms within a civil society.[51]

In this Frederick may be compared with a contemporary who dominated another discipline and priorized another old tradition: Johann Sebastian Bach, who came to Potsdam in 1747 to visit his son Carl, a harpsichordist at Frederick's court. Learning of the great musician's presence, Frederick invited the senior Bach to meet with him, an awkward event as it turned out, because Frederick challenged the reluctant but compliant Saxon court composer to try his hand at one of the king's musical favorites. Frederick also asked his guest to improvise a fugue, a request Bach fulfilled two months later by sending a "Musical Offering" from Leipzig.

That a meeting between the two might be uncomfortable was predictable for two reasons. The philosopher-king of the German Enlightenment was also a forward-looking man musically. He preferred the lighter rococo style, which the Austrians Haydn and Mozart would popularize by century's end, to Bach's traditional, churchly baroque.[52] Secondly, and more important, in these two men a principled old German tradition sure of its steps (Bach) confronted a new experimental one trying to find its legs (Frederick). This was true not only musically but philosophically and politically as well, a conflict the German nineteenth century, still following Frederick's comparatively cautious lead, would drive to the extreme.

On the other hand, both men were cosmopolitan and eclectic in their respective crafts, each blessed and cursed by living literally and culturally at Europe's crossroads. The philosopher-king of Sanssouci was an intellectual and cultural omnivore, who wanted his realm to be *au courant*, which meant French. The Saxon musician was no less a borrower, having built up his own repertoire by mastering and improving French and Italian models, as Handel, Haydn, and Mozart were doing over the second half of the eighteenth century. Even the musical style deemed classically German at this time derived from older Bohemian tunes.[53]

For more than twenty-five years, between 1723 and his death in 1750, Bach had worked in Leipzig composing cantatas for the city's churches.[54] His patrons expected his music to be both theologically and politically correct, which meant a true and exultant expression of Lutheran doctrine. As a condition of his hire, he had been required to swear an oath of allegiance to the sixteenth-century Formula of Concord, the definitive Lutheran creed written at the conclusion of the culture war between Gnesio (conservative) and Philippist (liberal) Lutherans. As a devout Lutheran, Bach brought deep theological knowledge and a loyal political will to these conjoined responsibilities. The resulting compositions, approximately three hundred cantatas, were complex statements of two hundred years of mainstream religious and national faith.

They were not, however, Enlightenment music, and especially not French Enlightenment music. What distinguished Bach's work and made it lasting was the musical-emotional demonstration of humankind's need for transcendence and majesty, yet utter inability to encompass and master either. By contrast, the new Enlightenment faith, especially as it found its voice in the nineteenth century, believed in humankind's ability to resolve the riddle of history, both to mock and to play the gods. Here the ambition that had driven modernizing movements since antiquity, when the prelapsarian Adam and Eve were its models and the uncorrupted light of reason its tool, reached what were arguably its greatest heights yet. By contrast Bach's music reasserted the dialectical character of reality and the bipolarity at the center of the human heart, each mysterious and complex beyond all human fathoming.

Bach conveyed this musically by subjecting fixed and invincible themes to alternating consonance and dissonance, repeatedly demolishing and reconstituting any audible fortress the listener might hope to build. In the process, variety challenged unity, and disorder order, and each contested the other in return. The alternating loss and restoration of harmony left the auditor with an intermittently pleasurable, but never final or secure, sensation of reconciliation, which was also the intention of the juxtaposition of Law and Gospel in the contemporary Lutheran sermon: oneness only in division, righteousness only in sin.[55] Very similar also, and within the same mainstream German tradition, would be Goethe's cautionary warning to the Enlightenment not "to tarry with the present moment," no matter its beauty.[56]

III

ENLIGHTENMENT, REACTION, AND A NEW AGE

6

TROJAN HORSES

From the French to the German Revolution

BY COMPARISON with the American and French Revolutions, the enlightened initiatives taken by the courts of Prussian king Frederick the Great, Austrian empress Maria Theresa, and the rulers of lesser German states seem modest. In America and France tyrants were overthrown, citizens endowed with new liberties, and governments fundamentally restructured. By contrast national unity, a freely elected transregional parliament, and constitutionally assured individual rights faced an uncertain future in Germany at the approach of the nineteenth century.[1]

In the late eighteenth and early nineteenth centuries, the French presented the Germans with a model of a liberal society and gave them a strong push toward it. Earlier, during the Thirty Years' War, they had helped rescue Germans from the future emperor, Ferdinand of Hungary, one of the butchers of Nördlingen in 1634, only thereafter to wreak their own havoc on them.[2] Now, again, the French crossed the Rhine as liberators, this time bearing an epochal

Enlightenment and a social Revolution that promised to free Germans from both Austrian Hapsburg and Prussian Hohenzollern rulers.

The only parallels to the French Enlightenment and Revolution the Germans had in their own history were the Renaissance and Reformation of the fifteenth and sixteenth centuries. Then they successfully asserted their linguistic, political, and cultural-religious independence from Italian papal and Spanish Hapsburg rule. Like earlier German reforms but far more radically, the revolutionary French government secularized monastic lands and religious orders, transferring control of schools and marriage from the Church to the state. New secular laws ensured the equality of citizens before the law and the priority of merit over birth in employment and career advancement.[3] Although contemporary German intellectuals believed French culture shallow and artificial by comparison with their own, the Germans clearly had some catching up to do.[4]

WARRING MODELS OF ENLIGHTENMENT

From a distance France in 1789 was Western civilization's brightest light. In the French Enlightenment and Revolution, Germans confronted a new world more challenging to their own than any previous competitor or predator. Would they join that modern world, cling to their old, or seek a middle way? Germans were not alone in addressing such questions. From Sweden to Italy and England to Russia, virtually every major European country had its own Enlightenment, most in response to the French. In each a more accurate measure of man was believed to have been gained, and with it the promise of freedom of thought and liberation from political tyranny and social injustice. Thenceforth the surest path to truth would be through the sovereign, correcting mind of man.

The movement began in England and France, where seminal thinkers of the Enlightenment posited a natural world governed by verifiable laws. In the place of abstract hypothesis and historical principle, an "exact analysis of things," in Voltaire's words,[5] was said to reveal both God and the world as they truly were. Immanuel Kant wrote of this new freedom from inherited, especially clerical, authority:

> Enlightenment is man's exodus from his self-incurred tutelage [or] inability to use his [own] understanding without the guidance of another. This tutelage is self-incurred if its cause lies not in any weakness of the understanding, but in his own indecision and lack of courage. "Dare to know! Have the courage to use your own understanding": this is the motto of the Enlightenment.[6]

No contemporary thinker's initials were chiseled more deeply into the bricks paving the roads to enlightenment and revolution in France than those of Jean-Jacques Rousseau. "Everything is good when it leaves the hands of the [Creator]," he declared in his educational novel, *Émile*, "however, everything degenerates in the hands of man." Transplanted from nature to civilization, man, who had been born true to self and self-loving, was transformed, thenceforth false and divided against himself.[7] Such hyperbole showered primitive human nature with more goodness, and developed civilization with greater harm, than either arguably exhibited. Yet in this basic notion revolutionaries across the social spectrum found a sanction for their actions.[8]

Over the last decade of the eighteenth century, a succession of French politicians—Pierre Jacques Brissot, Georges Danton, Jean-Paul Marat, Maximilien Robespierre, and Louis de Saint-Just—turned enlightened French thought into sociopolitical lightning. All of them died violent deaths: Marat, stabbed in his bath, Brissot, leader of the Girondists, guillotined in 1793, the others in 1794. "If man is now corrupt," Robespierre paraphrased Rousseau, "the responsibility lies with vicious social institutions." In the storming of the Bastille and the execution of the French king and queen four years later, Robespierre beheld the birth of a new "kingdom not of this world," one in which "Messianic dreams" would be fulfilled.[9]

German thinkers were drawn early and enthusiastically to the French Enlightenment. From the mid–eighteenth century, the Prussian court of Frederick the Great displayed that Enlightenment alongside the German, whose great patron and exemplar was the king himself. Although he spoke French better and more often than German, and favored Frenchmen at his round table in Sanssouci, Frederick, like other contemporary German intellectuals, believed that Berlin had as much to teach the French as Paris the Germans. That belief was only strengthened by the indiscipline and recklessness of the visiting Voltaire, who brazenly pitted self-rule against royal rule, the freedom of the individual against the authority of the state in the person of the king.

The German alternative found revealing expression in a prize essay contest conducted by the Berlin Academy in the 1780s. Instigated by Frederick, who would not live to see its conclusion, its subject attracted more participants than any other such contest in the academy's history. The debated question was: Is It Useful to Deceive the People? Should a ruler, secular or religious, treat his subjects as enlightened, or simply command them? Might he trust them to discover the truth on their own, or must he methodically instill it in them? Some essayists believed that the empowerment of reason and the freedom to act on one's own were more important than any truth that might be discovered in the process, while for others everything hung on declaring the truth and enforcing its observance. The storming of the Bastille in 1789 lit up an issue implicit for all essayists, and very much on the mind of the enlightened German despot who posed the question: With what likelihood of success, and at what risks, does government enlighten the masses?

Unlike France, Germany's social and political history were not then being turned upside down in the name of the new god, Reason, nor had the Germans yet fully contemplated the consequences of pursuing Enlightenment in the French way.[10] That the Berlin Academy's prize was shared equally by the best essays on *both* sides of the question makes clear that Germany in 1792 had not yet become France. For the Germans, individual enlightenment (reason and freedom) and objective truth (higher authority and submission to it) were properly coexistent, and it was a moral imperative to treat them as such. The French Enlightenment, Revolution, and occupation of Germany did not overturn that principled belief, nor would Germany's own democratic revolution a half century later.

What drew Germans to the French Enlightenment and Revolution were the latter's liberation clauses: equality at law, the abolition of clerical and noble privilege, and the hiring and promotion of workers on the basis of ability and skill rather than social class. Those rights and freedoms had also been part of Germany's own history of protest and reform, going back to the Middle Ages. Thus could German intellectuals debate in Berlin pubs and salons the question of whether the French, by their Enlightenment and Revolution, were "trying to establish a state based on sound Prussian principles"—a question Austrian intellectuals also raised with reference to "sound Austrian principles" in their pubs and salons.[11]

The differences were certainly greater than the similarities. Prussian schools did not confront future citizens with a "vicious society," nor were French-style revolutions against "unnatural" political authority encouraged. The education of the enlightened German was not the revolutionary *"liberté, égalité, fraternité"* of the enlightened Frenchman.[12] The purpose of education was individual maturation under a government and within a society deemed essential to and supportive of it.

What the cautious Kant was to enlightened German philosophy, the Interior Ministry's director of school and church affairs, Wilhelm von Humboldt, was to enlightened German education. His reflections on the state's power over the individual, first published in 1792, updated sentiments expressed in a treatise of similar title written three centuries earlier by Martin Luther, in which the Protestant reformer warned rulers not to extend their political authority into the private realms of soul and conscience.[13] For Humboldt safeguarding the right to individual growth and maturation was the state's primary role in forming its citizenry. By allowing youth to "unfold their essences" freely and become what nature intended them to be, the state also served its own best interest, the presumed result being citizens true to themselves and loyal to the state. Individual freedom thus was not, as with the French, an end in itself to be pursued primarily within the public arena and against established political authority.

In comparing the French and German models of enlightenment, many historians have deemed the German to be education for self-realization rather than for self-government—an aesthetic, or spiritual, preparation rather than a proper training for modern political life.[14] Embracing a more positive relationship between the individual and the state, Germans rejected political violence on the French scale and deferred more readily to king and country. In doing so they were expressing a greater collective fear of anarchy than any preference for despotism. From the German point of view, the French construction of liberty threatened the balance between freedom and authority, and the individual and the state. From Luther's "justified believer" to Kant's "enlightened man" and Humboldt's "naturally unfolded" person, the proper German led both a sovereign private and a self-sacrificing public life. And each presumed him to be religiously free, philosophically informed, and socially educated in the service of his neighbor and the state.

For all the things Germans liked about the French Enlightenment, no other Europeans greeted the upheaval that followed it with greater alarm, nor found their misgivings about the French model more surely confirmed. Having made liberty a supremely individual political matter, the French, in the end, veered far off Enlightenment's course.

THE FRENCH DISEASE

With other French neighbors, Germans watched intently in June 1789 when a revolutionary National Constituent Assembly replaced the Estates General of the old regime in France. By that change the first two social estates, the clergy and the nobility, became subordinate to the more populous third: the propertied commercial and professional classes, which included many government officials. With the grudging consent of the French king, the new governing body convened and voted not as a hierarchy of social orders but as equal members of a classless parliament. July brought the storming of the Bastille by small artisans and shopkeepers, August the abolition of serfdom and the Declaration of the Rights of Man and Citizen, which guaranteed every Frenchman the pursuit of life, liberty, and property. In October armed Parisian women joined the masses outside the palace at Versailles to demand the king's capitulation to the Revolution.

In the summer of 1790, the French assembly abolished trade guilds, confirming German suspicions that liberty, equality, and fraternity had not been the Revolution's only, or even its true, aim. For ordinary people the new egalitarianism became very expensive, making France an out-migration land during the revolutionary 1790s.[15] In July the new government paid the Revolution's mounting bills with bonds secured by confiscated Church lands. Dwarfing the earlier pillagings of the Church by Carolingian and Salian kings, the Civil Constitution of the Clergy, as the new confiscatory legislation was named, made the French state the virtual owner of the French Church, able to reduce the number of priests and transform them into a new species of civil servant. That legislation drove Catholics away from the Enlightenment and into the arms of reactionary rulers. Therein also lay the roots of the so-called modernist conflict between Church and state, a German version of which would torment the later decades of German national unification.[16]

No revolution sees farther into the future, or is more frightening to observers, than one that does not know where it is going. Concern over the direction of the French Revolution brought bitter rivals Austria and Prussia briefly into alliance, after French soldiers massed on Germany's western borders. Apparently in the belief that the enemy of one's enemy is one's friend, Prussia had initially promoted Jacobinism—the organized, antimonarchic republicanism then churning France—in southern and northern (today's Belgium) Austrian lands. Belatedly recognizing the foolishness of that policy, Prussian king Frederick William II and new Austrian Hapsburg emperor Leopold II struck a diplomatic accord, the Convention of Reichenbach, in 1790, agreeing to cooperate in the eradication of the new French disease, revolution, fatal to both monarchies.

Over the next two years, 1790–92, the two Germanies extended safe conduct and refuge to French émigrés in flight from the Revolution, welcoming persecuted Huguenots and Catholics into their lands. The new allies also threatened to invade France, should its royal family become imperiled. By 1792, with French armies massing on the Rhine, Austria broke a thirty-six-year nonaggression pact with France. The diplomatic accord of two years was soon thereafter replaced with a mutual defense treaty between the two German powers.[17]

Upon first acquaintance, not every German intellectual had looked favorably on the French Enlightenment and Revolution. In notable instances the embrace was cautious. The father of the German Enlightenment, Kant, qualified his support by rejecting any right of citizens to rebel against properly constituted government. Lawyer Justus Möser was also wary, warning that the notion of "abstract rights belonging to everyone" seemed to put individuals in the service of self and encourage "dangerous illusions," certainly unsociable.[18] Goethe was initially taken with Napoleon, who publicly honored his work in Paris. He did not, however, want Germany to imitate France. Expressing a greater fear of folly than of modernity, he paired France's record of "exacerbating troubled times" with Lutheranism's disruption of "peaceful study."[19] For such seeming aloofness in an age of revolution, modern historians have accused him of "fleeing the responsibilities of power." As James J. Sheehan scolds: "[Goethe] believed radical change was risky, ideals illusory, and the populace a fickle mob. He much preferred the sort of political neutrality possible in a well-run, benevolent authoritarian regime—a neutrality . . . tantamount to accepting the status quo."[20]

Goethe's preference for "the sweet fruit of private bliss" over "intruding political forces," in this instance the French army, can just as plausibly be interpreted as a precocious warning of where such forces might take the world. Recalling Germany's "wretched history" of unification, he doubted the wisdom of a German political movement in imitation of the French, perhaps fearing that Germans would become even more adept at imperialism.[21] With Hegel, he remained a firm opponent of post-Enlightenment romantic nihilism, which believed that the transcendent force behind reality was hostile, not benevolent.[22] Friedrich von Schiller also sensed "false ideals" in the revolutionary age, with its "deeply rooted destructive urges . . . threatening mankind's long, perilous journey from barbarism to civilization."[23] For many other German intellectuals and ordinary people, the dark side of the Revolution became clear only after it had turned tyrannically on itself at home and on the Germans in the Rhineland.

If, in the end, the French Enlightenment was ideologically jarring for Germans, a French-style Revolution was sociologically impossible. German society lacked the dramatis personae for an uprising on the scale and in the manner of the French. There was no comparable commercially successful, property-owning German bourgeoisie to attack, nor masses of *sans culottes* ready to hurl themselves against the rich and the privileged.[24] Despite the confidence of young intellectuals in the 1790s, the devastation of both the Thirty and the Seven Years' Wars was still in easy reach of memory, and few Germans remained as optimistic as the French about humankind's ability to leap beyond itself.[25]

It was for that reason that more copies of Edmund Burke's exposé of the French Revolution were sold in a more populous Germany than in England. When the leaders of the German Enlightenment read Burke, Luther's princely mirror for Saxon elector John Frederick likely flashed before their well-read minds. There Luther, like Burke, pondered the question of whether contemporary politics needed "a Luther," an uncompromising reformer, only to perish the thought, fearing that society might instead empower "a Müntzer," a catastrophic revolutionary. Also like Burke, Luther had reminded his age's firebrands of history's long odds against millenarian makeovers, proposing more modest, and dogged, amelioration in their place. "Because there is no hope of getting another government in the [Holy] Roman Empire . . . it is not advisable to change it. So let [each] who is able rather darn and patch it up, punishing the abuse and putting bandages and ointment on the smallpox."[26]

French Masters

Between the summer of 1792 and that of 1794, the Revolution's irrepressible need to reinvent itself diverted European attention back to Paris. Amid scheming Jacobins and their steaming allies, the *sans culottes*, a new round of revolution had begun. This second revolution, determined to hold the first to its original utopian charter, resulted in massacres in the streets, the serial executions of the king and the queen, and the so-called Terror that accompanied Robespierre's rise and fall.

While the causes of freedom and enlightenment were pressed at home by massacre and guillotine, the French began exporting their Revolution north and west. Declaring war on Austria and its fainthearted ally Prussia in April 1792, the Grand Army marched up the German Rhineland, "liberating" the cities of Speyer, Worms, and Mainz. Then, turning eastward, it began a military expansion across Europe that would end perilously two decades later in deepest, darkest, coldest Russia.

Together Austria and Prussia possessed the military might to halt that offensive in its early years. However, at the time when their combined efforts might have made a difference, the two were hoggishly dividing up Poland with Russia and fighting over the spoils, mostly to Prussia's advantage. Emperor Francis II did not declare war on France until March 1793. Thereafter the armies of the individual German states proved to be no match for the French, who now made the Rhineland a new laboratory for their Enlightenment and Revolution.

There, as in every land they subsequently conquered, the French planted the Revolution by suppressing the local nobility, abolishing serfdom, and putting new, elected governments in place by universal male suffrage. Consoling the larger German states they defeated by allowing them an open season on smaller ones, the French hit upon an efficient way to begin the consolidation of the German Rhineland and coopt its rulers. Such fanning of territorial self-interest also dampened German national feeling and unity, further facilitating the occupation and exploitation of conquered German lands. But as time would also prove, this streamlined and more governable Rhineland, cleverly reconfigured during the French occupation, also made German resistance easier, once Germans were again in a position to reclaim their fatherland.[27]

Prussia's early decision to withdraw altogether from the conflict ensured French control. Preoccupied with Jacobin threats in its new Polish territories, and lacking the resources to fight a two-front war, Prussia simply swapped its occupied Rhenish lands in the west for French neutrality in northern Germany and the promise of new lands east of the Rhine (Peace of Basel, 1795). By thus stepping out of the French maelstrom and going it alone, Prussia bought a decade of relative peace that allowed it to pacify and consolidate its newly acquired lands.

Regardless of the name the Prussian action was treachery, and it provided a baleful example for other German states (Baden, Bavaria, and Württemberg followed suit in 1796), increasing Austria's vulnerability and hastening the empire's demise.[28] Within two years Austria abandoned its Rhenish, Belgian, and Lombard possessions to a conquering France, falling back on its more immediate empire. Like the Franco-Prussian Peace of Basel, the Franco-Austrian Peace of Campo Formio in 1797 exalted regional identity over a common German one, sacrificing empire to state.[29]

After suffering a second great defeat at Hohenlinden in 1801, Austria conceded the western Rhineland to the French. France now had a firewall on its eastern front and an unobstructed pathway to eastern Europe.[30] With Napoleon as its draftsman, the realignment of the Rhineland ran apace, humiliating to the displaced but delighting the new masters. The boundary changes became official after the Imperial Diet accepted a made-in-Paris, written-in-Regensburg "Deputation Report," sanctioning the mammoth French reorganization and annexation of German lands during the occupation. Emperor Francis II proclaimed that report law on April 17, 1803. All but three Rhenish ecclesiastical principalities were secularized; forty-five of fifty-one free imperial cities ceased to exist; and the larger states cannibalized the private lands of the imperial knights. Also vanishing forever were 112 small southern and western states, most absorbed by Baden, Bavaria, Württemberg, and Hesse-Darmstadt. By eliminating so many of the political jurisdictions into which Germany had been divided since Hohenstaufen times, the more than three hundred sovereign entities the French encountered in 1800 had been consolidated into thirty-five at the time of their departure.[31]

Last Straws and Finishing Touches

With Prussia observing a neutrality pact with France, and France breaking treaty promises with the Hapsburgs, Austria made new alliances with Russia and England in a last attempt to save the empire. That contingents from Baden, Bavaria, and Württemberg fought alongside Napoleon in the new Franco-Austrian war, while

Prussia and the other German states again remained neutral, attests to the diminishment of the Hapsburg-led empire by the turn of the eighteenth century. The great battle of that war occurred at Austerlitz in 1805, perhaps Napoleon's greatest victory. Among the German states receiving Austrian spoils was his silent ally, Prussia.

In 1806 the Holy Roman Empire was formally dissolved. Napoleon might have taken the imperial crown for himself after Francis II surrendered it in August. But out of the ashes he created the Confederation of the Rhine, another buffer between France and its eastern enemies for the immediate future. From an initial sixteen ex-imperial, middling Rhenish states, the new confederation grew to thirty-nine, adding those of the old empire along with Prussia, Austria, Danish Holstein, and Swedish Pomerania.

Having stolen peace and prospered during the French occupation, Prussia now had the rudest awakening of all the German states. In October 1806 French armies, having already imposed their will in the south, crushed Prussia in twin battles at Jena and Auerstädt. At the eastern end of the Prussian kingdom, they occupied Königsberg (now Kaliningrad), while at the western, they created the new state of Westphalia, compounding west Prussian lands, Hannover, and twelve smaller states, over which Napoleon's brother, Jerome, ruled as king. The final settlement of the war in 1807 allowed Prussia to keep only its eastern lands (Brandenburg, East Prussia, and Silesia), cut its population in half, and left four occupying French soldiers for every Prussian. Had the czar not required this rump of Prussia as a buffer between Russia and France, Prussia might well have vanished altogether.[32] Such were the wages of Prussian neutrality in the continuing German war with the French.

Over the next six years the French rebuilt occupied Germany from its foundations, particularly in the Rhineland. The Code Napoléon encouraged comparatively open societies, with greater social equality and individual rights (peasants were emancipated throughout the Rhineland), free trade, and religious tolerance.[33] Under French pressure Austria and Prussia also introduced liberal reforms, mostly as temporizing measures favorable to their liberation. Recognizing that ordinary Prussians would more readily make the sacrifices necessary to remove the French if they were given a greater stake in their land and role in their government, Prussian ministers Baron Karl vom und zum Stein and Karl August Count Hardenberg moved to cut red tape, free serfs, and expand the middle class. To defeat Napoleon the diminished Prussian army, now only forty-two thousand, also needed to believe in the cause for which it fought. Here, too, greater individual freedom and self-reliance were introduced by basing rank and promotion more consistently on ability, merit, and self-sacrifice.[34]

While arousing territorial hatreds had long been a proven formula for defeating the Germans, it also had a history of awakening national sentiment. Smoldering in the ashes of German defeat was also hatred of the French. As the Rhinelanders learned early in the occupation, the French had come not to liberate and to teach but to dominate and to exploit. Contrary to contemporary French and many modern historians' portrayal of welcoming Rhinelanders, the great majority rather "saw their property looted and vandalized, their crops ravaged, their possessions requisitioned, their horses, carts, and persons conscripted, their churches desecrated, [and] their priests persecuted."[35]

While French reforms accelerated the legal and administrative modernization of German lands, the more the French changed things, particularly in Austria and Prussia, the more the Germans wanted them to remain the same. That reaction resulted more from the personal treatment Germans received at the hands of the French than from their reforms, which were neither completely new nor forbidden to Germans. But beyond ingrained German habit and tradition, the French army was its own worst enemy. If the French enlightened the Germans, consolidated their lands, streamlined their political institutions, and spurred their industrial development, they also plundered, displaced, imposed enormous taxes upon, and conscripted Germans involuntarily into the French army.

New trade barriers turned a previously international German economy into one narrowly focused on French markets. Along with new taxes Austria and Prussia also had to cope with war indemnities and large-scale conscription into the French army. And topping it all was the frequent contact with quartered French soldiers and high officials, who stood over Germans as lords and masters, disdaining native cultures and religions.[36]

Long-developed structural and temperamental barriers existed as well. If Germans were philosophically and sociologically ill-prepared for a French-style revolution, they were also historically ill-disposed to reforms that pursued impossible ideals and utopian goals. For most Germans the execution of the French king and queen and the rough justice meted out by French revolutionary tribunals suggested an Enlightenment and a Revolution run amok. Also working to keep Napoleonic absolutism at bay was Germany's politically layered society.[37] Historically, Germans had tiered political identities and allegiances, being at one and the same time self-conscious villagers or townspeople, subjects of a distinct land or state, and members of a transregional empire.

Germany's educated and professional classes also steered the nation away from the French model of revolution. From the clergy and humanists who advised princes and electors in medieval times to the academics and civil servants of the Frankfurt National Assembly and the shifting professional cabinets of the later Weimar Republic, Germany's educated elite both challenged and defended established society.[38] Therein lay a predilection for carefully controlled change, progress with good order—a society that could be both liberal and conservative at once.

Between the overbearing French army and the internal pressures of inertia and tradition, the success of the French Enlightenment and Revolution in Germany was understandably restricted. For all their appeal to Germans, the Declaration of the Rights of Man and Citizen and the Code Napoléon were not the cure-alls for what ailed Germany. If Germans were to make a great leap forward, more

French instruction was not what they required. What was needed most after 1813 was the freedom to make that leap out of their own history and on their own feet.

GERMANY RISING

When the Germans took another run at the French, a revived Austria was the first to engage and be defeated, leaving only the British on the offensive in Iberia, nurturing a Spanish revolt. The Russians made a better show of it, ultimately provoking Napoleon into one of the worst military decisions in the history of war: the sending of his Grand Army into Russia. At least seven hundred thousand strong for that mission, conscripted Germans made up a third of the army, joined by Italian, Dutch, and Polish contingents in addition to the French. Arriving in Moscow in September 1812, only to find the city torched and abandoned, the army began its withdrawal in the fall, with the Russian winter gathering before it and the Cossacks hot on their backs.

In December 1812 Prussian commander Ludwig von Yorck, sensing an opportunity, took his soldiers over to the Russians. In a losing battle the combined Prussian and Russian armies inflicted casualties sufficient to force an armistice and bring Napoleon to the negotiating table, where Austria acted as an honest broker for the Germans.[39] The failure of those talks set the stage for the Battle of Nations at Leipzig in 1813, where Austria and Britain joined Prussia, Russia, and Sweden in Napoleon's defeat. Although Napoleon broke the ensuing peace to fight and lose again, Leipzig had been his undoing.

Restoration

The Peace of Paris in 1814 returned a defeated France to its 1792 borders, and the Congress of Vienna redrew the map of Europe to reinstate prerevolutionary national boundaries almost everywhere. Invoking the principle of national independence and the sovereignty of states, the congress restored even France to great power status, allowing it to keep Alsace. Among the winners, Prussia gained the most, retrieving its lost Rhineland all the way to Westphalia.

In the postwar task of restoring old Europe, Austrian foreign minister Klemens von Metternich spoke for the old guard. After twenty years of war and three million dead, what all now feared most was the rise of a new imperial power capable of waging war again on a Napoleonic scale. Perceiving a united Germany to be such a power, the European community, with Britain, France, and Russia leading, sought a temporary solution by creating a new, politically hamstrung German Confederation, which counted Austria and Prussia among its members. Composed of thirty-five member states and four major cities (Bremen, Frankfurt, Hamburg, and Lübeck), the new organization was a nonthreatening successor to the defunct Holy Roman Empire. Its legislative assembly met in Frankfurt, presided over by the multinational Austrians, who had their own eastern empire and were not about to be absorbed into a greater Germany at its own cost. Between the enabling legislation and the international watchdogs who sat at its table, the confederation had little opportunity for loud self-assertion, much less any concerted action. Many issues before it required a two-thirds vote, some even unanimous passage, virtually ensuring stalemate. And the kings of Britain, Denmark, and the Netherlands, by virtue of their accessory titles to confederation lands, could insert themselves at will into its affairs.[40]

Prince Metternich famously justified the restoration's reactionary agenda by declaring the "transition from old structures to new" to be more precarious than the "retreat from new structures to crumbling old ones."[41] Too divided to pose a threat to its neighbors, the new tripartite Germany of Austria, Prussia, and the German Confederation seems a throwback to the divided Frankish empire after the Treaty of Verdun and the old Holy Roman Empire after the Peace of Westphalia. That perception, however, is deceptive, for Austria and Prussia were now great powers nursing large grudges against peer nations and even larger ones against each other. The resolution of those grudges would drive European conflicts until the middle of the twentieth century.

Social-Domestic Order

A reassertion of old social and domestic hierarchies accompanied the return to old geographical and political boundaries. At mid-century, liberal critics applied the term "Biedermeier" (literally, an honest, conventional steward) to post-1820s restoration society. Connoting ordinariness and simplicity, the term became code for apolitical, inward-looking, cog-in-the-wheel middle-class life aloof from both the hardscrabble agrarian and hurly-burly industrial worlds. At the center of the "Biedermeier family" a contented paterfamilias, the stolid,.kind, and trusting "German Michel," was portrayed. Taken derisively, such images suggested a Germany no longer keeping up with the times and easily taken advantage of by its enemies.[42] By the turn of the century, however, Germans looked back wistfully to the Biedermeier era's perceived comfort and peace.[43]

Looking forward, such caricatures magnified a part of German history that was not necessarily its destiny. The tight-knit, docile burgher family and principled society they portray had long been a German ideal, and no more or less successful and uniform in the nineteteeth century than in previous and subsequent ones.[44] The Biedermeier decades of the nineteenth century were as mixed as any in German history, tethered at one end by a fixed-estate society based on birth and privilege, yet at the same time reaching out to a meritocratic, enterpreneurial-class society at the other. Over the nineteenth century individual talent and achievement increasingly determined who Germans were in the workplace, a development contemplated in the educational and civic reforms of the Reformation era, and having gained some ground in the agrarian and military reforms of late-eighteenth-century Prussia.

Still, the old nobility possessed the means—land, money, and contacts—to maintain its hold on public life. Even in defeat, when forced to emancipate peasants on their lands, aristocrats received very generous compensation for their lost free labor. Among the layers of nobility posing the greatest obstacles to middle class advancement in the civil service were those staffing the royal courts, administration, and army. Yet resistance to reform might also come from those who had much to gain from the demise of the old aristocracy. Ambitious members of the rising middle class were not immune to the allure of the latter's privileges. On the other hand not a few aristocrats supported reforms that advanced burghers.[45]

In the more open and fluid society of the nineteenth century, the middle class formed its own elite civil service corps in the 1830s and 1840s. Their success resulted less from the egalitarian rhetoric of the freedom movement than from the economic power they amassed as a highly productive group. However, as ostracism and loss of employment were the price of whistle-blowing in the decades of restoration, being closer to the center of power inhibited middle-class criticism. Nonetheless, burgher civil servants could not close their ears to the pleas of reformers and revolutionaries pressing their causes.[46] Petitions for greater freedom of the press and association, as well as a judicial system blind to class and privilege, were frequently before them.

The middle class had its own self-promoting intelligentsia outside the civil service corps in the persons of unaffiliated writers and poets, journalists and editors, and lawyers and doctors—all professionally interested in a more open and just society. Unlike the middle-class civil servants on the inside, these professions could criticize the government with abandon from without, as Heinrich Heine and Karl Marx did. As outsiders they also made common cause with the lower middle class, whose foremost concern was material security. Threatened both by competition from the working classes beneath them and soaring numbers in their own ranks, craftsmen and shopkeepers zigzagged in both socially conservative and revolutionary directions. During the volatile 1830s and 1840s, the middle-class intelligentsia and a lightly educated lower middle class became the German revolution's most willing recruits.[47]

TOWARD 1848

Despite two decades of restoration, Germany still had a rendezvous with its own "1789." Pulled historically in both conservative and liberal directions, Germans were the least likely Europeans to find incompatible the sociopolitical alternatives of the nineteenth century. Despite the efforts of the Congress of Vienna to turn back the clock, too many Germans had seen the blessings of increased opportunity and freedom to return quietly to Prince Metternich's fixed, hierarchical world. The big question now for the Germans was the degree to which the old world and the new might accommodate one another, for Germans had enduring attachments to aspects of both.

Wartburg, 1817

The first significant rallying of the postwar nation occurred at Wartburg Castle in Eisenach in Thuringia, the site of Luther's translation of the New Testament into German and, for many, the birthplace of a modern, pan-German culture. There, on October 18–19, 1817, a cross-section of Germans celebrated three path-breaking events: the third centenary of the Protestant Reformation, the recent founding of the national student fraternity movement, and the fourth anniversary of Napoleon's defeat at Leipzig.

The fraternity movement was a new student generation's reaction to French occupation and the Congress of Vienna's seeming attempt to freeze German national development. It drew mostly idealistic Protestant youth intent on preserving a genuine German culture within a free, reformed, and united German state. Although French refrains echoed in their songs, theirs was a Germanic tune versifying medieval and imperial German history.

The number of students who joined the movement was comparatively small, and the contingent attending the festival smaller still. Nonetheless, they represented a segment of society with influence beyond their numbers and were deeply committed (many grew beards and dressed in the style of earlier German generations).[48] Amid nationalist fervor deemed revolutionary by Prince Metternich, the Wartburg celebrants marched under the red, black, and gold flag of Adolf Freiherr von Lützow's Prussian unit, the heroes of the Battle of Nations. That flag would later fly over the three national assemblies to which modern German democracy traces its lineage: the Frankfurt National Assembly of 1848–49, the Weimar Republic of 1918–33, and the post–World War II Parliamentary Council of 1949.

The nationalism displayed was narrowly chauvinistic. With rare exceptions, the fraternities excluded unbaptized Jews, moving them to form their own. During the celebrations at the Wartburg, a spectrum of "foreign" books was burned: the Prussian police laws, the Code Napoléon, and rabbinical writings.[49] In this, the Protestant fraternity brothers appear to have been following Martin Luther's example of three centuries earlier. In December 1522, Luther and his students had burned books of canon law, papal decretals, and scholastic theology in Wittenberg in protest of papal and imperial condemnations of the Reformation.[50]

In 1819 a radical student named Carl Sand assassinated a popular reactionary writer, August von Kotzebue. That action gave the princes a pretext to ban university fraternities and shut down urban newspapers, then the twin media of revolutionary speech. Meeting in Carlsbad (today Karlovy Vary) in 1819, the princes, again led by Prince Metternich, imposed new repressive measures that remained law until 1848.

Although the students' primary goal was a united Germany with great-power status, their political liberality was genuine, making the movement a progressive force in the years immediately after the Congress of Vienna's conservative retreat. Driven underground by the princes after 1819, the movement would resurface in the 1840s in an older and more cautious generation.[51]

The July Revolution in France

In the 1820s and 1830s dormancy was the most prudent state for German liberals and revolutionaries, while in Switzerland, Italy, Poland, and France, sporadic protests and uprisings kept national freedom movements both alive and in peril. Of the latter the failure of the Bourbon dynasty in France particularly unnerved reigning governments. The stage was here set for the so-called July Revolution of 1830, a reaction to King Charles X's overturning of an unexpected liberal election victory. His unabashed crushing of dissent and rigging of a new election turned middle-class opinion against the monarchy bringing poorer Frenchmen into Paris streets, where fighting took almost two thousand lives. In the aftermath a liberal faction of French deputies arranged for the king's abdication and put a new constitutional monarchy in his place. Although flying the revolutionary tricolor, the new government favored the middle class and a political middle way, the specter of a successful proletarian revolt having made the underclass as loathsome as the overbearing king.

Like a contagion the July Revolution inspired protests and precautions. Although Berlin and Vienna were largely passed over, police and soldiers went on alert in numerous German lands. In the north (Brunswick, Hesse-Kassel, Hannover, and Saxony) and the south (Baden, Württemberg, and Bavaria), local democracy movements backed the protests. Beyond the legislative outcome, neither Frenchmen nor Germans soon forgot the scary days in July, when kings and the middle class rediscovered the powers, both legal and anarchical, of the masses. Among those taking that lesson to heart was future German chancellor Otto von Bismarck, then fifteen.[52]

Young Germany

Watching the struggle in France were influential groups of Germans ready to send Germany in a democratic direction. The Young Germany movement demanded for all Germans, including women and Jews, the rights and freedoms then being contested in other lands. Among its leaders was poet and essayist Heinrich Heine, a converted Jew and vocal supporter of the July Revolution, whose popular travelogues in praise of radical democracy made him a Parisian exile after 1830. His was not the only voice silenced in Germany. Like the German fraternity movement in 1817, Young Germany also had its provocative castle demonstration, in Hambach in the Bavarian Palatinate in 1832. There perhaps as many as thirty thousand marched in protest and exultation around the castle ruins in what has been called "the high point of early German liberalism."[53] Within a year reemerging members of the fraternity movement raided the government military depot in Frankfurt.

During these decades of escalating protest and repression, the freedom movement had a silent ally in the captains of industry, who pounded as hard on the doors of progress and change in their professional world as the age's social and political reformers did in theirs. In the second quarter of the century, gaslights transformed Berlin into a city that no longer had to sleep. The first passenger trains ran between Nuremberg and Fürth in the south and between Berlin and Hamburg in the north. Spinning and weaving mills sprang up like dandelions across southern Germany. And the first steamship crossed the Atlantic from Bremen to New York.

Equally vital to German progress and modernization was the

freeing up of trade. Prior to 1834 thirty-eight tariff and customs zones bogged down interregional traffic and threatened new commerce in deference to local trades and industries. Like medieval castles dotting the land, those barriers signaled "particularism" and invited conflict. At Prussia's initiative, a Customs Union was created in 1834, integrating lands with a total population of twenty-three million, with Austria ominously excluded.[54] The result was rapid economic growth for the members and a lasting reminder of the benefits of unity and free trade.

THE REVOLUTION OF 1848–49

By the mid-1840s a largely middle-class leadership had embraced the social and political goals of Germany's pioneer freedom movements. At stake for the revolutionaries was a direct role in the formation of the state through open elections, and in its operation in the courts, the civil service, and the military. To those ends several vital rights pertained: universal male suffrage, the freedoms of speech, press, religion, and work, and trial by jury.

Although the demands varied from protest to protest, the basic grievances and longings of the revolutionaries remained clear and distinct. They found eloquent expression in a mid–nineteenth-century German-English guide for newly arrived emigrants, who fled the fatherland before and after 1848. Prepared by a German émigré pastor settled in Boston, the guide was as flattering of the new world as it was condemnatory of the old in its promise of "a great blessing" to emigrants reaching North American shores. Yet it also pointedly conveyed the Old World message of authority and order amid freedom and equality:

> The German emigrant . . . comes into a country free from . . . despotism . . . privileged orders and monopolies . . . intolerable taxes, [and] constraint in matters of belief and conscience. Everyone can

travel . . . and settle wherever he pleases. No passport is demanded, no police mingles in his affairs or hinders his movements. . . .

Nothing can be . . . more dangerous and pernicious than the prejudices [of] monarchies [which assert] that some are born princes and nobles . . . while others are born subjects, from which [condition] neither they nor their posterity can ever rise. [These are] very erroneous views [of] the natural equality of man and must be forever extinguished. . . . Fidelity and merit are the only sources of honor here. The rich stand on the same footing as the poor; the scholar is not above the most humble mechanic; and no German ought to be ashamed to [pursue] any occupation. . . .

[Here] wealth and possession of real estate confer not the least political right on its owner above what the poorest citizen has. [Nor are there] nobility, privileged orders, [and] standing armies to weaken the physical and moral power of the people, [or] swarms of public functionaries to devour in idleness the bread of the poor. Above all, [there are] no princes and corrupt courts representing the so-called 'divine right of birth.' In such a country the *talents*, *energy* and *perseverance* of a person . . . have far greater opportunity for display than in monarchies. . . .

As much as the laborer deserves his reward . . . we strongly disapprove of those who, by violation of law, attempt to maintain a presumptuous right. If the claims of the working classes are well founded, legal means . . . are at the command of the people to secure their rights. . . . Freedom of speech and of the press, universal suffrage and the unlimited right of association [cancel] every pretext for violent opposition to the law. . . . The people themselves [are] the ruler, and the ballot-box, the courts of justice, the legislative halls, and that venerable Capitol at Washington [are] the . . . arenas where bloodless contests are waged for the public welfare.[55]

After 1846 agrarian and economic crises set the larger stage for revolution. Throughout Germany, local parliaments pressured rulers to convene a national parliament to write a national constitution, while workers and students took to the streets to demand political reform. In March 1848 these combined forces sent Prince Metternich fleeing to London and drove Austrian emperor Ferdinand out of Vienna.[56]

In Berlin, Prussian king Frederick William IV bitterly watched as blood was shed on his palace lawn. Belatedly and in desperation, he offered constitutional concessions to the revolutionaries, only to be put under house arrest and see his government placed in tenuous liberal hands. At the insurgents' instruction, he approved the May Day election of a new national parliament. In these months future German chancellor Otto von Bismarck made his political debut, decisively on the side of royalty.[57]

On May 18, 1848, a national parliament met in Saint Paul's Church in Frankfurt to debate its relationship to the monarchy, define the basic rights of the German people, and determine the member states of a new German empire. Those debates continued in Frankfurt until May 1849, thereafter to fizzle out in a rump parliament in Stuttgart in June.[58] The delegates came from all German regions and represented a cross-section of middle-class society and the professions. The guidelines permitted 649 delegates to serve, although fewer were actually elected. With one exception, no more than 450 delegates sat at any one session. The vast majority were educated civil servants and academics, more than 600 had university degrees, 80 percent of them in law, and all were beholden to the state for their jobs.[59]

These factors may explain the alternating audacity and indecision of the delegates. In addition to the ingrained German belief in both individual freedom and state authority, the delegates also had personal reasons not to overreach. Reflecting the times, representation among the less vested classes was minuscule. The lower middle class was hardly there at all, while not a single working-class person sat among the delegates. Yet, if liberal, educated Germany dominated the Frankfurt National Assembly, they did not forget the social and political welfare of the general populace in the laws they wrote.

Declaring itself the sovereign voice of the German people, with political authority superior to that of any member state, the assembly became the provisional central power, or official national government, assuming command of the army and the state's war- and treaty-making powers. It intended to rule in tandem with a provisional imperial regent, or national executive, empowered to command the army and appoint ministers of state on the assembly's behalf. Despite the lofty title and the concession of executive power, the regent was in fact to be a junior partner in the new constitutional monarchy.

Initially the political goal was the largest possible German confederacy, including German-speaking Austrian lands, under a Hapsburg regent, an honor extended to Archduke John of Austria. Before Austria could join and lead this "greater Germany," the assembly required it to spin off the non-German lands of its Austro-Hungarian empire, which the Austrians refused to do. Even if they had been willing, good reasons still existed to oppose a larger German confederation. Although promising a larger tent, with seventy million Germans, how tight could such a tent be? What the assembly wanted most was an impregnable German state, and that militated against Austria's prominent presence. With or without its non-German empire, Austrian Hapsburg leadership meant continued Austro-Prussian rivalry for German hegemony, the recent history of which had been division and disaster. In March, 1849, a majority of the assembly opted for a smaller and closer-knit Germany under Prussian Hohenzollern leadership in the person of Frederick William IV.[60]

As with previous German unions and confederations, success depended on the recognition of the great European powers, which was slow in coming and modest upon arrival. Those powers had no desire to see Germany united and its military and economic strength increased. Only the United States recognized the assembly as Germany's official government. Even more discouraging was the silence of the major German powers—Austria, Prussia, Bavaria, and

Hannover—none of which would recognize the imperial constitution as superior to their own.[61] Germany's many heads of state believed the Frankfurt assembly to be a tower of Babel rather than any clarion call to nationhood. The large German states, with much popular support, rejected the assembly's assumption of supreme military authority. So even as the new national government prepared to take to the seas, its most powerful constituents deemed it a steamless ship of state, unlikely to survive Europe's troubled waters, and hence best left in dry dock, which they made sure happened in the spring of 1849.

Basic Rights

In December 1848, the Frankfurt National Assembly enshrined the decades-old freedom movement in a fourteen-article Basic Rights Law. Abolishing agrarian serfdom, this omnibus protection of personal, political, and property rights has been called, with some hyperbole, "the end of the Middle Ages in Germany."[62] Not only had much that was medieval ended in earlier centuries, the modern abolition of serfdom was neither strictly principled nor as definitive as "abolition" suggests. Noble landlords received handsome compensation for emancipating their peasants, and while the latter's freedom was no small gain, the new class society that replaced it was almost as stratified and punishing as the estate society from which Germans had been trying to escape since the Middle Ages. A prosperous agrarian and industrial society continued to confront huge numbers of dependent workers near or at the bottom of society, unhappy masses who created new opportunities for revolutionary political parties. In real social and economic terms, the Middle Ages did not end in Germany in 1848–49, they just moved into the suburbs and the cities.[63]

In line with the French Enlightenment and the Napoleonic revolution, the Basic Rights legislation segregated Church (canon law) and state (secular law). Precedents for doing so existed as early as the Reformation. However, unlike the Frankfurt assembly, which would have allowed citizens to elect local clergy much as they did members of parliament, the laicized religion of the Reformation never contemplated a completely secularized state.[64] Also unlike post-Enlightenment Europe, rulers and clergy in earlier centuries traced their respective powers to the same divine source and sanction, making them partners in a joint civil-religious enterprise, rather than rivals in a zero-sum Church-state competition.

From a long historical perspective, the Frankfurt assembly revived high-medieval royalist arguments intended to render the Church a docile department of state. By updating that earlier confrontation, the Revolution of 1848–49 set the stage for a modern culture war, *Kulturkampf*, between Rome and Berlin, and with a Protestant fury to match that of Rome.[65] In this, as with so much of the nineteenth century, 1848–49 ran counter to mainstream German history, which never favored abject subordination of religion to society, or of the Church to the state. Historically Germans had preferred dualism: distinct, but linked and cooperative civic and religious spheres.

Avoiding the most radical proposals then abroad in the land, the Basic Rights Law sought to advance society by an incremental education in freedom—that is, to bring as many Germans as possible into the middle class simply by expanding equality and opportunity. That sensible approach did not, however, prevent a special assembly session in Berlin, in May 1848, from provoking both kings and public opinion. Given the task of accommodating the Prussian king constitutionally, its first item of business was a motion to immortalize the revolutionaries of the 1840s—that is, themselves—as "servants of the Fatherland." Although defeated, the very offering of such a motion sent the wrong message to the Prussian king, who had grave misgivings about the constitutional convention in Frankfurt from the day he was forced to convene it. Did the Forty-Eighters now intend to rewrite history as well as law?[66]

Given the times, the assembly's refusal to entertain a constitution written solely by a king was defensible enough. That it expected the king of Prussia to revere its own draft constitution was not. In December 1848, Frederick William dismissed the ambitious Berlin assembly and promulgated his own constitution. In doing so he cited as justification the subordinate position to which the assembly's constitution intended to relegate him. Detecting what he called the "whorish smell of revolution," he privately scorned any crown it might offer as a dog collar. When, on April 3, 1849, an assembly delegation did offer him a crown, he responded by asking it to poll the kings, princes, and free cities of the empire on the matter. That was a rhetorical reminder that he, as monarch, stood in the centuries-old succession of German rulers who received their crowns directly from God.[67]

Thereafter the Frankfurt National Assembly could only disintegrate. The Austrian delegation resigned on April 5 and the Prussian on May 14, leaving behind a small leftist faction to turn out the lights in Stuttgart, whither the rump had moved, in June. Although sympathetic historians acknowledge "revolutionary excess" and "dubious democracy" in the Frankfurt assembly's constitution, the modern story line has faulted the inertia of monarchy and its addiction to power for the failure of German democracy in 1849.[68] That, however, ignores the fright the assembly's political dreams had given a secure middle class and the more vulnerable lower-middle and working classes striving beneath them. In these progressive-regressive decades, Germans did not want to put what they had at risk by embarking on unsure political and social change. For all its precedential value and bright future prospects, the Revolution of 1848–49 divided and politicized contemporary Germans.

Falling Forward

On June 18, 1849, Prussian soldiers closed the doors on the remnants of the Frankfurt National Assembly lingering in Stuttgart. In German history this royal rejection of the democracy movement has frequently been compared to the suppression of the great peasants' revolt in 1525, each a benighted turning back of history's clock.[69] That judgment, however, does scant justice to the complexity and progress of German history prior to 1848. After 1525 mild reforms and some redressing of peasant grievances in fact occurred. In many places unnegotiated tithes, labor services, and death taxes were cancelled. Streams, forests, meadows, and fields were returned to common use. And the right to fence in crops and run dogs in fields—measures against animal foraging—was reinstated.[70] More important, each side gained a new appreciation of the other's breaking point: for the peasants, arbitrary and unbending reversals of customary rights and privileges, for the princes, anarchic and utopian revolution from below.

Germany 1848–49 is a story of political and social reconstruction, both sought and opposed, and of repression by both kings and revolutionaries. The years leading up to and from the Frankfurt National Assembly saw kings put to flight and arrested, and parliaments and constitutions arbitrarily overturned. If in its aftermath monarchs and aristocrats were as strong as ever, the German middle class had become even more so, henceforth the solid center of a society seeking increased opportunity and security. Many German lands still had constitutions under which rulers and parliaments shared a common power of governance. And, as with princes and peasants in 1525, both sides of the conflict had learned what the other could and could not tolerate, which was also not so different from 1525.[71]

That the Frankfurt assembly did not get its way calmed as many fears as it raised. Most Germans were relieved to know that their country had not jumped onto the high-speed tracks of a highly experimental sociopolitical and economic future. And once again, as throughout German history, the European great powers rejoiced in the knowledge that a united greater Germany was still not in the cards.

The years 1848–49 are not a sad tale of German democracy

undone, but another in a long series of clashes between the two souls of Dr. Faustus—that is, of Germans deeply at odds with themselves.[72] To the extent that the Frankfurt National Assembly failed, it was not because the delegates were too academic or philosophical, or the opposing princes hopelessly backward, or the German people pathologically driven to hierarchical rule. In the end the assembly's enemies were both royalty and the middle class, both conservatives and liberals. The Revolution of 1848–49 faltered for the same reasons as many an earlier German reform or revolt—because contemporaries believed it had not gotten the proportions of authority and freedom, security and equality, right. Insofar as the assembly's work had addressed progressively the most basic of German needs, it would be remembered and revived when later parliaments resumed the search for the elusive German political mixture.

The nineteenth-century memorial statue to Arminius, near Detmold in the Teutoberg Forest. *(Courtesy of Martin Wieland, Archäologisches Institut der Universtat zu Köln)*

First-century German slaves taken captive by the Romans near Mainz. *(Courtesy of Landesmuseum Mainz)*

The Merovinginan Frank Clovis, on horseback, calls out to Jesus Christ to give him victory over the Alemanns, promising to become a baptized Christian in return. *(Courtesy of Bettmann/Corbis)*

Hans Holbein's portrayal of Martin Luther as the German Hercules. Slain at his feet are the philosophers and scholastics on whose work the false doctrine of the medieval Church had been built: Aristotle, Peter Lombard, Saint Thomas Aquinas, William of Ockham, and Nicholas of Lira. Jakob Hochstraten is about to be slain, while the pope, hanging from Luther's teeth, is the next to go. *(Courtesy of Zentralbibliothek Zürich)*

Dürer self-portrait, in 1500, as Jesus Christ. *(Courtesy of Bayerische Staatsgemäldesammlungen)*

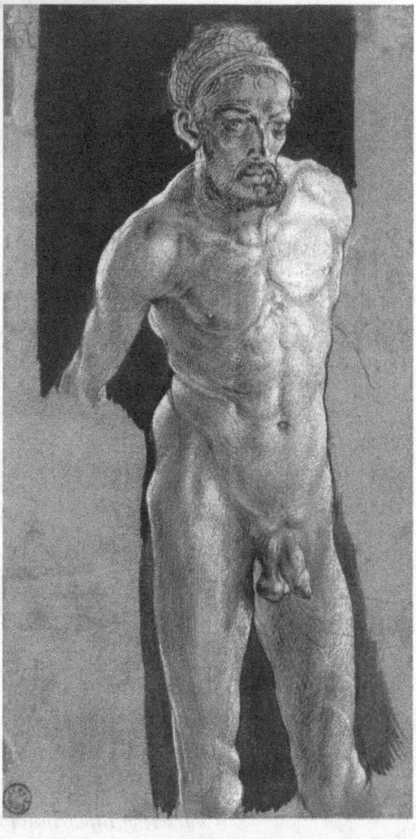

Dürer self-portrait in 1502–3, as he recovered from plague. *(Courtesy of Bettmann/Corbis)*

Voltaire enlightens Frederick the Great in a garden at Sanssoucci.
(Courtesy of Bettmann/Corbis)

After the Battle of Nations in 1813, Napoleon crosses the battlefield at Leipzig with his generals, among them a Mameluke. Observing some of the thirty-seven thousand French bodies that litter the field, he tells the grateful crows to "pack it in," while he flees the scene with the Cossacks in hot pursuit.
(Courtesy of Bildarchiv Preussischer Kulturbesitz)

Personified in the simple, honest German Michel, a freer and unifying Germany rises up in 1848 against the European powers that would divide and exploit it—the French knocked to the ground, the Russians brought to their knees, the English hastening away, the papacy completely withdrawn, and self-serving German aristocrats in retreat as well.
(Courtesy of the Germanisches Nationalmuseum Nürnberg)

The German royal family (*from left to right*): Crown Prince Frederick William, later Kaiser Frederick III (ninety-nine-day rule in 1888); Kaiser William I (1871–88); (child) Prince William (b. 1882, eldest son of Kaiser William II); Prince William, later Kaiser William II (1888–1918).
(Courtesy of Bettmann/Corbis)

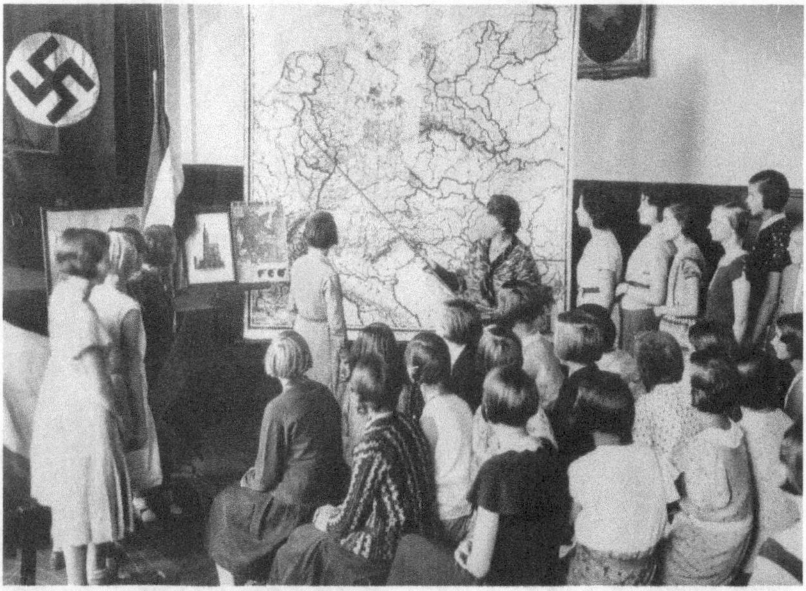

The signing of the Treaty of Versailles on June 28, 1919, was remembered by Germans. Here, in a schoolroom fourteen years later, as the new Nazi regime was proceeding to undo the treaty, a teacher explains to her class what the Allies had taken from their country after World War I. *(Courtesy of Bettmann/Corbis)*

In 1923, with one American dollar buying 4.2 million deutsche marks, German children turned their worthless currency into playhouse bricks. *(Courtesy of Bettmann/Corbis)*

A weary Hitler discussing strategy with Nazi press agent "Putzi" Hanfstaengl and new parliamentary president Hermann Göring on the day before Kurt von Schleicher became chancellor. Seven weeks later Hitler was chancellor.
(Courtesy of Bettmann/Corbis)

7

ABSOLUTE SPIRIT AND ABSOLUTE PEOPLE

The Intellectual Torrents of the Nineteenth Century

IN THE FIRST HALF of the nineteenth century, numerous German lands saw democracy movements flourish as rulers were either put to flight or voluntarily stepped down, permitting the creation of new parliamentary governments. By French comparison, the German revolution pales. Terrified of organized Jacobin anarchy, Germans, liberal and conservative alike, did not allow French freedom to move very far down the social ladder. When a clear choice had to be made, Germans prefered political gridlock or subservience to revolution from below. Critics, however, existed on both the left and the right, the one condemning the German Enlightenment as insufficiently reformist, the other damning it as inadequately restorationist.

Future German chancellor Otto von Bismarck would orchestrate this debate after mid-century. Emerging as a national political figure during the death throes of the Frankfurt National Assembly, he became the lightning rod for the German struggle in the political sphere, playing rival liberal and conservative parliamentary factions against an often shifting—yet to his mind—nation-saving middle course.[1] In the intellectual realm, a succession of brilliant thinkers, almost all lapsed Lutherans, aggressively addressed vital issues of thought and culture, beginning with a comparatively cautious Immanual Kant and peaking with the ferocious Friedrich Nietzsche. These were linked developments, as German religion and philosophy did not stray far from society and politics. In the end the revolt of the intellectuals helped turn the German political stalemate into one of the most productive—and destructive—transitions in German history, one that still runs deep in the early twenty-first century.[2]

FROM KANT TO NIETZSCHE

Kant's Copernican Revolution

Königsberg philosopher Immanuel Kant may have been the greatest mind of the German Enlightenment. His arguments opened eyes long closed but also put new blinders on them. A dialectical thinker in the German dualist tradition, Kant restricted knowledge by making it rigorously scientific—what he called "pure reason"—yet set it soaring by demonstating its transcendental moral side, or "practical reason." Exalting human nature by putting the voice of God at its core, he also pulled it up short by confining that voice to an introspective conscience, thus making the individual, not society and politics, the target of its critical shouts. For a conservative Germany facing change, Kant's teachings, straddling both the old world and the new, appeared to be the perfect philosophy.

In a series of provocative studies, Kant analysed the powers of human reason, will, and judgment. For ordinary mortals his conclusions were, again, both flattering and deflating. They were flattering because he demonstrated the known world to be more a creation of the mind than any mirror image of reality itself, yet deflating because what the mind could reliably know was shown to be limited and subjective. The sphere of true knowledge, while never more sure, was, by the rigor of pure reason, never so small.

Philosophers and theologians who wished to talk authoritatively about vital spiritual realities—God, the soul, freedom, and immortality—found the new Kantian limits discouraging.[3] To be sure, man's sensory and rational powers could reliably perceive, process, and categorize objects in the world around him. But those mundane realities were knowable only as "phenomena;" their defining identities, or "essences"—*Dingen an sich*—remained forever hidden. Beyond the feathers and the scales, what is a chicken or a fish? Reason could not definitively say; the inner identities of things remained "noumenal," beyond sensory perception and certain grasp. The human mind, in a word, knew only what was directly in its eye, and that only on its surface. For Kant this was no skepticism or atheism, only a clear-eyed recognition of human limits.

Yet, while pure, or scientific, reason quickly hit a wall, reason in its full expanse had capacities of will and judgment that allowed it to soar beyond the empirical. Kant thus posited a "practical reason," a kind of moral intelligence privy to an imposing if indemonstrable spiritual and transcendental world. The threshold of such knowledge lay beyond pure reason, yet practical reason could "intuit" that world. The one, pure reason, knew lesser things more surely, while the other, practical reason, perceived better things less well.

Kant deduced the transcendental powers of reason from a felt predisposition to good, which he deemed to be universal in humankind and hence prima facie evidence of an irrepressible moral law within: "Act so as to make your act by your will universal law." Whenever practical reason confronted a moral dilemma, Kant believed that internal maxim became a constant drumbeat, revealing humans to be accountable to a higher law and able freely to choose the good or follow an equally strong inner propensity for evil. This internal law became the basis for inferring the existence of vital spiritual realities beyond pure reason's ken: God, the soul, freedom, and immortality.

Unlike the French *philosophes*, Kant and the German Enlightenment could not let traditional religion go. They did, however, initiate its moral reconfiguration and ultimate secularization. Kant called it "a religion within the limits of [practical] reason alone," in which Jesus Christ became the "historical archetype" or perfect embodiment of what practical reason intuitively knew. In turn the Holy Spirit was the perfect shorthand for humankind's "good and pure disposition to good," and the biblical Golden Rule was grandly renamed the "Categorical Imperative."[4]

Trenchant Warfare

In the years leading up to the German revolution of 1848–49 and German unification in 1871, liberal thinkers fanned the sparks of political change while conservatives threw up firewalls from the German past. The political battles had their complement in equally fierce academic ones, with philosophers and writers attempting to draw the lessons of both the radical French and the conservative German Enlightenments. The struggle was pursued on both parallel and crossing fronts. At the academic heights a succession of philosophers, following Kant's lead, progressively deconstructed traditional Christianity. One, philosopher Ludwig Feuerbach, did so with counterintuitive arguments from classic Lutheranism. Closer to the street, reactionary intellectuals, with their own brew of romanticism, nationalism, racial theory, and Social Darwinism shaped a new-age chauvinistic culture. Together these parallel academic and popular movements fed a sociocultural revolt against the past that contributed substantially to Germany's twentieth-century catastrophes.

Fichte and Hegel

Kant's division of reason drew opposition from both romantics and kindred idealists. By putting absolute truth out of reach, the new critical philosophy undermined the unity of reality those thinkers presupposed, and threatened the bona fides of their transcendental flights.[5] Jena philosopher Johann Gottlieb Fichte became the first to propose a rational way around Kant's impenetrable phenomenal world. He reunified reason and reestablished its long reach by declaring acts of human consciousness ultimate reality. The phenomenal world thus became the ego's own self-objectification: The "reality" behind reality was not, as Kant had argued, untouchably "noumenal" but the all-creating and all-knowing human ego itself. With that argument, Fichte endowed reason with the absolute creative power medieval philosophers had attributed only to God. In a word, man posited and supremely knew the world around him.[6]

The full measure of the romantic-idealist revolt against the Enlightenment became most visible in Georg Wilhelm Friedrich Hegel's philosophical unveiling of the history of "absolute Spirit," *Geist*, by which he meant the ultimate force and meaning behind everything. Expressing the belief that the rational is the real and the real the rational, his *Phenomenology of Spirit* was an audacious scholarly romp through the noumenal world in the face of Kant's cautionary studies of the limits of reason.[7] At the distant end of that run stood Friedrich Nietzsche, the prophet of the death of God, who awaited the coming of an "Overman," *Übermensch*, the so-called superman, or man beyond man—a self-made, new species of humankind able to take God's place and powers.

For ordinary Germans being "the measure of all things" and "going it alone" in superman fashion did not have the protections and privileges of a university chair. Yet the man on the street also wanted to be one with the "world spirit," which he might do by becoming "collective man"—modestly, by joining a choral society or a hunting club, assertively, by becoming a member of a political party, and—as increasing numbers did megalomaniacally over the nineteenth century—by merging with the transhistoric, pan-Germanic *Volk* (people), the popular equivalent of "absolute spirit."

Hegel's Great German Project

Kant and the Enlightenment modernized the age-old conflict between faith and knowledge—now practical and pure reason—by drawing a deeper line in the philosophical and theological sands. As a philosopher intent on raising the unitive experience of religion from primitive feeling to rational consciousness, Hegel saw his life's work jeopardized by Kant's isolation of pure and practical reason. That Kant had also made the individual master of his limited domain was small comfort. Taking up the Kantian challenge, Hegel became the philosopher of his age.

He was, however, something of a throwback to the medieval scholastics, whose integrative motto, Faith Seeking Understanding, had been a more humble version of his own. With them, Hegel believed that a God who could not properly be understood by reason would be forgotten in an enlightened world. Only as God and the moral law were grasped at the highest human level, which for Hegel was philosophical consciousness beyond religion and art, did man gain the knowledge to which he was destined.

> If there is to be no knowledge of God, the only realm that remains of interest to the spirit [of man] is that of the ungodly, the limited, the finite. [Because man must also live in that lesser world] it is an even greater necessity that he have a Sabbath in his life [on] which he may transcend his workaday affairs . . . devote himself to what is truly real, and become [rationally] aware of it.[8]

Though Hegel was portrayed as a child of the Reformation, his great fear was more akin to that of the scholastics with whom Luther had fought. That fear was the unknowability of God, and hence his possible nonexistence, neither of which had haunted Luther, for whom God's transcendence and reality were assured by simple biblical faith. What troubled the Lutherans was the nagging possibility of misplaced trust in the divine will. In the specter of a God who both existed and lied, and hence, was a true, eternal evil Other, lay the sixteenth-century Lutheran vision of nihilism, one that not only left man ignorant and alone in the universe, but at the mercy of an uncertain and overwhelming force. Lutheran faith was, above all, reassurance that God was true to his Word and might confidently be trusted.

The atheism and nihilism Hegel and Goethe saw stalking the nineteenth century echoed that envisioned by the old scholastics (no knowledge of God, no God, and no God, no human future)—only now a new generation of philosophers embraced them as a *liberating* opportunity for humankind. Given the strict Kantian limitations on reason, post-Enlightenment thinkers believed they confronted a world without transcendence or truth beyond individual human consciousness. With the denial of any objective standard for knowing or evaluating the world beyond the human mind, the world itself could only be as real and as good as that mind deemed it to be.[9] For Hegel such conclusions were fraught not only with epistemological danger, but existential and political as well, in the face of which he endeavored to salvage transcendence by demonstrating its existence philosophically, or by a rational critique.

It was Friedrich Nietzsche, writing in the last quarter of the nineteenth century, who picked up on the even more threatening nihilism envisioned by Luther and the Reformation, which left man completely to his own devices in a world ruled by a mendacious God. Through Zarathustra, his imaginary prophet of the "superman," Nietzsche exposed the Judeo-Christian God as the very specter Luther had feared—a fake with no staying power, who lost interest in and withdrew his mercy from humankind as soon as it fell short of his expectations. In this Nietzsche saw no God who had died for humankind but rather one who had died *because* of humankind, out of pity and shame for what nineteenth-century bourgeois society had made of his original creation.[10]

After Hegel

By voluminously arguing reason's transcendental connections, Hegel believed he might salvage the primordial unity of God, man, and the universe. And by raising that unity to full rational consciousness, he gave new life to the expansive worldview of the romantics from Johann Gottfried von Herder to Goethe. Both the idealists, for whom Hegel spoke, and the romantics, who despised the Enlightenment even more, aspired to a unity and certainty of knowledge Kantian philosophy denied. Led by its own modernizing wing ready to rationalize and moralize its history and teaching away, the Church also joined these philosophical discussions.[11] In published speeches to the "cultural despisers" of religion, Berlin theologian Friedrich Daniel Schleiermacher, soon to become the most famous Lutheran since Luther, accused the "cold worldly mind" of the Enlightenment of tossing up a religion as if it were "a mess of metaphysical and ethical crumbs."[12]

These newly allied groups—romantics, idealists, liberal Catholics, and Pietistic Lutherans—faced more formidable enemies than Kant and the Enlightenment, with whom, despite heated exchanges, they still had something in common. Hegel sensed the larger danger and, being even more ambitious than the Enlightenment, he exalted reason still higher—beyond Kant, Scripture, and history—subjecting every authoritative voice to philosophical reason. By such extravagant claims he naively put a large pickax in the hands of the subversive children of the Enlightenment, whose namesake he became—the so-called young, or left-wing, Hegelians, an unsentimental succession of thinkers, ready to turn the cultural and social world upside down.[13]

Initially Hegel stood tight with Goethe in support of mainline German dualism, which always preferred incompatibles, a reflection of the belief that human life was oppositional at its core. Nicholas of Cusa, who celebrated the "coincidence of opposites" in the fifteenth century, and Luther, for whom man at his best remained "simultaneously righteous and sinful," were early examples.[14] Here, God and man, eternity and time, good and evil, coexisted dialectically, the one as irradicable as the other and indispensable for understanding humankind.

Both philosophically and politically the new radical thinkers looked to simplify and resolve. Assuming reason's absolute sovereignty and declaring independent transcendental realities nonexistent, they sorted out and declaimed over a demystified, post-Enlightenment world. In rapid succession the core beliefs of the old regime, beginning with classical Christianity, came under attack. Unlike Kant and Hegel, who rationalized and moralized Christianity, the left-wing Hegelians dismissed it as mythical and even harmful.

David Friedrich Strauss and Ludwig Feuerbach

In his *Life of Jesus*, published in 1835, David Friedrich Strauss, a Church historian and student of Hegel, denied the historicity of Jesus and portrayed classical Christian beliefs as historical myths no different than those of other world religions. For many at the time, his book was unsettling, and it cost him a professorship in Zurich. To a warm reception from Friedrich Engels and Karl Marx, Erlangen philosopher Ludwig Feuerbach's *The Essence of Christianity*, published in 1841, argued that theology was anthropology, man himself both origin and referent of statements about God. The divine attributes (powerful, wise, good, righteous, merciful) "projected" what man believed or intended himself to be. Feuerbach cited a well-known statement from Martin Luther in support of his thesis: "One receives from God to the extent that one believes in God," concluding that those words meant that faith, construed as human projection, created God.[15]

Feuerbach's exposé of Christianity targeted Christian individualism and political authoritarianism, which had been compatible over the course of German history. Their exaltation of the individual over the community was said to pose the greatest threat to a progressive bourgeois society and liberal democracy.[16]

As a doctoral student Feuerbach had learned from Hegel that reason was not limited and individual but universal and social (Hegel's main point against Kant). "Insofar as I think," Feuerbach wrote in his dissertation, "I am no longer an individual."[17] With utopian foresight he projected an enlightened community of love, equality, and sharing, once Christian personalism had been successfully exposed and rejected. From such reflections he formulated a new social imperative, perhaps with Kant's more individualistic one polemically in mind:

> "Think in existence, in the world as a member of it, not in the vacuum of abstraction as a solitary monad, an absolute monarch, an indifferent, otherworldly God."[18]

Karl Marx

Like Feuerbach, Karl Marx was a rapt but critical student of Hegel. Neither gained a salaried academic post after completing his doctoral thesis due to the controvesial nature of his work. After a stint as an unsalaried university lecturer, Feuerbach managed his father-in-law's porcelain factory, while Marx bypassed the academic world altogether, working as a political reporter for the liberal-left *Rheinische Zeitung* before the government suppressed it in 1843.[19] During the revolutionary 1840s, both men lived in a welcoming Paris.

Although embracing Feuerbach's theory of projection and anti-Christian social program, Marx believed that Feuerbach and Hegel shared the same failing. Having endowed men and women with godlike powers of reason, neither then sent them into apocalyptic battle against injustice in the real world. Of the two, Hegel had come closer to doing so by praising political man, or man as he lived and worked in the state, as humanity's highest incarnation. However, unlike Rousseau and Robespierre, with whom Marx agreed, Hegel could not recognize in the state the individual's fiercest enemy, but rather praised it for giving individuals stability, grandeur, and purpose beyond what they might collectively achieve on their own.[20] In Hegel's outline of history, civilization originated with the Persians, who passed it on to the Jews, who handed it down to the Greeks, who transferred it to the Romans, who shared it with the Germans, who perfected it in the modern Prussian state.[21] For Marx, that was Hegel's great "castle in the sky"—mistaking the despotic Prussian state and its pliant Christian citizenry for humankind's supreme political collective.

Despite such criticism Hegel knew as well as Marx that work in the state was "alienating," a term Marx lifted from Hegel's work and applied to the new industrial age. In the philosophical tradition Hegel represented, transcendental "absolute spirit," *Geist*, beyond the individual, was life's most necessary part. Without it, neither work nor government had any legitimacy, nor could any worker or ruler who believed himself the ultimate reality be counted on to do his duty.[22]

The left-wing Hegelians had no tolerance for reality short of perfection and let the world know its failings. Marx's critique of German society and culture became the most romantic and relentless yet. While agreeing that collective political life was human life at its fullest, he rejected Christian ideals as any proper part of it. By its exaltation of the individual, religiously sanctioned transcendence had been the source of arbitrary social and political power, undermining rather than securing the communal and ethical foundations of society. On this score Marx fully agreed with the left-wing Hegelian critique of Christianity. Like Feuerbach before him and Nietzsche after, he traced everything he disliked about contemporary society to the "transcendental Christian state," much as Hitler would also do in the 1930s, when he made scapegoats of the Jews and their beliefs and put Christians in their camp as well. Bourgeois democracy and the liberal state were, for Marx, the legacy of the marriage of Church and state,[23] in which the individual triumphed over humanity, in a tragic loss of collective life and ethical community.[24]

In seeking a final solution, Marx targeted private property, the source of the division between the haves and the have-nots,[25] which would never have occurred without the success of Christian individualism. The survival of the species was thus seen to hang on the recovery of communal, or mass, man, which only the elimination of individual religious and political freedoms—the death of God and of liberal democracy—could bring about.[26] A new political collective was envisioned in which civil servants and workers, bourgeoisie and proletariat alike, lived together in a classless society.[27]

Marx looked to the revolution of 1848 to make the clarion call. From Brussels, whence he had moved in 1845, he watched the suppression of the Frankfurt National Assembly. There he and Friedrich Engels organized the Communist Party and published the final version of its *Manifesto* in 1848. Expelled from Brussels, Marx made England his home, where, with others, he led the international Communist movement, writing among other works the first volume of *Das Kapital*. That critique of capitalism described the "depersonalization" of workers and "barbarization" of civic life, crimes against humanity to which Marx believed the age's philosophers and politicians turned a blind eye.[28]

Where Hegel and Feuerbach had empowered man in theory, Marx turned abstract constructs into real protest, exhorting the masses of poor workers to plunge into politics—a proletarian version of changing history by blood and iron. In the Marxist seizure of power, workingmen and -women saved both themselves and the higher social classes by creating an egalitarian community beyond the hierarchical nation-state. Marx cast his description of that event in terms his old teacher and adversary Hegel would have read as parody: "True communism is the genuine resolution of the conflict between existence and essence, depersonalization and independent activity, freedom and necessity, individual and species, *the riddle of history solved.*"[29]

These words were fanciful and ominous but not quite visionary. One must say fanciful because most Germans in the nineteenth century did not believe that history's meaning could ever be made completely manifest, certainly not by a proletarian revolution. To argue that the proletariat, given control of the means of production, would kindly liberate the middle class—something the latter had never done for them—was as self-serving a myth as any of Hegel's.[30] On the other hand one must say ominous, because over the course of the nineteenth century a critical mass of people did begin to subscribe to such millenarian dreams. Finally those words must be deemed less than visionary for failing to foresee the possibility of a moderate political Marxism, pragmatically embraced and successfully applied, by the Social Democrats during and after the 1870s.[31]

Accompanying these radical currents of Enlightenment, Romanticism, and post-Hegelian criticism were reinforcing technological leaps—gaslights, telegraphs, railways, and steamships—which also suggested unbounded human mastery of life. In the universities and the civil service, talk about perfect human beings and societies became respectable in Marx's lifetime, challenging Germany's historic view of man and society as always penultimate and flawed. In lieu of any hard evidence to the contrary, old Germany counseled amelioration through education and self-sacrifice, rejecting any notion of a final resolution of human conflict this side of eternity.

The moral universe promised by a successful proletarian revolution invoked a new collective imperative, one that rang out in the streets as well as in conscience and urged a complete sociopolitical makeover of society and politics. For Germans with a long historical memory, such ambition echoed the failed visions of Meister Eckhart and Thomas Müntzer, heroes of the late Middle Ages who were being rehabilitated by romantics and Marxists as forerunners of the nineteenth century's sociocultural revolt. These early revolutionaries had also sought a final solution to the contradictions of history—Eckhart by a spiritual unity "beyond all division," Müntzer by a "bloody cleansing" of the sociopolitical establishment.[32] Both projects, deemed Icarian by contemporaries, died aborning.

Friedrich Nietzsche

"The world is deeper than Day had ever been aware." Thus spake Friedrich Nietzsche's Persian prophet of the anti-Christian lifestyle.[33] Therein lay a scolding of the Enlightenment for underestimating the enormity of man's plight in the contemporary world. In Nietzsche's new language, nineteenth-century man had become the "last man," humankind beyond salvage either by the Enlightenment or left-wing Hegelian critics.[34] Humankind's only hope was now to leap to a new species, beyond that produced by bourgeois, Christian, liberal democratic society.

Nietzsche invoked his new man from the ashes of Judeo-Christian myth, a failed Enlightenment, and codependent liberal democracy.[35] Endowed with an absolute will to power, the superman was free to refashion himself and the world as he pleased. Eternal recurrence was his creed—a life without trajectories and increments. No longer a docile Christian created and redeemed by a transcendent God, the new man was himself alpha, omega, and everything in between, and without apology, doubt, or regret.[36]

Such special individuals, undeterred by life's meaninglessness, would scout the way for all.[37] Nietzsche found a namesake for them in the Greek god of wine and fertility, Dionysus. In his construction Dionysus was indestuctible, the polar opposite to Jesus "the Crucified," who died. The new man survived modern nihilism by life-affirming, orgiastic ecstasy. Nietzsche compared the experience to the power of music, at once elevating and tragic, as it momentarily reconciled antithetical forces meant to be kept "eternally apart."[38] Luther's moment of faith had been similarly conflicted, and remained such in Bach's musical rendition of it.[39] However, unlike the ecstasy of the Nietzschean superman, Lutheran faith left an indelible affirmation of transcendence, reconciling, however so briefly, persons meant to be eternally together.

Like his contemporary Bismarck, Nietzsche believed that Prussia's military and parliamentary successes had been less the result of ideas than of blood and iron.[40] However, in the twentieth century, Nietzsche's own ideas played no small role. In the cafés of Belgrade the assassins of Austrian archduke Francis Ferdinand discussed his works.[41] And *Thus Spake Zarathustra* was carried in the knapsacks of countless German soldiers. In 1914 a special edition of 150,000 copies was distributed at the front along with copies of the *New Testament* and Goethe's *Faust*—therein the full, polarized spectrum of old and new Germany.[42]

If the new gospel of Zarathustra and Dionysus helped propel soldiers into the trenches and consoled them once they were there, it did nothing to get them out. Germany's modern culture failed the generation of 1914 as completely as did its military might. That generation, unable to forget the horror of defeat and surrender, reparations and deprivation, would in time take a superman's revenge.

ABSOLUTE PEOPLE

High philosophy's pursuit of a new age was joined by that of popular culture. What Hegel called "absolute spirit" and Schleiermacher "the universal existence of [the] finite in and through the Infinite," lesser academics, public intellectuals, publishers, journalists, and drummers simply called "the people," *das Volk*.[43] Whereas the former roamed the history of ideas and played influential mind games, the latter reacted spontaneously to the dislocations of war, the upheavals of the Industrial Revolution, and the intrusions of the new German state.[44] But "the people," too, were a noumenal essence in and through which any individual German might become Everygerman.[45]

By giving Germans a much-wanted revenge for the French occupation and spoilation of their lands, the defeat of Napoleon in 1813 evoked a chauvinistic popular culture determined to see Germany united and a European great power. That ambition had hardly taken hold before the Congress of Vienna agreed to return postwar Europe to its monarchical status quo ante, an effort at restoration that provoked nearly a half century of protest and revolution in Germany.[46]

Among the early brain trust of popular nationalism were Ernst Arndt and Friedrich Ludwig Jahn. Writing under the influence of Herder and Fichte in the wake of the wars of liberation, these men tapped into German roots that ran far deeper than those of any political state. Bonn theology professor Arndt wrote rhapsodically of Germans in the year of Napoleon's defeat. Calling them an "original *Volk*" who still retained their ethnic purity, he invoked a transhistoric German culture to inspire allegiance to the fatherland. Founder of the national fraternity movement and creator of the modern gym, Lutheran Pietist Jahn merged physical fitness and nationalism into an ethnic gospel appealing to university students.[47]

Still another transitional figure in the German *völkisch* movement was Munich professor William Heinrich Riehl, a public intellectual and journalist, who perceived the "essential" Germany in the hometowns and villages of every German's youth. A contemporary of Richard Wagner, Riehl found none of the simplicity and warmth he associated with being German in Bayreuth's great operas, and recommended German folk songs in their place.[48] Riehl's counterpart to Hegel's philosophical grasp of "absolute spirit" was an emotional rootedness in the *Volk*, which gave ordinary Germans comparable self-esteem and self-transcendence. Pointing to a primordial "Germanness" that he believed all Germans shared, he played down estate and class differences as grounds for social conflict or political division. In doing so he excluded from the favored German pool "chronically restless people" said to resist assimilation—namely, the working poor, migrant workers, Jews, and journalists.[49]

As a chauvinistic popular culture grew over the century, Riehl's argument replicated itself. If a transcendental Germanness existed beyond estate and class, so too did a primordial Germanic faith beyond historical religious confessions.[50] In that faith the German people were themselves Revealer and Revealed, the collective German *Volk* as ultimate reality. For all its seeming crudity and presumption, the notion of a transhistoric people's religion was a consistent step from Kantian and Hegelian transformations of Christianity, and no great leap from Nietzsche's gospel of eternal recurrence.

In the search for German identity, influential eccentrics and visionaries joined sober preachers and organizers like Arndt, Jahn, and Riehl. A striking example was Jena publisher Eugen Diederichs. Dressed in zebra-skin pants and a Turkish turban, attire that projected the universal person he fancied himself to be, he hosted Dionysian feasts. He and his colleagues led a new generation of romantics, many of them recruited from the German youth movement begun in 1817.[51] Neither narrowly chauvinistic nor anti-Semitic, Diederichs took a religious model for humankind from the mystical teachings of Meister Eckhart. Along with Eckhart's works, he published numerous substantial works on ancient and medieval German culture intended to document the transhistoric German *Volk* and muster popular nationalism.[52]

The search for everlasting racial-ethnic roots ended as easily in darkness as in light. If it inspired "world citizenship" in romantics like Diederichs and ethnographer Bogumil Goltz, it also gave rise to bigoted efforts to typify and rank the peoples of the world culturally and biologically.[53] Among the more ominous results was nineteenth-century racial profiling. In a culture less credulous of utopias and this-worldly perfection, such fantasies would not have succeeded as well. "Two souls, alas! within my breast, and each withdraws from and repels his brother" was Goethe's reminder to the new century that unrelieved ambiguity and conflict remained the human condition.[54] That the perfect had always to meet the imperfect halfway was a difficult axiom to square with the "new-age" fiction of unlimited human and social advancement.

German racial theorists took a first building block from Kant, who hypothesized a connection between geography, racial characteristics, and what he called a people's "life force." Like theology for Feuerbach, geography became anthropology for Kant: different places, different races, motivation, and behavior. To this modest linkage of race and culture, racial scholar Joseph Arthur, comte de Gobineau, a favorite of Nietzsche, added different destinies: The purer races survived and overwhelmed the mixed and waning. A second racial cornerstone was the discovery of the so-called Aryans, a postulated Indo-European people believed to have migrated west from homelands in central India during the second millennium B.C. From studies of native peasant cultures, contemporary English and German philologists concluded that these slippery and possibly fictional people were the original forebears of the Anglo-Saxons.[55]

As all these racial pieces were jiggled into place, a predictable question emerged: Who among the peoples of the world are the purest and the strongest? Many Germans believed it to be the Nordic Aryan race, or themselves. Richard Wagner's son-in-law Houston Stewart Chamberlain, who wrote extensively on the subject in the second half of the century, made the Wagners' home base of Bayreuth a mill for such biological racist/nationalist thinking. The wealthy son of an English admiral turned German citizen, Chamberlain was a major authority on the world's races, with a special interest in the history of German-Jewish relations, a subject on which he published a bestseller in 1900. No crude anti-Semite, he nonetheless identified German Jews as the chief antagonists of Aryan purity. While small in numbers and a waning race, their devout adherence to the Law empowered Jews and made them a credible threat to Germans.[56] Unlike Gobineau, Chamberlain believed that pure races did not occur naturally, but could be bred "like race horses and fox terriers."[57] How ominous such scholarly speculations were was confirmed decades later, when Adolf Hitler, then a struggling Nazi Party leader who had read Chamberlain's books, met the old man on his deathbed and kissed his hands.[58] Although no one could have imagined it at the time, that kiss began the long descent of German racism into Jewish persecution and genocide.

ALTERNATIVES

The German nineteenth century did not lack powerful contrarians who confronted new-age fantasies with the mainstream German past. Two who stepped into the revolutionary fire to remind their contemporaries who Germans had been were Ludwig von Beethoven and Johann Wolfgang von Goethe, the latter emerging less scathed from the effort than the former.

Between Enlightenment and Utopia: Ludwig von Beethoven

Like Bach, who musically preserved the German dualist tradition in the experimental eighteenth century, Beethoven grew up in a musical family that served the Cologne elector in Bonn. Unlike Bach's family, Beethoven's was dysfunctional. Later in life he tried to flee it altogether by pretending to be, alternately, the illegitimate son of Frederick William II or Frederick the Great. At the Bonn court the young Beethoven came under the spell of the French Enlightenment and Kant's high-minded gospel of the categorical imperative. These formative influences went with him to Vienna in 1792, there to inform the flightful, heroic music he conjured.[59]

Prior to General Napoleon's hubristic leaps, from first consul of the Republic in 1799 to Emperor of the French in 1804, Beethoven, with the vast majority of German and Austrian intellectuals, admired the French general, and he apparently intended to dedicate his Third Symphony to him. He withdrew that salute, however, after the new emperor denigrated the French Enlightenment and Revolution by his expansive, imperial rule. Beethoven nonetheless remained devoted to the promise of a secular, fraternal utopia, which he sought to fulfill at least in musical fantasy.[60] In the process he, like Napoleon, appears to have evolved from an enlightened to a new-age self-perception. That conclusion is suggested by the mottos displayed prominently under glass on his writing table in later life, apparently self-referential. Taken from ancient Egyptian sources, they read:

> I am that which is.
> I am everything that is, was, and will be—no mortal man has lifted my veil.
> He is of himself alone, and it is to this aloneness that all things owe their being.[61]

In the original Egyptian these had been statements of human autonomy and self-sufficiency, the first two spoken by women, the third by a male. Transposed into the culture of nineteenth-century Germany, they became claims to self-deification. In the Old Testament "I am that I am" was God's reply to Moses when asked his name (Exodus 3:14). Such proto-Nietzschean claims had popped up earlier in the young Beethoven, then inspired by the Enlightenment.[62]

Beethoven's utopianism found its most memorable expression in the Ninth Symphony's "Ode to Joy," whose words actually derived from the lyrics of a student drinking song written by Schiller. Acting as a kind of musical Napoleon fulfilling the original dream of the Revolution, Beethoven created a symphonic foretaste of the Elysian fields, the mythical abode of the blessed dead. There, as the ode movingly conveys, a united humankind momentarily celebrates fraternal and sororial harmony beyond all earthly contradiction and conflict, a foretaste of eternal unity and peace.[63]

In the charity of his late-twentieth-century biographer, that fraternal and sororial dream is said to excuse its utopianism, since without the impossible dream, humans have "no counterpoise against the engulfing terrors of civilization, nothing to set against Auschwitz and Vietnam as a paradigm of humanity's potentialities."[64]

In these words the utopianism of the nineteenth century leaps into the twentieth, with the new-agers of both centuries finding in Beethoven's Ode weaponry to defeat modern tragedy. What rather excuses the utopian dream in Beethoven, but not in Napoleon at the beginning of the century, nor in Nietzsche at its end, is Beethoven's confinement of it to a brief experience of exultant faith, musical ecstasy, or self-sacrificial love—moments that do not last but also cannot be defeated. He had no illusions that such saving moments would carry over into real life and resolve the riddle of history. In the classic German tradition, the temptation to do just that was deemed a totalitarian moment—one in which a mere human fancied himself a god, as Beethoven ruefully condemned Napoleon for doing.

The belief that momentary feelings of unity or visions of perfection can survive permanently into everyday life this side of eternity is the ante-room of nihilism and fascism. Such beliefs give rise to ahistorical fantasies, which can never materialize beyond the notion. To the extent that they are relentlessly pursued, they progressively crush the solace that precious moments of grace can in fact convey. Historically such fantasies have spawned generations of cynics, misanthropes, and failed revolutionaries who, having glimpsed resolution, cannot forgive the grinding years of imperfect life that still must be lived.

Reality Simple: *Johann Wolfgang von Goethe*

Auschwitz and Vietnam are reality: A world beyond all contradiction and conflict is the stuff of dreams, and for those who cannot awaken from them, of nightmares as well. No German better stated the difference between utopia and reality and the predictable consequences of abandoning oneself to either than Johann Wolfgang von Goethe. His enduring study of the man who would be God—*Faust, A Tragedy*—was classic Germany's most impressive modern challenge to the steady evolution of new-age thought and culture between Kant and Nietzsche. Having begun it in 1775, Goethe completed it over a lifetime. The first part, published in 1808, retold the story, dating back to the sixteenth century, of a learned Dr. Faustus who sold his soul to the devil for knowledge and power beyond humankind. The second part, appearing twenty-four years later, in 1832, followed the doctor's life to its resolution in both time and eternity.

One need not read far into Goethe's *Faust* before discovering that it is no modern story but a conscious updating of a medieval one, a reprise of the German dualist tradition for a modern audience that had forgotten the lessons their history and tradition so clearly taught.[65] Beginning with a prologue in heaven, Mephistopheles, the devil himself, observing with delight humankind's divided nature, questions the goodness of God's creation and subjects the Enlightenment to a critique straight out of the Reformation.

> *The little god of the world [Reason] sticks to the same*
> *old way,*
> *And is as whimsical as on Creation's day.*
> *Life somewhat better might content him,*
> *But for the gleam of heavenly light which Thou has*
> *lent him:*
> *He calls it Reason—thence, his power's increased,*
> *To be far beastlier than any beast.*[66]

Weighed down on the one hand by a morally imperiled humanity, while longing on the other to rise by worthy deeds to the heights of the gods, Faust describes the undying conflict that is the human condition.

I am not like the gods! That truth is felt too deep:
The worm am I that in the dust doth creep . . .
This godlike rapture, this supreme existence,
Do I, now but a worm, deserve to track . . . ?
Yes, let me dare those gates to fling asunder. . . .
It is time, through deeds, this word of truth to thunder:
That with the height of gods man's dignity may vie![67]

God wagers with Mephistopheles that man, a once-good creation, is still good, and permits his adversary to put Faust to the test. Although Faust, by his own fallen nature, is trapped in a life of "unrelieved [moral] ambiguity," God is confident that he will stay the course, fight the good fight, and receive divine forgiveness commensurate with his striving. Faust knows all too well, and freely confesses, that he is neither a satisfied nor a good man. His scholarly attainments have brought him no nearer to the Infinite nor given him tranquillity. He longs to delve deeper into life and resolve its mystery, to which end he accepts "the Devil's tether." With God's leave Mephistopheles makes that very offer—his personal guidance through, and dark power over, life—which Faust, his will to power at full throb, accepts on the promise of his soul.[68]

When thus I hail the Moment flying,
"Ah, still delay, thou art so fair!"
Then bind me in thy bonds undying,
My final ruin then declare![69]

In the end Faust found a mortal moment of true peace not in any personal merger with the Infinite, or loss of self in "one great one," nor in anything else that would last forever. He rather discovered the peace he sought in a selfless moment of mundane moral action. Having made the most of the powers lent him by Mephistopheles, he had gained a position in life that permitted him to act magnanimously on behalf of others, which he did by building protective moats and reclaiming marshlands around his neighbors' properties, from which anonymous service he derived a personal satisfaction unknown to him before:

> *[These] were now my latest and best achievements.*
> *To many millions [they] let me furnish soil. . . .*
> *Green, fertile fields, where men and herds go forth . . .*
> *Yes! to this thought I hold with firm persistence . . .*
> *He only earns his freedom and existence,*
> *Who daily conquers them anew. . . .*
> *And such a throng I fain would see,*
> *Standing on free soil among a people free!*
> *Then I dared hail the Moment flying:*
> *"Ah, still delay, thou are so fair!"*[70]

By the terms of their agreement, those concluding words entitled Mephistopheles to Faust's soul. However, God abrogated their bargain, sending angels to claim Faust's "immortal part" for heaven.[71] This was, however, no grandiose utopian ending. Faust had only hailed the fleeting moment; he did not lobby or mobilize for its enforcement. Nor did he become an unequivocally good man, or anything more than man. He remained the flawed, divided person he had always been, only now with truer knowledge of self gained from his failings and moments of service to others. Nor was the gift he gave his neighbors anything divine. Yet, as God had bet the devil Faust *would* do, he had put others before self, and that made all the difference.

8

REVOLUTIONARY CONSERVATISM

The Age of Bismarck

NO MODERN GERMAN LEADER divides opinion more than Prince Otto von Bismarck-Schönhausen, during whose years as minister-president of Prussia and as German reich chancellor, from 1862 to 1890, Germany became a united nation for the first time in its history. Depending on whom one reads, Bismarck either blocked Germany's political modernization or ushered it in. One bloc of historians sees the new age of science, industry, democracy, and parliamentary government simply passing him by. For another, he was the witting tool of the "invisible hand" moving Germany forward despite distasteful compromises, and beyond the ability of the "true partisans of the future" to do so.[1] Did this mediocre student and failed civil servant balance order and freedom more successfully than the elite academics and professional civil servants who made up the Frankfurt National Assembly? Or was his chancellorship the most fateful defeat yet of modern German nationhood?

The future count and prince grew up in a divided parental world, in which both parents prominently bent the twig. His urbane, ambitious mother pointed him toward a career in government, enrolling him in the best Berlin schools, while his easygoing father immersed him in the rural life of a Pomeranian Junker. After struggling through school and a short, unhappy career in the civil service, he returned to the paternal world for solace and new direction.[2] He would, however, continue to keep a foot in both worlds, and at increasingly higher levels of power and influence.

RELIGION AND POLITICS

Confirmed a Lutheran at sixteen by Pastor Schleiermacher, Bismarck drifted spiritually in his early twenties, finding gloomy consolation in brief encounters with the works of Shakespeare, Heine, and the young Hegelians. Pomeranian Pietists opened the door to a new life by introducing him to Johanna von Puttkamer, the daughter of a Pomeranian squire, whom he married in 1847.[3] During their courtship Bismarck underwent a religious conversion that deepened his belief in historical forces beyond the will of any individual, thenceforth a basic tenet of his political philosophy.

In later life he carried with him a calendar of biblical verses annotated by Luther, and he frequently aphorized the Lutheran-Pietist belief that service to one's fellowman was possible only through a self-denying religious faith. That heritage also inspired his rejection of the Enlightenment belief in the power of reason to perfect humankind, another classic German tenet he shared with Goethe. In June 1847 a youthful, provincial Bismarck defended a German "Christian" state and opposed the political emancipation of Jews. While claiming to be no enemy of Jews, and confessing "perhaps even to love them," he worried that their first loyalty would always be to a nonconforming religious nation,[4] much like that of the ultramontane Catholics with whom Bismarck bitterly fought in the 1870s.

At this time German Jews were no more credible a threat to the German state and Christendom than they had been in the sixteenth century. By 1870 Jews were only 1.25 percent (roughly five hundred thousand) of a German population that was otherwise Christian, two-thirds of that Protestant if Austria is excluded.[5] But, like the minuscule numbers of Anabaptists living in Luther's age, Jews angered Bismarck's majoritarian society far beyond their numbers. In the sixteenth century sudden substantial Anabaptist migrations to German cities, most prominently Münster in Westphalia, created suspicion and persecution.[6] In the second half of the nineteenth century, a disproportionate prominence and influence of minority Jews drove resentment and repression. Urban Jews filled slots in schools and universities far out of proportion to their numbers in society. Their prominence in banking, the professions, business and trade, the press, and liberal-left political parties was just as lopsided.[7] German Christians perceived an elite with power and influence sufficient to usher in a threatening new future, making the Jew, in Harvard historian David Blackbourn's words, a "perfect symbol of the disturbingly modern." Amid such circumstances the term "anti-Semitism" was coined.[8]

Contrary to Bismarck's youthful wish, Jews progressively gained full legal and civic equality in German states over the 1860s, helped along by a partially philosemitic Frankfurt National Assembly.[9] In 1869 the North German Confederation recognized the equal rights of all German citizens, "independent of religious denomination." Despite longstanding Christian fences around the civil service, commissioned military ranks, and denominational schools, that recognition became the law of the empire in 1871.[10] Whereas twenty years earlier Bismarck had believed Jews serving in public office "belittled" a Christian state, as new chancellor he proclaimed their political emancipation. He also praised Jewish skills at statecraft, something he observed during a decade of collaborative work with the National Liberal Party.[11] In private conversations, he recommended interfaith marriages and praised Jewish-Christian offspring as special—particularly when the husband was Christian and the wife Jewish.[12]

On another vital matter an older Germany also pointed the way for Bismarck during his formative years, pairing his traditional religious beliefs with classic political ones. In May 1847, amid a stream of protests swelling to the Revolution of 1848, Bismarck, thirty-two and self-emancipated from a civil service career, spoke out as a new, conservative Junker member of the Prussian Diet. In a prepared statement he challenged the argument that post-1813 Germany owed its unity and progress to liberal reforms then being pressed by German revolutionaries. Not social philosophy or political propaganda but "maltreatment and humiliation" by the French—visceral historical forces beyond anticipation and control—had inspired German unity and progress.[13]

The naïveté of such a belief was later demonstrated in a letter to his wife after the French surrender at Sedan in 1870. On that day Bismarck had visited the captured emperor Napoleon III, who asked him to arrange a meeting with the Prussian king. "Our conversation was difficult," he wrote to Johanna, "if I would avoid touching on things which must be painful to those whom God's mighty hand had overthrown."[14] Bismarck thought it not in Germany's national interest to treat either its victories or its defeats as eternal keys to history. Both were thrust upon Germans, or their adversaries, by unpredictable Providence. Thus a nation was best advised to stay alert to what history still had in store for it, for which reason Bismarck strongly condemned zealots who threatened public order in the years leading up to the Revolution of 1848–49.

In the latter's aftermath he never forgot that, for all their ideals and philosophizing, the liberal legislators of the Frankfurt National Assembly increased German division and intensified Austro-Prussian competition for German leadership. As Berlin's envoy to the federal diet in Frankfurt in 1851, he had witnessed the new international challenge. There he commented, provocatively and prophetically, that Germany was not big enough for both Austria and Prussia. At the time Austria was far the larger and more powerful, and was attempting to intrude itself into the Prussian-led Customs Union.[15]

PRIME MINISTER AND CHANCELLOR

Despite Frederick William IV's annulment of the Frankfurt Assembly's national constitution and careful pruning of his own, parliamentary governments continued to exist alongside monarchies in the German states. Industrial and economic growth also continued to push modernity along, despite the tides of politics. In 1862 new Prussian King William I, having observed in Bismarck an "unerring instinct for the politically possible," made Bismarck his prime minister. When William became emperor in 1871, Bismarck became his chancellor, a position he would hold with extraordinary powers for nineteen years, the longest of any German chancellor.[16]

From the first year of his reign, William was much in need of such a man. Since the late 1850s disagreements with parliament threatened a constitutional crisis, particularly over control of the military budget. By 1860 Prussian manpower and readiness had fallen behind those of major rivals France and Austria. Unfortunately for a king eager to expand his army, a liberal majority controlled parliament and, as the constitution prescribed, jealously oversaw the army budget. Because those budgets were approved on an interim basis, the king could not unilaterally strengthen the military, although members of parliament suspected, correctly, that he and his prime minister did so surreptitiously.

The May 1862 elections made the matter a crisis by increasing the number of liberal-left Progressive Party delegates. Determined to have his way, William threatened to suppress his parliamentary enemies, or resign his kingship.[17] He was saved from having to do either by Bismarck's ministry, a perfect wedge between the king and his parliamentary enemies. Each side feared Bismarck—the liberals because they believed him to be the dead hand of the past, the king because he knew that his prime minister had the greater power in the present circumstances.

Despite his principled roots in the old Germany, Bismarck promised a constitutional middle way—something he could do in good conscience because he had accepted a reality William and other restoration kings could not: The French Revolution had changed the world, and parliamentary government was in Germany and other European states to stay. Appropriate to that recognition was Bismarck's skill at bringing countervailing forces into equilibrium—in this case, confederational and centrist polities, states, and empire.[18]

On the vital matter of the Prussian army, Bismarck did not disappoint his king. For years he found ways, often serpentine, and on at least one occasion unconstitutional, to fund the army at the levels the government required.[19] After conceding to parliament in 1867 the right to set the military budget annually after 1871, Bismarck gained in the target year a seven-year parliamentary review. That remarkable turnabout kept the parliamentary opposition in the game, while freeing the government to develop Prussian military power on its own timetable.[20]

With a military buildup assured, Bismarck was free to pursue his main objective: a united federal German state under Prussian leadership. To that end he had to reckon with Austria, still the contender in the German-speaking world. Having suffered an ignominious defeat at the hands of the Italians in 1859, Austria had become a waning international power in the early 1860s.[21] Still Bismarck, diplomatically, insisted on joint Austro-Prussian leadership of the German Confederation. He also embraced the idea of a new federal parliament, hoping both to placate and gain support from the post-1848 democracy movement. By the mid-1860s, these conciliatory moves put Prussia in a position to unify Germany, in Bismarck's words of September 1862, by "blood and iron."[22]

He was greatly assisted in this by Denmark's incorporation of the far-northern duchies of Schleswig and Holstein. Both had a German-speaking population, predominant in Holstein, which was a member of the German Confederation. With the strong support of the larger German world, Hanoverian and Saxon soldiers occupied Holstein in anticipation of an Austro-Prussian invasion the following year. Badly outmatched, Denmark surrendered both duchies to Austria and Prussia in October, 1864. In the following year, the Convention of Bad Gastein placed them under joint Austro-Prussian administration, even though Austria occupied Holstein and Prussia Schleswig.[23] As both duchies lay in Prussia's backyard, it was logical that the Prussians ultimately administer them, which Austria, being financially strapped, was prepared to concede in exchange for slices of Prussian-occupied Silesia on its northeastern border. Silesia, however, had been hard won by Prussia in the previous century, although that was not the main reason Bismarck refused to dice it up. Having long believed that the two powers could never coexist amicably in a greater Germany, he rejected the Bad Gastein agreement, withdrew from the German Confederation, and marched Prussian soldiers into Holstein.[24]

In a failed effort to take back its new possession and maintain a northern presence, Austria mobilized an army from sympathetic confederation lands. Hapsburg and Hohenzollern had their showdown on the battlefield at Königgrätz in Bohemia in 1866. In the largest single battle of the nineteenth century, Prussia trampled the federated Austro-Saxon army. The Treaty of Prague in August 1866 removed Austria from Germany, thenceforth to be the new monarchy of Austria-Hungary, and dissolved the German Confederation. In its place came a new North German Confederation that embraced Saxony and "Greater Prussia"—that is, Prussia with its annexed lands of Schleswig-Holstein, Hannover, Hesse-Kassel, and Frankfurt, an impressive union of eastern and Rhenish lands.[25]

As the defeat of Austria cleared one great hurdle to a new German empire, another, higher one was placed in Prussia's path. Historically France had been the state most sensitive to changes in

Germany on the magnitude of Königgrätz. Now the weaker of the two, the French had all the more reason to be wary, and mobilized in anticipation of Hohenzollern expansion.

In the end a relatively harmless development brought the belligerents onto the battlefield in what became the Franco-Prussian War of 1870–71. A relative of King William, Leopold of Hohenzollern-Sigmaringen, had been invited to ascend the Spanish throne. Foreseeing themselves in German pincers, the French complained loudly to the Prussian king, who was initially inclined to discourage Leopold. However, the French demanded a Hohenzollern commitment *never* to occupy the throne of Spain, something the Prussian king could not promise.

William's communique diplomatically rejecting the French king's demand fell into Bismarck's hands like a zebra into the crocodile-infested Zambezi River. Unifying Germany by way of war with France was then foremost on Bismarck's mind, and putting a Hohenzollern on the Spanish throne seemed a useful diversion of the French. The king's message gave him still another opportunity to provoke the French. Before telegraphing it on to the French ambassador, he rephrased it to maximize the insult to French pride, ensuring the war he correctly suspected the French would neither avoid nor win.[26]

Six days later, on July 19, 1870, France and Prussia were at war, and four months later, after German armies had besieged Paris, French armies surrendered at Sedan and Metz. The final peace gave the Germans Alsace and Lorraine and saddled France with war reparations of five billion francs—reasonable damages to Germans, who remembered French looting of Germany in previous wars and occupations. Although the French paid off their war debt within a few years, it was not soon forgotten, ensuring that future wars and reparations between the two countries would remain memorably punitive.[27]

SHAKING EUROPE

With Prussian victories over Denmark, Austria, and France, German nationalism was aglow in the 1870s, and the North German Confederation growing under Prussian leadership (Württemberg and Bavaria had quickly joined). What the European great powers had feared most now seemed to be happening: Germany was united and strong enough to assert its will across Europe. In Benjamin Disraeli's incisive words, the German revolution from above was "a greater political event" than the French one from below, a comment that proved to be particularly true with regard to Germany's ability to realign the states of Europe.[28]

German Unification Around Prussia Under Bismarck

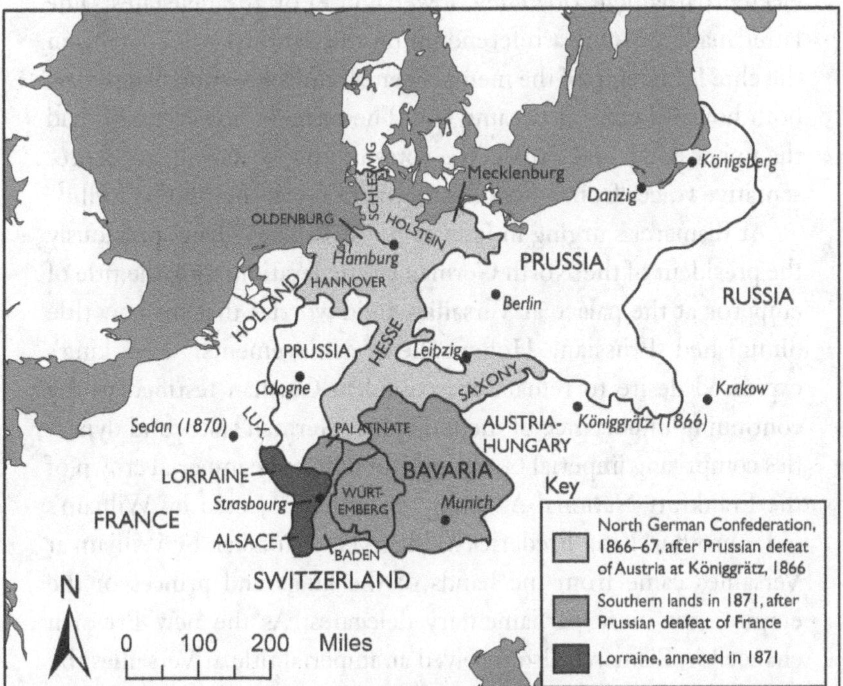

With its new political and military success, Germany also came face to face its own worst fear: the formation of great power coalitions against it. What kept the German leadership awake at night was the specter of an Austro-Russian-British or an Austro-Russian-French alliance, either of which presented an impossible three-front war. Throughout the 1870s Germany's main foreign policy objectives were to contain Russia and isolate France.[29]

In April 1871 the constitution of the North German Confederation became, with minor alterations, that of a new, united imperial Germany.[30] From a historical perspective it was a good constitution for the times, as it attempted to balance both monarchical-executive-authoritarian elements with federative-legislative-democratic ones. The new government had a controlling federal council (*Bundesrat*, upper house) of fifty-four princes and a freely elected parliament (*Reichstag*, lower house) of 382 delegates. The latter made possible a referendum on the national will apart from the elite leadership of the member states, and legislation had to pass both houses before it became law. The princes, however, still had the upper hand, and Prussia the votes to impose its will, yet representative voices from across the new nation had their say as well.[31]

At Bismarck's urging in January 1871, King William, previously the president of the North German Confederation, took the title of emperor at the palace at Versailles amid worries that his new title diminished Prussian, Hohenzollern achievements. The king's expressed desire to remain the complete German testified to the continuing importance of the individual German states and dynasties comprising imperial Germany. But unlike the imperial crown of the Frankfurt National Assembly, so rudely rejected by William's older brother, King Frederick William IV, that taken by William at Versailles came from the hands of the kings and princes of the empire, not mere parliamentary delegates. As the new Prussian chancellor, Bismarck also received an imperial title at Versailles. By this ceremonial transformation of the North German Confederation into an empire, his "smaller Germany" gained the historically appealing appearance of an older and more inclusive realm.[32]

Once dismissed by historians as narrow, artificial, and illiberal, the latter a reference to Bismarck's heavy-handedness,[33] the new imperial Germany has been recognized more recently for the opportunities it opened. Even for Bismarck the new empire was always a work in progress, never a nation set in stone. Reflecting his philosophy of history, which viewed leaders and states as mere instruments of larger providential and collective human forces, he deemed the new empire to be the creation of its people, including the liberal members of parliament, and not the work of a king or a chancellor.

Despite the new constitution's Prussian mold, contemporary liberals were as positive about it as could be expected. Not a few gave Bismarck credit for achieving what the Revolution of 1848 could not: a government with both a strong executive and a strong representative parliament. If, as they believed, Bismarck gave the army too much independence, he also made it effective for the times, strong enough to ensure the new nation's political survival and evolution. Liberal attraction to and repulsion from Bismarck's policies between the triumphs of 1866 and 1871 were memorably summarized by contemporary philosopher-historian Rudolf Haym.

> Sometimes . . . he has gone too far in the direction of liberalism [as in his support of universal and equal suffrage], at other times he has regrettable tendencies toward and sympathies [for] conservatism. At yet other times he encourages interest-group politics which . . . slight the nobler motives in political life and must have a corrupting effect. But . . . I remind myself that nobody else has such a lively regard for the idea of making the young empire vital, permanent, and resilient. . . . All his twists, turns, and inconsistencies can be explained by the power of this idea.[34]

That Prussia's predominant influence (its king, prime minister, and army were now the core of the German empire) was not crushing is attested by the independent governments and armies that continued to exist in the twenty other German states.[35] For all Bismarck's executive authority, especially in matters of foreign policy, he still had to work his will within defined constitutional limits. The emperor and the army acted independently of him, and no legislation passed parliament without a majority vote of all members.

During the 1870s that meant a majority of liberal votes, as a spectrum of liberals held as many as three out of four parliamentary seats. Despite their successful vote-getting rhetoric, Bismarck believed that the true design of the National Liberals and the Progressives was an interventionist state—a conservative version of which they also accused him of pursuing.[36] Although he could lash out fiercely at the opposition, labeling Social Democrats "subversives," in his first decade as reich chancellor he more often bit his tongue and stroked the powerful men with whom he disagreed. His modern reputation as the consummate Machiavellian, playing the liberal when ruling party coalitions required it, and taking heartfelt conservative revenge when circumstances permitted, overlooks his devotion to pragmatic lawmaking and preference for half a loaf rather than none.

THE CHURCH DEFENSIVE

By creating a new German empire around Prussia, Bismarck scuttled the imperial dreams of many devout Roman Catholics, who envisioned a larger German empire under Austrian leadership. Those same enemies also nursed grudges against a modernist Protestant culture dating back to the French occupation, when Church lands had been confiscated and clerical authority diminished in the Rhineland. That culture acknowledged a God only "within the limits of reason alone" (Kant), or one who was a self-projection—salutary, according to some (Feuerbach); harmful, according to others (Marx); and in one stark portrayal, recently deceased (Nietzsche).[37]

The Catholic Church's response to modernism was the same in the nineteenth century as it had been in the sixteenth: a flight *ultra montes*, beyond the Alps, to the authority of the pope in Rome. By the 1870s only papal authority seemed to offer a sure refuge from the avalanche of modernism. First invoked in the eighteenth century by the Jesuits, ultramontanism had undergone a revival in Germany in the aftermath of the Napoleonic revolution, encouraged by a papacy that saw its spiritual mission jeopardized by the smallest compromise with the new secular world. Some Catholic clergy and laity, however, wanted a more streamlined and enlightened Christianity, and found vernacular masses and a less juridical and ceremonial cure of souls appealing.[38]

This new crisis in the Church prompted popes to reassert their authority in questionable new dogmas and appoint ultramontane clergy to vacant German positions. In 1854 Pius IX proclaimed the Immaculate Conception of the Virgin. That doctrine did for the Church of the nineteenth century what the doctrines of eucharistic transsubstantiation and penitential absolution had done for that of the Middle Ages—confronted the laity and rulers with the pope's extraordinary transcendental powers over this life and the next. Distancing the Church from "progress, liberalism, and civilization as lately introduced" by the state, Pius's encyclical *Syllabus of Errors* in 1864 shocked liberals and conservatives by its condemnation of some of the secular world's proudest achievements: separation of Church and state, nonsectarian schools, and religious pluralism and toleration. A final blast came with Papal Infallibility in 1870. In this doctrine, reminiscent of Pope Boniface VIII's *Unam Sanctam* in 1302, Pius made a desperate protest against French expansion at Church expense, declaring kings, as lay Christians, inferior and subject to popes in all matters of faith and morals.[39]

During the ensuing "war for civilization" (*Kulturkampf*), as renowned pathologist and Progressive Party delegate Rudolf Virchow named the conflict, both Church and state believed their institutional survival to be at stake.[40] To the National Liberal Party, the pope's claims and condemnations were an attack on a still fledgling democracy movement, while Bismarck thought they exposed the Roman Curia as just another predatory foreign state. He rebutted Center Party leader Ludwig Windthorst's special pleadings for Catholics with bittersweet humor, declaring on one occasion that two things sustained his life: "my wife and Windthorst—the one for loving, the other for hating." Invoking the separation of Church and state, Bismarck concluded it best that religion and theology be kept as far away from parliament as possible.[41]

German Catholics who supported the *Syllabus* and Papal Infallibility were treated as hyphenated Germans, their primary allegiance presumed to be not to the new German state but to a threatening foreign power in Rome. On similar grounds Bismarck criticized opposing Center Party conservatives and Social Democratic liberals as "subversives," alleging greater allegiance to political ideology than to the new German constitution.[42]

Refusing to "go to Canossa" (pay homage to the pope), Bismarck sided with the modern critics in rejecting the historical collaboration of the German state and Church. That collaboration, in existence since the Reformation, had created a politically cohesive bureaucratic state church, which expedited and chastened the undertakings of both. During the *Kulturkampf* the government confined the Christian churches to a strictly moral-sacramental-spiritual sphere, removing the clergy from public schools and banning confessional political lobbies. A new Department of Religious Affairs oversaw both confessions, and a "pulpit paragraph" forbade clerical commentary on politics during the cure of souls. Finally the "May Laws" of 1874 subjected all clerical candidates to a qualifying state exam.[43]

A majority of German bishops and Catholic laity opposed the *Syllabus of Errors* and Papal Infallibility. That gave the government an important wedge to divide local Catholic authority from the papal kingdom beyond the Alps. German clergy who publicly sided with the pope risked the loss of their bishoprics or parishes. On the other hand lay Catholics proved to be far less critical of the Church when they voted, giving the Center Party three-quarters of the Catholic vote. Eventually, the government's foolhardy battle with the Center Party and the Church fell prey to the ballot box, as conservative Protestants, who knew they might be next, voted against Bismarck as well. Effective also in restraining the government's assault on the Church was Center Party leader Windthorst's shaming of Bismarck for branding his political enemies as enemies of the state.[44] It was the death of Pius IX and the succession of Pope Leo XIII that permitted a face-saving retreat for both sides. Turning his papacy toward Christian social action and away from political confrontation, the new pope accommodated the changing world more realistically than his predecessor had done.[45]

Who won the culture war? Because the main players were absolutists, each side got some of what it wanted. Indelible lines were drawn during the conflict, and in the aftermath, both the papacy and the German state confronted a more disciplined German Catholic Church, while Bismarck and the liberal parties found themselves at the helm of a truly interventionist state. Although the likes of Bismarck's bullying of German Christendom would not be seen again until the 1930s,[46] the government was in a stronger position to enforce its laws on both believers and citizens. It did so, however, at a great loss of national unity and trust, with many citizens leaving Germany for the Americas and other free lands.[47]

TRUE COLORS

Three developments during the 1870s conspired by decade's end to allow Bismarck's expedient rule to become a more principled one. They were a mounting economic crisis, the increasing leftward drift of the National Liberal Party, and two assassination attempts on Emperor William's life.

The Domestic Front

The economic crisis emerged early in the decade, and together with the *Kulturkampf*, turned conservatives against the chancellor. Under the circumstances Bismarck's only realistic alternative in the legislative process was the majority National Liberal Party. He had made common cause with it earlier during the military budget crisis, and it supported his strategy of a Germany united around Prussia. However, because of its left faction, the Social Democrats, whose leader, Eduard Lasker, Bismarck came to hate even more than he did Center Party chief Windthorst, the alliance remained as uncomfortable as it was necessary.[48] During the early and mid-1870s, Bismarck was something of a hat-in-hand chancellor, forced to compromise with several parliamentary factions to get his programs passed.

The economic crisis hit industrial and agrarian interests hard, particularly ironworkers, farmers, and woolen-makers, and foreign imports made matters even worse. Mounting pressure for tariff protection put the government on a collision course with the National Liberal Party, whose signature platform article was untrammeled trade. Although tariffs promised badly needed government revenues, Bismarck straddled the fence on the issue as late as 1877. Then, between Pope Leo's willingness to end the *Kulturkampf* and the Center Party's support of new iron duties, a more congenial constituency for tariffs seemed to beckon.[49]

Bismarck fired the first shot in the tariff war by proposing a government monopoly on tobacco. In response Social Democrats bogged parliament down in verbal class warfare, accusing the government of favoring rich farmers.[50] Bismarck's animus toward this liberal faction was both philosophical and from the heart. While backing basic health, accident, disability, and old-age insurance,[51] he believed the more generous measures of his liberal opponents only raised expectations unrealistically and threatened to tip the delicate social balance toward a proletarian revolt. Belief became conviction after a successful but short-lived proletarian uprising in Paris in

1871. Ten years later Bismarck was still warning that Germany, too, could spin as quickly out of control as Paris, should men with "unshakable optimism and unlimited faith in social progress" gain power. The times, he believed, called for tamping down the flames of social progress rather than causing them to flare higher.[52]

After the personal attacks Bismarck sought a confrontation with the National Liberals, hoping to isolate the party's radical wing and draw the majority closer to the government. Two assassination attempts on the eighty-one-year-old emperor within the space of two months in 1878 provided the needed pretext. On both occasions, the assassins fired on him as he rode along the avenue Unter den Linden. The first try, with a pistol, missed altogether, while the second, with a shotgun, found its mark, seriously wounding William.[53] Bismarck had earlier turned to political advantage two unsuccessful assassination attempts on his own life, the first at point-blank range on the eve of the Austro-Prussian war, the other a near miss fired in protest of the anti-Catholic May Laws. Making office trophies of both weapons, he waved the first when bolstering the war with Austria, and he made a useful prop out of the second when whipping up anti-Catholic sentiment during the *Kulturkampf*.[54]

Although no evidence implicated Social Democrats in the attempts on the emperor's life, hard times and street protests made it easy for Bismarck to point an accusing finger at his political enemies. A week after the first attempt a draft anti-socialism bill ("Against Social Democratic Outrages") was submitted, which denied freedom of assembly and speech to all socialist organizations. Although defeated five to one, the bill climaxed a three-year crusade against "subversives" and had the intended chilling effect. After the second attempt Bismarck invoked his extraordinary emergency powers and dissolved parliament with its unanimous consent. However, cabinet ministers denied his requests for martial law, a thousand new policemen, and police checkpoints for entry to and exit from Berlin.[55] In the new elections that followed, the National Liberals lost one seat more than the conservatives gained, bringing the two sides roughly to parity. The following year, 1879, new tariffs went into effect, completing Bismarck's break with the National Liberals.[56]

In the late 1870s Bismarck could pursue his programs with fewer political compromises. Although historians see something of a "turnabout," his more deliberate and proactive rule seems rather to reflect the new strength of his government after the wars with the liberals and the Church.[57] He now enacted his long-pursued anti-socialist law, in effect from 1878–90. Yet his strengthened hand did not prevent a more evenly divided parliament from becoming as deadlocked as ever. As before, either the chancellor's goals fell short of what the opposition wanted, or those of the opposition exceeded what the chancellor believed to be feasible or desirable—his critics accusing him of holding back the times, he accusing them of trying to outrun them. Given the requirements of the age, Bismarck's tempering of the new Germany with the old was arguably a better way to hold together a diverse young nation with intense growing pains.[58]

The Congress of Berlin

Imperial Germany raised both European fears of German expansion and German fears of preemptive European strikes. Echoing Frederick the Great's feeling of always being "surrounded by rogues," Bismarck spoke of "nightmares about coalitions."[59] As in the years following the Thirty Years' War, when foreign powers held both legal right and military might within Germany, discipline and vigilance on the home front and beyond was vital to German survival. This preoccupation with homeland security severely handicapped Germany's race for foreign colonies and international prestige—an embittering self-denial for the proud new empire.

Shortly after the assassination attempts on Emperor William in the summer of 1878, fear of pan-European conflict brought Austria,

France, Great Britain, and Russia together with Germany in the Congress of Berlin—a salute to Germany's new standing in the world. The great issue before the congress was Russia's successful military advance through Bulgaria and the Ottoman Empire, which positioned it to dominate the Balkans and sail its warships through the Dardanelles into the colonial world—opportunities conveyed to the Russians by the Treaty of San Stefano in March 1878 in the wake of Turkish defeat. Austria, Britain, and Germany had worries enough about what the others were doing, and each was determined to restrain Russian expansion at Turkey's and Austria's expense. As none of the great powers wanted to go to war over the Balkans, the congress was convened to persuade Russia to modify the treaty voluntarily. The statesman chosen by the great powers to lead that difficult diplomacy was Bismarck.[60]

Beyond the Balkan crisis the congress also met to reiterate the rules by which each member state would conduct itself toward the others—a message especially intended for the new German empire. The guiding principle was to have and to let have, each member agreeing not to tread on the vital interests of another, while pressing its own interests on the world stage. Small bites might be taken from lesser lands, but not to the point of provoking the formation of great-power packs and a subsequent pan-European frenzy. Germany's two concerns were Russia, which Bismarck restrained by tilting diplomatically toward Britain, and old enemy France, whose foreign alliances had historically brought Germans grief.[61]

Between Bismarck's statesmanship and the agreements reached independently among the principals the peace was saved. The German chancellor departed the congress something of a hero. Later, during his retirement and at his death, the European community would remember and honor his successful diplomacy there.

Emperor William II

In 1888 the ailing eldest son of William I, Crown Prince Frederick William, succeeded his father as Emperor Frederick III—but only for ninety-nine days. At twenty-nine, Frederick's eldest son, William, whose mother was the daughter of Queen Victoria, succeeded his father as Emperor William II. Politically liberal like his father young William thought himself a thoroughly modern man, ready to plunge headlong into the future—and over Bismarck or parliament if either blocked his way. Despite the inequality in political experience, the seventy-three-year-old Bismarck was now the more vulnerable of the two. Having doubted his political will throughout the 1870s, the hard conservatives now held him responsible for the new strength of the anti-Junker socialist movement and the Catholic Center Party, tracing the former to his support of universal male suffrage and the latter to his relentless prosecution of the *Kulturkampf*.[62]

Once William II was emperor, Bismarck tried to make himself indispensable by crying wolf, that is, by raising the specter of imminent proletarian revolt and government chaos, which he alone had the experience to prevent. However, the emperor's idealism and inexperience made him fearless in the face of danger and timid in the enforcement of domestic policy, reactions that disarmed Bismarck. And adding insult to injury, he fully shared Bismarck's self-confidence and confrontational style.[63]

A year and a half of spitting across two generations ended with Bismarck's resignation. The great man ensured his own firing by overriding a labor protection bill the emperor had docketed, while pursuing another vindictive bill of his own against the Social Democrats. William's grandfather, who had recognized Bismarck's genius, might have given him his head, whereas the upstaged grandson now demanded it.[64] Ordered by the emperor to retract his bill, Bismarck, who had recently suffered an impressive defeat at the polls, recognized that his time had come and submitted his resignation in March 1890. The issue, as William phrased it, was "whether the Hohenzollern dynasty, or the Bismarck dynasty, would reign."[65] Bismarck's exit was not graceful. His avuncular resignation bore a warning to the emperor of just where his policies would likely lead the nation, namely, into war—advice that proved to be prescient.[66]

A Paladin of Germany Past

A basic flaw of Bismarck's chancellorship was his inability to believe wholeheartedly in liberal, middle-class, parliamentary government. As he wrote in his youth when denouncing robotic bureaucrats and legislators he swore he would never become: "[Government] is cancerous in head and limbs; only its belly is sound, and the laws it excretes are the most straightforward shit in the world."[67]

Bismarck believed that the nation he governed by the extraordinary powers of chancellor could not be secure under such a government. To maintain national unity and security amid the possible coalitions of Germany's rivals required an authoritarian polity—an agile and disciplined monarchy and bureaucracy.[68] The pursuit of such a state made him many enemies, and once out of office, he fell vulnerable to their long-harbored contempt. On his eightieth birthday in 1895, parliament denied him the expected celebratory greeting, a slight for which the emperor later apologized after protests poured in from rulers around the world, who remembered Bismarck as a friend of international stability and peace.[69]

The insult was as much a rejection of the classic German past as it was of the chancellor. To contemporary and modern critics, Bismarck's Germany was lesser in more than just size. Most argue that the progressive developments accompanying his chancellorship—national unity, an industrial economy, an interventionist state, and an international system of governance—would have occurred without him.[70] Given his philosophy of history, which scoffed at the notion that great men manufacture great events, he might well have conceded the thought, even though many contemporaries believed that his being there had made all the difference—both for good and for ill.

Today even sympathetic biographers view Bismarck ironically, as the man who carried Germany into the modern world, while doing everything he could to hold it back. That characterization is especially misleading with regard to the age's economic and technological progress, which he thoroughly embraced. His own investments, well-managed by bankers Rothschild and Bleichröder, made him a wealthy man and one of Germany's biggest landowners.[71] On the other hand the features of the age he hated most were also bound up with the modern, particularly the vaulting social expectations of Social Democrats, which only baited revolutions whose goals exceeded society's grasp. In this regard he believed he lived in a benighted age in flight from reality.

Recalling King William's salute to him in 1866 after Germany's triumph in Schleswig-Holstein, Bismarck encapsulated what he deemed to be the wisdom of the ages. At the time the king had given him all the credit for Prussia's victory over Austria, while Bismarck rather pondered it as something Providence had thrust upon him—calling it "a lesson one learns well in this business [of politics and war]," namely "that one can be as wise as the wise ones of this world, and yet at any point find oneself in the next moment walking like a child into darkness."[72]

Confronted by the unpredictable turns of history, the world-perfecting dreams of philosophers and revolutionaries were no match for what animal passion and raw power might do with blood and iron, given a real objective. Germany had became a great empire in his lifetime not because of the teaching of Voltaire or Kant, or the Revolutions of 1789 and 1848, but because Germans had responded creatively to the elemental suffering inflicted on them by their enemies.

IV

GERMANS IN THE MODERN WORLD

9

THE LAST EMPIRE

From Wilhelmine to Weimar Germany

GERMANY WAS NEVER more in need of a Bismarck than after he was gone, yet when the old chancellor resigned, the time for him to go had long since come. Unstable and paranoid at the end, he despaired of the government he had created and even contemplated toppling it. He left behind well-entrenched parliamentary factions of Catholics, socialists, and left-liberals, among whom the Social Democrats were his match. In his absence they posed a formidable challenge to young Emperor William II, who possessed none of Bismarck's charisma or skill at building and outfoxing coalitions. The new emperor was also tone-deaf in foreign policy. In his vaulting ambition to advance Germany on the international stage, this impulsive grandson of Queen Victoria counterintuitively targeted the British, on whose trust and neutrality both Germany's survival and the European balance of power depended.

THROWBACKS AND TRANSITIONS

At first William seemed the monarch of every liberal's dreams. To all appearances a Forty-eighter devoted to the legacy of the Frankfurt National Assembly, the emperor in his early reign was socially enlightened. He supported progressive legislation for working women and children (fewer hours, better conditions, increased benefits, and new grievance procedures) and he opposed Bismarck's antisocialist laws, in effect from 1878 to 1890. Despite a shrunken left arm, damaged during birth, he was the complete German male: the father of six sons and a daughter, a Prussian militarist, and an avid hunter. However, behind the political bluster his private life was kinder and gentler, revealing a far more complex person.[1]

Like his imperial predecessors, he believed himself a Hohenzollern emperor by the direct hand of God, and his unsentimental firing of Bismarck made it clear that he would be no Social Democrat doormat either. Inserting himself directly into the work of parliament, and able to challenge it virtually at will, he weakened representative government while taking great power into the hands of a ruler unable to build consensus.[2]

But if William wanted to be emperor, chancellor, and parliament, so too did the political parties and career bureaucrats who opposed his policies. Wanting to dominate the legislative agenda and command the emperor's ministers, oppositional Social Democrats and left-liberals aspired to a virtual elective monarchy. The result was a commanding, factional parliament that was no less a throwback to the Middle Ages than was the often blustering William.[3] The growth of both the military budget and liberal voter turnouts attested to these two opposing directions of state, centrist on the part of the emperor, particularizing on that of the ruling parties.

During the forty-three years between unification and the outbreak of World War I, German population rose 60 percent, to sixty-eight million. Only the United States had greater productive capacity. And in terms of shared values and self-assurance, Germans were then reaching across social lines.[4] Despite the persisting obstacles to political unity and colonial expansion, they believed their culture to be the most historically rooted and destined of the European states. In 1890 "Deutschland über Alles" began to be sung in the schools and on national holidays, a transregional German anthem that nurtured a national identity.[5]

Turn-of-the-century Germans took pride in another old virtue historically synonomous with their name: good order. In 1590 an English diplomatic message sent from Nuremberg to the queen of England marveled that the city's streets, unlike those of London, had no standing dunghills; also that one who lost a purse, a bracelet, or a ring by day might expect to have it returned by nightfall.[6] Despite its greater poverty and violence, the late-nineteenth-century German city aspired to a similar order. Modern historians detect in such vigilance what the postmodern French philosopher Michel Foucault called a "carceral society"—historically connective steps on the path to twentieth-century fascism. Even if nineteenth-century Germans were not innately docile, it is argued, they nonetheless surrounded themselves with disciplinary institutions (schools, asylums) conducive to a "subject mentality." In one year, writes a shocked historian, the police of Düsseldorf, a city of 91,000, visited and questioned 13,500 parents about their children.[7]

Although written almost four centuries earlier, Martin Luther's exposition of the Fourth Commandment in his *Large Catechism* offers a less anachronistic account of, and perhaps also a truer heuristic for, the Düsseldorf police action. A primer for generations of German Lutherans and still in use today, that religious guidebook put forth an urban magistracy bound by its oath of office to act "honorably" toward its citizenry and be "dutifully" obeyed by them in return. In the classic German tradition, what Luther's catechism called the vigilance of all authority (*alle Obrigkeit*) lay at the heart of a vital compact between people and government, a sentiment also shared by German Catholics. Children, Luther taught in a remarkably modern vein, did not belong only to their parents. Every adult with authority over a child, be it the teacher at school, the master in the shop, or the magistrate at city hall, had a duty to protect, correct, and rear children placed in their care, while the children, in turn, had a duty to heed their instruction as if they were being spoken to by their parents.[8]

German historians, politicians, and pundits writing in the eighteenth and nineteenth centuries drew similar justifications of good order from prior examples of social and political disintegration, particularly that of the Thirty Years' War.[9] Such historical religious teaching and cautionary tales offer less pejorative explanations of German discipline and vigilance than arguments spun from ideology or alleged pathology.

Whatever the ultimate trigger, German civic culture cracked during the 1890s. Inward-looking professional associations and leagues multiplied in trade and industry, agriculture and farming, the civil service, and the military. Political parties developed hard-core constituencies among such groups, which in turn created their own government lobbies. Among socially rising groups, the industrial proletariat found a home in Marxist Social Democracy, which, after 1890, became the largest German political party, taking a third of the vote in 1912.[10]

By the end of the nineteenth century, these affiliations and lobbies had widened the fissures within German politics. Having left the old estate society behind, new entrepreneurial success brought new political, social, and professional groups into power, which in turn provoked factions and threatened the progress made since 1871 toward a cohesive national culture.[11] Like the emperor and the parliament, the late-nineteenth-century body politic, too, was something of a throwback to an older, fragmented Germany, but now with ominous new elements in the mix. Rarely in German history had a ruler carried a bigger, yet less practiced, stick than did Emperor William II, nor were the moral and religious truisms that had guided Germans in the past more riddled with doubt and scorn than at the beginning of the twentieth century.

Playing with Fire

Wilhelmine politics and society had a disintegrating, fin-de-siècle intellectual culture to match. Two major spokesmen, philosophers Arthur Schopenhauer and Friedrich Nietzsche, despaired of both the new Germany and the old, and exalted individual human will as the only sure reality. These precursors of modern existentialism dismissed the liberal-moderate Enlightenment of the late eighteenth and early nineteenth centuries (Kant, Hegel, and Goethe) as roundly as they did the German reform movement of the sixteenth (Dürer, Pirckheimer, and Luther). Equally omnious, a disenchanted, post-1871 generation of idealistic youth traded the culture of their parents for a presumed purer, truer, mythological world of their own. Free and at risk in a new "postunification" world, young Germans wandered from soapbox to soapbox, on which influential demagogues, militarists, nihilists, and racists increasingly climbed,[12] much as they would also do, in even greater numbers, in the 1920s.

Few Germans, however, wished to surrender the positive achievements of modernization, certainly not those made in science and technology, nor the hard-won individual and social freedoms then enjoyed by all. Accompanying these advances was a constructively critical frame of mind that made invention and change both possible and ongoing. Yet even at its most useful and noncontroversial, the new materialism worried minds and soured souls in a land whose historic religious and philosophical values, shared by Protestant and Catholic alike, never forgot the inner life. Living in a young nation that was suddenly an economic, industrial, bureaucratic, and military behemoth, many Germans asked if that were all there is.[13] And while it is probably an exaggeration to say that Germans suffocated under the Wilhelmine state, or longed for the cleansing apocalypse that World War I would be, a great many Germans looked for what was missing in the wrong places.[14]

When a society frays at the seams, as happened in late imperial Germany, remedies native and foreign, proven and novel, lie at hand.

For millennia the Roman Catholic Church had cared for German souls, and, even in the "godless" 1860s and 1870s, could count a third of the German population its own. During the *Kulturkampf* the Church, as it had done since the Middle Ages, still offered devout Germans both a transcendental alternative to the modern world and a political alternative to the German state.

Secularists, most Protestants, and not a few German Catholics believed that the Church's stance against modernism was backward and superstitious. Apart from traditional Christianity, new-age philosophies and cure-alls abounded. They appealed to Germans of all social classes and led many away from mainstream religion and reasonably enlightened worldviews.[15] If not Europe's most deeply religious land, Germany had been its most theologically engaged since the Reformation. Because of, or perhaps despite, such literacy, increasing numbers of inward Germans abandoned the traditional spiritual refuges for those promised by enlightened reason, empirical science, or post-Enlightenment fringe movements. Behind this transfer, which was occurring Europe-wide, lay centuries of excessive familiarity with, and estrangement from, mainstream religion. In Germany the propulsive forces were the exuberance and idealism of a proud, young, can-do nation seemingly at its *Stunde Null*, a new beginning in its history.

That such wishful thinking ran against reality is suggested by the varieties of shelters thrown up for pilgrim souls in flight. Many joined the romantic rush to the past, some pursuing comparatively tame ultramontanism, others a mystical or racist chauvinism. Untold others sought to calm minds and lift souls by thoroughly modern escapes, immersing themselves, as David Blackbourn calculated, in "psychology, sexology, physical culture, holistic medicine, anthropology, the paranormal, spiritualism, Buddhism, [and] Tolstoy's vision of rural bliss."[16] In such searching beyond history and tradition, sizable numbers of previously docile Germans spread new wings as they fanned, at close proximity, the new-age fires.

In his own modernized version of Germany's great cautionary

tale, *Doctor Faustus*, Thomas Mann, whose life spanned Imperial, Weimar, National Socialist, and postwar Germany, reached back into the German past to memorialize the transition he had witnessed over his lifetime. In updating the Faust story in 1947, he endowed the famous protagonist who sold his soul to the devil with attributes of Friedrich Nietzsche and incidents from his life. In this modern incarnation, Dr. Faustus appears as composer Adrian Leverkuhn, who contracts syphilis in a sexual sealing of his pact with the devil, thereafter to suffer serial paralysis, insanity, and death.[17] Evidently siding with the classic German tradition against nineteenth-century nihilism, Mann created a good German narrator, Dr. Serenus Zeitblom, a principled man at peace with himself, much as Goethe's Faust turned out to be in the end.

STUMBLING INTO WORLD WAR

Culturally the Austro-German world of the late nineteenth century was one of iconoclasts who became icons: Nietzsche in philosophy, Sigmund Freud in psychology, Albert Einstein in science, Richard Wagner in music, Mann in literature, and Max Weber in sociology. A grand patron of the arts and a grander meddler in them, William II, the last Hohenzollern emperor, possessed none of the talent of such men, although he thrust himself upon the political world as one who was larger than life.[18] His firing of Bismarck in the second year of his reign was more anticlimactic than heroic. More noticed by contemporaries was William's failure to learn from history, a point made by the old chancellor himself in his condescending letter of resignation.

Bismarck made Germany strong by centering it around Prussia and keeping its foreign policy focused. In doing so he defeated efforts by the Austrians and the Bavarians to perpetuate the old sprawling empire with its ancient divisions and rival states. His compact empire gave the chancellor a freer hand in dealing with parliament and the European great powers. Instead of casting a hated imperial shadow across Europe, Germany became its honest broker, turning its geographical position in Middle Europe to international advantage in keeping the peace.

By contrast Emperor William provoked international conflict by projecting an expansive Germany. Determined to see Germany become a world power, he plunged the empire into Europe and the developing colonial world. Although no one knew what the future held, the imperial government's every commanding step in that direction was one toward war.

However, if Bismarck's balanced Europe began to look like a house of cards, Emperor William was not solely to blame. In the end the miscalculations of the Foreign Ministry, on which the emperor's new chancellor, Leo von Caprivi, relied, had more to do with Germany's foreign policy slide than the emperor's interference and bravado. Caprivi, a former chief of the Admiralty, had been a poor choice for the rapidly changing 1890s. He fell quickly under the spell of Bismarck appointee and hater Frederick von Holstein, who now controlled the ministry. On Holstein's recommendation, Caprivi did not renew the Reinsurance Treaty with Russia, which since 1887 had guaranteed Russian neutrality in the event of a western, or southern, invasion of Germany. Claiming that the treaty favored Russia, the ministry rather counted on historic ally Britain, then Europe's superpower, to intervene diplomatically with belligerents and to come to Germany's aid in the event of attack.

Within five years of the treaty's lapse, France and Russia had become trading partners, and before two more had passed, they were defensive allies, each promising the other to strike Germany should Germany mobilize against either.[19] Suddenly Germany was in the great power pincers it so feared, a peril the renewal of the Reinsurance Treaty might have averted. When the time came for the British to choose sides, the Germans had unfortunately become their economic and military rivals.

In 1894 William revealed his hand to majority Social Democrats and left-liberals, who had earlier thought him an ally. To their dismay he expressed the fears of the captains of industry, sponsoring new antisocialist legislation and censorship laws, neither of which exited parliament. Between parliament's own infighting and the emperor's readiness to favor, or betray, liberal and conservative members alike, the 1890s saw little of the democratic government Germans had alternately pursued and undermined since mid-century.[20]

Competing smartly with France and Russia in the colonial world, Britain opened diplomatic doors for a Germany desperate to establish its presence there. Without British neutrality Germany's forward leaps during the 1890s, both colonial and European, would have been impossible. But after the turn of the century, Britain progressively ceased to be Germany's friend. William's steady buildups of the German army, now Europe's largest, and, still more provocative, its navy, gave the Europeans a scare. Making battleships a national obsession—no fewer than thirty-eight were approved by the turn of the century—Admiral Alfred von Tirpitz took dead aim at British naval power in a competition Germany had no chance of winning.[21] After boldly testing Britain's mettle in colonial South Africa, the Germans confronted a newly cooperative Britain and France, which entered an Entente Cordiale in 1904 that would only strengthen and broaden.

As early as 1907, British diplomats described Germany as "out to dominate Europe," while Russia, more fearful of Germany than ever, began closing ranks with Britain.[22] Agreeing on their respective possessions in colonial Asia, the two great powers joined with France to create an informal, but scary, association of Germany's most feared rivals, something Bismarck's diplomacy had spared the Germans. If and when war broke out, Germany now faced attack on both its eastern and western fronts, with only a self-preoccupied Austria-Hungary and an ever-retreating Italy for allies (the aged and weary Triple Alliance). Largely by its own saber rattling, and to its peril, Germany had made itself the center of great-power attention.

The German man in the street could measure the height of the tightrope on which the government had placed his nation by an interview Emperor William gave to the London *Daily Telegraph* in October 1908. Acting as if he were an insider, William lectured the British on their colonial failings, while at the same time protesting the innocence of Germany's military expansion and colonial forays. That transparent lapse in state discipline and veracity so embarrassed both governments that William was forced to sacrifice Chancellor Bernhard von Bülow, who had signed off on the interview.[23] By 1909 the worldwide commercial rivalry between Germany and Britain had intensified to the point of confrontation, a prospect nervously discussed within both countries' diplomatic corps and high command.[24]

No one, of course, was yet calling for what became the Great War. And when that war spontaneously broke out, it was not in northern Europe but in the long crisis-ridden Balkans—and not with the great powers attacking one another but with smaller ones, long squeezed by Austria-Hungary and the Ottoman Empire, venting local grievances. For decades, a Serbian-led pan-Slavic nationalism had been beating on Austria's gates, which, unhappily for Serbia, enclosed Bosnia and Herzegovina after 1908. Austria's annexation of the latter had occurred with the blessing of Serbian ally Russia and Austrian ally Germany, for which support Austria promised the Russians warship passage through the Dardanelles and another chance to become a Mediterranean power—an old dream Britain and France would not allow to become reality.[25] The result was Serbian and Russian rage at Austria, and a shaking to the core of the Triple Alliance.

German overreaching in the colonial world further poisoned inter-European relationships. Twice, in 1905 and 1911, the Germans trolled French Moroccan waters. In 1911 they angled for a catch in the French Congo, which proved in the end to be not only small fry but were taken at a far greater diplomatic price than their worth. Claiming a German naval presence in Morocco to be necessary to protect German citizens there, a gunboat was stationed in the port of Agadir and forced modest concessions from the French. The action alarmed the British, inflaming cordial British-French relations, warming since 1904, into a formal alliance against the Germans.

Germans also left innocuous marks on the colonial map of the Near and Far East. An impressive decades-long construction of a railroad between Berlin and Baghdad opened Ottoman trade and made Middle Eastern oil accessible. The venturesome Germans also acquired a coal depot in China and built a lager brewery there.[26] Those feats did not, however, dampen the tinderbox created by Austro-Serbian conflict in the Balkans and new German provocations in the colonial world. When Winston Churchill, then First Lord of the Admiralty, publicly expressed his discomfort at knowing that the government commanding the German army and navy believed itself to be above its own parliament, it seemed a prophecy of war.[27]

Between 1912 and 1913 the Balkans were at war again, both with Turkey and among themselves, with the Serbs the big winner. Thereafter, Serbia, in search of an Adriatic port to add naval power to that of its army, provoked a new crisis with Austria. Amid Austrian cries for a preemptive strike on Serbia, Emperor Francis Joseph and his heir, Archduke Francis Ferdinand, surprised many of their fellow countrymen by pleading for a peaceful resolution short of war. Condemned as pro-Slavic, the two became targets of Austrian and Serbian militants. On June 28, 1914, Bosnian terrorists, acting with evident Serbian support, assassinated the archduke and his wife in Sarajevo—two royal peacemakers, whose deaths made war inevitable. Suddenly Austria found itself in a position to stabilize its Slavic interests with presumed German support.

Germany, of course, also wanted to assert itself within Europe, although not necessarily in a prolonged and expanding Balkan war. But with the Austrians, Adolf Hitler among them, fervently reaching out to their fellow Germans, blood and history pulled, while ambition and opportunism pushed Germany into Austria's war with Serbia. It has been much argued that domestic-political problems at home lay at the root of Germany's entry, the war presenting it with an opportunity to establish new markets in a German-controlled Central Europe, the desirability of which German elites had discussed in the prewar years.[28] It was not, however, until late September 1914, after the German army had bogged down in trenches along the Marne, that the German high command, foreseeing a much longer war than originally planned, approved extensive annexations.[29]

A deliberate German program to occupy Central Europe came after, not before, the outbreak of the war, which at its inception was to be a defensive war, despite an offensive strategy to that end. Many in states beyond Germany had been willing to risk war as a solution to the problems they faced.[30] However, neither the Germans, nor anyone else at the time, had a special plan to dominate Europe. By 1917, however, the postwar aspirations of all participants had blossomed. Germany's harsh treatment of Russia after the latter's defeat on the eastern front suggests what Germans were prepared to do across Europe, had they also won the war on the western front.[31]

However, in July 1914, before the guns started firing, Germany weighed its support of Austria against Russia's reaction. The Austrian high command counted on its German allies to give Russia pause before it rushed to Serbia's aid, thus ensuring a quick Austrian conquest of Serbia, which the Germans gave every appearance of preferring as well. On July 19 Austria presented Serbia with a ten-article ultimatum phrased in the most prosecutorial terms, with forty-eight hours to respond. Among the demands were the immediate suppression of anti-Austrian propaganda and the arrest of Serbian officers complicit in the assassination of the archduke, with a list of the accused attached.[32]

Like the mobilizing Serbs, the Russians read the ultimatum as a declaration of war and began to mobilize as well. With both Austria and Russia preparing for war, German eyes fixed on Russia's ally France. On July 29 the Russians went on a full war-footing. The next day everyone's bluff was called when Germany answered in kind, the last of the major combatants to do so. German support of Austria had not stopped the Russians, nor had Russian support of Serbia deterred the Austrians and the Germans. With all hopes of peace now dashed, the four great powers moved their ambitions, ultimatums, and armies onto the battlefield.[33]

The German military had a long-standing plan for the confrontation it feared most: a two-front war with Russia and France. Field Marshal Alfred von Schlieffen had prepared a preemptive strike stategy in 1905, which he updated regularly until his death in 1913. It called for an offensive war that would send calibrated waves of German soldiers sweeping west through Belgium and south into Paris. From Paris they would march eastward to meet a hoped-for snail-paced Russian mobilization on the latter's western front—all in all a blitzkrieg designed to catch unawares and crack in twain the great-power pincers squeezing Germany.[34]

The success of the plan depended on three contingencies: German ease in positioning its forces (bogging down was not an option); maintaining the supply lines for an army traveling west to south to east in multiple units; and continued British neutrality after German soldiers crossed into Belgium en route to France. Inasmuch as Britain, France, and Prussia had respected Belgium's neutrality for three-quarters of a century, the Schlieffen Plan seemed a long shot from the start.

THE TOLL OF WAR

Avoiding fortifications protecting France's eastern flank, the Germans occupied Belgium in the first three days of August, but not quickly enough to dash on to Paris and defeat the retreating French. As German soldiers caught their breath on the fourth day, the British sent an expeditionary force to meet them, further interrupting the Schlieffen Plan. Long convinced that war was coming, Britain, France, and Russia had found ways to assist one another in stopping the Germans. Although blame for the beginning of the war may be laid at the feet of several nations, only a most impulsive Germany could have drawn together the reluctant alliance of the Triple Entente that engaged the German army in the late summer and fall of 1914.

The war remained close for three of its four years due largely to the slow pace of trench warfare, into which the combatants settled within a month of its launch. In September 1914 both sides had dug in along the river Marne, where French and British forces made their stand. Beyond that boundary the war against France never penetrated. In succeeding years its pace picked up with the advent of tanks, unrestricted submarine warfare, and the arrival of the Americans. By then its romance and glory had died a frightful death amid barbed wire, machine guns, and mustard gas.

The German army was more successful on the eastern front, where it had greater mobility and superior commanders in Paul von Hindenburg and Erich Ludendorff, the army high commander and quartermaster-general, respectively, after 1916. Between their victory at Tannenberg in 1914, where five Russians lay dead for every German slain, and the Treaty of Brest-Litovsk in March 1918, Hindenburg and Ludendorff became household names with future roles in the postwar Weimar Republic.

The unexpected hardship of the war and its shocking outcome discredited the imperial government and left Germans disheartened and degraded. In 1914 one-fifth of the German population was under arms, or in some war service. By war's end a third of the male population had been killed, maimed, or incapacitated by injury or illness, putting six hundred thousand war widows on the government payroll. Over its four years and for several thereafter, female population growth remained normal, while the male deficit was jarring. In numerous households, industries, and trades, the gender imbalance turned traditional structures of authority upside down. German women, who had not been strangers to the workplace before the war, filled traditional male roles at home, on farms, and in industry, doubling their prewar numbers in factories and on railways.[35]

For the many Germans who had been well off before the war, the sudden hardships created by falling trade, inflation, "turnip winters," and sheer physical vulnerability were unforgettably shaming and embittering. Even before the war's end, Germany was sinking in debt; by September 1923, one American dollar bought 240 million German marks.[36] Lowering morale and morality, the suffering sowed cynicism and undermined discipline and obedience.

Together with the civilian population, soldiers returning from the front stomped about in denial, as if they might at any moment kick over and repossess their previous lives. The one thing most had in common was the inability any longer to trust their government.[37] Behind the outrage, dashed hopes, and sense of futility was the shock of betrayal by previously trusted authority. Although not the first time Germans felt themselves crossed by their leaders, the fact that so many, who only a short time before had been well off, had lost everything created an undying need to get even and to make right.

After the war Germans found themselves between a failed and, to many, ill-begotten imperial monarchy, and a hastily created and vaguely promising Weimar Republic.[38] The first had let too much slip away, and for that reason had to go with it, while the second offered something untried by Germans: a liberal democracy. Could a new government stay the course and compensate for what had been lost?

THE WEIMAR REPUBLIC

Four years after rushing confidently into war, Germany endured what has been called "calamity such as the world had never seen before."[39] In the immediate aftermath the shock and humiliation of the war loss triggered an internal revolution across the sociopolitical spectrum. In the ruins three camps vied with one another for control of a nation in political free fall. One was the government that had waged the war and now sought to preserve as much of its former power as the new chaos would allow. Directly opposed were newly formed political councils, *Räte*, which represented the masses of unemployed soldiers and civilians, among them future National Socialists, who demanded a clean break with the past. Finally there was the Spartacus League, later to become the German Communist Party (KPD), which wanted to remake Germany into a Soviet-style state. Opposing the remnants of the imperial regime, as well as one another, these new movements of the right and the left became locked in a civil and cultural war for Germany's body politic and soul.[40]

In the immediate aftermath of war, official power to govern fell briefly to war hero Erich Ludendorff. Knowing the imperial government to be in its last throes, he cynically appointed a conciliatory prince, Max von Baden, to be chancellor of a new government consisting of Social Democrats, liberals, and the Center Party. As historian Hagen Schulze has put it, Germany's first democratic government was the product of "a general staff at its wit's end."[41] In the wake of defeat and with the army demobilizing, no prominent remnant of the imperial government could last long, and Prince Max resigned after only a month, in November, 1918. As he stepped down, he announced the abdication of Emperor William and the crown prince from the Hohenzollern throne and designated Social Democratic leader, Friedrich Ebert, to be his successor as chancellor. The emperor and crown prince retired to the Netherlands, while Ebert become the first president of the Weimar Republic.[42]

Even before the latter's constitution existed, the transitional government's first acts of great moment did not win it any public confidence. In November 1918 it signed the armistice ending World War I and accepting unconditional defeat. It was no accident that a delegation from the new civilian government, and not one from the German high command, signed that hated document. Prescient generals and politicians had foreseen German defeat as early as summer, 1917, and had begun even then to cast about for a face-saving peace. Independently but ultimately in vain, liberal and center parties pursued a peace proposal put forward by the revolutionary Russian government. By spring 1918 the German high command privately accepted the inevitability of defeat, yet kept it from a still-trusting German public completely unprepared for the harsh consequences of an unconditional surrender.

Having promised a quick victory to a nation never given any reason to contemplate defeat, the high command—which had been entirely responsible for the conduct of the war—knew that explanations would be demanded and revenge exacted. The generals determined early that the new civilian government, not the military, would bear the bad tidings to the public. To that end they were both helped and thwarted by President Woodrow Wilson's demand that parties independent of the war-era political and military machines sign the peace. Its terms required the Germans to embrace and practice President Wilson's Fourteen Points: idealistic principles of freedom and self-government derived from the American democratic experience (these would be reiterated to the Germans even more emphatically in 1945).

As the military had calculated, those who signed the instruments of peace became "criminals" in the eyes of many of their fellow countrymen, who accused them of stabbing Germany in the back. The leader of the delegation, Center Party member and Acting Secretary of State Matthias Erzberger, became the hated messenger and was assassinated two years later, in 1921. If, however, a fatal stabbing of the German nation had occurred, it was arguably frontal, to the eye, not to the back, and came from the hand of General Ludendorff, later to be among Hitler's original allies. Believing defeat to be inevitable, Ludendorff approached the Allies—precipitously, it is argued—to ask for an immediate "armistice to avoid catastrophe." In doing so, he subjected Germany to far harsher terms (unconditional surrender) than would have been the case in a negotiated truce between active belligerents.[43]

In the aftermath of the Great War, no government could have acted quickly enough to meet the urgent and unforgiving demands of so stricken a nation. Blamed for the war loss, the harsh conditions of surrender, and the new chaos of postwar life, the new government began its life under attack.

Although he came to office unconstitutionally, Ebert, a saddler by trade, offered the new German experiment with democracy its best chance of success. But, confronted by the revolutionary councils on the one hand, and newly formed socialist and proto-communist parties on the other—each challenging his authority and eager to lead a new government itself—the principled Ebert found it impossible to govern.[44] He could, however, call for the election of a new parliament, which he quickly did. Although the National Constituent Assembly did not convene until January 1919, and its new constitution did not take effect until the following August, the Weimar Republic was conceived within that body, its name taken from the city in which the final version of the constitution was written.

In fifty-six articles the Weimar constitution laid out the "basic rights and obligations" of the German people in a future democratic state. Under the new law both the president and the parliament were to be popularly elected, and the chancellor was subject to a majority vote of parliament. For the first time women, having earlier been admitted to universities as auditors, got the vote. And they cast it to install 41 of their own among the 423 elected representatives, a greater percentage than in any subsequent German parliament or post–World War II federal assembly.[45]

The constitution contained ominous new articles as well. In an exuberant democratic gesture and coalition-building tactic, fringe parties were given seats proportional to their share of votes. Executive sovereignty continued in the president's right to appoint his own chancellor and assume "sovereign legislative and executive authority" during a state of emergency, which he alone might proclaim. Known as Article 48, this powerful measure would later allow

President Hindenburg's chancellors to rule briefly as strongmen, and the last of them—Adolf Hitler—to do so indefinitely.[46]

Coming into existence without fanfare, the parliamentary leadership of the new republic was decidedly socialist, however not in a modern revolutionary, or communist, sense.[47] In the January 1919 election, moderate Social Democrats and their allies, the Center Party and the German Democratic Party, took better than three-quarters of the vote, a victory that gave postwar Germany a fresh new political look. Yet, before a year and a half had passed (June 1920), a moody electorate would take back more than a third of that mandate, a jarring turnabout for the liberal coalition, and a first glimpse at the roller-coaster politics that lay ahead for the Weimar Republic in the 1920s.

The Treaty of Versailles

Whatever realistic hopes the new government may have raised, the Treaty of Versailles, which presented the Allies' peace terms, threatened them all. Those terms shocked Germans as much as the war loss and the armistice and were imposed without any previous negotiations, or even so much as the presence of a proper German delegation. For these reasons Versailles became a recurrent rallying cry for resistance, rearmament, and the retirement of the new government, casting a shadow over the 1920s that reached all the way to 1933.

The treaty had separate parts, signed over several months beginnning in May 1919. The final ceremony in June 1919 was intentionally held in the Hall of Mirrors at the royal palace in Versailles. There, in January 1871, Germany had earlier humiliated a conquered France by proclaiming German King William I emperor. Now it was the turn of the French to remind the Germans who they were. In the persons of Social Democrat Hermann Müller and Center Party member Johannes Bell, the new government once again held center stage in the signing of another abject surrender.

By this point in its brief history, the government's strongest critics believed it to be no less a foreign predator than the new League of Nations, designated by the Allies to enforce the treaty terms.[48] As the League had no collective army, its member states—Britain, France, Italy, and Japan (the Germans and the Soviets had been expressly excluded)—let the task of enforcement fall to the state most able and willing to do it, France.[49]

The treaty ended the Hapsburg, Hohenzollern, and Ottoman empires and reduced prewar German territory by 14 percent. The annexed lands included vital areas of heavy industry. The Allies reconfigured attractive slices of Silesia and East Prussia to create a "Polish Corridor" to the North Sea, a humiliation the Germans would harshly revenge in the 1930s. Gone also at this time were Alsace-Lorraine, the city of Danzig, and the coal-rich Saarland, whose ultimate destiny hung on a later plebiscite. With these lost lands went 10 percent of Germany's population, several million absorbed by Poland. Lost also were Germany's colonies, half of its iron, coal, and dairy cattle, five thousand locomotives, and a quarter of its chemical and pharmaceutical production.

Capping the German army at one hundred thousand men and the navy at fifteen thousand, Versailles banned all heavy weapons, tanks, airplanes, and submarines. Germans found themselves hard pressed to find ways to expand their military strength to maintain their internal security. A solution lay at hand in the large numbers of former soldiers and officers ill-disposed to return to civilian life. Organized into local volunteer armies known as *Freikorps*, they originally supplemented, and eventually exceeded, local police and state armies. Denied engine flight, Germans perfected gliders for purposes of surveillance, thus keeping their aviation skills sharp.[50]

Holding Germany solely responsible for the war, Versailles levied reparations for war-related damages in all German-occupied territories, including the costs of Allied war pensions, an unusual punitive damage. Having originally estimated reparations at 480 billion imperial marks—more than 1,700 percent of annual national

German income—the Allies reduced that figure in two stages: to 269 billion in January 1921, and to 132 billion the following spring. The payments were to be spread over thirty years, with Belgium and France using their shares to pay down American debt incurred by the war effort.[51]

At the time prominent English economist John Maynard Keynes denounced the magnitude of the damages as a "shakedown" that promised a future Armaggedon, once the Germans were in a position to strike back.[52] Exiting a still needy and dangerous Europe without joining the League of Nations, the isolationist Americans also thought Allied reparations to be arbitrary and bellicose. Apart from France, historically the most frequent and successsful poacher on German lands, the members of the League had little enthusiasm for imposing or enforcing the original reparations.[53]

Assessing German reparations macroeconomically, in terms of population growth and industrial expansion over the 1920s, historians have argued that those payments were not as burdensome as the Germans alleged. Also factored in was the flexibility in payment the Germans might theoretically expect from an international community that had no desire to cripple so productive a subject people.[54] It is noteworthy that Germany imposed even harsher reparations on Russia in l918, demanding at least three-quarters of its coal, iron, oil, and cotton, and annexing a third of its population and railways.[55]

Between November 1923 and April 1924, the American-led Dawes Commission secured German reparations by tying them to annual German economic performance and underwriting them with short-term American loans.[56] With the Wall Steet crash in 1929, these accumulated loans caught the Germans well short, creating still more hardship. However, during the intervening five years, from 1924 to 1929, the borrowed billions did stabilize the German economy, enabling the highly leveraged German, like the highly leveraged American, to know at least a portion of the 1920s as "golden" and "roaring."[57]

Before the great crash another American-led delegation, the

Young Commission, rescheduled reparations at a fixed annual rate well within Germany's projected annual exports, replacing Dawes's cascading 1 to 2.5 billion marks per annum with a firm 1.6. billion.[58] However, the new plan startled Germans by running scheduled payments out to 1987–88. The issue was soon made moot by the world recession, which left Germany unable to pay reparations or any other debt. Postponed in 1931, reparations ended in the summer of 1932.[59]

It has been argued that Versailles' reparations provided a needed stimulus for the weakened German economy.[60] Whether that is true or not, price tag alone did not make reparations a peacebreaker for the Germans. More important was the serial humiliation of being forced to bear sole responsibility for the war, the denial of any German role in the armistice and treaty talks beyond submission, and a seven-year moratorium on membership in the League of Nations.[61] On the eve of the Great War, Germany had been a world power second only to the United States, and by the war's end two million Germans had died on European battlefields. Even though treating Germany thereafter as a slave nation among presumed purer master nations was within the traditional parameters of victory and defeat, it struck Germans with any historical memory as their most unforgiving put-down yet.

Achievements and Failures

The Weimar Republic's alternating conservative and liberal directions reflected the political spectrum of modern German history, and its fourteen-year span has been described as an effort to subject imperial Germany to the French and German Revolutions.[62] Although the conservative-regressive elements survived in the end, magnifying the politics of the right, Weimar's distinctive achievement was the constitutional expansion of a liberal welfare state. Before the 1920s only revolutionary Russia had been bold enough to promise to meet the basic social needs of all of its citizens.

Weimar's quantum leap in government services for families and protections for workers sprang neither from the Russian nor the German revolution, but found its footing in the progressive social insurance laws passed under Bismarck in the 1880s.[63] The republic's ambitious legislation envisioned solutions to virtually every social problem, from health and housing to anti-social behavior and even genetic abnormality. It extended benefits of unprecedented generosity to the needy and the unemployed in a welfare program described by one admiring historian as "the culmination of the Enlightenment's utopian dream to secure the greatest good [for] the greatest number."[64]

Dreamers, however, are often poor bookkeepers, and Weimar liberals passed social insurance laws without totaling the cost. Although hard times prevented the delivery of much that was promised, enough got through to more than double the welfare budget between 1915 and 1925. Borrowing heavily from American banks to pay for those benefits and services, the government piled up a mountain of new debt while the German economy worsened.[65]

Beyond the welfare state were structural problems no less difficult to resolve. The inability to forget the war loss continued to generate suspicion and distrust of a government many deemed complicit. Having given the nation a new, democratic political structure, Weimar's implementation of it remained tentative and abstract. With Germans desparately in need of paying jobs, family assistance, and postwar reconstruction, the new parliament seemed preoccupied with constitutional issues and legalities, aloof from the primal imperatives of daily life.[66] New political parties of the left and the right stood ready to replace the republic by undemocratic means at the first opportunity. An entrenched old guard, rife with antirepublican sentiment, ensured confrontation and stalemate by clinging to key judiciary and administrative positions. As early as March 1920, a revolt led by the founder of the right-wing East Prussian Fatherland Party, Wolfgang Kapp, foreshadowed the violence that would stalk the Weimar Republic intermittently throughout the decade.

And to this perilous standoff the new constitution added a structural problem of its own, when it gave the republic's president the power to dissolve parliament and rule directly through his chancellor in time of crisis.[67]

Closer to the government, antirepublican sentiment also increased over the decade within the German high command, which despaired of ever getting the military it desired from an SPD-led parliament. With an eye to the contracts an expanding military would generate, big business and industry, particularly those of iron and steel, pressured the government to shift investment away from the welfare state to the production of armaments.[68]

Against this background the failure of the Weimar Republic can be followed year by year and event by event. Even at its inception in 1919, a countervailing wind was evident in the 75 of 337 National Assembly members who voted against its creation. The first parliamentary election in 1920 gave critical or hostile parties a slight edge over the previously ruling liberal coalition.[69] Many of the dissenting votes came from East Elbian estates, who watched wheat prices fall 40 percent between 1919 and 1922.[70] Most ominously the government began early on to lose the support of the middle class. Fearing costly intervention from the new liberal government and costly competition from a militant working class, mainstream craftsmen and shopkeepers became as skittish as the lower classes and vulnerable sectors of high society. Perceived mounting threats to their livelihood also made these groups susceptible to what Detlev Peukert has called the "wildest ideological and quasi-mystical notions" of what harmed and helped Germans. With rural voters, the urban middle class progressively lost its faith in the liberal parties and, after 1928, they abandoned the conservative German National People's Party as well. Led by press magnate Alfred Hugenburg, that party joined with the National Socialists in 1929 to protest the Young Commission's schedule of reparations, a conjunction that moved not a few of its members into Hitler's party.[71]

As if wishing it otherwise, the German electorate brought to power under Hermann Müller the last Social Democratic coalition before that of Willy Brandt (1969–74) in what proved to be the republic's longest ruling cabinet, from 1928 to 1930. To this point Weimar owed its limited success to Friedrich Ebert and his equally principled chancellor and foreign minister, Gustav Stresemann. Between 1923 and 1929, Stresemann maintained cordial relations with other nations by economic cooperation and shared risk, evidenced particularly in his support of heavy German borrowing from the United States. The stability and normality Germans enjoyed between 1924 and 1929 was a direct result of that successful diplomacy.[72]

The Perfect Storm

Looking back on the developments that undid the Weimar Republic and set the stage for National Socialist rule, one finds both human blunders and forces beyond human control converging everywhere. Believing that Serbia, Russia, and France had a combined, crippling first strike capability, the German government was preparing for war at least as early as 1912. Both high German officials and vigilant foreign diplomats attest to "numerous megalomaniacal . . . schemes of expansion" making the rounds in Germany. Historians long believed that the imperial government had been the main disturber of the peace and started World War I primarily to evade the domestic-political challenge posed by popular democracy and socialism.[73] Today Germany's need to accommodate growing population and industrialization, so-called *Lebensraum* and buffer zones, is a better recognized part of the story, along with its overweening desire to catch up with peer states in the colonial world. These were also period-appropriate reasons for contemporary nations to wage war.[74]

The shattering defeat of 1918 started an internal revolution in German lands to determine what kind of nation would rise from the remains of vanquished empire. Created in 1919 to resolve that national conflict, the Weimar Republic came instead to embody it, and in the end was unable to prevent the escalation of factional political warfare into fascist mass democracy and a National Socialist state. To a Germany faced with the dissolution of the imperial monarchy and the stern dictates of the Allies, the Weimar experiment was the only promising political course of action. That so many came so quickly to view the new government as the enemy within, and to make it a scapegoat for wounded pride and irretrievable loss, does not change that fact.

A popular argument has been that the Germans worsened their plight by refusing to take responsibility for the war, choosing rather to cast blame on others and pursue pipe dreams.[75] However, postwar Germans held no monopoly on make-believe, and illusory worlds of innocence and blame preexisted the twentieth century both in Germany and in other lands. Whatever degree of self-deception and wishful thinking may have inspired the new political organizations and governments that emerged in the aftermath of war, the Weimar Republic began soberly enough and with reason for hope.

What happened thereafter was less a retreat into an illusory world than a plunge into a perfect storm.[76] During the 1920s three fronts, one economic, another political, and a third sociocultural, each abuilding since the late nineteenth century and potentially fatal in itself, converged over Germany. The economic broke first in the unprecedented inflation at the beginning of the decade and again in the unprecedented unemployment at its end. The political then struck in the form of Weimar's inability to secure a liberal democracy, creating a progressive and unprecedented collapse of social order and public safety. Finally the long nineteenth-century deconstruction of German history and tradition, particularly the unprecedented intellectual and spiritual assault on mainstrean morality and religion, had taken its toll by the 1920s, leaving many Germans confused, cynical, and exploring dark and unfamiliar pathways, not least that leading to National Socialism.[77]

Each of these fronts bore its own special destructiveness, and their million-to-one convergence in the 1920s made the unthinkable real. The result was the creation of an undefined third Germany beyond imperial Germany and the Weimar Republic. For the next twelve years, from 1933 to 1945, Germany would remain a work in progress. With the German people largely in tow, the National Socialists proceeded to fashion a new age, one whose structure and values would be determined ad hoc by the strongest along the way.[78]

10

THE BARBARIAN PRINCE

The Rise and Fall of National Socialism

LEGITIMATE GERMAN GOVERNMENT remained left to center during the 1920s, while popular politics shifted ominously center to right. At both the beginning and the end of the decade, Social Democratic coalitions prominently governed. In the early 1930s a new hard-right party, the National Socialists, and an upstart fascist leader, Adolf Hitler, methodically took charge of a tired and outmaneuvered German government. Both that seizure and its aftermath were unprecedented breaks with German political and cultural tradition.

Unprecedented conditions preceded the unprecedented event. Between 1922 and early 1923 hyperinflation cast deathly shadows across Germany, the result of overspending in the optimistic war years and the uncontrolled printing of money thereafter to support German strikers in the French-occupied Rhineland. In the space of a single year, 1921–22, the wholesale price index shot up 1,800 percent. The first crisis year, 1923, ended with that index at an incomprehensible 1,261 billion times the base year 1913, when inflation was not yet a serious concept for Germans. Those shadows seemed to disperse during the Stresemann government, only to return darker than ever at decade's end. After Wall Street's crash in 1929, a Germany that had long relied on short-term American loans to pay its debts stood alone with turned-out pockets.[1]

In the four years between 1929 and 1933, German unemployment jumped as high in human terms as the German currency had fallen in monetary ones: from 1.3 million jobless to more than 6 million. Many of the affected still had vivid memories of good jobs, while others had been on assistance, or simply scrounging, for as long as five years—all deeply embittering experiences.[2] With the new Weimar government overwhelmed by and occasionally exacerbating the crisis,[3] each painful passing year made radical political solutions more credible and the recruitment of Germans into the parties advocating them easier.

HITLER

Although a laughable prospect at its founding, the National Socialist Party and its obscure leader, Austrian-born Adolf Hitler, soon gave every indication of having an epochal destiny. Despite the Hindenburg government's efforts to prevent it, Hitler came more quickly and surely to power in Germany than anyone had imagined, except perhaps himself.

The fourth child of a strict-disciplinarian father, Adolf, according to his sister, had been thrashed daily. As a schoolboy he left no high marks on his student records, flunking out of the Linz *Realschule* (high school), where he pursued a course of science and technology, and failing to graduate from a technical school in Steyr. During his late teens he idled away his time in Linz, whose large German population supported Austria's return to the German empire. At twenty he worked at odd jobs in Vienna, where, in pursuit of his ambition to be a painter or an architect, he twice failed the entrance exam to the Viennese Academy of Fine Arts.[4]

Thirty years after that fact, Hitler remained in denial, claiming to have impressed his examiner at the time as one who possessed an "indisputable talent for architecture."[5] His immediate response had been defiance, escapism, and compensatory daydreaming about alternative careers even farther beyond his mastery, while indulging in Wagner's music—balm for many proud and angry youths.[6] The wound seems to have been a lasting one. Observing him closely after 1931, Albert Speer, Hitler's chief architect and armaments minister, described a man so defeated and estranged that he preferred the company of dogs to that of people.[7]

Vienna was a school of hard knocks for Hitler in both body and soul. Rife with social and religious conflict, and dotted with busy anti-Semitic presses, the city shaped his early prejudices against Jews, who lived there in greater numbers than in any other German-speaking city (8.6 percent of the population in 1910).[8] Hitler lived in homeless shelters in the district most densely populated by Jews, earning money by drawing postcards, which two Jewish partners helped him sell. He also watched with alarm the growing Marxist Social Democratic Party, whose political philosophy increasingly became his bête noire.

Munich

Hitler left Vienna a dodger, with the Linz police on his heels because he had evaded his mandatory Austrian military service. In Munich he discovered his true talent: argument and propaganda, or revolutionary politics. During these years he was a keen observer of life on the streets, acquiring what we today call emotional intelligence. His was an uncommon ability to perceive and articulate what people wanted to hear, or acquire, regardless of propriety, or feasibility.[9] After Mussolini, and to greater effect, he was the first twentieth century politician to put the cult of personality at the center of politics.[10]

Confessionally, Hitler was a lapsed Catholic, ready to point out the contradictions between faith and reason, and an eager "new ager," unencumbered by traditional religious beliefs and deep historical knowledge. From the beginning, he believed the eternal rules of life were still to be made. In their history, Germans had not seen a pluckier, luckier comeback kid, or a more dogged can-do political party, than Hitler and the National Socialists.[11]

In Vienna and Munich, Hitler absorbed the existentialism of Arthur Schopenhauer, who taught that nothing exists beyond the individual will. Hitler claimed to have carried his books on his person throughout the war years. Two books by Nietzsche, *Thus Spake Zarathustra* and *The Anti-Christ*, both essays on the death of God, echoed in his table talk whenever he inveighed against Judaism and Christianity.[12] In Vienna he had personal relations with Viennese Jews, immersed himself in the city's anti-Semitic pulp fiction, and observed local Christian Social Party leader Karl Lüger's anti-Semitic activities. Also fanning his native Christian prejudices against Jews in these early years were the works of racial theorists Joseph Arthur, compte de Gobineau, and Houston Stewart Chamberlain, and newly popular Social Darwinism.[13]

World War I

After years of idling and wandering, the twenty-five-year-old Hitler found structure, discipline, camaraderie, and a cause in the military. Despite his foreign citizenship, in Munich he enlisted in a Bavarian regiment—a mistake on the part of German authorities, who were required by law to deport Austrian fugitives.[14] This was the first of several twists of fate, which, had they met the odds, might have changed the course of history.[15]

Hitler served the four years of the war on the Western Front, mostly as a dispatch runner. Performing with unusual valor, he was twice wounded, first in his thigh and two years later in his eyes, with mustard gas, for each of which he received Iron Crosses—a rare achievement for one at his rank. He honed his native political skills in those years, gaining the respect and affection of his comrades, who knew him as "Adi" or "Dolphi." Even then he was preparing for postwar conflict with rival liberal and Communist parties and, beyond them, the high-stakes negotiations that would bring National Socialism to power.[16]

THE PARTY

Throughout Germany, fragmented government and civil strife marked the postwar years. In Bavaria, government evolved from left-liberal to right-conservative in the year and a half after the war. After assassinating its provisional Jewish president, Kurt Eisner, a short-lived soldiers' council displaced the revolutionary Social Democratic coalition.[17] Conciliar rule was in turn crushed by the national army (Reichswehr) with the assistance of local military units (*Freikorps*). A residue of the Great War, these fighting units consisted of veterans who, like Hitler, were reluctant to return to the few options civilian life still offered. Although unpredictable, the *Freikorps* gave German states additional police and armed forces beyond the limits allowed by the Treaty of Versailles. It was with *Freikorps* assistance that reactionary military governments came to power in Bavaria, turning the state into a magnet for unhappy veterans across Germany.[18]

Hitler, still in uniform, worked for two years in Munich as a communications officer for both the ruling Social Democratic coalition and the interim political council that succeeded it. In that role he investigated alleged subversives and disseminated state propaganda. His political career began in earnest after he joined and rapidly gained control of the local German Workers' Party (DAP), one of more than seventy *völkisch* groups born of the war. Created in March 1918, it was one of a few select parties to field candidates for the National Constituent Assembly that met in Weimar in January 1919 to write a new constitution.[19]

With this modest base, Hitler entered an inspired, if star-crossed, political marriage with the revolutionary captain Ernst Röhm. The staff commander of the Munich Army District and an open homosexual, Röhm was popularly known as the "machine-gun king." Putting their stamp on the party, the two of them renamed it the National Socialist German Workers' Party (NSDAP) in 1920. Hitler personally designed its swastika, modeled on that of an Austrian party of the same name. Röhm's contribution was the storm troopers (SA, for *Sturmabteilung*), mostly hard-core *Freikorps*. Originally the party's bouncers, they would grow over the decade to rival the German national army. In this partnership between Hitler, the party's wordsmith, and Röhm, its enforcer, a new kind of German government was born.

The party's twenty-five-point platform promised the masses what its authors perceived they wanted, while attacking what it thought they opposed. Among the former were a "greater Germany" (inclusive of Austria), for which Hitler pleaded emotionally in the opening pages of *Mein Kampf*; new land and colonies, both for living space and international prestige; and economic breaks for small merchants, the party's initial base.[20] The platform attacked the Treaty of Versailles, reparations, the liberal press, capitalism, Jews, big industry, and big landowners. In these early years National Socialists and Communists targeted the same audience: the working and lower middle classes. Hitler's strategy was twofold: to fan class envy and resentment and to stigmatize wealthy, liberal opponents with the war loss. Over the years the party would win more white- than blue-collar voters, while demonstrating a substantial appeal across the social spectrum.[21]

Gatekeepers

Between 1921 and 1923 Hitler became the most successful barker on the political right, playing John the Baptist to a still to be discovered new political leader, who would inaugurate a new German age.[22] Unlike the crowds at his early stump speeches, his close associates had means, media, and connections in high places. Beyond Röhm, his military friends included Rudolf Hess, who had served in the same regiment during the war, and Hermann Göring, another war hero and household name. Journalist and bon vivant Dietrich Eckhart, one of the few men on intimate terms with Hitler, proselytized successful members of the middle class, who endowed the party newspaper, the *Völkischer Beobachter* (the National Observer), which Eckhart edited.[23]

Two wealthy couples—pan-Germanists Hugo and Elsa Bruckmann, he a publisher, she a Romanian princess, and Carl and Helene Bechstein, he a top piano manufacturer, she a socialite who became one of many Hitler "mothers" who doted on and coached the socially awkward politician as he was introduced to German high society. Among Bruckmann's authors was Houston Stewart Chamberlain, whom Hitler later met and revered on his deathbed.[24] On a day in October 1923 that he never forgot, the Bechsteins introduced him to the Wagners of Bayreuth. Still another door-opener to high society for the budding Nazi party was Munich-born Ernst "Putzi" Hanfstaengl, who had an American mother, a Harvard degree, and two Civil War generals in the "maternal" family tree. Finally there was Nuremberg publisher and anti-Semite Julius Streicher, who extended the range of the party's propaganda after Hitler stole him from the rival German Socialist Party.[25]

The French Occupation

Between the summer of 1921 and the winter of 1923, Bavaria contemplated a conservative challenge to the national government in

Berlin, a coup d'etat strongly favored by Hitler's party. A series of propulsive events, connected with the enforcement of the Treaty of Versailles, emboldened that treason. In 1921 the final reparations figure was set and a Polish corridor carved out of eastern German lands. In August 1922 Germany declared itself insolvent, its foreign debts unpaid and mounting. The final blow was French and Belgian occupation of the Ruhr in January 1923 after treaty-mandated shipments of German timber and coal fell short.[26]

The Germans fought back by walking out of the mines and the factories and off the rails. But while such defiance appeased national passions, it also put the Berlin government in the increasingly impossible position of having to support striking workers. With Ruhr industries shut down, workers elsewhere lost related jobs, enlarging the government dole. Given Germany's foreign obligations, payouts to the unemployed could be made only with inflated currency. So successfully was that done that marks became worthless by the end of the year, adults bundling them into fire logs or papering walls with them, while children turned them into playhouse blocks.

Although bookended by unprecedented inflation at the beginning of the decade and unprecedented unemployment at its end, the middle and late twenties saw comparative stability and even a culturally creative golden age. Still, the collective pain of 1923 proved to be a nation-altering experience. Unperceived, the roots of a great national vengeance had been put down in this unprecedented year of economic collapse and futility.[27]

Because German suffering and National Socialist success went hand in hand, the French and Belgian occupation of the Ruhr was a mixed blessing for Hitler's party. It was bad because Germans were moved to support their government against the armies of occupation. But it helped the party after an economically busted government ordered Ruhr workers back to their jobs. The spectacle of the government's caving in to the enemy gave critics the opportunity once again to accuse it of backstabbing.

Stresemann

Hitler's emergence on the historical stage coincided with the appointment of German Peoples' Party (DVP) member Gustav Stresemann as chancellor and foreign minister in 1923. Beyond the coincidence of their rise to national prominence, the two had little in common. Stresemann, who would survive numerous parliamentary coalitions and cabinets, believed in the Weimar Republic and appealed to the higher German soul. After the government forced workers in the Ruhr to abandon their popular strike, that appeal became more difficult, and his chancellorship was cut short. Later he sent federal troops to crush regional coups d'etat in Saxony and Thuringia, also in Hamburg and Munich, where the government provoked hostility by banning complicit Communist and National Socialist parties.[28]

Beyond the conflict in the Ruhr, the Stresemann government stabilized the German economy by printing a new mark secured by gold reserves and mortgage investments. Despite subsequent layoffs in the civil service, the new fiscal discipline gave Germany some breathing room on reparations.[29]

Stresemann had other political successes as well. He ended the occupation of the Ruhr in the summer of 1925, gained Allied recognition of the inviolability of German borders by the Locarno Pact, and saw Germany take a seat at the League of Nations in 1926. In recognition of his normalization of German relations with peer nations, Stresemann shared the 1926 Nobel Peace Prize with his French counterpart, Aristide Briand.[30]

The Munich Putsch

It was during Stresemann's brief chancellorship that National Socialists made their grab for regional power. By 1923 Bavaria had become a conservative military bastion with national ambitions rising in tandem with Weimar's problems. Under the combined leadership of Bavarian president Gustav von Kahr and the commander of the Bavarian national army, General Otto Hermann von Lossow, the National Socialists envisioned a new political union strong enough to challenge Berlin.

Believing those authorities to be of one mind with him, but hesitant out of fear of General Hans von Seeckt, commander of the Bavarian contingent of the German national army, Hitler thrust opportunity upon them. He picked November 8–9 for his coup, two days when President Kahr, General Lossow, and Bavarian police chief Hans Ritter von Seisser were scheduled to be in Munich for the celebration of the fifth anniversary of the postwar revolution against the imperial government. The festivities had just begun when Hermann Göring and a contingent of storm troopers escorted Hitler to the podium where Kahr, Lossow, and Seisser sat. Taking the microphone and declaring a national revolt against the Weimar Republic, Hitler proclaimed a new provisional government and named Kahr, Lossow, and Seisser to top positions in it.

Knowing the poor odds against the coup's success, the new appointees took the first opportunity to exit the hall and alert General von Seeckt. Confronted thereafter with their peril, the National Socialist leadership chose to make a bravado show of force. At noon the next day, rank-and-file members, two thousand strong, marched arm in arm through the city before being stopped by the army. Fourteen were shot dead, including the party member who had marched at Hitler's side—another shot, but for a few inches, that might have changed history. Göring took a bullet in the leg, while Hitler fled with a dislocated shoulder to Putzi Hanfstaengl's house, where he was later arrested.[31]

Between February 26 and March 27, 1924, the state put the National Socialist leadership on trial for treason. Because the trial occurred in reactionary Munich and not in Berlin, the leaders did not pay with their lives. Hitler, wearing his Iron Cross, stood in the dock as a war hero and accused his accusers—Kahr, Lossow, and Seisser—of being the real traitors for having betrayed the Munich putsch. Scornfully portraying Hitler as "only a drummer"—an agitator or propagandist—Lossow played into his hands, for many in the courtroom, unhappy with the times, did not think that "drumming" so insignificant.[32] At trial's end Hitler was a regional figure to be reckoned with.

The Leader

Because the political winds of Bavaria blew rightward in 1925, Hitler served only thirteen months of a five-year mandatory sentence that, if fully served, would likely have meant political oblivion.[33] During the months in Landsberg Prison, he dictated what would become *Mein Kampf*, originally a stream-of-consciousness autobiography in defense of his life, mostly since the end of the war. First entitled *Four-and-a Half Years of Struggle Against Lies, Stupidity, and Cowardice*, the first, more biographical volume was followed by a second, more programmatic one in 1926. Published together in the 1930s, they made Chancellor Hitler a rich man. The overarching theme was a racial, Social Darwinist play on the Nietzschean motif of the highest and the lowest man, which, for Hitler, meant "the Aryan" and "the Jew" (or "the Jew-Bolshevik"), respectively. In contrasting the two, he echoed numerous nineteenth-century new-age dissertations, from Feuerbach to Nietzsche, and from Riehl to Wagner and Chamberlain, while scorning the core teachings of classic German philosophy and theology, which portrayed Everyman as the highest and the lowest.

After his release in December 1924, Hitler quickly reestablished his authority over his still-banned party. During his imprisonment, he had come to believe that he was himself "the superleader" he had earlier prophesied. A newfound abstinence from alcohol and meat may have been an outward sign of that enlightenment, although the reasons he alleged were a desire to lose weight and avoid foods harmful to his body.[34] He became a fervent vegetarian, yet took care not to push his views on the great majority of hunters and carnivores who made up the rank and file of National Socialism—although he did not hesitate to tease them about the inequitable nature of their blood sport.[35]

Respecting the threat he posed, the Weimar government banned Hitler from public speaking for two years (three in Prussia). In the enterprising spirit that would continue to win the party popular support, the National Socialists held more than two thousand public meetings during his first year out. Banned from the public forum, Hitler turned adversity to advantage by scheduling nonstop private talks with influential groups.[36]

In 1925, the year of his release, Field Marshal Paul von Hindenburg became the second president of the Weimar Republic after appendicitis took Friedrich Ebert's life. With the inauguration of Hindenburg, a principled, conservative leader, there began a political shift of the government from left to center-right.[37] Because of the stability he and Stresemann brought to Germany in their different ways, a shocked nation appeared to get its bearings and sail smoothly. Yet any significant rise in German spirits and security during the remainder of the decade had foreign loans rather than political breakthroughs, or reforms, to thank.[38]

RENOVATING A NATION

By the end of the decade, amid the Wall Street crash, the European depression, and the tripling of German unemployment, Hitler's criticism and predictions of doom in the preceding years seemed prescient to many. As division deepened within the states and the national parliament, and increasing numbers of landowners, farmers, industrialists, and workers voted National Socialist, another great splintering of the German electorate occurred. By the early 1930s Hindenburg's chancellors were unable to deliver a parliamentary coalition capable of passing the government's programs.[39]

Center Stage

Stalemated in parliament, Hindenburg exercised his constitutional right to dissolve it in July 1930, ruling thereafter by presidential decree. The invocation of Article 48 was, in effect, a reversion to hierarchical rule, with Hindenburg acting as a kind of latter-day emperor through his chancellor. In place of old-guard Social Democratic chancellor Hermann Müller, he entrusted his programs to Center Party leader Heinrich Brüning in March 1930.[40]

Government by emergency decree was unpopular, and Hitler denounced it with his familiar fury and sarcasm. Yet in three short years his party would also install such a government, one that made Hindenburg's desperate post-1930 regime seem the soul of reason. En route to that goal, the National Socialists continued to draw members and support from the other right-wing party, the National Peoples' Party, and a reactionary veteran's group known as the Steel Helmet. This shift of power to the hard right became especially visible in the September 1930 election, when the number of National Socialist delegates shot up from 12 to 107, in excess of six million voters.[41]

Encouraged, Hitler reined in the impatient Röhm and resolved to gain total power "legally." By that he meant methodical criticism of the government, the scapegoating of unpopular Communists and Jews, and generally scaring the electorate. His tactical restraint notwithstanding, he knew that a great part of his appeal, especially after 1929, lay in his clearly conveyed intention to ignore the law, if ending Germany's plight and punishing those responsible required it. By 1930 a vote for National Socialism had become a vote to subordinate means to end.

Foremost in the minds of most ordinary Germans was relief from economic crisis and ineffectual government. A model study of Northeim in Lower Saxony, a town with a population of ten thousand, has dissected the tactics and appeal of Hitler's party as it "plunged a civilized democracy into nihilistic dictatorship."[42]

Divided between a cohesive, conservative middle class wanting stability and control, and a tight-knit working class demanding radical change, the town was ripe for Nazi propaganda. Hitler's party widened the fissures by constant marches, gatherings, disruptions, and harassment. In doing so they found a careless ally in the local Social Democratic Party, whose left-liberal rhetoric did much to stampede Northeim's middle class into the arms of the National Socialists. In the end two-thirds of the electorate voted National Socialist in the belief that the party would both end the depression and prevent a Marxist takeover of local and state government, the success of which promised the middle class only more austerity. In voting Nazi the citizens of Northeim did not vote for what the Third Reich became, but for what it promised to do by way of ending the present political and economic crisis.[43]

Northeim's story may be read as that of Germany writ small. In times that cried out for resolution and retaliation, the National Socialists succeeded in portraying themselves as incomparable doers and winners. Germans voted for Hitler in growing numbers because he conveyed, like no other, the image of a leader more outraged over their plight than they, and possessed of the will and wit to end it—something Hindenburg and the Weimar Republic had long since lost the ability to do.[44]

Courting Hitler

Confronted with National Socialism's rapid growth (party membership more than doubled in 1931) and its own unpopularity, the Hindenburg government opened discussions with an adamant Hitler in the autumn of 1931. At the time Chancellor Brüning asked only for a pledge of neutrality during the remainder of Hindenburg's term. A second meeting on the subject occurred in early January 1932, with Hitler still wanting everything—namely Brüning's dismissal and new elections.

In advance of his first meeting with Hindenburg on October 31,

1931, Hitler recalled that Secretary of State Otto Meissner, who would later also serve Hitler in that position, confided to him that Hindenburg was repelled by everything he stood for.[45] The stench, however, was masked by his party's ability to provide the Hindenburg government with the parliamentary majority it coveted. By July 1932 National Socialists made up more than one-third of the Reichstag, and their storm troopers were three hundred thousand strong and still growing.

General Staff officer and future chancellor Kurt von Schleicher led the government push for Hitler's inclusion, convinced that an alliance with the National Socialists would secure the government, strengthen the national army, and banish the threat of Communism.[46] In private talks he promised Hitler Brüning's resignation in exchange for National Socialist support until the economic crisis ended, implying that the chancellorship would then be his for the taking. That, however, could have meant enduring yet another Hindenburg presidency, an unacceptable prospect given Hindenburg's opposition to Hitler.

Having rejected the Brüning-Schleicher pleadings, the only way left for Hitler to realize his ambitions was to run for president in the April 1932 election.[47] Using airplanes (the campaign was called "Hitler over Germany") and film commercials for the first time in a German political campaign, he took 30 percent of the vote to Hindenburg's 49 percent, rising to 37–53 percent in the runoff in May. Although they lost, it was an impressive showing for Hitler and his party, which held 230 seats after the July national elections.[48]

That Hitler had become the dominant political force in Germany was made clear in the election's aftermath, when Hindenburg banned all paramilitary groups, including the storm troopers and Hitler bodyguard and Gestapo chief Heinrich Himmler's new SS (*Schutzstaffel*, "protective squadron").[49] Hitler and SA leader Röhm immediately demanded the lifting of that ban as the price of National Socialist cooperation, something a tired, scrambling Hindenburg government would soon do.

Three weeks after the election of May 5, 1932, the unpopular Brüning resigned, a victim as much of his own deflationary policy as of opposition politics. Having bet that an insolvent Germany would more quickly be relieved of reparations, he intentionally allowed joblessness and destitution to ratchet up, earning him the nickname of "Hunger Chancellor." Unfortunately German reparations were not rescinded until July 1932, by which time austerity had become every nation's policy.[50]

With Hitler's consent, Hindenburg replaced Brüning with Franz von Papen, a trusted Center Party member. As there was no love lost between Papen and Hitler, the latter's consent was given much as the fox recommends the chicken. After July fully half of parliament's votes were in the hands of National Socialists and Communists, who demonstrated their combined ability to create havoc in the streets as well. With Papen, like Brüning, fearing a coup and unable to gain a ruling coalition in parliament, Hindenburg again invoked Article 48 and ruled by presidental decree. That procedure, however, was poison to democracy and could not be sustained. If the government was going to pass its programs through parliament, it would have to form a majority coalition, and that meant bringing the National Socialists on board.

Lobbied by Schleicher and assured by his cabinet that Hitler could be controlled, Hindenburg invited Hitler to rule, with Papen as vice-chancellor. Sensing victory, Hitler agreed only to cooperate with the new government—and only on the conditions that it lift the ban on his storm troopers and hold new elections, the first of which occurred in mid-June, the second in late July.[51] He had now positioned himself to grasp his true goal: the chancellorship with the near-absolute powers Hindenburg had bestowed on Brüning and Papen.

Hitler Ascendant

With Göring as the president of the parliament, the National Socialists joined ranks with their archenemies, the Communists, to ensure the most ignominious no-confidence vote possible on Papen's chancellorship in December 1932.[52] Despite Hitler's moving to take Hindenburg's place, the president's obstruction of the man he called a "Bohemian corporal" was not over yet. His hand strengthened by National Socialist slippage in the November elections, Hindenburg, pointing to the party's lack of a parliamentary majority, reinstated Papen.[53] In the end Hitler's advocate Schleicher, now plotting to gain the support of the National Socialists and lose Hitler in the process, maneuvered himself into the chancellorship.[54]

In January 1933 Hitler and Papen successfully made common cause against Schleicher, bringing his brief chancellorship to an end and setting the government adrift again—a painful development for Hindenburg, whose choices had long been Hobsonian. On January 30, 1933, Hitler became chancellor.[55] In a kind of throwback to the ritual celebrations of sixth-century Goths and Franks upon attaining great power or victory over the Romans,[56] Hitler contemplated commemorating the new age he believed his chancellorship inaugurated by changing the German calendar in the French revolutionary fashion.[57] The German experiment with liberal democracy, begun in 1918, had now run its course. In the coming decade and a half, new and unimagined forms of dictatorship would take its place.

NAZIS ON TOP

In their first six months the National Socialists ground up the remains of Weimar's freedoms, and by the time of Hindenburg's death in August 1934, Hitler was the supreme master of Germany. Barely a month had passed when fortune handed him virtual carte blanche. On February 27, 1933, a mentally unbalanced twenty-four-year-old Dutchman, Martin van der Lubbe, set fire to the Reichstag. Crying "Communist putsch," Hitler put an emergency decree—"A Decree for the Protection of People and the State"—before the president the very next day. Designed for such Prussian troubles as arson, revolt, and terror, the decree was now extended throughout the Reich and secured the murky legal basis of National Socialist rule.[58]

In the early days of March 1933 the electorate helped by giving the new regime 43.9 percent of the vote—not a ruling majority but a definite increase. After the February 28 emergency decree and the March vote swell, the new parliament's passage of the Enabling Act of March 23—"A Decree for the Removal of Distress from the German People and Reich"—by a whopping four-to-one vote was anticlimactic.[59] For any who may have doubted the new regime's intent, its true colors now flew at full mast.

Beginning in April, Hitler dispatched his own imperial governors to the states to establish his official presence in all German lands. The governors oversaw locally the national policies of the chancellor. Unlike premodern imperial emissaries, who had to rely on fickle regional armies for enforcement, Hitler's governors had the services of local storm troopers, the SS, and Steel Helmet contingents in addition to the national army.[60]

Having ridden the law into power with the clear intent of breaking it once there, the party acted as advertised. As any reader of *Mein Kampf* would have known, the true Aryan in every culture is not the one who plays by the rules but the one who wins despite them. Hitler hated Christianity and Communism for their social leveling and static societies, and he identified the supremely hated Jews as the mother root of both plagues.[61] Although anti-Semitism had not been the spearhead of the new regime's propaganda and success, it tested anti-Jewish laws early. The first day of April saw a one-day boycott of Jewish businesses enforced over loud national and international protest. The week after the boycott, new laws excluded Jews from the civil service and the practice of law, denied Jewish physicians access to national insurance patients, and reduced the quota of Jewish children admissible to public schools. Roman Catholics, too, were muzzled; with Vatican concurrence, priests were forbidden to make any social or political commentary during their cure of souls.[62]

By July 1933, having imprisoned, exiled, or intimidated political opponents into silence, the National Socialists, now 2.5 million strong, effectively became the only German political party. Within just a few months, large numbers of Germans, from civil servants to local bowling clubs, had been successfully *gleichgeschaltet*, or brought into line. By mid-October the Reichstag was dissolved, and Germany, no longer a member of the League of Nations, was massively rearming in defiance of the Treaty of Versailles. When the new Reichstag convened again after the November elections, the National Socialists had the final tool they needed to wage a world war: every sitting deputy supported Hitler. The time had come, as the National Socialists had promised voters it would, to pay back those who had stabbed Germany in the back.[63]

Before doing so Hitler had his own housecleaning to do. His targets were the leadership of the storm troopers, who through the years had remained firebrands, and their chief, Ernst Röhm, who remained determined to see his soldiers become the main German army. There was also a possibility that Röhm might challenge the führer himself. This troubled the commanders of the national army, who now held the key to Hitler's success.

June 30, 1934, was known as the "night of the long knives." By daybreak on July 2 the SS had murdered the storm troopers' high command and other political opponents by the dozens, while other perceived opponents either fled or were imprisoned.[64] After the carnage a reduced number of storm troopers remained under SS command, the latter thenceforth Hitler's sworn bodyguards and henchmen. It is a commentary on the brutality of the times that the massacre received overwhelming acclaim from both parliament and the general public, helped along by rumors of a planned Röhm coup and cartoons about his homosexuality.[65] The killings served their intended purpose. Not until 1944 was there an equivalent threat to Hitler from the German military.

Undoing Versailles

Between 1934 and 1936 a remilitarized Germany reestablished its political and geographical status prior to the Treaty of Versailles. The greatest damage of World War I had been on Germany's western Rhenish flank, where a nonaggression pact with Poland now allowed German troops to concentrate. A year later the Saarland was returned to Germany by a previously stipulated plebiscite. After March 1935 the German air force, long forbidden engine flight, returned to the skies. Because the Allies were also rearming at their own pace, the League of Nations did not challenge these ominous initiatives. By March 1936, sword making turned to sword rattling, as German soldiers moved unopposed into the demilitarized Rhineland. The Allies' response was a fingers-crossed, eyes-averted acceptance of the aggression in the deluded hope that a first big bite might be the last.

By 1938 the bites had only gotten larger and the feeding insatiable. In further defiance of Versailles, the German army marched into a largely welcoming Austria, recreating the fabled "greater Germany" that had inspired Hitler as a schoolboy in Linz. This newly reunited, ethnically aware Germany proceeded to take by force the land it deemed necessary for its growing population—ultimately from the Czechs and the Poles. Czechoslovakia's Sudetenland, home to another majority German-speaking people, was the next to go, but, unlike Austria, it did so kicking and screaming, its cries heard but ignored by the Allies. Arriving in Munich in September 1938 to address Germany's seizure of the Sudetenland, British prime minister Neville Chamberlain blithely brokered away the Czechs' vital buffer, and within six months German soldiers were goose-stepping through Prague. Then, after signing a nonaggression pact, mortal enemies Germany and the Soviet Union launched a surprise attack on Poland in September 1939, conquering and dividing the hapless nation according to previously agreed-upon secret provisions. Thereafter, in 1940, the German military methodically made its way into Denmark, Norway, Belgium, the Netherlands, Luxembourg, and—accompanied by their Italian allies—France. Among Europe's great powers, only Britain remained free in the West.

Undoing Germany

On September 3, 1939, Britain and France declared war on Germany, yet did little for the greater part of a year. Without defeating Britain and Russia, Germany could not win the war. Had the Germans had their way, Russia would have become for Germany what India had been for England—*Lebensraum* for a "superior" people. Hitler deemed the Russians inferior even to the Jews, calling them "brutes in a state of nature" and comparing their organizational abilities to those of rabbits rather than ants and bees. Yet he also believed that "a drop of Aryan blood" still flowed in Russian veins, making them a people on whom order might be "thrust." The Jews were a more dangerous people by virtue of the discipline and focus instilled in them by their Law. Believing Bolshevism to be the illegitimate offspring of Judaism and Christianity, Hitler looked on the Russian people's defeat as their deliverance from three crippling ideologies.[66]

In late June 1941, with its immediate goals accomplished on the western front, the German army began its march east. Had it instead turned only ninety degrees and invaded North Africa and the Middle East, World War II might have ended differently. There the Germans might have struck the British more effectively, gaining control of the Mediterranean and the Suez Canal and access to Middle Eastern oil fields. However, the easy victory over France and the stalemate with Britain moved Hitler, illogically and against the advice of his generals, to plunge into Russia. Later he claimed to have acted on intelligence identifying a single Russian factory with greater tank production than all German factories combined.[67] Between the Russian winter and poor German timing and tactics, the German offensive ground to a halt on the outskirts of Moscow, allowing the Russians to survive the most horrific carnage yet.

A second German invasion in the summer of 1942, aimed at capturing Russia's southern oil fields, ended in the total destruction of the besieging German army at Stalingrad. That battle was the proverbial point of no return for both armies, and greatly diminished Germany's chances of winning the war. The great whale, Britain, and the great bear, Russia, had proved to be too much for the German army. With the Americans fully engaged in the war by the beginning of 1943, and the Allies then willing to bomb civilian populations, Germans became the hunted and Germany's collapse only a matter of time. After the Normandy invasion on June 6, 1944, Allied armies were back on the ground in force, slogging their way to Berlin, where, in May 1945, they found the Russians in possession of the city and Hitler a suicide.[68]

THE ROOTS OF EVIL: JEWS, CHRISTIANS, AND BOLSHEVIKS

German anger and vengeance put Hitler in power, but they did not give him any mandate to prey at will on largely helpless scapegoats, as the Jews soon became. That Hitler could invoke German Jews to denigrate his opponents and advance his agenda is not explained by preceding centuries of Jewish-Christian conflict and mutual rejection. By comparison with most other states, nineteenth-century Germany had been a good place for Jews to live. Their emancipation had begun early in the century, and the small number of German Jews, roughly 1 percent of the population, were a comparatively well-to-do group and highly visible before century's end. Prussian Jews, who were 37 percent of all German Jews, gained citizenship in 1808 and within a decade moved, worked, married, and bought land much as any Gentile. At mid-century the Frankfurt assembly emancipated all German Jews, a lead the individual states followed.[69]

Jews nonetheless found themselves in a controversial position. Despite tiny numbers many were prominent in the elite professions by the 1860s. Non-Jews noticed when Jewish children made up more than 8 percent of gymnasium students and 12 percent of university students in 1870s Prague and Vienna.[70] Traditionally strong in clothing and retail businesses, Jews were fully 17 percent of German bankers, 16 percent of lawyers, and 10 percent of physicians. Politically the great majority were left-liberal, and Jewish lawyers held high positions in liberal parties. Eduard Lasker, a chief critic of Bismarck during the 1870s, and widely blamed for the economic depression that began in 1873, led the National Liberals. A half century later, in 1922, Walther Rathenau, the Weimar Republic's foreign minister, headed the government team that implemented the Versailles reparation payments—representation that cost him his life, by assassination, before the year was out.[71]

Although hatred of Jews had long existed among German Christians, it was slow to become focused and developed into a systematic campaign—a commentary on both Jewish success and the slowness of Germans to react vehemently to it. Historically the spokespersons for the majority Christian population, two-thirds of whom were Protestant in the nineteenth century (excluding Austria), desired Jewish conversion and assimilation into Christian society.[72] The perception that German Catholics and Jews had a prior allegiance to a religious community deemed higher than the German state endeared them neither to their secular and areligious, nor their devoutly Protestant, fellow citizens.[73]

Still, as late as 1900, anti-Semitism was far rifer in France and Czarist Russia than in Germany. During World War I, 12,000 German Jews died for the fatherland, and no anti-Jewish riots or pogroms marred the years of the Great War. Nor did anti-Semitism play any great role in Hitler's seizure of power in 1932–33. The anti-Semitic actions of his government, both early and late, surprised and disturbed most Germans, who reacted with greater fear of their new government than of their Jewish neighbors. In fact,

Kristallnacht, "the night of Broken Glass" (November 9–10, 1938), divided even the Nazi elite, with Propaganda Minister Joseph Goebbels, its chief organizer, receiving much criticism. On that infamous night, the anniverary of the Munich Putsch, the genocide campaign began in earnest. In claimed retaliation for the murder of a German Embassy staff member in Paris by a young Polish Jew, the storm troopers killed scores of German Jews, burned their synagogues, and generally wrecked their businesses across Germany. Later, it was also telling behavior when the directors of the genocide campaign made every effort first to hide the fact of it, and then to explain it away, believing that most Germans would dissent.[74]

If, to some modern historians, the German high command appears to have been fighting World War II primarily to exterminate Europe's Jews, that was emphatically not the rationale of the war for German soldiers who engaged Allied armies on the Eastern and Western Fronts, or for those on the home front who worked on their behalf and awaited their return.[75] The original motives for the war were completely self-centered, not Judeocentric or anti-Semitic. Germans wanted to avenge and repair, by total victory, the draconian reparations they had been compelled to pay and the terrible suffering they had endured since World War I. At the beginning of World War II the victors of the first were believed to owe Germany a lot, and many Germans looked forward to the fruits of war-making much as Hitler had looked back to the German-Russian Treaty of Brest-Litovsk. By that treaty Germany relieved Russia of the Baltic states, Finland, Poland, and the Ukraine, along with three-quarters of its steel industry and a quarter of its textile mills. Confirming widespread German sentiment, Hitler declared Brest-Litovsk to be "infinitely humane" by comparison with Versailles.[76]

In 1941, when Polish ghettos began to swell with deported Austrian and German Jews, such fanciful solutions as deportation to Siberia and Madagascar were contemplated. Between the tides of war and the depravity of hearts, execution became the optimal solution, and gas chambers the most efficient and least stressful method for the appointed executioners.[77] When, in 1944, wholesale killings of Jews tripled in the concentration camps, the war had turned irretrievably against the Germans. As the Allies advanced into Germany, Jews and Jewish labor ceased to be relevant to their keepers, whose sole concern now became the speedy destruction of the camps and the stories they told.

The new massacres also addressed a long-building problem created and hidden by the Nazi presumption of invincibility. A besieged Germany could not at one and the same time provision the soaring numbers of Jews and slave laborers in concentration camps, supply a retreating army, and protect a civilian population in flight from Allied tanks and carpet bombing. As early as 1941, citing "laws that become valid in exceptional times," Hitler had ordered Himmler "to liquidate everything . . . in the concentration camps" at the first sign of "troubles" at home, thereby depriving the troublemakers of their leaders "at a stroke."[78]

Although German Jews, like Jews in other European lands, were only a tiny percentage of the population, no other people, Hitler believed, had inflicted more harm on the world or were more capable of still doing so than the Jews. However, during his rise to power and his regime's first months in office, it was the Communists, not the Jews, who dominated the National Socialist agenda. Before and after the burning of the Reichstag, Hitler's party exploited widespread fear of a Communist coup, not of any impending Jewish peril.

That changed abruptly, however, after the boycott of Jewish businesses. Between the specter of Communism and the ineptitude of the Weimar government, the National Socialists insinuated their own less salable, because so monumental, anti-Semitism into German party politics. Portraying Russia's left-wing Social Democrats, the devoutly Leninist Bolsheviks, as the "creation of the Jews," Hitler hung conspiratorial Marxism and Judaism around the necks of the German Social Democratic Party. Since 1920 these "German Bolsheviks" had been National Socialism's strongest political opponents and Germany's best hope for a modern democracy.

What bound Marxists, Social Democrats, and Jews together in Hitler's mind was a shared desire to level society economically and politically. In his vision of history, Bolshevism was born in the first century with the "Jewish mobilization of slaves" against the Romans. That revolutionary project exceeded the ability of the Jews but was successfully taken up by their more powerful offspring, the Christians. Setting class against class and inferior against superior, Judaism and Christianity succeeded in undermining the Roman Empire and gaining position and advantage neither merited.[79] In the twentieth century Hitler saw history threatening to repeat itself, now in the form of Bolshevism and social democracy and at the expense of the German empire. He variously lumped together as "Jewish creations" democracy, capitalism, liberalism, internationalism, and even modernism in art.[80] These were, he believed, the sundry yet kindred ways nobodies became somebodies—a perception of the undeserved success of others that had tormented him from his student days, when he was forced to confront his own failures.

Although Judaism held chronological and material priority over Christianity in Hitler's reading of history, Christianity enacted its sociopolitical fury. Modern Jewry was "the ferment that caused [a] people to decay," but modern Christianity "systematically cultivated . . . human failure," threatening much worse: "Pure Christianity . . . leads quite simply to the annihilation of mankind; it is . . . wholehearted Bolshevism under a tinsel of metaphysics."[81]

Thus, while Hitler subjected German Jews to a "final solution," he singled out the removal of the "rotten branch of Christianity" as the "final task" of National Socialism, with the removal of Slavs, Gypsies, and homosexuals in between.[82] Beyond the Jewish Holocaust lay the eradication of Christianity.[83] The "religious problem" was thus theoretically two-tiered. It was not Judaism but its more numerous and hearty progeny, Pauline Christianity—the prototype of Russian Bolshevism and German social democracy—that had destroyed the Roman Empire in antiquity and now threatened its successor, the German Reich, in the modern world. In Hitler's reading of history that empire had been a great friend of Germanic peoples. The marriage of Roman and German, Aryan with Aryan, had rejuvenated Rome and extended its rule in late antiquity. Christianity, by contrast, suppressed the Roman religion "common to all Aryan peoples," replacing its belief in social solidarity and ethnic unity with a novel notion of the equality of all people under one God, regardless of social standing and race. Whereas Jesus had led "a local movement of Aryan opposition to Jewry" and sided with the Romans in their conflict with the Jews, the rabbinically trained Paul of Tarsus turned the masses against the Romans, unleashing Jewish vengeance, through Christianity, on both Roman and subsequent European civilization.[84]

The National Socialist elite believed that traditional Christians would, in the end, oppose party "principle[s] of racism . . . unlimited aggressive war . . . and the complete subservience of church to state."[85] Unlike minority Jews, Christians were also too many, too powerful, and too German to be directly attacked. Party leaders also believed that the churches, having historically always adapted to the goals of reigning political power, might come in time to embrace National Socialism. That hope underlay Article 24 of the National Socialist program, which embraced historical Christianity sufficiently to leave the door open for swayable Christians. For this reason Hitler ordered party leaders, regardless of any sincere commitment to the faith, to remain in the churches, as he himself did until his suicide.[86]

The liberal Protestant theology of the Enlightenment and the left-wing Hegelians was far more vulnerable to being coopted by National Socialism than was traditional Christianity.[87] In the early years a great many churches, Protestant and Catholic, were silent about human rights and civil liberties and sought ways to accommodate the new regime while they weathered the storm. In exchange for control of its own schools and organizations, the Vatican silenced its priests in July 1933, hoping thereby to preserve a base from which to fight principled moral battles. One such battle was over the euthanasia program which killed, by injection, malnutrition, or gassing, an estimated 72,000 physically or mentally impaired children and adults between 1939 and 1941.[88]

In 1933 a pro-Nazi Protestant-led German Christian Movement came close to merging the leadership of Germany's majority Christian religion with that of its new politics. Among the movement's tenets was the exclusion of non-Aryan pastors and those with non-Aryan wives from the churches. When a German Christian reich bishop was elected in 1933, only seven thousand of the eighteen thousand Protestant clergy joined the opposing Pastors' Emergency League.[89] However, in May 1934, the anti-Nazi Protestant-led "Confessing Churches," loyal to the Bible, condemned the notion that either Hitler or his party might in any way be construed as revealing God's will.[90]

In the new age envisioned by National Socialism, biblical Christianity was politically subversive, even a "rebellion . . . against nature."[91] Its perceived absurdity had been impressed on Hitler during his Austrian schooldays, when, as he mockingly recalled, students attended a catechism class at ten A.M. to hear the biblical story of Creation, only then to listen, at eleven A.M., to Darwin's version of it in a natural science class—the latter winning hands down.[92] During the war years Hitler recommended a slow "natural death" for Christianity by exposing its dogmas to the light of science.[93]

Believing history documented a leap from Paul of Tarsus to Karl Marx, a Roman Empire "bolshevized" by Christianity to a Russian empire "bolshevized" by V. I. Lenin, Hitler feared that an incautious German Reich would be the next victim of the Jewish-Christian-Bolshevik juggernaut. In the winter and spring of 1933, he raised the specter of an imminent "renewal of the [ancient Christian] experiment" with a new "vitiation of racial integrity," as he believed had happened in late ancient Rome. In the autumn of 1941, recounting such fears in his table talk, he expressed a belief that Bolsheviks were at that very moment deporting hundreds of thousands of Russian men, while delivering perhaps equal numbers of Russian women into the beds of inferior non-Russian males imported from other lands.[94] Such intentional mongrelization of the races threatened Europe with inferior offspring and was being pursued benightedly in the name of Christian and Bolshevik egalitarianism.[95] Thus, through Christianity and Bolshevism, the ancient, empire-destroying power of the Jews lived on in the modern world. Therein lay, for Hitler, the imperative of a "final solution" for the Jews and of a postwar terror for the Christians.

WHY HITLER?

Weights and Measures

"Yes, we are barbarians! We want to be barbarians! It is an honorable title. We shall rejuvenate the world!"[96] Thus did Hitler declaim at table in 1933, embracing an epithet Germans historically associated with belittlement and subjugation. Successful leaders do not blindly follow tradition, nor do they simply pull the plug on the past. That was true of the governments of Frederick the Great, Bismarck, Gustav Stresemann, and Paul von Hindenburg. Although Nazi propaganda placed Hitler himself in the company of three of those Germans, he was the supreme counter establishment leader, finding only failure and doom in the past and the present, while promising Germans a perfect new age. An Austrian who did not become a German citizen until 1932, he was rootless, volatile, self-absorbed, and had little interest in German history beyond its use to advance his career. As late as 1928 he was, in the words of a modern biographer, "a small-time politician, little known outside of southern Germany, and . . . part of the lunatic fringe of Bavarian politics."[97]

His seizure of power in 1933 was no clear German victory.[98] Never did his party have the backing of a majority of Germans, and its success came only in time of crisis and by virtue of the lopsided support of vulnerable social groups and well-organized lobbies. No one group voted more consistently for National Socialism than did the lower middle class (*untere Mittelstand*), which, on average, made up more than 50 percent of party members between 1925 and 1932.[99] Germans who supported National Socialism before the March 1933 election—the last free election before Hitler's Enabling Act transformed Germany into a one-party state—voted their pains and grievances. Theirs was a positive response to a then seemingly credible program of economic relief, political reform, and national security. While vengeance and reparations were foremost in many minds, few can fairly be said to have voted to fight a world war to the last man or to slaughter six million German and European Jews.

However, the 43.9 percent National Socialist share of the March 1933 vote, the party's highest, cannot so easily be defended as only the result of individual self-interest. Coming less than a week after the burning of the Reichstag, and amid brazen Nazi intimidation visible to all, few observant voters could have failed to notice, if additional examples were needed, the dark and reckless side of National Socialism.

Ambivalence continued to shroud Nazi success. While some claim that as many as nine of ten Germans were "führer believers" by 1938, there is also no denying widespread individual and institutional resistance to the regime over twelve years of Nazi rule—from worker foot-dragging on production lines, to church condemnation of immoral programs, to an aristocratic effort to blow Hitler up.[100] The party ruled supreme only by fear and terror, and never succeeded in making Germany the voluntary, cohesive national community that its propaganda desired.[101]

Yet, for a people with so long and obsessive a history of foreign and self-predation, the resistance pales before the actions or inactions of so many Germans in bringing the most destructive predator ever into their midst. In its background lay extraordinary conditions, which arguably could have brought any other contemporary nation to the breaking point. Ignominious military defeat in 1918, after mythical expectations of what the war would bring, was compounded by punitive war reparations in 1921. To those shocks were added economic collapse and unemployment at levels never before seen, while a new government, over thirteen years of liberal-conservative rule, could provide no sure refuge from the cascading crises.

Had such overlapping disasters not befallen Germany, and the Weimar government been less inept at rescue, the National Socialists might have remained a lunatic fringe. The results of the annual elections after 1925 make it clear that their support rose and fell with the government's success at resolving crisis. A problem-solving Weimar government would have mesmerized far more Germans than all the ranting speeches of Hitler. However, neither the Ebert liberals nor the Hindenburg conservatives were able to deliver the German people in their darkest days. In the end it was that fact that gave Hitler, a politician who knew how to stuff a void with promises, a decisive advantage.

The specter of a successful Communist coup particularly frightened middle- and lower-middle-class Germans, who knew that such rule would further reduce their personal property and livelihood. Most Germans also had reason to believe that a Communist coup was more likely with a left-liberal government than with a right-conservative one.[102] With Hindenburg's succession to the Weimar presidency in 1925, a barrier had been thrown up against that possibility—one, however, that favored a National Socialist seizure of power in the event of Hindenburg's failure.

Ignoring legalities and comfortable with violence, Hitler's party presented itself as incomparable problem solvers and relentless righters of wrongs. Seeing no way out of the Weimar undertow, and holding both Hindenburg and foreign powers responsible for their plight, increasing numbers of voters simply looked to Hitler's magic for deliverance and punishment. For a great many proud Germans, who had lost everything or had precious little left to lose, this all-or-nothing approach seemed, at endgame, to be the perfect message. Collectively those who embraced it had to have known that it would mean at least war with enemies abroad and fifth columns at home.

Thoroughly Modern Nazis?

Blaming National Socialist success on a persisting authoritarian German past has become ingrained in the historiography of modern Germany. Even today one can find a debate on its chronological depth: whether the fatal step was taken in the age of the Hohenstaufen Fredericks, Luther, Frederick the Great, or Bismarck. Whence and whatever its distant precedents, most historians find a fateful conjunction in the Wilhelmine empire.[103]

A recent, contrarian answer to the question, "Why Hitler?" has suggested modern motives for embracing National Socialism, pointing to its egalitarianism, or mass democracy, and fervent promise of a more perfect people and state. Repudiating both imperial Germany and the Weimar Republic, Hitler's party looked neither to the past nor to the present for instruction, but forward to a yet-to-be-defined future. It invited all Germans to become equal partners in "fashioning a populist-nationalism"—a big-tent approach that welcomed both aristocrats and the lower middle class and embraced both chauvinism and social awareness.[104]

If Hitler was the culmination of an old, authoritarian Germany and the pied piper of a communally renovated one, he was also the first political leader of the twentieth century to embrace to the core the previous century's sociocultural revolution, with its breakaway existential values.[105] His party's goal was to replace a firmly principled past, which both imperial Germany and the Weimar Republic had been, with a completely experimental future. Suffering the cuts of a thousand post-Hegelian illusions, much of the old political and cultural Germany had died on the killing fields of the nineteenth century. Like disaffected Wilhelmine youth, who pursued lesser sociocultural, racial, and utopian worlds under the spell of trendy academics and *völkisch* gurus, a spiritually depleted and vocationally deprived Weimar generation became easy prey for National Socialist propaganda.[106] Fantastical notions of waxing Aryans and waning Jews, and of political and economic paybacks, mesmerized audiences in universities, boardrooms, and beerhalls, sanctioning the wildest departures from what Germans historically had deemed sane, moral, and humane. For all the clinging eggshells of the old Germany, here was a new fluid mentality, both confident and desperate, ready to entertain Hitler's speeches.

11

THE COMPOSITE GERMAN

Germany Since World War II

MAY 8, 1945, MARKED THE OFFICIAL END of the war in Europe, the unconditional surrender of all German forces to General Dwight D. Eisenhower having occurred the day before in Reims. By this time Allied bombing had laid waste to Germany's great cities, and the total German war dead would climb to 4.5 million. Of those, 500,000 were civilians incinerated in the cities, 2 million soldiers who died on the battlefields, and another 2 million refugees forced from German-occupied Hungary, Poland, and Czechoslovakia between 1944 and 1946 in what has been called "the greatest migratory movement of modern times."[1]

The victorious Allies who now sought to pacify and unite a defeated Germany were themselves divided by different histories, polities, and cultures. Those differences, later driven home in the occupied zones during the Cold War, also shaped the future of Germany. The French and left-liberal German intellectuals believed a solution to the German problem lay in the permanent division of

Germany. In the end, however, it was the Allies' need to resolve their own differences that created the two Germanies.

At a meeting in Tehran in November 1943, Britain, the United States, and the Soviet Union agreed to divide Germany into occupied zones. A second meeting at Yalta, in February 1945, addressed the imperative of disarming and denazifying Germany to the fullest extent. In the three Western zones, the allies proceeded to turn Germans into democrats, while in the Eastern the Soviets sought to make socialists of them. In all four zones the Germans were reluctant converts, the great majority of them hoping for a democratic-socialistic "third way" that would keep German lands united and accessible to all Germans.[2]

The Potsdam Conference implemented the Allied agreements in the summer of 1945. Meeting under the leadership of President Harry S. Truman and British Prime Minister Clement W. Attlee, the Allies adopted a pragmatic rule that had saved Germans after another pan-European crisis centuries earlier: the ruler of a land or, in this case, the commander of an Allied military zone, would govern that zone as he deemed best.

Among the divisive issues were reparations. The Soviets occupied the territorially largest but least populated and industrialized zone, moving the better endowed Western Allies, whose zones included the industrial Ruhr, to pledge them an additional 10 percent of their reparations. The needy Soviets dismantled far more German factories for transport and reassembly at home, suggesting that they had not intended to occupy Germany for long. The French also stripped their zone during the first four years of occupation. However, by 1948, the Western Allies, with France by then in agreement, remembered the aftermath of Versailles and chose a policy of recovery and reconstruction over one of punishment and pillage. Empowered by the Marshall Plan, a four-year strategic investment of $1.4 billion in rapid European recovery, West German unity and productivity ran impressively apace.[3]

With few true democrats existing in West Germany at war's end and equally scarce committed Communists in the East, the Allies in both Germanies had their work cut out for them. Viewing the Germans collectively as Nazis, the Western Allies initially denied existing antifascist groups a role in rebuilding their country. In doing so an opportunity to jump-start German democracy sooner and place it under native political leadership was arguably missed.[4] Also keeping Germans on the sidelines in the Western zones were zealous Allied efforts at denazification and reeducation. The Nazi-ferreting questionnaires of the Americans cited 136 mandatory reasons for excluding a German from postwar employment. For interrogated Germans four possible categories of guilt and only one of exoneration existed.[5] Such postwar scrutiny and tutelage, which continued in different forms during the Cold War, created red-tape nightmares for both the hapless and the guilty, leaving much repressed German resentment.[6]

The Soviets, by contrast, targeted German sociopolitical structures rather than individuals. In place of the old Nazi regime came a Marxist-Leninist collective, into which preexisting Social Democratic and Communist parties were funneled. Established in 1946, the new Socialist Union Party (SED) thenceforth became the only legal East German political party. Repressing individual freedom and entrepreneurship, the new Soviet-style command economy progressively undermined the political stability top-down control had won.

Despite initial screening, a sizable number of former Nazi Party members gained important positions in Germany's reconstruction. In many instances they had the better skills and experience, and in the larger scheme of things their employment was arguably more practical. During the strict Nazi years, many jobs and positions required a party affiliation, which forced untold numbers of Germans to become nominal Nazis not out of ideology but necessity. In the first months of reconstruction, Allied determination to identify and punish real Nazis created a conflict that still continues today—namely, how to balance the humane responsibility of remembering with the vital need to move on. The first, of course, weighed more heavily on the Allies, the second on the Germans, who had suffered the most devastating defeat of their history within short memory of another like it.[7] Here was a crossroads all too familiar to the Germans, whose inability to put 1918 and the bitter years of Weimar behind them had paved the way to 1933.

In May 1949, under Allied mandate, a German constituent assembly ratified a new provisional constitution for the Western zones known as the Basic Law. Assembly president Konrad Adenauer, a seventy-three-year-old former lord mayor of Cologne, Catholic and anti-Communist, signed the legislation into law three months before taking office as West Germany's first postwar chancellor. More in need of stability than of change, West Germany was ruled for two decades by the conservative Christian Democratic Union Party, an ecumenical postwar reconfiguration of the old Catholic Center Party. Between 1948 and 1952 the Marshall Plan allowed the tough and clever Adenauer to stand even taller, practicing what some unadmiringly called "Chancellor democracy."[8] The intention was to rebuild Western Europe's industry and labor into an economic wall against Eastern zone Communism, the first of two great walls to be thrown up between the two Germanies.

In December 1946 the British and Americans merged their zones ("Bizonia") and were joined two years later, in June 1948, by the French ("Trizonia"). In June 1948 Western currency reform, the brainchild of Economics minister Ludwig Erhard, gave the converging Western zones a second big push toward West German statehood. After minting a new German mark in the United States and introducing it into their zones on forty-eight hours' notice on June 20, the Western Allies proceeded to extend the new currency into the sectors of Berlin they occupied, which lay well inside the Russian zone. From there it found its way into the Soviet zone and East Berlin, where a separate currency, the East German mark, was introduced by the occupying Soviets the following week. The western action broke an understanding with the Soviets, and triggered a blockade of the major western roads into Berlin. Three months earlier, after discovering Allied plans to create a separate Western German state, the Soviets had resigned from the Allied Oversight Commission. Out of this confrontation, which saw Allied planes fly 277,000 sorties in less than eleven months to supply the 2.5 million people unprovisioned in the western sectors of Berlin, East and West Germany were born.[9]

MIRACLES AND REVERSALS

The great majority of Germans had hoped for a hybrid union of East and West. The new governments instead took their respective states in opposite political directions set by the occupying powers. The new regimes did, however, have this much in common: Unlike the Weimar Republic and the Third Reich, each became a highly predictable and productive state.

Adenauer's German counterpart, Walter Ulbricht, had spent the war years in the Soviet Union, whence he returned to eastern Germany as head of the Communist Party in 1945. By the end of that year, the large agricultural estates had been nationalized and the privileged Junker class abolished. During his twenty-two-year tenure as premier of the German Democratic Republic, from 1949 to 1971, Ulbricht nationalized East German finance and industry, converted the five separate eastern German states into party districts, and collectivized agriculture. On June 17, 1953, East Berliners revolted against the Soviet occupation, only to be brutally suppressed. After joining the Warsaw Pact (the East European military alliance) and Comecon (the East European economic union) in 1955, the new Stalinist state became the most important cog in the Soviet empire. In 1960 a new round of agricultural collectivization sparked new protests, quickening the flight to the West. By the time the Berlin Wall was built the following year, 1.65 million East Germans had moved to West Germany.[10] By 1968 the SED proclaimed its sovereign rule in a new constitution.

The Federal Republic mirrored the Western democracies with its competitive party politics, unabashed materialism, and ban on the Communist Party.[11] Between 1950 and 1980, the West German mark increased in value at an average annual rate of 8 percent, while the GDR counterpart rose at 3 percent—a very respectable growth rate given East Germany's more jarring transformation.[12] In addition to its economic success, the Federal Republic won its citizenry to democracy by achieving what the Frankfurt National Assembly could only blueprint and the Weimar Republic realize in intermittent stretches: an effective government and bankable security. The Basic Law contained new provisions designed to prevent the anarchy and fascism that destroyed the Weimar Republic. It denied seats in the Bundestag, Germany's Federal Parliament, to splinter parties with less than 5 percent of the vote, and recognized the durability of a vulnerable chancellor until parliament had agreed on a successor.[13] The Federal Republic thus became a more stable democracy, whose principles and goals did not overreach or scare anyone.

Undergirding the West's thirty years of industrial boom, from 1950 to 1980, was a policy of joint decision making between industry and labor. In addition to that consensus, German success owed much to German labor's ability to do more and better work in a thirty-five-hour week than many competitors in forty.[14] In East Germany a similar work ethic, both marshaled and repressed by collectivization, nationalization, and political conformity, set the pace of productivity within Comecon.

West Germany

While a new materialistic society dismayed some West Germans, the rising standard of living and freedom from risky, ideology-driven policies buoyed most. However, in the 1960s and 1970s, the economic miracle became the object of mounting left-liberal criticism, which also targeted the government's slowness to address the Nazi past in the schools and universities. Such criticism helped retire Kurt-Georg Kiesinger's three-party coalition—CDU/CSU (Christian Social Union) and SPD—and bring Willy Brandt and a new SPD/FDP (Free Democratic Party) coalition to power in 1969, the beginning of fourteen years of left-liberal rule. An outspoken, and hence endangered, socialist, Brandt spent the war years in Norway aiding Nazi resistance movements in- and outside of Germany. Prior to becoming chancellor, he had been the popular mayor of West Berlin and a scene-stealing foreign minister in Kiesinger's government.

Kiesinger, by contrast, had been a Nazi Party member throughout the 1930s and 1940s, working in the Foreign Ministry as a radio propagandist. Interned in 1945, he was declared innocent of any war crimes in 1947. That so seemingly odd a couple could create a coalition government was a true snapshot of postwar Germany in transition. When Brandt defeated Kiesinger in 1969, thirty-nine years had passed since the last SPD chancellor. Given Brandt's role in the resistance, it was poetically just that that chancellor, Hermann Müller, had led the last coalition to work in true partnership with a German government prior to the Nazi seizure of power.

Postwar Germans East and West lived in a society largely shorn of power elites, although the SED represented a very privileged group in the classless GDR. In the West only the remnants of an old aristocracy, a sizable segment of which had resisted Hitler, kept Germany's noble past alive in the public eye.[15] Rather than an ethnic-political union, or the old hierarchy of fixed estates and rankable classes, postwar Germans viewed themselves and their nation pragmatically, as a society of professions (*berufständische Gesellschaft*), citizens grouped around, and defined by, freely chosen productive labor.[16]

With the Berlin Wall incarcerating East Germans after 1961, meritocratic and egalitarian ideals asserted themselves in the West during the 1960s, particularly in the universities.[17] Between 1959 and 1988 university enrollment climbed almost eightfold, from two hundred thousand to 1.5 million, and grew especially rapidly during the chancellorships of Brandt (1969–74) and Helmut Schmidt (1974–83), who steadily expanded the opportunity for a college education.[18] This convergence of large numbers of students from diverse backgrounds on theoretically open and liberal universities still staffed by a very conservative professoriate—many professors at the time refused to answer questions in their lectures—was a sure recipe for generational conflict.

That, however, was only one reason why German universities became hotbeds of dissent in the late 1960s. The decade also saw the rapid growth of an autonomous youth culture across both Europe and the United States. Large numbers of idealistic youth, with their own money, music, sexual freedom, and unprecedented mass political power, found themselves no longer bound to, or necessarily destined for, the vocational and social worlds of their parents. In addition to many local "tyrants" begging attack, an "imperial" enemy also emerged on the international stage, giving disaffected youth everywhere a rallying cry: the American army in Vietnam with its napalm and B-52s. (When I left the University of Tübingen in the spring of 1968, I watched students spray painting "USA" as "U-[swastika]-A" on university buildings.)

In 1967 the stakes of the generational battle rose even higher after police shot to death a student protester during a state visit by the shah of Iran—an episode made all the more inflammatory after media mogul Axel Springer's newspapers blamed the death on the protesters. The following year "Red" Rudi Dutschke, an East German pacifist and Marxist turned West German student protest leader, was left a cripple by a right-wing assassin's bullet, further provoking youthful reaction. For a radical few those two acts of carnage transformed protest into terrorism. The most violent group active in the 1970s was the Red Army Faction (RAF), popularly known as the Baader-Meinhof gang in romanticized honor of pioneer terrorists Andreas Baader and Ulrike Meinhof—the former a professor's son, the latter a pastor's daughter, journalist, and mother of two—who happened also to be lovers. With other kindred groups, the RAF killed 28, wounded 93, took 162 hostage, and robbed thirty-five banks of 5.4 million marks before being neutralized.[19]

The late 1960s and 1970s also saw heightened conflict between parliamentary conservatives and liberals. Willy Brandt spent his political capital on normalizing relations with East Germany—*Ostpolitik*—diplomacy popular with the voters, who always wanted more contact with family and friends on the other side of the Wall. Brandt's political overtures to the East not only brought the two Germanies closer together, they elevated East Germany onto the European and international stage, leading to its membership in the United Nations and normalcy as a European state. To Brandt's critics his *Ostpolitik* was just another word for giving aid and comfort to the enemy, and they enjoyed a sweet vindication when one of his top aides was discovered to be an East German spy.[20]

Another major problem whose seeds were sown in the early 1960s also stemmed from the rapidity of postwar reconstruction, and not least that of the physical separation of the two Germanies epitomized by the Berlin Wall. The booming Western economy created many largely menial jobs undesirable to West Germans, and with the building of the Wall, the steady stream of cheap East German labor on which the West relied ceased to flow. In its place came foreign guest workers (*Gastarbeiter*) from the east and the south, mostly Turks and people of Mediterranean descent.

Those who came took full advantage of Germany's postwar generosity and emotional need to show kindness to strangers. Given pay, benefits, and human rights beyond those in their homelands, new immigrants arrived in ever-increasing numbers, and often with little desire ever to return to the unblessed life they had left behind. By 1990 the new work force had become a problem for a reuniting Germany. Some 4.8 million foreign workers and their ever-growing families, a third of them Muslim Turks, lived in Germany. For the most part they integrated themselves poorly into German society and culture, while successfully replicating their own on German soil.[21] In 2000, 30 percent of Frankfurt's population were Muslim Turks, who worshiped in the city's twenty-seven mosques.[22]

In German history the hyphenated German and the predatory foreigner have often merged into one, and they have done so again in the persons of these modern foreign workers. The workers coming in recent decades, however, cross German borders from the south and the east not as aggressors or invaders but as invited "guests" to help maintain the German economy and way of life—hence, more as federates than as aliens. Yet, with the passage of time, their permanence, proliferation, and nonassimilation have also burdened the economy and threatened German unity and cultural identity. With them have also come hundreds of thousands of economically motivated asylum seekers (*Asylanten*), who take advantage of postwar Germany's penitential need to be a refuge for the politically persecuted of the world. By German law any foreigner, simply by stepping on German soil and claiming to be in flight from tyranny, received an asylum hearing at state expense, including room and board for the duration of the process. Among other postwar immigrants invited to Germany after the dissolution of the Soviet Union were Eastern Jews, who faced renewed persecution there, and nearly two million ethnic Germans.

The Blood Law of 1913 (aka the Nationality Act) had based German citizenship on lineage rather than land of birth. The Aliens Act of 1990 changed that by giving German-born residents with fifteen years of residency, and their children born on German soil, the right to petition for naturalization—a tough scrutiny that only 5 percent of applicants passed.[23] As in the United States and other fat lands, roughly two-thirds of those denied permanent residency became illegal aliens, disappearing into established foreign-worker communities.

By the new law implemented on January 1, 2000, any child born in Germany is today legally a German citizen, provided that one parent has been a legal resident for eight consecutive years and has held a valid resident permit for at least three.[24] However, the new law discourages dual citizenship. Foreign-born German citizens must choose one or the other nationality by age twenty-three. In cases where the surrender of non-German citizenship may be impossible or inadvisable, dual citizenship can be petitioned up to age twenty-one. The new citizenship law thus prioritizes German acculturation in an apparent effort to minimize large numbers of "hyphenated" German citizens. Assuming Germans can find the will to embrace larger numbers of such citizens, their ability to pay for them and to maintain a unified German culture in the process remains a large, unanswered question.

East Germany

In the 1950s West Germany's political stability and economic success exceeded the expectations of both the Allies and the Germans. During the 1960s and 1970s, student protest and terrorism, amid unprecedented foreign immigration, threatened the loss of that unity, freedom, and prosperity. Such foreboding played a sizable role in making Helmut Kohl's sixteen-year conservative rule the longest of any German chancellor since Bismarck.

Egalitarian East Germany threw up a more protective shell from the start by installing single-party rule in 1946. That rule steadily tightened through the 1950s and 1960s with the dissolution of East Germany's five separate states, its membership in the Warsaw Pact and Comecon, the building of the Wall, and a hard-line, Soviet-oriented constitution that magnified the German Democratic Republic's separate nation status vis-à-vis the West.[25] Although no Nazi dictatorship, the GDR was a police state from the start, with its own security forces—the so-called *Stasi* (STAatsSIcherheitspolizei)—who were backed up by Soviet soldiers. After 1960 East Germans could not travel freely to the West, thenceforth bound to their fatherland not only by patriotism and free choice but also by brick walls and bullets—desperate measures taken by a Communist state fearful of losing its vital work force and raison d'être to the West.[26]

In the 1970s, after two and half decades of totalitarian rule, the GDR stepped up its dialogue with the West. Its most liberal action during the decade, however, was one the Communist Party came to regret. In 1978 the SED recognized the independence of the Protestant Church, allowing it to become a refuge for the forces of protest and reform, thereby indirectly taking the first steps toward unification with the West.[27]

Contrary to appearances the state's recognition of the Church did not amount to appeasement or cooptation on the part of either side, but was a step taken from deep within German history, with both sides venturing and gaining. Like many East German intellectuals and writers, the Protestant clergy also improved the success of their own mission by cooperating with the state.[28] In 1971 East German bishop Albrecht Schönherr, speaking for the League of Protestant Churches, described the East German church, already then indispensible to the operation of the state's welfare system, as ready to "work within rather than 'against' or 'alongside' socialism."[29] The accord thus reached with the state fulfilled mutually self-interested religious and political goals. Rather than signifying ideological pluralism within the SED, the agreement attested the overriding force of historical cooperation between German Church and state dating back to the Middle Ages. In an effort to facilitate a spiritual mission in even direr need of political support, Luther, centuries earlier, had declared Saxon rule and the Christian cure of souls to be independently tasked yet similarly destined[30]—a latter-day version of which Bishop Schönherr appears to have articulated in 1971.

Church-state cooperation was not the only part of the German past East Germans embraced to advantage. In the late 1970s historical Saxon and Prussian strongmen—Luther, Frederick the Great, and Bismarck—had wide popularity.[31] Within their own history East Germans found resources to fashion a state of their own beyond Soviet and American models. Both Germanies thought the latter to be flawed, the Soviet by its suppression of individual freedom and collectivism, the American by its heightened individualism, materialism, and social divisions. The classic German past also offered an alternative to the political universalism then being served up to a new generation in the West by left-liberal intellectuals, who encouraged Germans to think of themselves in European and global terms and not as citizens of a particular nation-state. This may have been the development West German president Richard von Weizsäcker had in mind when he credited East Germans with a "more stable, serious, and truthful consciousness of German history," notwithstanding Communist Party lapses into "ideologization."[32]

While SED officials exploited the past to shore up a failing political system, many East Germans, counting lost freedoms and taking every opportunity to flee to the West, believed relevant answers to individual and national identity loomed large there. For those in flight, the past told a story of German men and women, who, from age to age, had embodied their nation's will in forceful action. In this, the Saxons of the second half of the twentieth century had something in common with those of the first half of the sixteenth. Then, too, a national reform movement explored a largely unknown German past in search of telling examples and native counsel, around which church and state might realign their respective endeavors.

The East Germans' more positive reading of their history contrasted sharply with that of prominent West German intellectuals, who read the past as merely prelude to latter-day horrors—particularly in the ages of strong rulers. Believing the past to be tainted and nowhere magisterial, not a few postwar German historians, philosophers, and writers dismissed its polities, societies, and culture much as the sages of the nineteenth century had. The most critical heard the pleas of postwar chancellors for normalcy as the siren calls of Bismarck's Reich and Kaiser William II's Germany.[33]

GERMAN UNIFICATION, 1990

The union of the two Germanies and the return of self-exiled Germans from foreign lands made German identity an even more pressing matter. Throughout twenty-eight years of separation, divided families had kept reunion hopes alive. Straws, fanned by the churches, began blowing steadily East to West during the 1980s. In both lands evangelical and Catholic churches had continued to preach an appealing gospel of spiritual freedom and equality beyond the secular confines of Marxist-Leninism and capitalism. That gospel rang true with both Eastern communal and Western democratic ideals. At the same time Mikhail Gorbachev pressed his program of *glasnost*, the freedom to question, and *perestroika*, the right to reform, on the Soviet bloc. After East German leader Erich Honecker's agreement in 1987 to allow his citizens to make brief visits to the west without the usual bureaucratic harassment, the push West became unstoppable.

As the Cold War created the division of Germany, its conclusion made possible its repair.[34] Between the soaring expense of the arms' race and the failure of showcase Communist states, the Soviets had no option but détente. Having arguably pursued a collectivist society beyond common sense and human ability, eastern-bloc states became demoralized dictatorships, their citizens alienated from both their labor and their governments.

The first crack in the Iron Curtain came in 1989 when newly democratic Hungary, left to its own devices by the Soviet Union, opened its border to Austria. Soon the Czech border was porous as well. In East Germany smaller curtains began falling, despite the integrity of the Berlin Wall. Rediscovering itself, the SPD challenged the SED, and a new intellectual lobby, the New Forum, made a compelling case for political change. Under the banner "We Are the People," revolutionary protests and marches, particularly those in Leipzig in the summer of 1989, became too numerous and persistent to be crushed by the state. Influential citizens—among them Kurt Masur, then music director of the Leipzig Gewandhaus Orchestra—successfully counseled détente rather than tanks. With a push from Gorbachev, Honecker resigned on October 1, eventually to become an exile in Chile. In the first week of November, the new government of Egon Krenz recognized the right of its citizens to travel at will to West Germany and even promised them a democratic election. On November 9, the Berlin Wall was breached, with thousands going back and forth on that day, to be followed the next weekend by a throng of 4 million.[35] By New Year's the GDR was crumbling, and Krenz's West German counterpart took notice. While events were moving beyond everyone's expectations, Helmut Kohl positioned himself to put the two Germanies back together.

The Germans called his election in 1982 the *Machtwechsel*, or "change of power"—namely, from the fourteen-year liberal SPD/FPD rule of Brandt and Schmidt to the sixteen-year conservative CDU/CSU rule of Kohl, with center-liberal FDP help. Kohl stuck to his campaign promises of normality and stability. Once breaking events made the unification of the two Germanies a viable option, he stepped under the yoke and never looked back, having correctly read the minds of the majority of Germans, who wanted their country united immediately. Promising East Germans verdant landscapes, and assuring West Germans that it could be done with little pain—neither of which proved true—Kohl threw his full weight behind "unification now."[36]

Within months of the fall of the Berlin Wall, Kohl won the March 1990 election on the promise of immediate German unification, the SPD, to its electoral peril, having campaigned on caution. Kohl and his CDU counterpart in the East, Lothar de Maziere, began reunion talks almost immediately. The *Machtwechsel* was succeeded by *die Wende*, "the turn," as the two Germanies now united on their own without the hovering, dictating allies. Kohl sweetened the prospects for East Germans by offering a one-to-one currency exchange on the first four thousand marks of wages and pensions (the rate thereafter being adjusted according to age and wealth).

While a boon to East German pocketbooks and unification, that bit of economic parity threw East German industries into an impossible competition with their West German counterparts.[37]

Germanness

Since Roman times Germans have struggled to define themselves as a people. Today, when meeting a foreigner, the citizens of no other European land are more likely to know, or quickly to speak, the foreigner's language—or to do so as well as the Germans. One may see in such behavior only the will to power. More likely it is the reflex of a people hard pressed throughout their history to demonstrate their abilities and worthiness to powerful, distrusting, and dangerous neighbors.

Between the fall of Rome and the creation of the Frankish and Saxon empires, culturally challenged Germans embraced the institutions, languages, laws, and customs of the superior Greco-Roman and Judeo-Christian worlds they served and conquered.[38] Germans have ever since been careful students of other people, today going more often to foreign lands when they vacation than the citizens of any other nation.[39] From the beginning geography and history made centralized German lands crossroads of international trade and culture, and thus also classrooms with many nonnative teachers. During and after the Thirty Years' War and then, again, with Napoleon, Germans demonstrated their ability to embrace and rework foreign models. In both cases the scope of foreign conquest and occupation gave them reason to doubt their continued existence, politically and culturally, as a people. During both those wars and into reconstruction, large numbers of defeated Germans lived on native lands reconfigured by foreigners. Making the most of their surroundings became the German way of survival and self-discovery.

This story is particularly well told in the history of German music, where borrowing Germans exceeded their foreign masters. Beginning with the hymns of the Reformation, which set a new theology to both old religious and new popular music, Germans pioneered inclusive musical arts.[40] During the baroque period, master German composers improved on other peoples' signature tunes and songs. Bach and Handel and their Austrian counterparts, Haydn and Mozart, pirated Italian operas—Bach finding additional models among the French masters, while Handel adapted the oratorios of his adopted England, a few of which celebrated the ancient Hebrews.[41]

Such inquiry into the culture of others was not confined to the musical arts. In their studies of early German language and folklore, Jakob and Wilhelm Grimm compared many non-German examples. Jakob had been a student of Friedrich Karl von Savigny, perhaps the age's greatest legal scholar, who sought to fathom German culture through the study of law codes. With similar motivation the Grimms probed the international folk literature, writing to Sir Walter Scott and his counterparts in Ireland, England, Norway, Denmark, Czechoslovakia, Serbia, and Russia.[42] In the aftermath of the French occupation, many Germans feared that they were witnessing the end of their culture, for which reason they took reassurance and inspiration from the studies of Savigny and the Grimms.[43]

In the nineteenth century Richard Wagner, director of the Dresden Opera House at thirty and a fervent supporter of the German Revolution of 1848–49, wore the latter's failure proudly on his baton. Joining the romantic reaction in the wake of democracy's defeat, he looked inward for the heights politics had been unable to reach. In doing so he reflected more powerfully than any other nineteenth-century musician the new critical culture pointing the way to the twentieth. On the one hand he feared "foreign intellectual products," both musical and non, believing that they would corrupt the purer German. Yet this most *völkisch* of German composers strove to render foreign talent universal.

At thirty-seven, he pseudonymously wrote a minor dissertation ridiculing "Jewishness in Music," the impact of which, upon the discovery of his authorship, brought him public criticism and even ostracism.[44] From it he apparently learned a small lesson. Thirty-two years later, he invited German Jewish maestro Hermann Levi to conduct the first performance of *Parsifal* in 1882, giving musical talent a belated and, unfortunately, exceptional priority over new-age anti-Semitism.[45]

Unknowingly preparing the way for the darker side of the 1930s, nineteenth-century German musicologists doggedly pursued the search for "Germanness" in antiquity by attempting to document a race-specific "Nordic musical feeling." That search focused on the ancient Alemanni tribe and the widespread popularity of the lyre (*lur*) among the Germanic tribes generally, an instrument that suggested polyphony, which implied musical ingenuity. That conclusion, however, was as erroneous as popular racial profiling was perilous. The classic style of German music appears rather to have derived from Bohemian roots, not precise, identifiable German ones.[46]

In the 1860s the quest for German unity intensified speculation on German identity. Among the nets then being cast, none was larger or retrieved a more various catch than that of the widely traveled nineteenth-century ethnographer, Bogumil Goltz. A self-taught student of world cultures, Goltz wrote on such wide-ranging subjects as the natural history of women, the genius of Shakespeare, German pubs, and Egyptian small towns. These studies provided context and contrast for his exploration of the traits of Germans, which he found to exist both outside German lands and beyond the nineteenth century.[47] In casting about for models of the "universal people," which he believed Germans to be, he was not alone. Between the seventeenth and nineteenth centuries, German scholars were among, if not *the*, world experts on ancient Greece and Rome. And they devoted even greater study to contemporary French, English, and American societies.[48]

Writing in the decade of the *Kulturkampf* and national unity, Goltz extrapolated German identity from Germany's historical role as the bearer of Greco-Roman and Judeo-Christian cultures to

Europe. And by connecting the dots that led beyond Europe, he discovered a cosmopolitan people (*Weltbürgerlichkeit*), who knew both too much and too little about themselves:

> As man stands above all other creatures, the German is privileged within the human race, for he unites in himself the characteristic properties, talents, and virtues of all races and nations. . . . We are . . . a cosmopolitan, world-historical people . . . and for that reason cannot be chauvinistically herded and driven like dumb animals. . . . We are the people in whom all other people and races of the earth may find their roots and treetops.
>
> We are as hard-working, diligent, and skillful as the Chinese and possess . . . their reverence for parents, old people . . . and princes, [also] their respect for learning and the ways of the past. . . .
>
> In our scholarship and other endeavors, we exhibit a Jewish-Talmudic subtlety, organizational skill, toughness . . . and indestructability, [also] Jewish slander, calumny, envy, and quarrelsomeness in our private life, yet without prejudicing Jewish sociability, warmth, sympathy, and tender family feeling. . . .
>
> We are disposed both to the separatist-temporal caste-spirit [of India and] to its polar extreme, the formless, Arabic, fairy-tale fantasy and brooding myth-theosophy of the ancient Indians. . . .
>
> We await the reconciliation of dynastic autocracy and democracy, backwardness and forwardness, pedantry and discovery, refinement and the primordial brew, immanence and transcendence, the centrifugal and the centripetal, [old] authority and [new] ideas, socialism and individualism. . . .
>
> If there is one people who from the [early European] migrations until today have mastered and preserved a world culture in all circumstances, it is the Germans. Roman history flows in German veins, because Germans assimilated Roman law and customs, and thereafter were raised to new powers by Christianity, which allowed the German people to become a new reality. . . .[49]
>
> [Thus] the German, who cannot unify his own land politically, and has so much difficulty grasping the concepts of a nation-state

> and a balance of power with other states, that same German helps establish states and cities in faraway parts of the world. . . . And he does so because he identifies so easily with the characteristics of every other people, while not giving up his own.[50]

In a decade when brainstorming a new German state was in vogue, Goltz has been credited with creating the "longest list of improbable models."[51] The thrust of his argument, however, was to derive German identity from a historical amalgam of Judeo-Christian, Greco-Roman, and ancient-medieval Germanic cultures, thus putting Germans at the center of European and colonized world cultures. Classic German dualism appears in juxtapositions of German desires and the irony of a people who presume to speak for every other, yet cannot create a lasting political union of their own.

The author's constructed German is as presumptuous as he is preeminent, yet this "Everygerman" was no Aryan superman. In a decade when anti-Judaism, racial profiling, Social Darwinism, and philosophical nihilism combined to make anti-Semitism a proper noun, the strengths and failings of no other people were more at the center of Goltz's composite German than those of the Jews. By contrast the mythic superman who materialized at the far end of left-wing Hegelian criticism[52] looked neither backward nor sideways, but only forward to a future alone, choosing not to study man as he had been or to join him as he is, but to leave him completely behind.

A German Democracy

Given the horrors of the twentieth century, few today readily think of Germans as a mirror of humanity. For many, Germany remains a land of late, perhaps permanently arrested, political and moral development—not an exemplary world people, but a special breed the world must always worry about. The mere disagreement with American foreign policy in Iraq recently brought damning American doubts and suspicions of Germans rushing to the surface, which the Germans repaid in kind. Sympathetic historians and famous Germans themselves have long made a case for the backward German, whose time in the sun has not yet come. From 1076, when the emperor Henry IV watched the German princes and the Roman Church divide his kingdom, to the 1930s and '40s, when National Socialism left Germany in ruins, the long history of Germany has seemed, in the words of Geoffrey Barraclough, "a story of development cut short, of incompleteness and retardation."[53]

Against the euphoria that greeted the fall of the Wall and the unification of the two Germanies, previous attempts at creating a unified and free Germany seem more prophetic than rudimentary. Yet what the Federal Republic, with hindsight, calls "milestones of [German] democracy,"[54] many historians view ambivalently, as they also do Germany's future prospects. Looking back from 1989–90, the Frankfurt National Assembly of 1848–49 appears to have been searching for a polity more congenial to elite revolutionaries than to a divided land recovering from French occupation and a reactionary, post-emancipation restoration. When, in 1871, Germans achieved national unity for the first time, it was a Prussian solution, with Germany's most powerful state muscling the weaker ones into line. In 1918–19, the Weimar Republic gave Germans a true democracy, yet its constitution was fatally flawed and its leaders unable to reassure a defeated and strapped nation that it had a viable future.[55]

The postwar Basic Law also invoked these earlier precedents of German democracy. Imposed on Germans by allied military governors in 1945, Germans, again under Allied patronage, provisionally ratified it in 1949. The Allies dictated democracy to the Germans in the Western zones much as the Soviets did Communism in the Eastern. A true, native German constitution had to await the unification of the two Germanies in 1990, a goal the Basic Law had pledged West Germany would pursue.[56] Fifty-two years of sequential National Socialist and East German dictatorship preceded that epochal event. Once reunited and free, the German people put in policy, at their own initiative, a democratic government of, by, and for themselves. With that new, united government, Germany became one of the world's youngest democracies.

In nation-building years the German democratic experiment is a work in progress, and therein lies the difficulty for Germany's friends and enemies. Unification was a mighty revival of previously defeated liberal nationalism. So far there have been no ominous signs of a pan-Germanic utopianism likely to revive a dark German past. Despite close elections and disagreements with close allies, Germans have turned inward without breaking apart or lashing out. Present-day industrial and economic policies give every appearance of conforming to democratic imperatives.[57] From a long historical view, post-1990 Germany appears on the verge of securing what Geoffrey Barraclough called the only lasting solution to its political problems: "a limited democratic Germany within historic boundaries."[58]

Since reunification, it has been easy to forget that earlier German attempts at liberal democracy not only failed, but did so miserably. While the new German polity gives every hope of resolving Germany's history of political division and strong-man rule, it has been a long time coming and, until recently, prompted mostly from without. As the abiding old Germany and the brash new nation continue to thrash things out, one can only speculate on the outcome. If the long history of Germany is any guide, it is likely to be a tighter democracy by comparison with that of today. Over the long sweep of their history, Germans have prized authority and order as much as they have freedom and equality, convinced that the best polity requires and protects both.

The ability to act collectively—national unity—and the right to act individually—political representation—have been the twin concerns of Germans since at least the sixteenth century, the first demanding self-sacrifice and conformity, the second permitting self-assertion and dissent. A historically informed, mature German polity will likely be more limiting of freedom than are the egalitarian democracies of France and the United States, which have arguably forgotten how to discipline freedom and consequently lost control of the individual. In the evolution of Rousseau's and Robespierre's France, and Jefferson's and Emerson's America, individual freedom appears to have become a right of self-absorbtion, threatening the citizen's responsibility to the public sphere and the believer's obligation to God. The Germans do not believe that true freedom must be untidy, or that a free people have the right to run amok. The new German democracy will likely tolerate more radical, but shorter-lived, dissent and resistance to the state. To the extent that the waning of authority and order has become more problematic to the world's older democracies than the expansion of freedom and equality, the new German democracy may offer a solution for liberal democracy's modern ills.

In light of German history, one must also ask whether polity alone has been, or can be, a German cure-all. That question is pushed to the fore by the largely successful revolt of the moderns against the ancients during Germany's nineteenth-century sociocultural wars. While a new imperial Germany was constricting a struggling democratic one, a powerful, deconstructive left-liberal intellectual culture was undermining the German Enlightenment, which, unlike the French, had endeavored to fold hard-won moral and religious lessons from the past into modernity. Contemptuous of the beliefs of the old Germany, especially those informed by Judeo-Christian teachings, the spokesmen for that culture proclaimed a new age in which the individual would renovate the world, free of any tutelage from the past.

The fires of twentieth-century liberation movements have since chastened the remnants of nineteenth-century imperial government, racism, and Social Darwinism, and a powerful egalitarian ethos now thrives throughout much of the West. However, the radical individualism, atheism, elitism, and utopianism of that century's intellectual and cultural revolt have also survived into the twenty-first. The ambitions of that revolution, still strong today, are as great a threat to a sustainable democracy as any credible revival of fascism.[59] Against both, the best defenses are old and proven: facts and evidence, skepticism and common sense, sobriety and honesty, humility and strength.

Fear of Germans and German Fears

With German reunification on the horizon, the March 26, 1990, issue of *Time* magazine asked in its cover story: "Should the World be Worried?" Some 61 million West Germans, Europe's largest state, were uniting with 17 million East Germans, to which untold numbers of Germans scattered around the world would gradually be added. Despite their political and cultural differences and the staggering costs, most commentators at the time envisioned the rapid emergence of a political and economic juggernaut. Yet, with the exceptions of Israel and Poland, opinion polls indicated overwhelming approval of unification, even in the Soviet Union, where the war had taken an estimated 26 million lives.

To West Germany's credit, *Time* noted the failure of right-wing parties since the war to gain the 5 percent needed to be seated in the Bundestag. Helmut Kohl pointedly remarked that the majority of Germans living in 1990 had not been born during the war years and could not be blamed for them. Much like Chancellor Gerhard Schröder, he pointed out to those sitting in judgment Germany's positive actions since the war, not least of which has been the $33 billion then paid in reparations to Israelis and other Jews—a sum that had nearly doubled by the year 2000 and is still climbing.[60]

Despite the euphoria of 1989–90, postunification Germany remains a troubled and divided land. The citizens of the Federal Republic share a twentieth-century legacy that will never be put completely out of mind, certainly not along the lines of earlier East German rationalizations. Declaring Nazism a variant of capitalism, of which its polity was free, the GDR disassociated itself completely from the crimes of the Third Reich, on which grounds it paid no reparations to Israel after the war and offered only an apology upon reunification.[61]

Beyond the spiritual and economic burdens of war and the Holocaust, the two sides brought almost three decades of oppositional politics and cultures into their union, heavy baggage for a remarriage. After the Berlin Wall was gone, the so-called wall in the head remained.[62] Many East Germans missed the security of the all-provident GDR, especially in jobs, while the West Germans resented the high cost of salvaging the old Stasi state and resettling so many ethnic Germans in their lands. In 1989, 370,000 East Germans moved to the FDR; between 1990 and 1992, more than 1 million settled there. By contrast West Germans moved eastward in a trickle, yet one that had the force of rapids, as not a few were there to reclaim property confiscated by the Soviet regime after the war, or to convert state industries to the Western market economy. This was often viewed by the East Germans as more unwelcome, post-unification pillage.[63]

As the excitement of unification diminished, each side found reasons to be unhappy with the other. In the eyes of West Germans, the repressive East German Soviet state, while taking no responsibility for National Socialism, had far greater political continuity with it than the democratic West. Given their postwar advances, West Germans who came to instruct their fellow Germans in political and economic freedom brought with them an air of moral superiority. The East Germans called them "Besserwessis," a play on "*Besserwissers*," or know-it-alls.[64] For their part, East Germans, believed themselves to be the truer antifascists, and took pride in their German heritage with an ease many West Germans could not. Today, left-liberal gadflies urge both sides to transcend their national identities and lead historically anonymous and politically neutral lives as Europeans and citizens of the world.

During the 1950s and 1960s, liberal-left German academics and public intellectuals continued the earlier denazification and reeducation efforts by subjecting German history and society to a radical critique. The children of Feuerbach, Marx, and Nietzsche, these native critics inquired not after the classic German past but after men and women capable of making the freshest of starts. The goal was less to recover and repair a fallen fatherland than to create a new German state powerful in penance and prostrate before the world. In narrowly construing the German past as protofascist and incapable of enlightening a modern world, an attempt was rather made to bury it.

Many of the harshest critics had grown up during the war years, some having been in the Hitler Youth, while others served briefly in the Wehrmacht. All believed they lived in a land with a "democratic deficit"[65] and felt duty bound to confront their parents with war crimes and the abnormalities of German history. Prominent among the new critics were philosopher and social theorist Jürgen Habermas and writer and political activist Günter Grass. Unlike other prominent left, liberal figures who now serve the German government in peace and in war—for example, Chancellor Gerhard Schröder, a former Marxist, Foreign Minister Joschka Fischer, a former student protest leader and long time Green Party member, and Interior Minister Otto Schily, cofounder with Petra Kelly of the Green Party and the defense attorney for the leaders of the Baader-Meinhof gang—Habermas and Grass maintained their youthful idealism and outside criticism of the state into their seventies.[66]

As the leading intellectual of the Marxist Frankfurt School, Habermas espoused a philosophy of "constitutional patriotism" requiring absolute loyalty to a transcendental political ideal that always trumps realpolitik.[67] Those possessing and exercising such principled knowledge are the state's truest patriots and properly judge its actions on behalf of and for the good of all. Much as with Lutheran preachers in the sixteenth century, only less compromisingly, the task of these modern critics has been to arouse the public whenever rulers transgress a once divine, but now strictly citizens', mandate to rule. Here was a new breed of hyphenated Germans—not those beholden to another community, nation, or ruler beyond the German state, but self-appointed, native citizen monitors with a prior allegiance to a supreme moral imperative.

Grass wrote speeches for Willy Brandt in the early 1970s and, like him, became a Nobel laureate—in 1999, for a body of work begun forty years earlier with *The Tin Drum*, a ferocious exposé of the Nazi mind. Grass also opposed German reunification as a new *Anschluss*, believing that a reunited Germany would soon devour Europe as it had done after annexing Austria in March 1938. As penance for its war crimes, Grass wanted Germany to forgo the normal ambitions of statehood: power, security, and wealth. The good Germany would remain a divided, decentralized, apolitical state, with the dimmer East playing the "contrapunctal suffering nation" to the brighter, hedonistic West.[68]

What Grass proposed was historical Germany's worst nightmare. Being an internally divided and externally resented people had been the burden of German history. To have saddled postwar Germans with such a fate, both as a matter of principle and as far as the eye could see, was the most dangerous course Germany could have taken, both for itself and the peace of the world. As with the earlier conservative turn of the Adenauer government, Social Democratic wavering on German unification helped make Helmut Kohl Germany's longest ruling chancellor since Bismarck. In a more recent reaction to the peril of Grass's utopianism, Marcel Reich-Ranicki, critic and literary editor of the *Frankfurter Allgemeine*, appeared on the cover of the German weekly *Der Spiegel* in 1995 literally shredding Grass's latest version of it—a history-roaming novel set in postunification Berlin.[69]

Because Germany's strength is so great and its cooperation vital to Europe and the world, a retreating, self-doubting Germany is a worst-case scenario.[70] To date neither the spiraling costs of reunification and immigration nor the durability of "the wall in the head" have stampeded Germans. Far from shrinking from new responsibilities in Europe and the world, the governments of chancellors Kohl and Schröder have embraced them at the highest European and international levels.[71] That Schröder refused to rubber-stamp American foreign policy in Iraq was no reneging on such commitments, much less any dark, new *Sonderweg* ("special path"), as American and German critics were quick to allege. Even if politically expedient, or misguided, that contrarian stance was a proper action for a normal nation, and supported by a solid majority of Germans mindful of their own historical experience.[72]

Where, then, does the danger lie for, and from, the Germans? The present-day German is five persons in one, three of whom remain ineradicably German, while the other two are comparatively new experiments. Each has developed chronologically from the other, and each transcends the other in scope, if not in attachment and loyalty. One is the citizen of a village or a town, the most basic German self. Running close behind is the German who is a citizen of one of Germany's sixteen states. Since 1871 every German has also been a citizen of a united German nation, governed by an elected, transregional parliament. More recently, Germans have become part of a transnational European Union beyond their native urban, state, and national identities. Finally Germans are today global persons, ubiquitous by virtue of international trade, immigration, and communications.

For all the power and attraction of the new European and global personae, they pose no threat to the native German. That truism popped up memorably in an interview with German filmmaker Roland Emmerich, who became known to his countrymen as the "king of Hollywood" after directing the American box-office hit *Independence Day*. Working back and forth between high-tech studios in Los Angeles and Ludwigsburg, he confessed frequent longings for nothing so much as his mother's Swabian *Maultauschen*, literally "mouth pockets," stuffed pasta that resembles ravioli.[73]

In a needed effort to reassure a fearful world of German power, Helmut Kohl declared Germany's first identity to be European and global. Germany, however, possesses an irradicable history and destiny as a nation-state, which must be embraced and asserted in both glory and shame, if it is to become a normal nation. Attempts to cloak national identity in European and global ones threatens to hyphenate Germans and raise again the specter of predators within—a problem as old as the Germanic tribes and one the Schröder government appears to have taken more seriously than Kohl's.[74]

Europe and the world have both realistic and unrealistic fears of Germans. Foremost among the former is Germany's potential to disrupt important segments of their economies. Between 1998 and 2000 major German companies bought major foreign ones—Volkswagen acquiring Rolls-Royce Motor Cars, Deutsche Bank Bankers Trust of New York, Daimler-Benz the Chrysler Corporation, and Mannesmann, cellular telephone manufacturers in Britain and Italy. At the same time the Germans threatened to take over the London Stock Exchange.[75]

More worrisome has been Germany's ability to dominate the European Union. Chancellor Schröder's 2001 plan to increase EU centralization on the German federal model, which would have strengthened both the parliament's authority over member states and the latter's rights, brought excited flips from the British and indignant croaks from the French. Because Germany is the EU's most populous and richest member and pays a disproportionate share of its bills, the proposal gave rise to fears of even greater German influence.[76]

Underlying such fears has been a suspicion that Schröder's government is not as Eurocentric or global as Kohl promised the world Germany would be. Concurrent with his proposals to revamp the EU, Schröder has insisted on the world's recognition of Germany as a normal nation-state. By the latter he means one that may freely pursue its national interests in proportion to its strength, free to be selfish and to err—a delicate if not taboo subject for Kohl, who had to prepare a skeptical world for German unification. Taken together Schröder's initiatives suggest a new German patriotism determined not to leave Germany mired in a crippling twentieth-century past.[77]

Beyond realistic fears of German economic and political power within Europe is the arguably unrealistic fear that Germans are congenital anti-Semites and recidivist Nazis, who require the world's constant scrutiny and vigilance. Even when Germans argue among themselves, the issue of the good German is quick to surface. Looking backward and forward from Germany's provocative role in the years leading up to World War I, twentieth-century historians tied imperial Germany closely to the Third Reich. This has more recently seemed an unfair assessment of what had been a complex, if far from glorious, imperial Germany. Likewise historian Ernst Nolte ignited a bitter "historians' quarrel" in the 1980s by placing National Socialism and the Holocaust within a larger, generic twentieth-century pattern of fascism and genocide, suggesting that the German example was different only in scale. From Jürgen Habermas to the editorial page of the *New York Times*, the uniqueness of Nazi criminality was restated, and Nolte condemned for "whitewashing" the Nazis.[78]

The skittishness over resurgent neo-Nazism was also demonstrated in February 2000, when the conservative Austrian Freedom Party, having won 27 percent of the vote, the most yet for a West European postwar rightist party, took its seats in the Austrian government. European and world reaction was immediate. For the first time in its history, the European Union imposed sanctions on one of its fifteen member states, and the *New York Times* printed three major cautionary pieces on the event within a five-month period.

The story became large because a man named Jörg Haider had led the Freedom Party to victory. The son of prominent Nazi parents from the same region as Hitler, Haider gained fame and infamy by refusing to make blanket condemnations of either Germany's or Austria's wartime pasts. Haider also insisted that good Germans had served not only in the Wehrmacht but even in the Waffen SS. A handsome globetrotter who burnished his image in California and at the Harvard Business School, Haider attacked the growing influx of foreign workers in Austria and opposed Austrian payment of reparations to Israel, a position that won him the support of large numbers of blue-collar workers and youth.[79] Critics who rebutted him with accusations of neo-Nazism, a crime in Austria, found themselves at the losing end of lawsuits. With 80 percent of Austrians opposing the EU's sanctions, and smaller member states also protesting the heavy hand of Big Brother, the EU lifted its sanctions on Austria after seven months.[80]

Despite the hand-wringing at the time, the main lesson of the Haider affair may be neither carte blanche neo-Nazism in the larger German world nor moral cowardice on the part of the European Union. It may rather be the unwillingness at the time of Austria and other European states to subject their national politics to the new Brussels collective, a sentiment both predictable from history and compatible with evolving democracies.

In the same summer of 2000, as the EU debated lifting sanctions on Austria, Chancellor Schröder reacted to a pathetically small but highly disturbing outbreak of neo-Nazi violence in eastern Germany. Touring towns with large numbers of foreign workers and successful far-right parties, he tried to remind their citizens who true Germans were. In Eggesin and Wolfen-Nord, he told audiences to "take stronger grasp of their destiny . . . and stick up for the weak, the old, and the foreign." His government subsequently demonstrated its determination to end skinhead violence by offering generous incentive packages to members willing to leave the gangs: up to $45,000 per individual, including cash, a new name and job, relocation, and counseling.[81]

Since unification of the two Germanies, the German government has conducted its affairs with every appearance of good faith and endeavored to make a larger European identity alter ego to the German. Despite repeated threats on the life of Germany's finance minister, the mighty and beloved mark gave way to the euro.[82] Although Germans hold the lion's share of power within the EU today, the Federal Republic's actions can leave little doubt that German intent is to be an active partner within, not a commanding power over it.[83] Germany also continues to pay reparations to Israel on what has been called "penance on a vast scale."[84] During Willy Brandt's visit to the Warsaw ghetto memorial, and, more recently, Schröder's to the new Berlin Jewish Museum, the German government literally fell to its knees in setting a national example of compassion. And former federal president Richard von Weizsäcker has urged postwar generations to accept collective responsibility for the Holocaust and continue to remember.[85]

Present-day Germans also have realistic and unrealistic fears of the world around them, which they address in signature fashion. In a cover picture worth a thousand words, the German magazine, *Wirtschaft Woche*, Business Weekly, re-created the Normandy invasion on its November 22, 1999 cover, depicting foreign businessmen and women charging ashore under the headline: INVASION! ATTACK ON THE CONSENSUS SOCIETY. There a new German predator, the global economy, threatened to divide and conquer the fabled integrated network of government, banks, industry, and labor that has sustained modern Germany.

The editors had two recent examples in mind. The first was the economic collapse and forced government rescue of Germany's leading construction company, 150-year-old Philip Holzmann A.G. The second was a pending hostile bid by Britain's Vodafone Air Touch for a controlling interest in German communications giant Mannesmann A.G. Holzmann was a mismanaged and highly leveraged company that German banks had earlier bailed out but now abandoned to market forces. When the Schröder government came at last to its rescue, a cracking of the "consensus society" was heard throughout Germany, moving one German commentator to complain again about "barbarians within our own midst."[86] Another shaking of Germany's carefully integrated economy came when the government failed to rally German interests behind bankrupt media giant KirchGroup, whose possible loss to foreign conglomerates threatened a further coarsening of German culture.[87]

The American economic model has also been something of a

bogeyman for Germans. While loving American freedom and prosperity, Germans hate "the shop-around-the-clock mentality, the chaos of the unfettered market, the huge gap between CEO pay and workers' wages, and [the unbridled] immigration."[88] However, these perceived American vices, particularly the latter, seem to be marching irresistibly Germany's way with the global economy.

The Canary in the Mine

Does Germany's long history offer any clues to its future course? Present-day observers scrutinize German reaction to ever-growing numbers of foreign *Gastarbeiter* and the impact of an often-reckless global economy. Attention is also given to mounting German exasperation with American, especially Jewish American, efforts to keep the Third Reich and the Holocaust in the forefront of German history.[89] The left-liberal critique from within has been no less trampling of German history, skeptical of German democracy, and alarmist with regard to future prospects. After a half century of continuing unprecedented reparations, responsive democratic government, and model service within the European and the international communities, Germans still remain latent barbarians, anti-Semites, and fascists in the unforgiving minds of many.[90]

Recently a new reparations front opened on yet another area of National Socialist criminality: the slave labor, Jewish and non, extracted by German businesses in wartime. In December 1999 the German government agreed to pay $5.2 billion to settle claims against three multinational German companies (Siemens, Daimler-Chrysler, and BASF), with government and business splitting the costs equally. In May 2000, under intense international legal pressure, the Austrian government created a $395 million fund to pay off similar claims. Since more than half a century has passed, the burden of these new reparations falls on workers and stockholders, foreign and domestic, who were not living at the time of the crimes or too young to have committed them.[91] More recently lawsuits have been filed against the American government and U.S. multinationals (General Electric, Chase Manhattan Bank—now JP Morgan-Chase—and IBM), alleging complicit action, or inaction, during World War II. These include IBM's sale of calculators used to manage the concentration camps and the failure of the American and British high command to bomb the railways leading to the death camps.[92]

Such attempted shakedowns have been roundly condemned by Gentile and Jewish critics alike, yet targeted companies choose to pay rather than face the threatened deluge of negative publicity and righteous litigation.[93] As U.S. journalist Holman Jenkins sees it, the demands are being paid "in obedience to a political consensus that atonement for Nazi crimes is necessary to ease the acceptance of German power in the world."[94] Thus originally uninvolved governments and generations living more than a half century after the crimes, and with most of the actual perpetrators long since dead, are forced to play the scapegoat for the sake of the normality Germany craves.[95]

Today the canary sings in the German mine, assuring everyone that the mine is currently safe. One development that might stop that song is postwar criticism, particularly the kind that escalated during the 1960s, intent on making National Socialism and the Holocaust, with their attendant war guilt and reparations, the bookends of German history. No more than Germans could or should live as the nontechnological, pastoral people the "Fundi" Greens would have them become can they be the perpetual penitential society literary and philosophical utopians demand.[96] Historically Germans have been haunted by the fear of becoming other nations' doormat, and innocent present and future German generations neither should nor can build a normal state on imputed guilt and penitential servitude. Should, however, such a point of view ever catch on in Germany, and a new generation of Germans attempt to create a democratic republic distinguished foremost by sackcloth and ashes, the resulting pain and suffering for Germans and the world might well approximate the past. Normal nationhood is Germany's best hope for the future.

The canary is also likely to continue to sing the all-clear if Germans who have learned Faust's lesson fill the mine. In Goethe's famous telling of the story, Faust pursued an insatiable will to power, which brought him personal tragedy and loss. In later life, however, he came to accept his human limitations, and in doing so found an inner peace in freely chosen, anonymous service to neighbors he also did not know.[97] The history of Germany, including the bloody twentieth century, is also a story of such deeds. Since 1952, when Konrad Adenauer and David Ben-Gurion reached the first accord on reparations, Germany has quietly assisted the new state of Israel, becoming, after the Americans, its surest trading partner and most reliable military ally—the source, for example, of its submarine fleet. While some Germans believe themselves to be the targets of what *New York Times* reporter Roger Cohen has called an "American 'Holocaust industry,' " German-Israeli friendship has remained strong.[98] And despite serious new strains placed on that relationship by Prime Minister Ariel Sharon's prosecution of the Israeli-Palestinian conflict, neither side is likely ever again to think of the other as illegitimate or, much less, an enemy.

Anecdotal evidence appears regularly in German and foreign newspapers recounting Faustian conversions of individual Germans. One such story is that of former convicted RAF terrorist, Silke Maier-Witt, who, in 1977, was party to the kidnapping and execution of German Employers president Hanns-Martin Schleyer. Today Ms. Maier-Witt is a social worker and trauma therapist in Kosovo. Addessing the congregation of a Lutheran church in Bonn in 2001, she was asked why her "youthful idealism" had turned her to terrorism. Her answer was that the "disillusionment of [my] ideology" demanded more of German society than it could reasonably give, leaving her with the cynical belief that nothing one did mattered or could make a difference. "I don't believe I will let that happen again," she told her audience, concluding rhetorically: "What else can I do?"[99] Such "darning and patching" of the social fabric—the phrase is Martin Luther's summary of his social ethics—has many precedents in German history.

Germany today is Western Europe's most populous state, and in 2000, it was also home to its largest immigrant population: 7 million and growing. As Germans have watched those numbers swell, they have made it clear that they do not want to become, as Roger Cohen kindly puts it, "a multi-cultural unit of the European union"—but then, neither do any of their peer nations.[100] Not surprisingly the seeming German drift in that direction has sparked right-wing protests. Relegating the potential for neo-Nazi ideas to a small, violent minority, Foreign Minister Fischer has expressed his own fears of "passive xenophobia" and even a revived Red Army Faction in eastern Germany.[101]

However, such modest fascist violence—just over a hundred people were killed in "xenophobic attacks" between 1990 and 2000—seems the least possible reaction the German government could expect at the end the Cold War, and is thus rather good news within and outside Germany.[102] The more revealing fact about Germany's new immigrant tinderbox has not been the small outbursts of xenophobia lamented by Fischer. It is the Federal Republic's faithful payment of $450 per month to each immigrant, providing food, lodging, education, and medical and dental care, as long as that immigrant is unemployed.[103]

There are clear signs that the foundations of the postwar welfare state, exceedingly generous to natives and foreigners alike, are shaking under the accumulated weight of what has been called egalitarianism. German wages and taxes, if not the world's highest, are among them, and they threaten both the viability of companies and the security of workers, who can pay as much as 70 percent of gross salary in state pensions, insurance, and taxes.[104] The good Germans are today being undone not by war crimes and war guilt but by their own postwar generosity and pursuit of a just society. Refusing on moral grounds to let theirs become a riven land of haves and have-nots like the United States, Germans seem unable to let go of the beleaguered consensus society and its increasingly coerced cornucopia. But if the latter are to continue, new ways must be found to discipline freedom and ration equality, so that less may still seem to be as much, if it cannot be more—a goal history suggests is well within the abilities of Germans.

Notes

Introduction: Looking for the Good German

1. Some 18.3 million claim full German ancestry. "You Told Us: Ancestry": www.census.gov/population/socdemo/ancestry/German.txt.
2. See below, chap. 11.
3. Cf. Richard J. Evans, *In Hitler's Shadow: West German Historians and the Attempt to Escape From the Nazi Past* (New York, 1989), pp. 11–40, esp. 114–15.
4. The phrase is Rolf Dahrendorf's. See chap. 1.
5. Georg G. Iggers, *New Directions in European Historiography* (Middletown, Conn., 1975), pp. 93–94, 96–98; Jan-Werner Müller, *Another Country* (New Haven, 2000), chap. 1; Isabel V. Hull, *The Entourage of Kaiser Wilhelm II, 1888–1918* (Cambridge, 1982), pp. 1–3. Leonard Krieger, "German History in the Grand Manner" (review of Gordon A. Craig, James J. Sheehan, Fritz Stern, and Hans-Ulrich Wehler), *American Historical Review* 84 (1979): pp. 1007–17. Wehler's three-volume, 2,300-page narrative: *Deutsche Gesellschaftsgeschichte, 1: Vom Feudalismus des Alten Reiches bis zur defensiven Modernisierung der Reformära, 1700–1815; 2: Von der Reformära bis zur industriellen und politischen 'Deutschen Doppelrevolution,' 1815–1845/49* (Munich, 1987); *3: Von der 'Deutschen Doppelrevolution' bis zum Beginn des Ersten Weltkrieges, 1849–1914* (Munich, 1995). Subsequent volumes carry the story forward to 1949.
6. Gordon A. Craig, *The Germans* (New York, 1982), p. 22.
7. David Blackbourn, *The Long Nineteenth Century: A History of Germany, 1780–1918* (Oxford, 1998), p. 275.

8. Edward R. Brandt et al., *Germanic Genealogy: A Guide to Worldwide Sources and Migration Patterns* (St. Paul, 1995), pp. 137–71; John A. Hawgood, *The Tragedy of German-America: The Germans in the U.S.A. During the Nineteenth Century and After* (New York, 1940), pp. 57–58. See also Mack Walker, *Germany and the Emigration, 1816–1885* (Cambridge, Mass., 1964), and Anne Galicich, *The German Americans* (New York, 1996), pp. 13–17.
9. F. W. Bogen, *The German in America* (Boston, 1851), pp. 39–41, 57.
10. Richard J. Evans, "Whatever Became of the Sonderweg?" in *Rereading German History: From Unification to Reunification, 1800–1996* (London, 1997), pp. 12–14; Krieger, "German History in the Grand Manner;" James Van Horn Melton, review of Wehler's *Deutsche Gesellschaftsgeschichte*, 1–2, *American Historical Review* 95 (1990): 189–90.
11. Eley defends "a less abject bourgeois role in modern German history"; Blackbourn cites advances in "property rights and ideas of competition, the rule of law, the emergence of philanthropy" as "substantial achievements amounting to a programme . . . which created . . . a new kind of public man." David Blackbourn and Geoff Eley, *The Peculiarities of German History: Bourgeois Society and Politics in Nineteenth-Century Germany* (Oxford, 1984), pp. 13, 164.
12. Harold James, *A German Identity, 1770–1990* (New York, 1989), p. 212. See below, chap. 11.
13. See the contributions to "The Continuity Debate," in James F. Harris, ed., *German-American Interrelations: Heritage and Challenge* (Tübingen, 1985), pp. 55–94; James J. Sheehan, ed., *Imperial Germany* (New York, 1976); Richard J. Evans, ed., *Society and Politics in Wilhelmine Germany* (London, 1978).
14. Cf. Charles S. Maier, "German War, German Peace," in Mary Fulbrook, ed., *Germany Since 1800* (London, 1997), pp. 539–55; cf. Evans, *In Hitler's Shadow*, pp. 104–7. In laying the road to 1933, nineteenth-century big business and capitalism have also proved to be less complicit than Marxist theory would lead historians to believe. The basic studies are Henry A. Turner, Jr., *German Big Business and the Rise of Hitler* (New York, 1985); Jeffrey Diefendorf, *Businessmen and Politics in the Rhineland* (Princeton, 1980); Rolf Dahrendorf, *Society and Democracy in Germany* (London, 1968). Nor did the imperial government under Bismarck and Emperor William I prove to be the protofascist juggernaut many historians allege.

Realistic foreign policy fears and colonial competition played as large a role in imperial Germany's decision making as did strife-ridden domestic politics and specters of rebellion. The critical historians' stress on domestic politics ("power structures," "social structural deformations") and continuity between imperial and National Socialist foreign policy especially rested on Fritz Fischer's pairings developed in his *Griff nach der Weltmacht* (Düsseldorf, 1961; English ed., 1967) and *Krieg der Illusionen* (Düsseldorf, 1969; English ed., 1975). See Hull, *Kaiser Wilhelm II*, p. 1.

15. Evans, "Nipperdey's Nineteenth Century," in *Rereading German History*, pp. 23–43. Nipperdey's volumes: *Deutsche Geschichte, 1800–1866* (Munich, 1983 [English, 1996]); *Deutsche Geschichte, 1866–1918* I: *Arbeitswelt und Bürgergeist* (Munich, 1990); *Deutsche Geschichte, 1866–1918*, II: *Machtstaat vor der Demokratie* (Munich, 1992).
16. Nipperdey, "1933 und die Kontinuität der deutschen Geschichte," in *Nachdenken über die deutsche Geschichte: Essays* (Munich, 1987), pp. 186–205, esp. 168; Thomas A. Brady, Jr., *Turning Swiss: Cities and Empire, 1450–1550* (Cambridge, 1985), chap. 7; Peter Blickle, *Gemeindereformation: Die Menschen des 16. Jahrhunderts auf dem Weg zum Heil* (Munich, 1985).
17. Nipperdey, "1933," p. 200.
18. Evans, "Nipperdey's Nineteenth Century," pp. 28–31. Evans considers Nipperdey the lesser evil among "conservative" German historians, yet devotes more attention to him in his historiographical retrospective than to the liberals' archvillain Ernst Nolte (roughly twenty pages to two). The latter sparked the bitterest "historians' quarrel" in the late 1980s when he attempted to treat Nazi crimes generically. The fact that Evans gives Nipperdey such attention suggests (properly) that he is the historian of record on the subject. "Beyond the Historikerstreit," in *Rereading German History*, pp. 221–22; see below, chap. 12, n. 84. On the so-called *Historikerstreit*, cf. Charles S. Maier, *The Unmasterable Past* (Cambridge, Mass., 1989).
19. Evans, "Nipperdey's Nineteenth Century," pp. 35, 41.
20. Thus Evans on Wehler, "After Reunification," in ibid., p. 238.
21. On this touchy subject, featuring other modern German historians, cf. Tim Mason, "Intention and Explanation: A Current Controversy About the Interpretation of National Socialism," in Mason, *Nazism, Fascism, and the Working Class* (Cambridge, 1995), pp. 212–30.

22. Ian Kershaw, *The Nazi Dictatorship: Problems and Perspectives of Interpretation* (London, 2000), pp. 185–87.
23. After Claus, Graf von Stauffenberg, who placed the bomb at Hitler's feet.
24. See chap. 10.
25. Kershaw, *Nazi Dictatorship*, pp. 188–89.
26. *Facts About Germany: The Federal Republic of Germany 50 Years On* (Frankfurt-am-Main, 1999), pp. 90–137.
27. Hagen Schulze, *Germany: A New History*, trans. D. L. Schneider (Cambridge, Mass., 1998), p. 202.
28. One forbade the president from suspending individual rights and freedoms, another assured the orderly transfer of power from one government to another, placing Germany on a surer democratic path. *Facts*, pp. iv–xxiii.
29. Ibid., pp. v, xxiv–viii.
30. See chap. 12.
31. Ibid.
32. Cf. Blackbourn and Eley, *Peculiarities*, pp. 55–59.

1. The Barbarian Complex: Roman-German Relations in Antiquity

1. Not, however, by "Germans" themselves. "A member of a German tribe, when asked about his or her affiliations, would have answered 'Langobard," 'Vandal,' 'Frisian,' or 'Goth,' not 'Germanus.' " Malcolm Todd, *The Early Germans* (Oxford, 1992), pp. 9–10. On documenting German tribes between the Rhine and Loire, Todd, "The Germanic Peoples," in *The Cambridge Ancient History*, vol. 13: *The Late Empire, A.D. 337–425*, ed. Averil Cameron et al. (Cambridge, 1998), pp. 464–71. A brief, up-to-date overview is Clifford R. Backman's "Early Germanic Society," in his *The Worlds of Medieval Europe* (Oxford, 2003), pp. 48–68.
2. Lester K. Little and Barbara H. Rosenwein, "The Fate of Rome's Western Provinces," in Lester K. Little & Barbara H. Rosenwein, eds., *Debating the Middle Ages: Issues and Readings* (Oxford, 1998), pp. 8–10; Walter Goffart, "The Barbarians in Late Antiquity and How They Were Accommodated in the West," in ibid., pp. 26, 38, 40.
3. Ethnic identity appears to have remained more fluid among the Huns, Alemanni, and Slavs. Patrick J. Geary, "Barbarians and Ethnicity," in Glen W. Bowersock et al., eds. *Interpreting Late Antiquity:*

Essays on the Postclassical World (Cambridge, Mass., 2001), pp. 108–9. "Goths, Vandals, Franks, even Huns were not enemies of the Roman Empire, they were its (initially external) members and federates, and their attacks were more of an upheaval than an invasion." Walter Pohl, "Conceptions of Ethnicity in Early Medieval Studies," in Little and Rosenwein, eds., *Debating the Middle Ages*, p. 18. See also Susan Reynolds, "Our Forefathers? Tribes, Peoples, and Nations in the Historiography of the Age of Migration," in Alexander C. Murray, ed., *After Rome's Fall: Narrators and Sources of Early Medieval History: Essays Presented to Walter Goffart* (Toronto, 1998), pp. 17–36, esp. 26. Also relevant are the comments of James J. Sheehan, "What Is German History? Reflections on the Role of the 'Nation' in German History and Historiography," *Journal of Modern History* 53 (1981): p. 4.

4. Todd, *Early Germans*, pp. 47–49.
5. Geary, "Barbarians and Ethnicity," p. 112; E. A. Thompson, *The Early Germans* (Oxford, 1965), pp. 1–16, 29–41.
6. "The devastation caused by barbarian raids into the empire paled in comparison with the wasting and slaughter meted out by Roman armies engaged in expeditions across the Rhine or Danube." Geary, "Barbarians and Ethnicity," p. 114.
7. See the frontier studies of C. R. Whittaker, *Frontiers of the Roman Empire* (Baltimore, 1994) and Benjamin H. Isaac, *The Limits of Empire: The Roman Army in the East* (Oxford, 1990).
8. Tacitus, *The Agricola and the Germania*, trans. H. Mattingly and S. A. Handford (London, 1970), pp. 113–14.
9. Thompson, *Early Germans*, pp. 48, 53–60; Todd, *Early Germans*, pp. 32–33.
10. Thompson, *The Early Germans*, pp. 18, 21–24, 28, 73–74, 79, 92–95; Todd, *Early Germans*, pp. 88, 90, 95, 100.
11. Geary, "Barbarians and Ethnicity," p. 110.
12. Between modern Bielefeld and Osnabrück in northern Rhine-Westphalia.
13. Tacitus's work was discovered in 1451 and printed in Venice (1470) and Nuremberg (1473) editions before appearing in a new edition of Tacitus's collected works (Rome, 1515). A 1458 Italian commentary on *The History of Germany*, translated into German in 1526, added to German interest in it. Todd, *Early Germans*, pp. 52, 256; Gerald Strauss, ed., *Manifestations of Discontent in Germany on the Eve of the*

Reformation (Bloomington, Ind., 1971), pp. 75–81. On the waning of the myth, see *Facts*, p. 90.

14. Thompson, *Early Germans*, pp. 73–85; Todd, *Early Germans*, pp. 84–86.
15. Tacitus, *The Germania*, pp. 102, 106, 108, 113, 116–18, 121, 132, 140.
16. Ibid., pp. 110–14, 119–120.
17. Ibid., p. 125.
18. Thompson, *Early Germans*, p. 104
19. When barbarians looked at the empire, they saw "the home of the great king [the emperor] . . . inexhaustible wealth, and . . . a powerful . . . treacherous ally"; in all their dealings with the empire, the Goths gained "neither peace nor parity." Geary, "Barbarians and Ethnicity," pp. 110–20.
20. Herwig Wolfram, *The Roman Empire and its Germanic Peoples*, trans. Thomas Dunlap (Berkeley, 1997), pp. 56–67.
21. Tacitus, *The Germania*, p. 104; Thompson, *The Early Germans*, pp. 63–66.
22. Arthur Ferrill, *The Fall of the Roman Empire* (New York, 1986), p. 26.
23. Todd, *The Early Germans*, pp. 53–57.
24. Geary, "Barbarism and Ethnicity," p. 115; Brent D. Shaw, "War and Violence," in Bowersock, ed., *Interpreting Late Antiquity*, pp. 135–36.
25. Ferrill, *Fall of Rome*, pp. 31–32, 41–43, 45–49; Shaw, "War and Violence," pp. 150–51.
26. Ferrill, *Fall of Rome*, pp. 59–60.
27. Cited by Wolfram, *The Roman Empire and Its Germanic Peoples*, pp. 83–84; see also Todd, *Early Germans*, p. 153.
28. Jordenes, *History of the Goths*, in Patrick Geary, ed. *Readings in Medieval History* (Peterborough, Ontario, 1997), chaps. 26–27, p. 89.
29. While acknowledging the "considerable proportion" of barbarians (especially Franks) holding the highest command positions in the Roman army by the end of the fourth century, Brent Shaw argues, apparently against Ferrill, that the northern barbarians entered Rome by invitation, not as invaders, and hence no "barbarization" of the Roman army occurred. It would thus be more correct to say, as Shaw seems to do, that the Roman military was not forcibly taken over by barbarians from without but by worthy allied federates from within: "There was not a single leader of such a large-scale ethnic force, from Alaric to Attila, who had not been invited into the empire

for the purpose of armed service." "War and Violence," pp. 151–52. That, however, does not lessen the ascendancy of barbarians within and over the Roman army.

30. Ferrill, *Fall of Rome*, pp. 60–61; Wolfram, *Germanic Peoples*, pp. 84–85; Jordenes, *History of the Goths*, chap. 16, p. 89.
31. Ferrill, *Fall of Rome*, pp. 80–85; Todd, *Early Germans*, p. 60 ("In the later fourth century it becomes difficult to identify holders of the most senior military posts who were certainly not Germans"); Wolfram, *Germanic Peoples*, pp. 85–88; Shaw, "War and Violence," p. 151.
32. Wolfram, *Germanic Peoples*, p. 66; Ferrill, *Fall of Rome*, pp. 71–72; Todd, *Early Germans*, pp. 59–61.
33. For what follows, Jordenes, *History of the Goths*, chaps. 29–31, pp. 90–92.
34. Maria in 400 and, after her death, Thermantia in 408.
35. Ferrill, *Fall of Rome*, p. 86–89; Wolfram, *Germanic Peoples*, pp. 89–90.
36. "If anyone offended him or his people, he became the barbarian who jumped up and ordered [a] march on Rome." Wolfram, *Germanic Peoples*, p. 100. On Gothic-Roman relations during Alaric's career and its aftermath, see R. C. Blockley, "The Dynasty of Theodosius," in Cameron, ed., *Cambridge Ancient History*, 13, pp. 118–32, and Peter Heather, "Goths and Huns, c. 320–425," in ibid., pp. 488–515.
37. Ferrill, *Fall of Rome*, pp. 71–75; Wolfram, *Germanic Peoples*, pp. 91–92.
38. Ferrill, *Fall of Rome*, pp. 75, 92, 95–97; Wolfram, *Germanic Peoples*, pp. 93–95.
39. Ferrill, *Fall of Rome*, pp. 99–101; Wolfram, *Germanic Peoples*, pp. 97–98.
40. Ferrill, *Fall of Rome*, p. 103.
41. Blockley, "Dynasty of Theodosius," p. 126.
42. Ferrill, *Fall of Rome*, pp. 103–4, 113, 121; Todd, *Early Germans*, pp. 158–59; Wolfram, *Germanic Peoples*, pp. 98–99. Jordenes has Athaulf seize Galla during a fourth sack of the city after Alaric's death and his own succession to the kingship. *History of the Goths*, chap. 31, p. 91.
43. Ferrill, *Fall of Rome*, pp. 113, 119, 121.
44. Jordenes, *History of the Goths*, chap. 31, p. 91.
45. Ibid.
46. Ibid., pp. 71–75, 122; Todd, *Early Germans*, pp. 160–61; Wolfram, *Germanic Peoples*, pp. 146–47; Blockley, "Dynasty of Theodosius," pp. 131–32.

47. Cited by Ferrill, *Fall of Rome*, pp. 121–22. See *Dictionary of the Middle Ages*, Joseph Strayer, ed., vol. 9 (New York, 1987), p. 281, and Walter Goffart's magnum opus, *Barbarians and Romans, 418–584: The Techniques of Accommodation* (Princeton, 1980).

2. *From Merovingians to Hohenstaufens: Germanic Rule in the Middle Ages*

1. "The great strength of the Frankish synthesis was the new creation within the Roman world of a unified society that drew, without a sense of contradiction, on both Roman and barbarian traditions." Patrick Geary, "Barbarians and Ethnicity," p. 125.
2. Richard E. Sullivan, "The Carolingian Age: Reflections on Its Place in the History of the Middle Ages," *Speculum* 64 (1989): pp. 281–97.
3. Pierre Riché, *The Carolingians: A Family Who Forged Europe*, trans. M. I. Allen (Philadelphia, 1993), pp. xviii, 4. On the sociopolitical evolution of the period, M. I. Innes, *Social Processes and the State: The Middle Rhine Valley from the Merovingians to the Ottonians, 400–1000* (Cambridge, 2000).
4. Nicholas Frérel, in 1714. Edward James, *The Franks* (Oxford, 1988), p. 239.
5. Ibid., pp. 235–43; cf. René Goscinny and Albert Underzo, *Astérix et les Goths* (Neuilly-sur-Seine, 1973).
6. George Holmes, *The Oxford History of Medieval Europe* (Oxford, 1988), pp. 65–66; James, *The Franks*, pp. 65–70.
7. *History of the Franks*, trans. E. Brehaut (New York, 1969), bk. 2, nos. 29–31, pp. 38–41.
8. James, *The Franks*, pp. 80–84, 86–90.
9. Ibid., pp. 163–68, 189–91.
10. Robert S. Hoyt and Stanley Chodorow, *Europe in the Middle Ages* (New York, 1976), pp. 69–72.
11. Gregory of Tours, *History of the Franks*, bk. 2, no. 38, p. 47; Michael McCormick, "Clovis at Tours, Byzantine Public Ritual and the Origins of Medieval Ruler Symbolism," in E. K. Chrysos and A. Schwarcz, eds., *Das Reich und die Barbaren* (Vienna, 1989), pp. 157–58, 166–67; James, *The Franks*, pp. 84–87.
12. Pierre Riché, *The Carolingians*, pp. 34–39, 44–49.
13. Paul Fouracre, "Frankish Gaul to 814," in *The New Cambridge Medieval History*, vol. 2, *c. 700–c. 900*, ed. Rosamond McKitterick (Cambridge, 1995), pp. 102–3.

14. Munz, *Life in the Age of Charlemagne* (New York, 1971), pp. 40–55; Riché, *The Carolingians*, p. 135; Dieter Hägermann, *Karl der Grosse: Herrscher des Abendlandes* (Munich, 2000), p. 634.
15. Munz, *Age of Charlemagne*, pp. 55, 90; Riché, *The Carolingians*, pp. 132, 135; Hägermann, *Karl der Grosse*, pp. 682–85; Rosamond McKitterick, ed., *Carolingian Culture: Emulation and Innovation* (Cambridge, 1994).
16. Hägermann, *Karl der Grosse*, pp. 445–48.
17. Munz, *Age of Charlemagne*, pp. 116–31, 150; Williston Walker, *A History of the Christian Church* (New York, 1959), p. 189; Riché, *The Carolingians*, pp. 117–18.
18. Riché, *The Carolingians*, 119, 199–200.
19. Ibid., pp. 121–23.
20. Munz, *Age of Charlemagne*, pp. 56–67; Riché, *The Carolingians*, pp. 125–29.
21. Fouracre, "Frankish Gaul to 814," pp. 107–8.
22. Paula Fichtner, *Protestantism and Primogeniture in Early Modern Germany* (New Haven, 1989).
23. James, *The Franks*, pp. 91, 169. On Merovingian, Carolingian, Ottonian, and Salian royal women, Edith Ennen, *Frauen im Mittelalter* (Munich, 1994), pp. 49–74.
24. Louis's arrangement for succession was "a direct borrowing from the unimplemented *Divisio* which Charlemagne had drawn up in 806." Janet L. Nelson, "The Frankish Kingdoms, 814–98: The West," in McKitterick, ed. *New Cambridge Medieval History*, vol. 2, p. 112.
25. Riché, *The Carolingians*, pp. 146–47; Janet L. Nelson, "The Last years of Louis the Pious," in Peter Godman and Roger Collins, eds., *Charlemagne's Heir: New Perspectives on the Reign of Louis the Pious (814–840)* (Oxford, 1990), pp. 147–61.
26. Later Louis's youngest son by Ermengard, Louis of Bavaria, married Judith's younger sister Emma, further brightening the Welf family's political fortunes within the Carolingian dynasty. See below.
27. Riché, *The Carolingians*, pp. 149–50; Elizabeth Ward, "Caesar's Wife: The Career of the Empress Judith, 819–29," in Godman et al., eds., *Charlemagne's Heir*, pp. 207–8.
28. Ward, "Caesar's Wife," pp. 213–14.
29. Nelson, "The Frankish Kingdoms," p. 117
30. Riché, *The Carolingians*, pp. 150–58; Nelson, "The Frankish Kingdoms," p. 118; Johannes Fried, "The Frankish Kingdoms, 817–911:

The East and Middle Kingdoms," McKitterick, ed., *New Cambridge Medieval History*, vol. 2, pp. 142–45.

31. Riché, *The Carolingians*, pp. 160–69.
32. Nelson, "The Frankish Kingdoms," pp. 118–19, 124.
33. Geoffrey Barraclough, *The Origins of Modern Germany* (New York, 1963), pp. 46–47; Nelson, "The Frankish Kingdoms," pp. 121, 136. The Frankish division of Western Europe created geopolitical boundaries that did not change dramatically until the end of World War II. After 1945 a divided Germany became the middle kingdom of Western Europe, over which new and greater Eastern and Western "kingdoms" competed: the Soviet Union and the United States with their respective allies.
34. Hajo Holborn, *A History of Modern Germany*, vol. 1: *The Reformation* (New York, 1961), pp. 27–28; *Facts*, p. 91.
35. Barraclough, *Origins*, pp. 14–25.
36. Ibid., pp. 27–30, 41.
37. Ibid., pp. 47–48, 53–58, 63.
38. Hoyt and Chodorow, *Europe in the Middle Ages*, p. 673.
39. Barraclough, *Origins*, pp. 77–79; Hoyt and Chodorow, *Europe in the Middle Ages*, p. 275.
40. These were the "provinces, palaces, and districts of the city of Rome and Italy and of the regions of the West" the Church claimed Emperor Constantine had donated to it. Henry Bettenson, ed. *Documents of the Christian Church* (New York, 1961), pp. 141–42.
41. Barraclough, *Origins*, pp. 85–90.
42. Ibid., pp. 35–36, 41–42; Brian Tierney, ed., *The Crisis of Church & State 1050–1300* (Toronto, 1996), pp. 33–44.
43. Barraclough, *Origins*, pp. 97, 103, 106; Tierney, *Crisis*, pp. 45–52.
44. Tierney, *Crisis*, pp. 53–73; see chap. 7.
45. Barraclough, *Origins*, pp. 109–10, 125.
46. Ibid., pp. 128, 131–33.
47. "The fantastic map of German particularism and the unlimited sovereignty of princes." Ibid., p. 153.
48. Hoyt and Chodorow, p. 673; Tierney, *Crisis*, pp. 46, 49, 100, 105.
49. Barraclough, *Origins*, pp. 169–71; Barraclough, "Frederick Barbarossa and the Twelfth Century," in *History in a Changing World* (Oxford, 1955), pp. 73–96.
50. Barraclough, *Origins*, pp. 176–77.
51. Norman Cohn, *The Pursuit of the Millennium* (New York, 1961),

p. 103. A more positive assessment is David Abulafia, *Frederick II: A Medieval Emperor* (London, 1988).

52. Barraclough, *Origins*, pp. 180–86, 188–90; Hoyt and Chodorow, *Europe*, pp. 354–64.
53. Barraclough, *Origins*, pp. 196–201; Hoyt and Chodorow, *Europe*, pp. 462–63.
54. Barraclough, *Origins*, pp. 204–11; Hoyt and Chodorow, *Europe*, pp. 463–69.
55. Barraclough, *Origins*, p. 214.
56. Ibid., pp. 219–24. Compare Prussian king Frederick the Great, another heroic German, who was shaped by, and loved, another culture (French) more than his native German. See chap. 5.
57. Ibid., pp. 236–37.
58. Ibid., pp. 227–33, 240.
59. Hoyt and Chodorow, *Europe*, pp. 623–25.

3. Man and God: Germany in the Renaissance and Reformation

1. The duke of Saxony, the margrave of Brandenburg, the king of Bohemia, and the Rhenish Count Palatine, and the archbishops of Cologne, Mainz, and Trier.
2. Karl-Heinz Blaschke, *Sachsen im Zeitalter der Reformation* (Gütersloh, 1970); Steven Ozment, *The Reformation in the Cities* (New Haven, 1975), pp. 125–29, 143–45; Bernd Moeller, "Imperial Cities and the Reformation," in *Imperial Cities and the Reformation: Three Essays*, trans. M. Edwards and H. C. Erik Midelfort (Philadelphia, 1972), p. 9.
3. Blaschke, *Sachsen*, p. 74.
4. Heinrich Schmidt, *Die deutschen Städtechroniken als Spiegel des bürgerlichen Selbstverständnisses im Spätmittelalter* (Göttingen, 1958), pp. 34–37, 69–72, 77; Blaschke, *Sachsen*, pp. 34, 49–55, 72.
5. Willy Andreas, "Die Kulturbedeutung der deutschen Reichsstadt zu Ausgang des Mittelalters," *Deutsche Vierteljahrsschrift für Literaturwissenschaft und Geistesgeschichte* 6 (1928): pp. 62–113; Moeller, "Imperial Cities," pp. 9, 13–15, 17; Mack Walker, *German Home Towns, 1648–1871* (Ithaca, 1971), chap. 4.
6. Gerald Strauss, *Law, Resistance, and the State: The Opposition to Roman Law in Reformation Germany* (Princeton, 1986), pp. 65, 80, 150.
7. Andreas, "Die Kulturbedeutung," pp. 55–56.

8. Gerhard Pfeiffer, "Das Verhältnis von politischer und kirchlicher Gemeinde in den deutschen Reichsstädten," in *Staat und Kirche im Wandel der Jahrhunderte*, ed. W. P. Fuchs, (Stuttgart, 1966), p. 85; Peter Blickle, *Communal Reformation*, trans. Thomas Dunlap (Leiden, 1998), chap. 5; Steven Ozment, *Protestants: The Birth of a Revolution* (New York, 1992), chap. 6.
9. Moeller, "Imperial Cities," pp. 35–38; Heinz Schilling, "Die Reformation in Deutschland," in Hans-Ulrich Wehler, *Scheideweg der deutschen Geschichte. Von der Reformation bis zur Wende, 1517–1989* (Nördlingen, 1995), pp. 15–27, esp. 20.
10. Ernst Borkowsky, *Das Leben Friedrichs des Weisen. Kurfürsten zu Sachsen* (Jena, 1929), p. 33.
11. Claus Grimm et al., *Lucas Cranach. Ein Maler-Unternehmer aus Franken* (Regensburg, 1994), pp. 309–13, 320–21; *Cranach und Picasso, Ausstellung, Nürnberg, 22. Sept.–20. Okt., 1968*, ed. Albrecht-Dürer-Gesellschaft (Nuremberg, 1968).
12. Borkowsky, *Leben Friedrichs*, pp. 6, 38. On Frederick's limits as a "Renaissance prince": Bernd Stephan, "Kulturpolitische Massnahmen des Kurfürsten Friedrich III., des Weisen, von Sachsen," *Lutherjahrbuch* 49 (1982): pp. 50–95, esp. 61–65.
13. Borkowsky, *Leben Friedrichs*, pp. 39–40, 44–46; Bernd Stephan, "Kurfürst Frederick III. der Weise," in Rolf Straubel et al., *Kaiser König Kardinal. Deutsche Fürsten 1500–1800* (Leipzig, 1991), p. 31; Jane C. Hutchison, *Albrecht Dürer: A Biography* (Princeton, 1990), 65–66, 69–70; Charles Nauert, *Humanism and the Culture of Renaissance Europe* (Cambridge, 1995), pp. 110–11; Georg Spalatin, *Friedrichs des Weisen Leben und Zeitgeschichte von Georg Spalatin*, in *Georg Spalatins historischer Nachlass und Briefe*, vol. 1 (Jena, 1951), p. 28.
14. This was the saint to whom Luther turned after being terrified by a lightning storm on the road to Erfurt, promising to enter a monastery if she spared his life.
15. Borkowsky, *Leben Friedrichs*, pp. 56–57; Ozment, *Reformation in the Cities*, p. 139.
16. Borkowsky, *Leben Friedrichs*, pp. 62, 71–72; Spalatin, *Friedrichs Leben*, pp. 28–30, 50; Stephan, "Kulturpolitische Massnahmen," 70.
17. Bernd Stephan, "Kurfürst Friedrich," pp. 26–27; "Kulturpolitische Massnahmen," 57–59.
18. Spalatin, *Friedrichs Leben*, pp. 58–59.
19. Borkowsky, *Leben Friedrichs*, pp. 18–20. On the entire episode, cf.

Spalatin, *Friedrichs Leben*, pp. 40–41, 57–59; Heiko A. Oberman, *Luther: Man Between God and the Devil*, trans. E. Walliser-Schwarzbart (New York, 1992), pp. 24–34.

20. "Beschwerlich genug gewest und wehe gethan . . . also soll umzogen werden." Spalatin, *Friedrichs Leben*, pp. 61–62.
21. Stephan, "Kulturpolitische Massnahmen," pp. 89, 95; Stephan, "Kurfürst Friedrich," pp. 33–34. On Luther's treatment and the threats to him: Borkowsky, *Leben Friedrichs*, pp. 64–65; Oberman, *Luther*, pp. 246–47, 299–300.
22. Stephan, "Kurfürst Friedrich," p. 33.
23. Ibid., pp. 33–34; Steven Ozment, *Mysticism and Dissent* (New Haven, 1978), pp. 79–97.
24. Borkowsky, *Leben Friedrichs*, pp. 66–67, 76; Spalatin, *Friedrichs Leben*, pp. 29–30; Stephan, "Kurfürst Friedrich," p. 34.
25. Spalatin, *Friedrichs Leben*, pp. 64, 68; Heinrich Bornkamm, *Luther in Mid-Career* (Philadelphia, 1983), pp. 376–77.
26. Borkowsky, *Leben Friedrichs*, pp. 75–77; Spalatin, *Friedrichs Leben*, pp. 42–43.
27. Spalatin, *Friedrichs Leben*, pp. 69–75.
28. "Albertus Durer Noricus," meaning, "from Noricum," between the Alps and the Danube—a non-Italian, a German.
29. After the Augustinian monk Johannes Staupitz, first dean of the University of Wittenberg and Luther's mentor and confidant; Luther occupied his chair of biblical theology in 1512.
30. Among its members were city council secretary Lazarus Spengler; city treasurers Hieronymus Ebner and Anton Tucher; city council lawyer and diplomat Christoph Scheurl; Andreas and Martin Tucher, owners of one of the age's great trading companies; and Jakob Welser, Nuremberg manager of the Augsburg-based Welser banking empire. Hutchison, *Albrecht Dürer*, p. 123; Oberman, *Luther*, p. 136; Lewis W. Spitz, *The Religious Renaissance of the German Humanists* (Cambridge, Mass. 1963), pp. 155–96; Steven Ozment, *Flesh and Spirit: Family Life in Early Modern Germany* (New York, 1999), chaps. 2 (Christoph Scheurl) and 4 (Sebald Welser).
31. "If God helps me come to Dr. Martin Luther, I will carefully draw his portrait and engrave it in copper for a lasting rememberance." Hutchison, *Dürer*, pp. 124–25; Martin Warnke, *Cranachs Luther. Entwürfe für eine Image* (Frankfurt-am-Main, 1984), p. 15. On Dürer's similar urging of Erasmus to protect Luther, Joseph L.

Koerner, *The Moment of Self-Portraiture in German Renaissance Art* (Chicago, 1993), p. 76.

32. Warnke, *Cranachs Luther*, pp. 15–20.
33. Later, in 1525, Cranach was a best man at Luther's wedding to Katherine von Bora; in 1526 he stood as a godfather to Luther's first son, Johannes.
34. Andreas Tacke, *Der katholische Cranach* (Mainz, 1992), pp. 9-15.
35. Strauss, *Manifestations of Discontent*, pp. 52–63; Ozment, *Protestants*, pp. 11ff.
36. What Warneke, in criticism of Robert Scribner, calls "die Angst der Obrigkeit vor der vollen Entfaltung der Wahrheit." Warnke, *Cranachs Luther*, p. 65.
37. So different from Cranach's first did the new portrayal of Luther appear, that Cranach's authorship was questioned by authorities as late as 1900. Warnke, *Cranachs Luther*, pp. 27–29; R. W. Scribner, *For the Sake of the Simple Folk: Popular Propaganda for the German Reformation* (Cambridge, 1981), p. 16.
38. Warnke, *Cranachs Luther*, p. 65.
39. Scribner, *For the Sake of Simple Folk*, pp. 14–34.
40. Strauss, *Manifestations*, pp. 3–34, 64–82, 196–207; Harold J. Berman, and John Witte, Jr., "The Transformation of Western Legal Philosophy in Lutheran Germany," *Southern California Law Review* 62 (1989): pp. 1575–1660; John Witte, Jr., "The Civic Seminary: Sources of Modern Public Education in the Lutheran Reformation of Germany," *Journal of Law and Religion* 12 (1995–96): pp. 173–223.
41. *Luther's Works* vol. 31, ed. H. G. Grimm (Philadelphia, 1957), p. 76; Ozment, *Mysticism and Dissent*, pp. 18-19.
42. "The Freedom of a Christian," *Luther's Works*, 31, p. 344.
43. *Das Buch der göttlichen Tröstung*, in *Deutsche Mystiker des 14. Jahrhunderts*, vol. 2: *Meister Eckhart*, ed. Franz Pfeiffer (Leipzig, 1875), p. 431; Steven Ozment, "Eckhart and Luther: German Mysticism and Protestantism," *The Thomist* 42 (1978): pp. 259–80.
44. Koerner, *Moment of Self-Portraiture*, pp. 40, 42, 122.
45. Koerner calls the 1502–3 portrait a "narcissistic crisis," the physical beauty of the 1500 portrait having come back to haunt the painter. *Moment of Self-Portraiture*, pp. 251–53, 268, 495, n. 44; Peter Parshall, "Albrecht Dürer and the Axis of Meaning," *Allen Memorial Art Museum Bulletin* 50 (1997): p. 20. For precedents in the medieval *memento mori/ars moriendi* tradition, see Alberto Tenenti, "Death in

History," and Donald Weinstein, "The Art of Dying Well and Popular Piety in the Preaching and Thought of Girolamo Savonarola," in *Life and Death in Fifteenth-Century Florence*, ed. M. Tetel et al. (Durham, N.C., 1889), pp. 88–104, and James M. Clark, *The Dance of Death in the Middle Ages and the Renaissance* (Glasgow, 1950), pp. 1–4, 22–24, 106–10.

46. *Luther's Works*, 31, pp. 3–34.
47. On the physical plant of the university, see E. G. Schwiebert, *Luther and His Times* (St. Louis, 1950), pp. 221–53.
48. "The Freedom of a Christian," pp. 347, 351; Ozment, "Luther and Late Medieval Theology," in R. M. Kingdon, ed., *Transition and Revolution: Problems and Issues of European Renaissance and Reformation History* (Minneapolis, 1974), pp. 109-51.
49. *Iacobi Hoochstrati Disputationes contra Lutheranos*, in *Bibliotheca reformatoria Neerlandica*, vol. 3, ed. F. Pijper (The Hague, 1905), pp. 609–10.
50. See chap. 7. On Luther's various perceptions of "madness," H. C. Erik Midelfort, *A History of Madness in Sixteenth-Century Germany* (Stanford, 1999), pp. 80–100.
51. Steven Ozment, *The Age of Reform, 1250–1550* (New Haven, 1981), pp. 269–70.
52. "Das eine christliche Versammlung oder Gemeinde Recht und Macht habe, all Lehre zu urteilen," ed. Otto Clemen, *Luthers Werke in Auswahl*, vol. 2 (Berlin, 1959): pp. 395–96; Ozment, *Protestants*, pp. 135–36.
53. Karl Holl, "Luther und das landesherrliche Kirchenregiment," in *Gesammelte Aufsätze zur Kirchengeschichte*, vol. 1 (Tübingen, 1923), pp. 361–69; Ozment, *Protestants*, pp. 91, 136.
54. "On Temporal Authority: To What Extent Should It Be Obeyed?" *Luther's Works*, vol. 31, pp. 77–130; Ozment, *Protestants*, chap. 7.
55. Herbert Wolf, "Pioneer of Modern German," in Thomas Nipperdey, *Martin Luther and the Formation of the Germans* (Bonn, 1983), pp. 30–31. "The Awful German Language" is the title of an essay by Mark Twain, cited in a chapter of the same title by Craig, *The Germans*, pp. 310–11.
56. Wolf, "Pioneer," pp. 26–28.
57. *Tischreden*, ed. Otto Clemen, *Luthers Werke in Auswahl*, vol. 8 (Berlin, 1950): p. 223, no. 4081 (1538).
58. "To the Councilmen of All Cities in Germany That They Establish

and Maintain Christian Schools," *Luther's Works*, 45, ed. W. I. Brandt (Philadelphia, 1962), p. 368.

59. Ibid., p. 370.
60. Ibid., pp. 368–70.
61. Ibid., pp. 376–77.
62. *Dr. Martin Luther's Large Catechism* (Minneapolis, 1935), pp. 35–36. On the impact of the reports on the reformers, cf. Gerald Strauss, *Luther's House of Learning: Indoctrination of the Young in the German Reformation* (Baltimore, 1978), chap. 12.
63. *Large Catechism*, p. 42.
64. "Crypto-theological core," in the words of Thomas Nipperdey, "The Protestant Unrest: Luther and the Culture of the Germans," in Thomas Nipperdey, *Martin Luther and the Formation of the Germans* (Bonn, 1983), pp. 8–14, 20.
65. Nipperdey, "Protestant Unrest," pp. 14, 16.
66. Blaschke, *Sachsen*, pp. 56-68; cf. Robert Jütte, *Poverty and Deviance in Early Modern Europe* (Cambridge, 1994).
67. For those of Wittenberg (1522) and Leisnig (1523), see Carter Lindberg, *The European Reformations* (Oxford, 1996), pp. 114, 118–20, 122–23; also Lindberg, *Beyond Charity: Reformation Initiatives for the Poor* (Minneapolis, 1993).
68. Heide Wunder, *"Er ist die Sonn,' sie is der Mond": Frauen in der Frühen Neuzeit* (Munich, 1992), pp. 59–63; Steven Ozment, *Ancestors: The Loving Family in Old Europe* (Cambridge, Mass., 2001), pp. 34–38.
69. Steven Ozment, *When Fathers Ruled: Family Life in Reformation Europe* (Cambridge, Mass., 1983), pp. 3–9; John Witte, Jr., *From Sacrament to Contract: Marriage, Religion, and Law in the Western Tradition* (Louisville, 1997), pp. 42–73.
70. Ozment, *When Fathers Ruled*, p. 45.
71. Ibid., p. 46.
72. Ibid., pp. 63, 90–93, 96–98.
73. "That Jesus Christ Was Born a Jew," *Luther's Works*, vol. 45, ed. W. I. Brandt (Philadelphia, 1962), pp. 195–230; Scott Hendrix, "Toleration of the Jews in the German Reformation: Urbanus Rhegius and Braunschweig (1535–1540)," *Archiv für Reformationsgeschichte* 81 (1990): pp. 189–215. On Jewish reaction to the Reformation: Hraim Hillel Ben-Sasson, "Protestant-Jewish Relations," *Diogenes* 61 (1968): pp. 32–51; "The Jews vs. the Reformation": *Proceedings of the Israel National Academy of Sciences* 4 (1971): pp. 652–713; and "Jewish-

Christian Disputations in the Setting of Humanism and Reformation in the German Empire," *Harvard Theological Review* 59 (1966): pp. 369–90. On social inclusion of Jews in the nineteenth century, see chap. 7.

74. "Against the Sabbatarians" (1538), *Luther's Works*, vol. 47, ed. F. Scherman (Philadelphia, 1971), pp. 59–62; Mark U. Edwards, Jr., *Luther's Last Battles, 1531–46* (Ithaca, 1983), pp. 125–26. No numbers of Christians involved in such philo-Judaic activities are provided.
75. "On the Jews and Their Lies," *Luther's Works*, vol. 47, p. 137.
76. Ibid., pp. 166–67, 192.
77. "On the Jews and their Lies," pp. 166–67, 192, 254, 260; on Catholic slandering of Luther's mother, Ian Siggins, *Luther and His Mother* (Philadelphia, 1981). On Korah, see Numbers 19.
78. "On the Jews," pp. 140, 144, 255, 259.
79. Ibid., pp. 141, 147–48, 175, 218, 226–27.
80. Ibid., p. 215.
81. Ibid., pp. 269–76, 288.
82. Ibid., p. 135; "Against the Sabbatarians," ibid., pp. 61–62; Hendrix, "Toleration of the Jews," pp. 201–2. On Josel of Rosheim, cf. Selma Stern, *Josel of Rosheim, Commander of Jewry in the Holy Roman Empire of the German Nation* (Philadelphia, 1965).
83. Johannes Wallmann, "Reception of Luther's Writings on the Jews from the Reformation to the End of the Nineteenth Century," *Lutheran Quarterly* 1, (1978): pp. 75–78.
84. Heiko A. Oberman, "Three Sixteenth-Century Attitudes Toward the Jews," in Heiko A. Oberman, *The Impact of the Reformation* (Grand Rapids, 1994), p. 115.
85. "Luther was anti-Jewish . . . but not anti-Semite or a racist of any kind because . . . for him a baptised Jew [was] fully Christian. . . . Not race, but belief in the law, in good works, makes Jews." Oberman, "Nazi Conscription," in ibid. pp. 69–78.
86. See chap. 8.
87. Wallmann, "Reception of Luther's Writings on the Jews," p. 135.
88. Oberman, "Three Attitudes," pp. 106–9; also, ed.'s introduction, "On the Jews," pp. 126, 132–34; "On the Lies of the Jews," pp. 126, 132–33.
89. See chap. 11.
90. Volker Press, "Germany Between Religion and Revolution," In

James F. Harris, ed., *German-American Interrelations: Heritage and Challenge* (Tübingen, 1985), pp. 67–78; Craig, *The Germans*, pp. 85–86.

91. See discussion in Ozment, *Ancestors*, pp. 31–32. On the alleged "sea change" for women, see Lyndal Roper, *The Holy Household: Religion, Morals, and Order in Reformation Europe* (Oxford, 1989), chap. 7.
92. Ozment, *Age of Reform*, pp. 281–84.
93. Peter Blickle, *The Revolution of 1525*, trans. Thomas Dunlap (Munich, 1975), pp. 155-61, 183-85; Brady, *Turning Swiss*, chap. 5; and Strauss, *Law, Resistance, and the State*, pp. 268-71. To the contrary, Ozment, *Protestants*, pp. 118–48.
94. See Introduction.
95. Karl Lüdecke, "Lucas Cranach in seiner Zeit," in *Lucas Cranach. Der Künstler und seine Zeit* (Berlin, 1953), pp. 104–8, 116–20; Ernst Ullmann, "Lucas Cranach der Aeltere, Bürger und Hofmaler," *Lucas Cranach, Künstler, und seine Gesellschaft*, ed., Cranach-Komitee der DDR, (Wittenberg, 1973), pp. 59–61.
96. The brothers Barthel and Sebald Beham, and Georg Pencz.
97. Hutchison, *Albrecht Dürer*, pp. 181–82, 200–204.
98. Germanisches Nationalmuseum, ed., *Martin Luther und die Reformation in Deutschland. Ausstellung zum 500. Geburtstag Martin Luthers*, (Frankfurt-am-Main, 1983), no. 338, pp. 262–63.
99. Hutchison, *Albrecht Dürer*, pp. 181–82; Ozment, *Mysticism and Dissent*, p. 143, n. 28.
100. Ozment, *Age of Reform*, p. 287.
101. Hutchison, *Albrecht Dürer*, pp. 200–204.
102. Friedrich Engels put Luther high on his list of history's "greatest bootlickers of political authority," while the anti-Semite and war criminal Julius Streicher invoked his anti-Jewish writings in his own self-defense at the Nuremberg trials. Günther Vögler, *"Die Gewalt soll gegeben werden dem gemeinen Volk": Der deutsche Bauernkrieg 1525* (Berlin, 1975), pp. 16–24; Oberman, "The Nationalist Conscription of Martin Luther," in *The Impact of the Reformation*, pp. 69–78.
103. "On Temporal Authority: To What Extent Should It Be Obeyed [1523]," *Luther's Works*, vol. 45, pp. 83–84. At the beginning of the Peasants' Revolt, Luther laid the blame directly at the feet of ecclesiastical and secular landlords. "An Admonition to Peace: A Reply to the Twelve Articles of the Peasants in Swabia [1525]," *Works of Martin Luther*, vol. 4 (Philadelphia, 1931), p. 220.

104. "Als die gerne menschlich und natürlich recht wollten haben," ibid., p. 234; Ozment, *Protestants*, p. 129.
105. "Admonition to Peace," pp. 241–42.
106. "Against the Robbing and Murdering Peasants [1525]," *Works of Martin Luther*, vol. 4, pp. 249–50. Much scholarship has followed Peter Blickle in seeing the revolt as larger than the peasants, a "revolution of the common man" in both villages and towns. Blickle, *Communal Reformation: The Quest for Salvation in Sixteenth-Century Germany*, trans. by Thomas Dunlap (Atlantic Highlands, N.J., 1985), chap. 7.
107. By century's end imperial reform had given the princes control of an imperial cameral court and a shorter-lived imperial governing council. On the evolution of the Holy Roman Empire, James A. Vann and Steven W. Rowan, eds., *The Old Reich: Essays on German Political Institutions, 1495–1806* (Brussels, 1974), and J. W. Zophy, ed., *The Holy Roman Empire: A Dictionary Handbook* (Westport, Conn., 1980).
108. Marc Forster, *The Counterreformation in the Villages: Religion and Reform in the Bishopric of Speyer, 1560–1720* (Ithaca, 1992).
109. Ozment, *Age of Reform*, p. 271. Instructed by court secretary Spalatin on behalf of Elector Frederick the Wise to curtail his protest against the sale of a new indulgence in Halle by the episcopal prince of Mainz, Luther professed his willingness to "lose" them both: "Your idea about not disturbing the public peace is beautiful, but will you allow the eternal peace of God to be disturbed by . . . that son of perdition? No, Spalatin! No, Elector." Letter to Spalatin, November 11, 1521, *Luther's Works*, vol. 48, ed. G. Krodel (Philadelphia, 1963), p. 326. On the development of resistance theory among early Saxon lawyers and clergy, Heinz Scheible, *Das Widerstandsrecht als Problem der deutschen Protestanten, 1523–46* (Gütersloh, 1969); cf. Quentin Skinner, *The Foundations of Modern Political Thought*, vol. 2 (Cambridge, 1978), chap. 7.
110. Julian H. Franklin, trans. and ed., *Constitutionalism and Resistance in the Sixteenth Century: Three Treatises by Hotman, Beza, & Mornay* (New York, 1969); Ozment, *Age of Reform*, pp. 270–72, 419–22; cf. David M. Whitford, *Tyranny and Resistance: The Magdeburg Confession and the Lutheran Tradition* (St. Louis, 2001).

4. *Europe's Stomping Ground: Germany During the Thirty Years' War*

1. Volker Press, "Germany Between Reformation and Revolution," in Harris, ed. *German-American Interrelations*, p. 70. For the modern political debate the war and its peace stimulated in nineteenth-century Germany, see Kevin C. Cramer, "Lamentations of Germany: the Historiography of the Thirty Years War, 1790–1890" (Ph.D. diss., Harvard University, 1998), pp. 270–78. For recent studies of the constitutional side of the conflict, Ronald G. Ash, *The Thirty Years War; the Holy Roman Empire, and Europe, 1618–48* (New York, 1997). The old classic, in large historical context, is R. J. W. Evans, *The Making of the Hapsburg Monarchy, 1550–1700* (Oxford, 1979).
2. Geoffrey Parker, ed., *The Thirty Years' War* (London, 1997), pp. 5–10. On the confessional side of the conflict and its background, Robert Bireley, S.J., *Religion and Politics in the Age of the Counterreformation: Emperor Ferdinand II, William Lamoraini, S.J., and the Formation of Imperial Policy* (Chapel Hill, 1981), and Menna Prestwich, *International Calvinism, 1541–1715* (Oxford, 1985).
3. John G. Gagliardo, *Germany Under the Old Regime, 1600–1790* (London, 1991), pp. 2–3; Parker, *Thirty Years' War*, pp. 12–14; Holborn, pp. 43–44.
4. Holborn, *Reformation*, pp. 244–45, 285; Parker, *War*, p. 17.
5. See chap. 4.
6. Holborn, *Reformation*, pp. 289–90; Gagliardo, *Old Regime*, pp. 16, 20–21; Parker, *War*, p. 18.
7. Simon Adams, "The Union, the League, and the Politics of Europe," in Parker, *War*, pp. 21–25, 28–29.
8. Michael Hughes, *Early Modern Germany, 1477–1806* (Philadelphia, 1992), pp. 86–87.
9. On Elector Frederick's motivations, legal-constitutional and religious, see Brennan Pursell, "The Constitutional Causes of the Thirty Years' War: Friedrich V, the Palatine Crisis, and European Politics, 1618–32" (Ph.D. diss., Harvard University, 2000).
10. Geoffrey Parker, "The War for Bohemia," in Parker, *War*, pp. 42–54; Simon Adams and Geoffrey Parker, "Europe and the Palatine War," in ibid., pp. 56–60.
11. Adams and Parker, "Europe and the Palatine War," pp. 61–63. On Maximilian and the Bavarians' changing roles in the war, cf. Dieter Albrecht, *Maximilian I. von Bayern, 1573–1651* (Munich, 1998).

12. On Christian and the Danish period of the war, Paul D. Lockhart, *Denmark in the Thirty Years War, 1618–48: King Christian IV and the Decline of the Oldenburg State* (Selinsgrove, Pa., 1996).
13. On the Peace of Lübeck, see E. Ladewig Petersen, "The Danish Intermezzo," in Parker, *War*, pp. 65–71; Holborn, *Reformation*, pp. 327–34.
14. R. W. J. Evans, "The Imperial Vision," in Parker, *War*, pp. 75–78, 82–84; Parker, "The Practice of Absolutism I: 1621–26," in ibid., pp. 82–84.
15. The church lands and imperial cities of Electoral Saxony and Brandenburg had been secularized before 1552 and thus escaped the reach of the decree. Gerhard Benecke, "The Practice of Absolutism II: 1626–29," in Parker, *War*, pp. 87–89.
16. Bodo Nischan, "On the Edge of the Abyss," in Parker, *War*, p. 101.
17. On the Swedish king and the Swedish phase of the war, see Michael Roberts, *Gustavus Adolphus* (London, 1992).
18. Parker, *War*, pp. 102–4, 106–9; cf. the description of Elector John George of Saxony (1585–1656) as a practitioner of "Lutheran pacifism, quietism, legalism, and xenophobia." Ibid., pp. 85–86. Hughes, *Early Modern Germany*, p. 90.
19. Hans Medick, "Historisches Ereignis und zeitgenössische Erfahrung: die Eroberung und Zerstörung Magdeburgs 1631," in Medick et al., eds., *Zwischen Alltag und Katastrophe: der dreissigjährige Krieg aus der Nähe* (Göttingen, 1999), pp. 377–407.
20. Geoffrey Parker, "The Intervention of Sweden," in Parker, *War*, pp. 112–16.
21. Geoffrey Parker, "1633–35: Oxenstierna vs. Wallenstein," in Parker, *War*, p. 155.
22. Ibid., pp. 117–20.
23. Hughes, *Early Modern Germany*, p. 91.
24. Richard Bonney, "France's War by Diversion," in Parker, *War*, p. 129.
25. The lower estimates are Parker's (*War*, pp. 147–48, 187–88), the higher, Hughes's (*Early Modern Europe*, p. 109). The most recent research favors the lower estimates, based on evidence that local authorities reporting postwar loss of life and damages often intentionally exaggerated both to gain tax cuts and increase their share of government restoration funds. John Theibault, "The Rhetoric of Death and Destruction in the Thirty Years' War," *Journal of Social*

History 27 (1993): 271–90, and "The Demography of the Thirty Years War Re-revisited," *German History* 15 (1997): 1–2.

26. Hughes, *Early Modern Germany*, p. 92, 98; Parker, *War*, 140–41, 159, 165, 194–95.
27. Hughes, *Early Modern Germany*, p. 94.
28. Ibid., pp. 95–96; Geoffrey Parker, "1647–50: The Making of Peace," in Parker, *War*, p. 163; Parker, "The War and Politics," in ibid., p. 195.
29. Press, "Germany between Reformation and Revolution," p. 70.

5. *Enemy Mine: Absolutism and the Rise of Prussia*

1. Mary Fulbrook, *A Concise History of Germany* (Cambridge, 1999), pp. 74–75.
2. Gagliardo, *Germany Under the Old Regime*, pp. 96–99.
3. Hughes, *Early Modern Germany*, pp. 115–16, 120.
4. Cited by Schulze, *Germany*, pp. 87–88.
5. Fulbrook, *Concise History*, pp. 83–84.
6. Schulze, *Germany*, p. 70.
7. Detlef Plöse, "Kaiser Leopold I," in Rolf Straubel et al., *Kaiser König Kardinal: Deutsche Fürsten 1500–1800* (Leipzig, 1991), pp. 188–89.
8. Gagliardo, *Germany Under the Old Regime*, pp. 2–3, 13; Hughes, *Early Modern Germany*, pp. 124–28, 131.
9. As ruler of Brandenburg, he was one of the eight German electoral princes who chose the Holy Roman Emperor.
10. Fulbrook, *Concise History*, pp. 76–81 (map); Schulze, *Germany*, p. 79; Philip Woodfine, *Frederick the Great of Prussia* (Huddersfield, 1990), p. 14; cf. C. A. Macartney, *The Hapsburg and Hohenzollern Dynasties in the Seventeenth and Eighteenth Centuries* (London, 1970).
11. Giles MacDonogh, *Frederick the Great: A Life in Deed and Letters* (New York, 1999), pp. 17–18, 24–25; Rolf Straubel, "Friedrich II von Preussen," *Kaiser König Kardinal. Deutsche Fürsten 1500–1800* (Leipzig, 1991), pp. 312–13; Fulbrook, *Concise History*, p. 79.
12. Hughes, *Early Modern Germany*, pp. 142–44.
13. F. E. Stoeffler, *German Pietism During the Eighteenth Century* (Leiden, 1973), pp. 24–27; Gagliardo, *Germany Under the Old Regime*, p. 191; J. V. H. Melton, *Absolutism and the Eighteenth Century Origins of Compulsory Schooling in Prussia and Austria* (Cambridge, 1988).
14. Editor's introduction, P. J. Spener, *Pia Desideria*, trans. T. G. Tappert (Philadelphia, 1964), pp. 8–21; Gagliardo, *Germany*, p. 183.

15. Gagliardo, *Germany*, pp. 107–10, 116. Here princely absolutism (the prince's unique authority to legislate) was not despotism (the absence of individual rights and the prince's ownership of everything and everybody). The ruler was always under divine and national law, making "duty and responsibility for the welfare of his people . . . inescapable parts of [his] entitlement to rule." Ibid., p. 121. Cf. Mary Fulbrook, *Piety and Politics: Religion and the Rise of Absolutism in England, Württemberg and Prussia* (Cambridge, 1983).
16. Stoeffler, *German Pietism*, pp. 37–38.
17. *Pia Desideria*, p. 80; Stoeffler, *German Pietism*, p. 69.
18. MacDonogh, *Frederick the Great*, pp. 29, 52–54; Straubel, "Friedrich II," p. 314.
19. MacDonogh, *Frederick the Great*, pp. 35, 42; David Fraser, *Frederick the Great: King of Prussia* (New York, 2000), p. 24.
20. Straubel, "Friedrich II," p. 314; Woodfine, *Frederick the Great*, p. 6.
21. MacDonogh, *Frederick the Great*, pp. 35, 50–53; Straubel, "Friedrich II," p. 315; Fraser, *Frederick the Great*, pp. 25, 37, 40.
22. Fraser, *Frederick the Great*, pp. 38–42.
23. MacDonogh suggests that, in 1729, seventeen-year-old Frederick's personal squire possibly "confirmed in him certain [sexual] ideas that were only then half-forming in his mind." *Frederick the Great*, pp. 48–49; on the cumulative evidence of Frederick's homosexuality, ibid., pp. 106, 169, 195, 202–4, 221–22, 242, 230.
24. Ibid., pp. 48–49; Fraser, *Frederick the Great*, pp. 28–29.
25. MacDonogh, *Frederick the Great*, pp. 63–75, 80–88; Straubel, "Friedrich II," p. 315; Fraser, *Frederick the Great*, pp. 29–31.
26. Frederick's brother William provided the dynasty's successor, future king Frederick William II (1744–97).
27. MacDonogh, *Frederick the Great*, pp. 99–100, 105, 135, 194; Straubel, "Friedrich II," p. 315.
28. In addition to Maupertuis, the German philosopher Christian Wolff, a Halle professor and leading figure of the German Enlightenment, and Count Francesco Algarotti, an Italian philosopher and Voltaire crony who supplied Frederick with the latest English books, were among the first resident intellectuals. MacDonogh, *Frederick the Great*, pp. 123–24; Fraser, *Frederick the Great*, pp. 33, 257–58.
29. Between 1770 and 1830 "Goethe, Schilling, Lessing, Kant, and Mozart made the German-speaking world the cultural cradle of Europe for half a century, ending the long dominance of French cul-

tural values." William Carr, *The Origins of the Wars of German Unification* (New York, 1992), p. 16; Fulbrook, *Concise History*, pp. 85–95.

30. MacDonogh, *Frederick the Great*, pp. 110, 137–39, 206, 323, 350, 370; Fraser, *Frederick the Great*, p. 608; Schulze, *Germany*, p. 89.
31. MacDonogh, *Frederick the Great*, pp. 124, 137–40; Straubel, "Friedrich II," p. 316.
32. Fraser, *Frederick the Great*, pp. 78, 80, 625.
33. Ibid., pp. 81–82; Woodfine, *Frederick the Great*, p. 2.
34. Macdonogh, *Frederick the Great*, pp. 145, 165–69. Daniel Gordon cites evidence suggesting that "Voltaire consummated his love for Frederick" in 1740, after being enchanted upon their very first meeting by Frederick's "large blue eyes and gentle smile," his head "swirling" in response to Frederick's "seductive gestures": "I gave myself to him with passion, with blindness, and without reasoning." Voltaire, *Candide*, trans. and ed. Daniel Gordon (Boston, 1999), p. 27.
35. Cited by Macdonogh, *Frederick the Great*, pp. 213–14, 234; Woodfine, *Frederick the Great*, p. 5.
36. Macdonogh, *Frederick the Great*, pp. 209, 217–21, 225–26.
37. Ibid., pp. 227, 229–30; Straubel, "Frederick II," pp. 316–17.
38. On Maria's career, Ingrid Mittenzwei, "Königin Maria Theresia," in Straubel et al., *Kaiser König Kardinal*, pp. 325–38.
39. See chap. 1; Woodfine, *Frederick the Great*, p. 14. MacDonogh claims that the Silesian wars began the blitzkrieg tradition. *Frederick the Great*, pp. 152–53.
40. Fraser, *Frederick the Great*, pp. 84, 89–94, 117–19; MacDonogh, *Frederick the Great*, pp. 155–58, 174–76; Hughes, *Early Modern Germany*, p. 140; Woodfine, *Frederick the Great*, pp. 12–13.
41. From Frederick's *Memoirs of the House of Brandenburg* (1746), cited by MacDonogh, *Frederick the Great*, pp. 196–97. "A monarch is not raised to his lofty rank . . . to grow fat on the people's substance and enjoy himself while everyone else suffers; the monarchy is the first servant of the state." Cited by Woodfine, *Frederick the Great*, p. 19.
42. Cited by MacDonogh, *Frederick the Great*, p. 247; Hughes, *Early Modern Germany*, pp. 129–31.
43. Simon Millar, *Kolin 1757: Frederick the Great's First Defeat* (Oxford, 2001), p. 41.
44. Albert Speer, *Inside the Third Reich: Memoirs*, trans. Richard and Clara Winston (New York, 1969), pp. 453, 463.

45. Hughes, *Early Modern Germany*, pp. 155–58; MacDonogh, *Frederick the Great*, pp. 260–66, 282–83, 286–89, 316–18.
46. Straubel, "Friedrich II," p. 318.
47. Nicholas Boyle, *Goethe: The Poet and the Age, II: Revolution and Renunciation (1790–1803)* (Oxford, 2000), pp. 26–27; Hughes, *Early Modern Germany*, pp. 145–46; Straubel, "Friedrich II," pp. 316–18.
48. See chap. 6, n. 11.
49. Hughes, *Early Modern Germany*, pp. 160, 164–66; MacDonogh, *Frederick the Great*, pp. 342–44, 347.
50. Fraser, *Frederick the Great*, pp. 599, 601, 614, 616.
51. See n. 15.
52. MacDonogh, *Frederick the Great*, pp. 198–99; Gagliardo, *Germany*, pp. 211–16.
53. Pamela M. Potter, *Most German of the Arts: Musicology and Society from the Weimar Republic to the End of Hitler's Reich* (New Haven, 1998), pp. 201–2.
54. Ulrich Siegele, "Bach and the Domestic Politics of Electoral Saxony," in John Butt, ed., *The Cambridge Companion to Bach* (Cambridge, England, 1997), pp. 17–34.
55. Cf. John Butt, "Bach's Metaphysics of Music," in ibid., pp. 46–59, and "Bach and the Rationalist Philosophy of Wolff, Leibnitz, and Spinoza," in ibid., pp. 60–71.
56. See chap. 6.

6. *Trojan Horses: From the French to the German Revolution*

1. Diether Raff, *A History of Germany, from the Medieval Empire to the Present*, trans. Bruce Little (Oxford, 1988), pp. 34–37.
2. Parker, *The Thirty Years' War*, pp. 126 ff, 137.
3. Hughes, *Early Modern Germany*, p. 171; Raff, *A History of Germany*, pp. 39–40.
4. Sheehan, *German History, 1770–1866*, p. 372; see n. 14.
5. Cited by Ernst Cassirer, *The Philosophy of the Enlightenment* (Princeton, 1951), p. 12. See also Norman Hampson, "The Enlightenment in France," in *The Enlightenment in National Context*, ed. Roy Porter and M. Teich (Cambridge, 1981), pp. 41–42; H. R. Trevor-Roper, "The Religious Origins of the Enlightenment" in H.R. Trevor-Roper, *Religion, the Reformation and Social Change* (London, 1967), pp. 193–236.

6. Cited by Cassirer, *Enlightenment*, p. 163.
7. Jean-Jacques Rousseau, *"Émile" or On Education*, trans. Allan Bloom (New York, 1979), bk. 1, p. 37; Cassirer, *Enlightenment*, p. 156.
8. On the revolution from below, see Robert Darnton, *The Forbidden Best-Sellers of Pre-Revolutionary France* (New York, 1996).
9. Hampson calls attention to Rousseau's influence on Brissot, Robespierre, and Saint-Just, "The Enlightenment in France," pp. 49, 51, 53. On German romanticism and the revolutionary age, Sheehan, *German History, 1770–1866*, pp. 330–39, and Darrin M. McMahon, *Enemies of the Enlightenment: The French Counter-Enlightenment and the Making of Modernity* (New York, 2001).
10. Joachim Whaley, "The Protestant Enlightenment in Germany," in Porter, *Enlightenment*, pp. 108–9.
11. Hughes, *Early Modern Germany*, p. 171; Sheehan, *German History, 1700–1866*, p. 372. Boyle, *Goethe*, p. 26.
12. Whaley, "The Protestant Enlightenment in Germany," p. 111; Gagliardo, *Germany Under the Old Regime*, p. 187.
13. Humboldt's 1792 tract was entitled, *Ideen zu einem Versuch, die Grenzen der Wirksamkeit des Staates zu bestimmen*, Luther's 1523 *Von welltlicher uberkeytt wie weytt man yhr gehorsam schuldig sey*.
14. Thus Boyle, *Goethe II*, pp. 18–31. Sheehan's liberal reading of this period places Humboldt "closer to the eighteenth-century ideal of moral reforms than to the nineteenth-century politics of liberalism," thus, with Justus Möser, Adam Müller, and Edmund Burke, whose writings on the French Revolution "helped [the Germans justify] the old order, which would be turned against the revolutionaries in France and the reformers closer to home." *German History, 1770–1866*, pp. 364–65, 368–70. Cf. Klaus Epstein, *The Genesis of Modern German Conservatism* (Princeton, 1966).
15. Boyle, *Goethe II*, pp. 8–9.
16. Williston Walker, *A History of the Christian Church* (New York, 1959), pp. 521–22. The story of the Revolution is memorably told by Georges LeFebvre, *The Coming of the French Revolution*, trans. R. R. Palmer (Princeton, 1967); Keith M. Baker, et al., eds., *The French Revolution and the Creation of Modern Political Culture*, vols. 1–3 (New York, 1987); and Patrice Higonnet, *Goodness Beyond Virtue: Jacobins During the French Revolution* (Cambridge, Mass., 1998).
17. Boyle, *Goethe II*, pp. 10–11.
18. Sheehan, *German History*, p. 214; Raff, *A History of Germany*, p. 51;

cf. Schulze, *Germany*, p. 106. On German intellectuals and the Revolution, see also Jacques Droz, *L'Allemagne et la Revolution Française* (Paris, 1949).

19. "Franztum drängt in diesen verworrenen Tagen, wie ehemals! Luthertum es getan, ruhige Bildung zurück." Cited by Sheehan, *German History*, p. 359.
20. Ibid., pp. 358–59, 385–86, 573–77.
21. Ibid., pp. 211, 384.
22. "Not God or nature, but a dark demonic force [was] behind phenomena." Michael Allen Gillespie, *Nihilism Before Nietzsche* (Chicago, 1994), pp. xvii, xix.
23. Sheehan, *German History*, pp. 360–61.
24. Boyle, *Goethe II*, pp. 24, 26–27; Hughes, *Early Modern Germany*, pp. 170–71; Blackbourn, *Nineteenth Century*, pp. 215–20. *Sans culottes*, "without breeches"—the name given the working classes who did not wear the fancy kneepants of the aristocrats.
25. "Germans were skeptical of the French precisely because of their confidence that the world could be set right by drafting the perfect constitution." William Carr, *The Origins of the Wars of German Unification* (London, 1991), p. 13.
26. *Exposition of Psalm 101* (1534), *Luther's Works*, vol. 13, p. 217. For Burke's 1790 "Reflections on the Revolution in France" and 1796 "Letters on a Regicide Peace," see *The Works of the Right Honourable Edmund Burke*, vol. 2 (London, 1855), pp. 277–518, and vol. 5 (London, 1861), pp. 152–355, 358-434; see also Boyle, *Goethe II*, pp. 6, 8–9.
27. Boyle, *Goethe II*, pp. 14–16; Hughes, *Early Modern Germany*, p. 174; Raff, *A History of Germany*, pp. 40–41.
28. Sheehan, *German History*, pp. 233, 239–40.
29. Raff, *A History of Germany*, p. 41; Hughes, *Early Modern Germany*, pp. 177–78; Sheehan, *German History*, p. 241.
30. Sheehan, *German History*, pp. 243–46; Carr, *Origins*, p. 9.
31. Hughes counts forty, Schulze thirty. Hughes, *Early Modern Germany*, pp. 179–81; Raff, *A History of Germany*, p. 42; Schulze, *Germany*, pp. 97. Sheehan calls the Reichsdeputationshauptschluss "one of the greatest territorial rearrangements in all of European history." *German History*, p. 343.
32. Martin Kitchen, *The Cambridge Illustrated History of Germany* (Cambridge, 2000), p. 152; Sheehan, *German History*, pp. 247–49, 259–61; Carr, *Origins*, p. 9.

33. Carr, *Origins*, pp. 10–11.
34. Schulze, *Germany*, pp. 103–4; Sheehan, *German History*, pp. 303–11, 421–22.
35. T. C. W. Blanning, *The French Revolution in Germany: Occupation and Resistance in the Rhineland 1792–1802* (Oxford, 1983), pp. 13, 16.
36. Hughes, *Early Modern Germany*, pp. 183–88; Raff, *A History of Germany*, pp. 42–44; Schulze, *Germany*, pp. 102–4; Kitchen, *Germany*, pp. 154–57; Carr, *Origins*, pp. 21–23; Sheehan, *German History*, pp. 255, 273.
37. Cf. Carr, *Origins*, pp. 13–15; Sheehan, *German History*, p. 217.
38. Carr describes the new professional classes (*Bildungsbürgertum*) of the late eighteenth and nineteenth centuries, who were given great power in the running of governments, as men "opposed to old-style absolutism [yet] mostly respectful of princely authority [and lacking the] bitter sense of underprivilege and social deprivation . . . felt by their French counterparts." *Origins*, p. 15. But were not such men ever thus? See the examples of Georg Spalatin (chap. 3) and Gustav Stresemann (chap. 10).
39. Later, with equally disastrous results, an imperious Hitler would twice repeat Napoleon's Russian blunder by sending a German army first to Moscow (December 1941), and then to besiege Stalingrad (January 1943), a strategic gateway on the southern route to the Caspian oil fields. In Stalingrad the three hundred thousand soldiers of the German Sixth Army, under orders to fight to the last, were surrounded and decimated, the few survivors surrendering abjectly in the end. Raff, *A History of Germany*, pp. 47–50, 309, see chap. 11.
40. Raff, *A History of Germany*, pp. 51–54; Schulze, *Germany*, pp. 106–10; Sheehan, *German History*, pp. 403–5.
41. Cited by Raff, *A History of Germany*, pp. 56–57.
42. Kitchen, *Germany*, p. 168; Schulze, *Germany*, p. 113; Blackbourn, *Nineteenth Century*, p. 270; Veit Valentin, *1848: Chapters of German History*, trans. E. T. Scheffauer (Hamden, Conn., 1965), pp. 428–29.
43. Sheehan, *German History*, p. 536
44. Steven Ozment, *Flesh and Spirit: Family Life in Early Modern Germany* (New York, 1999), esp. chaps. 2, 3, and 5.
45. Wolfram Siemann, *The German Revolution of 1848–49*, trans. C. Banerji (New York, 1998), pp. 15–16; Thomas Nipperdey, *Germany from Napoleon to Bismarck* (Dublin, 1966), 224–26.
46. The transformation from "an association of subjects to a society of

citizens." Nipperdey, *Germany*, p. 227; Siemann, *German Revolution*, p. 20.

47. Nipperdey, *Germany*, pp. 228–29, 231; Siemann, *German Revolution*, pp. 24–25, 34.
48. Eighteen percent of enrolled university students (fifteen hundred out of eight thousand) joined the movement; 486 of those attended the Eisenach Festival. Carr, *Origins*, p. 25; Kitchen, *Germany*, p. 166; Sheehan, *German History*, p. 406.
49. Mosse, *Crisis*, pp. 5, 191; Nipperdey, *Germany from Napoleon to Bismarck*, pp. 244–45.
50. "Why the Books of the Pope . . . Were Burned," *Luther's Works*, vol. 31, pp. 383–95.
51. Nipperdey, *Germany*, pp. 245–49; Sheehan, *German History*, p. 407.
52. Raff, *A History of Germany*, p. 64–67; Sheehan, *German History*, pp. 604–7; Gall, *Bismarck*, I, pp. 6–7.
53. Blackbourn, *Nineteenth Century*, pp. 126–27; Sheehan, *German History*, pp. 581–84, 610–13.
54. Raff, *A History of Germany*, pp. 62–63, 66, 96.
55. F. W. Bogen, *The German in America* (Boston, 1851), pp. 7, 39–41, 57, 61.
56. Siemann, *German Revolution*, pp. 82–85, 139.
57. See chap. 9.
58. Blackbourn, *Nineteenth Century*, p. 162; Sheehan, *German History*, p. 706.
59. Siemann, *German Revolution*, pp. 120–23; Schulze, *Germany*, p. 124.
60. Raff, *A History of Germany*, pp. 79–80; Siemann, *German Revolution*, pp. 189–93. On the forcing of this issue by Minister President Schwartzenberg, see Sheehan, *German History*, pp. 689, 712, 715.
61. Raff, *A History of Germany*, p. 77; Siemann, *German Revolution*, pp. 127–30.
62. Siemann, *German Revolution*, p. 132.
63. Nipperdey, *Germany*, p. 231. Emancipated peasants "traded one sort of dependence for another." Sheehan, *German History*, pp. 756–57.
64. Siemann, *German Revolution*, p. 132; John Witte, Jr., "The Civic Seminary," pp. 173 ff.
65. Nipperdey, *Germany*, pp. 359–71, 383. On the medieval story, see Brian Tierney, *The Crisis of Church and State, 1050–1300* (Toronto, 1988), pp. 172–210.
66. Siemann, *German Revolution*, pp. 134, 137–38.

67. Blackbourn, *Nineteenth Century*, p. 161; Siemann, *German Revolution*, pp. 196–98.
68. Siemann, *German Revolution*, 198; *Facts*, pp. 100–101; cf. Kitchen, *Germany*, pp. 84, 185–87.
69. Siemann, *German Revolution*, pp. 222–23.
70. Blickle, *Die Revolution von 1525*, pp. 217–23, 242.
71. Schulze, *Germany*, p. 129; Siemann, *German Revolution*, pp. 210–20.
72. See chap. 7.

7. *Absolute Spirit and Absolute People: The Intellectual Torrents of the Nineteenth Century*

1. See chap. 8.
2. Cf. Müller, *Another Country*, an incisive critique of post–World War II thinkers.
3. Karl Barth, *From Rousseau to Ritschl*, trans. B. Cozens (London, 1952), chap. 4.
4. Other formulations of Kant's maxim: "So act as to treat humanity, whether in thine own person or in that of another, in every case as an end withal, never as a means only"; "Act so that the maxim of thy will can always at the same time hold good as a principle of universal legislation." *Religion Within the Limits of Reason Alone*, trans. T. M. Greene et al. (Chicago, 1960), pp. 23–31, 54–56, 65; cf. Boyle, *Goethe II*, pp. 49–50.
5. Sheehan, *German History*, pp. 330–41.
6. "This 'I' replaces God as the transrational source of nature and natural law." Michael A. Gillespie, *Nihilism Before Nietzsche* (Chicago, 1994), p. xvii; "Individual ego opened onto the one immediate spiritual Life, which is the creator of all phenomena." Sheehan, *German History*, p. 344.
7. "A historical geography of the Spirit's evolution from the beginning of human history to the present . . . the rational pattern that gives meaning to [man's] tragic history." Sheehan, *German History*, pp. 350–51; Gillespie, *Nihilism Before Nietzsche*, pp. xv–xvi.
8. From *Reason in History* (1832), cited by Karl Löwith, *From Hegel to Nietzsche: The Revolution in Nineteenth-Century Thought* (New York, 1964), p. 331.
9. Gillespie, *Nihilism Before Nietzsche*, pp. xvii, xix.

10. *Thus Spake Zarathustra*, in *The Portable Nietzsche*, trans. and ed., Walter Kaufmann (New York, 1968), pp. 202, 208.
11. Barth, *Rousseau to Ritschl*, p. 224; Nipperdey, *Germany from Napoleon to Bismarck*, pp. 356–58, 375–76.
12. *On Religion: Speeches to its Cultural Despisers*, trans. J. Oman (New York, 1958), pp. 29–31.
13. See Warren Breckman, *Marx, the Young Hegelians, and the Origins of Radical Social Theory: Dethroning the Self* (Cambridge, 1999), pp. 2-10.
14. F. Edward Cranz, "Cusanus, Luther, and the Mystical Tradition," in *The Pursuit of Holiness in Late Medieval and Renaissance Religion*, ed. Charles Trinkaus and Heiko A. Oberman (Leiden, 1974), pp. 93–102.
15. Löwith, *Hegel to Nietzsche*, pp. 335, 338–41. For the range of Luther's statements on faith's creative powers, see Kurt Aland, ed., *Lutherlexikon* (Stuttgart, 1957), pp. 144–50. Feuerbach devoted a monograph to Luther, *The Essence of Faith According to Martin Luther* (1844). Luther described the experience of faith as being yanked into a world beyond oneself: *excessus mentis*, the momentary placement of the believer outside himself (*extra se*)—the very opposite of projecting a God. Steven Ozment, *Homo Spiritualis* (Leiden, 1969), pp. 105–8, 196–97, 204–5.
16. Brechman, *Marx, The Young Hegelians*, pp. 90, 96, 106, 109, 119.
17. Cited in ibid., p. 96.
18. Cited in ibid., p. 129.
19. Ibid., pp. 112, 272–73, 279–80.
20. Löwith, *Hegel to Nietzsche*, pp. 241–43, 307–8.
21. F. N. Magill et al., *Masterpieces of World Philosophy* (New York, 1961), pp. 593–600.
22. Compare Bismarck's near identical statement, chap. 8.
23. "Political democracy is Christian since in it man, not merely one man, but every man, ranks as sovereign, as highest being." Cited by Brechman, *Marx, the Young Hegelians*, p. 294. On Hitler's views of Jews and Christians, see chap. 10.
24. Ibid., p. 285.
25. Ibid., p. 278.
26. Ibid., pp. 292–95.
27. Cf. Löwith, *Hegel to Nietzsche*, pp. 169, 245–47, 307–8.
28. Ibid., 275–79.

29. Cited by Löwith, *Hegel to Nietzsche*, p. 114 (from *Das Kapital*). Italics mine.
30. Löwith, *Hegel to Nietzsche*, pp. 313–15.
31. See Bismarck's struggle with the Social Democrats, chap. 9.
32. Cohn, *The Pursuit of the Millennium*, pp. 251–71; Mosse, *The Crisis of German Ideology*, pp. 13, 42; Ozment, *Mysticism and Dissent*, pp. 61–97.
33. *Thus Spake Zarathustra*, pp. 227, 321; Löwith, *Hegel to Nietzsche*, pp. 368–71.
34. Gillespie, *Nihilism Before Nietzsche*, pp. 200, 212.
35. *Thus Spake Zarathustra*, pp. 122, 124–26, 189.
36. Ibid., pp. 199, 227, 253, 330–31.
37. Gillespie, *Nihilism Before Nietzsche*, pp. 199, 221.
38. Ibid., pp. xxi, 203–4, 210, 239–40, 248.
39. See chap. 6.
40. W. M. Simon, *Germany in the Age of Bismarck* (New York, 1968), pp. 155–57.
41. According to James Joll, his criticisms helped undermine "the values of contemporary bourgeois society," and his "calls for action and violence, toughness and ruthlessness [impressed] people in a position to influence the decisions of the rulers of Europe in 1914," thus contributing to the intellectual and emotional climate in which war broke out. *The Origins of the First World War* (London, 1984), pp. 188–89.
42. Rudiger Safranski, *Nietzsche: A Philosophical Biography*, trans. S. Frisch (New York, 2002), p. 329. My thanks to Bolek Kabala for this reference.
43. Schleiermacher, *Speeches on Religion*, p. 36.
44. On these dislocations, see Blackbourn, *Nineteenth Century*, pp. 272–81; Raff, *A History of Germany*, pp. 85–86.
45. "*Volk* signified the union of a group of people with a transcendental 'essence' [which] was fused to man's innermost nature and represented the source of his creativity, his depth of feeling, his individuality, and his unity with other members of the *Volk*." Mosse, *Crisis of German Ideology*, p. 4.
46. "Napoleon had only initiated the process of Germany's subordination; the Congress of Vienna completed it." Ibid. p. 14.
47. Sheehan, *German History, 1770–1866*, pp. 381–83; Mosse, *Crisis of German Ideology*, pp. 4, 14.

48. At mid-century, Wagner was a liberal supporter of the Revolution of 1848, while Riehl opposed it, something Riehl never forgave him for or forgot. Sheehan, *German History, 1770–1866*, pp. 839–40. On Wagner's Germanism in myth and music, see Robert Donington, *Wagner's "Ring" and its Symbols: The Music and the Myth* (New York, 1974).
49. Mosse, *German Ideology*, pp. 19–22, 27–28.
50. Ibid., pp. 33, 36–37, 43.
51. Ibid., pp. 53–57.
52. A striking example is Hans Boesch's illustrated history of German childhood between 1500 and 1800. *Kinderleben in der deutschen Vergangenheit 15. bis 18. Jahrhundert* (Leipzig, 1900; Düsseldorf, 1979).
53. See chap. 11.
54. *Faust, A Tragedy*, trans. Bayard Taylor (New York, 1950), Bk. I, scene 2, p. 39. Compare the far more sober utopian literature of the sixteenth century: Miriam Eliav-Feldon, *Realistic Utopias: The Ideal Imaginary Societies of the Renaissance 1516–1630* (Oxford, 1982), pp. 109, 119, 121–33; Ozment, *The Reformation in the Cities* (New Haven, 1975), pp. 91–107.
55. Mosse, *German Ideology*, pp. 89–91; Tacitus and Luther had earlier called attention to the purity of German peasant culture.
56. Paul L. Rose, *Revolutionary Antisemitism in Germany: From Kant to Wagner* (Princeton, 1990), pp. 358–76; Blackbourn, *Nineteenth Century*, pp. 432–33.
57. Richie Robertson, "Varieties of Antisemitism From Herder to Fassbinder," in Edward Timms and Andrea Hammel, eds., *The German-Jewish Dilemma: From the Enlightenment to the Shoah* (Lewiston, Maine, 1999), p. 112.
58. Mosse, *Germany Ideology*, pp. 91–96.
59. Maynard Solomon, *Beethoven* (New York, 1977), pp. 4–5, 20–22, 34, 85–89, 94–95.
60. Ibid., pp. 132–36.
61. Ibid., pp. 156–57.
62. Ibid., pp. 85–89.
63. Ibid., pp. 310–13.
64. Ibid., p. 315.
65. On its history, see *Faust, A Tragedy*, pp. vi–viii; cf. Richard Auernheimer and Frank Baron, eds. *Das Faustbuch von 1587: Provokation und Wirkung* (Munich, 1991).

66. *Faust, A Tragedy*, part I, scene I, p. 10; cf. Luther on reason as it is under either God's or the devil's control. *Luther's Tabletalk*, no. 439 (1933), p. 71.
67. *Faust, A Tragedy*, part I, scene I, pp. 24, 26.
68. Ibid., pp. xvii–xviii, xxi; part I, scene III, pp. 49–56; scene IV, p.
69. Ibid., part I, scene IV, p. 58.
70. Ibid., part II, act V, p. 241.
71. Ibid.

8. Revolutionary Conservatism: The Age of Bismarck

1. Raff, *A History of Germany*, p. 176; Katherine A. Lerman, "Bismarckian Germany and the Structure of the German Empire," in Mary Fulbrook, ed., *German History Since 1800* (London, 1997), p. 154; Lothar Gall, *Bismarck: The White Revolutionary: 1871–1898*, II, trans. J. A. Underwood (London, 1986), pp. 217, 234, 237.
2. Lothar Gall, *Bismarck: The White Revolutionary, I: 1851–1871* (London, 1986), pp. 13–17. Otto Pflanze, *Bismarck and the Development of Germany*, I, 2nd. ed. (Princeton, 1990), pp. 32–38.
3. Over their forty-seven-year marriage, Johanna was the recipient of a treasure trove of letters describing the comings and goings of the most prominent politician of the age. *The Love Letters of Bismarck, 1846–1889*, trans. Charlton T. Lewis (New York, 1901). Otto Pflanze, *Bismarck*, I, pp. 48–53. On Schleiermacher and the religious climate: Karl Barth, *From Rousseau to Ritschl* (London, 1959), chap. 8, and Nipperdey, *Germany*, pp. 376–78.
4. "For seventeen hundred years, from the fall of Jerusalem to the French Revolution, Jews had been able to equate religion with nationality." Peter Pulzer, "Emancipation and its Discontents: the German-Jewish Dilemma," in Edward Timms & Andrea Hammel, *The German-Jewish Dilemma: From the Enlightenment to the Shoah* (Lewiston, 1996), p. 11. As Blackbourn points out, "The Reformation was never far below the surface," and Germany's leading educator, Wilhelm von Humboldt, would have agreed. Blackbourn, *Nineteenth Century*, p. 293; Pulzer, "Emancipation," pp. 8, 12; Gall, *Bismarck*, I, pp. 29–32, 321; Emil Ludwig, *Bismarck* (Munich, 1927/1975), p. 93.
5. Blackbourn, *Nineteenth Century*, pp. 287.
6. James Stayer, *Anabaptists and the Sword* (Lawrence, Kans., 1972).

7. Blackbourn, *Nineteenth Century*, pp. 287–89; Pulzer "Emancipation," pp. 14–16.
8. In 1879. Blackbourn, *Nineteenth Century*, pp. 307–08. On the Jew as also a symbol for the disturbingly ancient and medieval, cf. Jeremy Cohen, *The Friars and the Jews: The Evolution of Medieval Anti-Judaism* (Ithaca, 1982), pp. 14–16. On the ability of the nineteenth century to manufacture its own original anti-Semitic and anti-Christian fantasies, Fritz Stern, T*he Politics of Cultural Despair: A Study in the Rise of the Germanic Ideology* (Berkeley, 1974), pp. xvi, 167–68, 283–89.
9. Brian Vick describes the assembly as neither "generally philosemitic" nor "radically anti-Semitic." It rather "accepted in principle both Jewish emancipation and the continuance of Jewish religion and cultural community." *Defining Germany: The 1848 Frankfurt Parliamentarians and National Identity* (Cambridge, Mass., 2002), p. 211.
10. Pulzer, "Emancipation," pp. 7-8, 12, 14.
11. National Liberal Party leader Eduard Lasker, whom Bismarck came to count as his chief enemy, was Jewish and the draftsman of his party's platform in support of Bismarck's "smaller German" empire. Ibid., p. 10.
12. Ludwig, *Bismarck*, pp. 353–54.
13. He later merged his religious belief and philosophy of history to conclude: "History . . . does not roll on like a railway train at an even speed [but] advances by fits and starts, and with irresistible force. . . . One must just be permanently on the look-out, and when one sees God striding through history, leap in, catch hold of His coat-tail, and be dragged along as far as one may. It is dishonest folly and outmoded political wisdom to pretend that [the outcome of history] is a question of weaving opportunities, stirring up troubled waters [and] then going fishing in them." Arnold O. Meyer, *Bismarcks Glaube im Spiegel der 'Lösungen und Lehrtexte'* (Munich, 1933), p. 64, cited by Gall, *Bismarck*, I, pp. xiv–xv, 28. This theme is also emphasized by Pflanze, *Bismarck*, I, pp. 52–53; ibid., III, p. 457.
14. *Love Letters* (Sept. 3, 1870, from Vendresse), pp. 416–17.
15. Cited by Raff, *A History of Germany*, pp. 114–17.
16. Ibid., p. 127; Gall, *Bismarck*, I, pp. xviii, 16.
17. Gall, *Bismarck*, I, pp. 159–60, 169.
18. Ibid., pp. 174–75, 186–88; Gall, *Bismarck*, vol. 2, p. 9.
19. Namely, the activities that gave rise to the Indemnity Act of 1866, a governmental acknowledgment, four years after the fact, of having

used, for military purposes, funds not approved by a stonewalling parliament. In the end the funds were, however, repaid. Gordon Craig, *Germany, 1866–1945* (Oxford, 1978), pp. 9–10; Pflanze, *Bismarck*, I, pp. 328–30.

20. Gall, *Bismarck*, II, pp. 64–66.
21. Blackbourn, *Nineteenth Century*, p. 238; Sheehan, *German History*, pp. 859–67.
22. Raff, *A History of Germany*, pp. 128–30; Schulze, *Germany*, pp. 138–40.
23. Pflanze, *Bismarck*, I, pp. 258–64.
24. John Breuilly, "Revolution to Unification," in Mary Fulbrook et al., eds., *German History Since 1800* (London, 1997). pp. 130–31; Pflanze, *Bismarck*, I, pp. 251–53, 264.
25. Raff, *A History of Germany*, pp. 131–37; Christopher Clark, "Germany 1815–1848: Restoration or Pre-March," in Fulbrook, *German History*, pp. 39–44.
26. Craig, *Germany, 1866–1945*, pp. 22–27; Carr, *The Origins of the Wars of German Unification*, pp. 178–80, 196–200.
27. Breuilly, "Revolution to Unification," pp. 136–37; Schulze, *Germany*, pp. 141–44.
28. Cited by Gall, *Bismarck*, II, p. 40.
29. Ibid., pp. 41–44, 49–52.
30. On the alternations, Blackbourn, *Nineteeth Century*, pp. 256–59; Raff, *A History of Germany*, pp. 146–48.
31. Raff, *A History of Germany*, p. 147; Schulze, *Germany*, p. 155.
32. Raff, *A History of Germany*, pp. 143, 147–48.
33. "A military monarchy, a pseudo-German constitutional state, a semi-constitutional state with parliamentary . . . additions, a Prusso-German semi-autocracy, and a pseudo-parliamentary regime." Lerman, "Bismarckian Germany," pp. 147–49.
34. Cited by W. M. Simon, *Germany in the Age of Bismarck* (London, 1968), p. 222; see sources from other leading liberals, ibid., pp. 99–122, 216–23.
35. Lerman, "Bismarckian Germany," pp. 149, 150–54.
36. "[In the name of] releasing individual forces and promoting free development of society . . . [liberalism] disguised and concealed what was really going on, namely, the step-by-step construction of the modern interventionist state." Gall, *Bismarck*, II, pp. 7, 10–11, 19; Schulze, *Germany*, pp. 160–61.

37. See chap. 7.
38. Gall, *Bismarck*, II, pp. 12–13; Nipperdey, *Germany*, pp. 263–64, 360–62.
39. Walker, *A History of the Christian Church*, pp. 523–24.
40. Craig, *Germany*, pp. 74, 202–3.
41. Gall, *Bismarck*, vol. 2, pp. 26, 78.
42. "At base . . . was [Bismarck's] conviction that Prussia was the object of a malevolent crusade on the part of ultramontane clergy and laymen." Pflanze, *Bismarck*, II, p. 196; Raff, *A History of Germany*, p. 151; Gall, *Bismarck*, II, p. 37.
43. Raff, *A History of Germany*, pp. 152–54.
44. Nipperdey, *Germany*, pp. 367–68, 371; Gall, *Bismarck*, II, pp. 17, 27.
45. Walker, *A History of the Christian Church*, pp. 525–26.
46. See Hitler's plan for undoing Christendom, chap. 10.
47. Cf. Gall, *Bismarck*, II, pp. 19–21, 31; Craig, *Germany, 1866–1945*, p. 77. On U.S. immigration in nineteenth century: Deward R. Brandt et al., *Germanic Genealogy: A Guide to Worldwide Sources and Migration Patterns* (St. Paul, 1995), pp. 139–43; Anne Galicich, *The German Americans* (New York, 1996), pp. 14–17, 78–79.
48. Gall, *Bismarck*, II, pp. 70, 78; Pflanze, *Bismarck*, II, pp. 222, 239–41; Pflanze, *Bismarck*, III, pp. 108–12. Lasker drafted the platform of the National Liberal Party, which was key to Germany's progress toward unification during the 1860s. Pulzer, "Emancipation," p. 10. On Lasker's politics, James F. Harris, *A Study in the Theory and Practice of German Liberalism: Eduard Lasker, 1829–84* (Lanham, Md., 1984).
49. Gall, *Bismarck*, II, pp. 59, 88–90; Craig, *Germany*, pp. 85–86, 90–93.
50. Gall, *Bismarck*, II, pp. 105–7.
51. Raff, *A History of Germany*, pp. 158–59.
52. Gall, *Bismarck*, II, pp. 12, 34–37, 101, 108–10.
53. Ibid., p. 93; Pflanze, *Bismarck*, II, pp. 391–93.
54. Pflanze, *Bismarck*, II, pp. 233–37.
55. Ibid., pp. 394–402.
56. Gall, *Bismarck*, II, pp. 99, 101, 105–7; Craig, *Germany*, pp. 96–97.
57. Gall describes Bismarck's "reversal" as seeking "to create and to preserve situations of his own making rather than adapt to those he found and turn them to his advantage." *Bismarck*, II, pp. 58–59, 88–90.
58. Cf. ibid., pp. 110, 113–14.
59. Raff, *A History of Germany*, pp. 161, 165, 170; see chap. 7.

60. Pflanze, *Bismarck*, II, pp. 434–38.
61. Gall, *Bismarck*, II, p. 57.
62. Hull, *The Entourage of Kaiser Wilhelm II*, pp. 79–80.
63. Gall, *Bismarck*, II, pp. 200–203; Hull, *Kaiser Wilhelm II*, p. 80; Pflanze, *Bismarck*, III, pp. 350–77. See the more recent study of William's character by Jan van der Kiste, *Kaiser William II: Germany's Last Emperor* (Gloucestershire, 1999).
64. Berlin wits dubbed Bismarck "William's last mistress," so successful was he in having his way with him. Pflanze, *Bismarck*, I, p. 309; II, pp. 276–78 (William's refusal to let Bismarck resign in 1875), pp. 507–8 (William's awe of Bismarck after the Congress of Berlin—"Bismarck is more necessary than I am"), pp. 514–16 (William's constraint of Bismarck after their "worst confrontation").
65. Raff, *A History of Germany*, p. 176
66. Gall, *Bismarck*, II, pp. 213–14; Raff, *A History of Germany*, p. 172.
67. Gall, *Bismarck*, II, p. 7.
68. Ibid., pp. 113–14.
69. Ibid., pp. 226–28.
70. Ibid. p. 234.
71. Ibid., p. 5.
72. Cited by Gall, *Bismarck*, II, p. 29.

9. The Last Empire: From Wilhelmine to Weimar Germany

1. Giles MacDonogh, *The Last Kaiser: The Life of William II* (New York, 2000), p. 69. According to Isabel Hull, William led a sexually homoerotic life without necessarily acting it out. He was reportedly an intimate of Count/Prince Philipp von Eulenberg, with whom he led the "Liebenberg Round Table," an annual hunting group among whose members were known bisexuals. *The Entourage of Kaiser Wilhelm II, 1888–1918* (Cambridge, 1982), pp. 21, 52–53, 133. Kitchen places William in a "circle of homosexual and transvestite intimates." *Cambridge Illustrated History of Germany*, p. 215.
2. William interfered in parliamentary decision-making "through personal vetoes, dissenting marginalia on official documents, and endless policy pronouncements." Blackbourn, *Nineteenth Century*, p. 403.
3. Ibid., pp. 402–5, 418–19; Raff, *A History of Germany*, pp. 187–93. Left-liberals and Social Democrats "hoped to create a parliamentary

monarchy in which ministers [of state] would be responsible to the Reichstag." Ibid., p. 192.

4. In the midst of class conflict and socialistic dissent, "common ground" bourgeois values existed, namely, "belief in property, achievement and law, attachment to rules, respectability, and 'correct' conduct, the place of family as haven and seat of ambition." Blackbourn, *Nineteenth Century*, pp. 351–52, 364. On labor and socialist movements, particularly the SPD: Dick Geary, "Socialism and the German Labour Movement Before 1914," in Dick Geary, ed., *Labor and Socialist Movements in Europe Before 1914* (Oxford, 1992), pp. 101–36.
5. Blackbourn, *Long Nineteenth Century*, chap. 8; cf. Roger Chickering, *We Men Who Feel Most German: A Cultural Study of the Pan-German League, 1886–1914* (London, 1984).
6. William Smith, "A description of the cittie [*sic*] of Noremberg . . . 1594 [English-German], trans. W. Roach, *Mitteilungen des Vereins für die Geschichte der Stadt Nuremberg* 48 (1958): p. 222.
7. E. G. Spencer, *Police and the Social Order in German Cities* (DeKalb, Ill., 1992), 65–66, cited by Blackbourn, *Nineteenth Century*, pp. 381–83; see also pp. 370, 374.
8. Ozment, *Protestants*, pp. l07–8; Ozment, *When Fathers Ruled: Family Life in Reformation Europe* (Cambridge, Mass., 1983), chap. 4. The surveillance of the young and of the general population was neither particularly suppressive or successful and may have prevented truancy and helped Germany attain its "enviable literacy rate." Blackbourn, *Nineteenth Century*, p. 383.
9. See Cramer's survey, "The Lamentations of Germany."
10. Lerman, "Wilhelmine Germany," in Fulbrook, *Modern Germany*, pp. 201–2; Raff, *A History of Germany*, pp. 181–82; Schulze, *Germany*, p. 175.
11. Nipperdey, *Germany*, pp. 228–29. Although the new social groupings also segregated the new class society, local clubs and associations did pull people of different classes together. Ibid., pp. 234–35.
12. Cf. Schulze, *Germany*, pp. 176–179. On the marginalization of youth in the Weimar years (1920s), Detlev J.K. Peukert, *The Weimar Republic: The Crisis of Classical Modernity*, trans. Richard Deveson (New York, 1989), p. 94.
13. For the impressive statistics, Blackbourn, *Nineteenth Century*, chap. 7. Hans-Ulrich Wehler, *The German Empire, 1871–1918*, trans. Kim

Traynor (Oxford, 1985): economic and industrial, pp. 32–51; military, pp. 146–70; and armament expenditures, p. 142.

14. Thus Blackbourn, *Nineteenth Century*, p. 385, and Schulze, *Germany*, p. 182. For the historiographical debate: Blackbourn, *Populists and Patricians* (London, 1987), pp. 45–54, 217–45.
15. See chap. 8. On the *Kulturkampf*, David Blackbourn, *Marpingen: Apparitions of the Virgin Mary in Nineteenth-Century Germany* (Oxford, 1993), pp. 85–91.
16. Blackbourn, *Nineteenth Century*, pp. 397–98.
17. Kitchen, *Cambridge Illustrated History of Germany*, p. 293.
18. Matthew Jeffries, "Imperial Germany: Cultural and Intellectual Trends," in Fulbrook, *German History*, pp. 186–87.
19. Craig, *Germany*, pp. 231–39.
20. A "progressive emasculation of the 'responsible government' which was simultaneously subjected to remorseless monarchical pressure." Lerman, "Wilhelmine Germany," p. 209; Kitchen, *Illustrated History of Germany*, pp. 217–18.
21. Kitchen, *Illustrated History of Germany*, pp. 220–23. On Germany's "annexationist and hegemonial schemes" in advance of the war: David Blackbourn and Geoff Eley, *The Pecularities of German History*, pp. 28–29; Lerman, "Wilhelmine Germany," p. 215; Geoff Eley, *From Unification to Nazism: Reinterpreting the German Past* (Boston, 1986), pp. 110–53 (against V. Berghahn).
22. Lerman, "Wilhelmine Germany," p. 224.
23. Blackbourn, *Nineteenth Century*, pp. 426–27, 443, 446; Kitchen, *Illustrated History of Germany*, pp. 223–24; Raff, *A History of Germany*, pp. 202–9.
24. Avner Offer, *The First World War: An Agrarian Interpretation* (Oxford, 1989), pp. 4–5.
25. See the Congress of Berlin, chap. 8.
26. Kitchen, *Cambridge Illustrated History of Germany*, p. 218; Raff, *A History of Germany*, pp. 198, 120.
27. Cited by Lerman, "Wilhelmine Germany," p. 224.
28. At the base of scholarly discussions of imperial and post-imperial German intentionality lie the classic studies of Fritz Fischer. See Introduction, n. 14 and the discussion by James Joll, *The Origins of the First World War* (London, 1984), p. 5, and Blackbourn, *Nineteenth Century*, pp. 457, 480.
29. Joll, *Origins*, p. 143.

30. Ibid., p. 196.
31. With ibid., Blackbourn, *Nineteenth Century*, pp. 454, 480–83.
32. Walther Schücking and Max Montgelas, eds. *The Outbreak of the World War: German Documents Collected by Karl Kautsky*, supplement 1 (New York, 1924), pp. 604–5; Joll, *Origins*, pp. 11–14.
33. Joll, *Origins*, pp. 10–14, 16–18, 21–22.
34. John Keegan, *The First World War* (New York, 1999), pp. 22–48.
35. Richard Bessel, *Germany After the First World War* (Oxford, 1993), pp. 10, 13–15, 18–19, 225. Ute Daniel stresses the continuity in women's work: *The War From Within: German Working-Class Women in the First World War*, trans. Margaret Ries (Oxford, 1997), chap. 3.
36. Ferguson, "German Inter-war Economy," p. 264; Schulze, *Germany*, p. 211.
37. Bessel, *Germany*, pp. 29–31, 41–42, 48, 223–40. On the impact of Weimar inflation on both institutions and morale, see among the many studies of Gerald Feldman, *Die Deutsche Inflation: Eine Zwischenbilanz* (Berlin, 1982). Offer stresses food shortages caused by the Allied blockade, leading to the unrestricted submarine warfare that brought the United States into the war. *The First World War*, pp. 354–67.
38. "A republican experiment [born] at the most unpropitious moment possible." Peukert, *Weimar Republic*, p. 6; Helmut Heiber, *The Weimar Republic*, trans. W. E. Yuill (Oxford, 1993), chap. 1.
39. Bessel, *Germany*, p. 252; Wolfgang Mommsen, "The German Revolution, 1918–20," in Richard Bessel and E. J. Feuchtwanger, eds., *Social Change and Political Development in Weimar Germany* (London, 1981), pp. 21–54.
40. Peukert, *Weimar Republic*, pp. 22–23.
41. Schulze, *Germany*, p. 197.
42. Heiber, *Weimar Republic*, pp. 4–9.
43. Bullock, *Hitler*, pp. 57–58; Peukert, *Weimar Republic*, p. 16; Niall Ferguson, "German Inter-War Economy," in Fulbrook, *German History*, p. 264.
44. Craig, *Germany*, pp. 401–3.
45. Ibid., chap. 2; Raff, *A History of Germany*, p. 183; Schulze, *Germany*, pp. 202, 207.
46. Peukert, *Weimar Republic*, pp. 38–39.
47. Blackbourn describes the SPD as "revolutionary, but not a revolution-making party . . . believing rather deterministically that history would deliver the future into its lap." *Nineteenth Century*, p. 422.

48. Schulze, *Modern Germany*, p. 204; Raff, *A History of Germany*, p. 215.
49. Later, in 1926, as part of Stresemann's successful diplomacy at Locarno, Germany became a League member. Raff, *A History of Germany*, pp. 252–53. On French enforcement of the treaty, see chap. 11.
50. Kitchen, *Germany*, p. 233–34; Ferguson, "German Inter-War Economy," p. 265; Peter Fritzsche, *A Nation of Fliers: German Aviation and the Popular Imagination* (Cambridge, Mass., 1992), pp. 104–6, passim.
51. Peukert, *Weimar Republic*, p. 53.
52. Ferguson, "German Inter-War Economy," p. 265.
53. Peukert, *Weimar Republic*, pp. 55, 57. France was "the most obdurate as well as the largest reparations creditor." Stephen A. Schucker, *The End of French Predominance in Europe: The Financial Crisis and the Adoption of the Dawes Plan* (Chapel Hill, 1976), pp. 23–24.
54. Peukert, *Weimar Republic*, pp. 54–55.
55. Blackbourn, *Nineteenth Century*, p. 481.
56. After American financier, Nobel laureate, and vice-president, Charles G. Dawes.
57. Peukert, *Weimar Republic*, pp. 60, 196–97.
58. After American financier and lawyer Owen Young.
59. Between 1919 and 1932, Germany paid 21.3 billion marks in reparations. Peukert, *Weimar Republic*, p. 197.
60. "Reparations did not . . . bleed the German economy. Indeed their net effect was to leave [it] in rather better shape." Ibid.
61. Ibid., pp. 42–43, 46, 55; Raff, *A History of Germany*, p. 227.
62. Karl Dietrich Bracher, "The Dissolution of the First German Democracy," in *Turning Points in Modern Times: Essays in German and European History*, trans. Thomas Dunlap (Cambridge, Mass., 1995), p. 103.
63. Peukert, *Weimar Republic*, pp. 130–32; see chap. 8.
64. Ibid., pp. 135–36.
65. Ibid., pp. 136–38, 145.
66. Bessel, *Germany*, p. 255.
67. Bracher, "The Weimar Experience," in *Turning Points*, p. 5; Peukert, *Weimar Republic*, pp. 223–25; Raff, *A History of Germany*, p. 242.
68. Peukert, *Weimar Republic*, pp. 226–30.
69. Bracher, "Dissolution," pp. 100–103.
70. Peukert, *Weimar Republic*, p. 235.

71. Ibid., pp. 156–57, 231–33.
72. Ibid., p. 198; Bracher, "Dissolution," p. 101.
73. Again, Fritz Frischer's influential argument about German war aims (1961), embraced by Wehler and V. Berghahn. On its influence and accuracy, Wolfgang J. Mommsen, "Domestic Factors in German Foreign Policy Before 1914," *Central European History* 6 (1973): 12–15; Lerman, "Wilhelmine Germany," p. 224; Müller, *Another Country*, pp. 51–52.
74. Lerman, "Wilhelmine Germany," pp. 222–24.
75. "Germans retreated into an illusory world in which their problems were invariably the fault of others." Bessel, *Germany*, p. 283.
76. Compare Bullock's metaphor of living through an "earthquake," with reference to the post-1929 crash and 1930-32 depression: "In such circumstances men are no longer amenable to . . . reason. . . . [They] entertain fantastic fears, extravagant hatreds and . . . hopes, [also] the extravagant demagogy of [a] Hitler." *Hitler*, pp. 132, 153.
77. "By the turn of the century and the time of the First World War . . . secularization had spread to wide sections of the population and Christian values were no longer universally accepted. . . . There was a search for new foundations and new values [which] took different political expressions: authoritarian conceptions of an autocratic state . . . left-wing visions of class dictatorship; a longing for a 'Volksgemeinschaft.' Another important political by-product was the sort of racialist utopia that played a central role in National Socialist ideology." Peukert, *Weimar Republic*, p. 242.
78. Cf. Peter Fritzsche, *Germans into Nazis* (Cambridge, Mass., 1998), pp. 199–211, and, below, chap. 11.

10. The Barbarian Prince: The Rise and Fall of National Socialism

1. Cf. Jeffrey Fear, "German Capitalism," in Thomas K. McCraw, *Creating Modern Capitalism* (Cambridge, Mass., 1997), pp. 135–82.
2. Detlev J. K. Peukert, *The Weimar Republic: The Crisis of Classical Modernity*, trans. R. Deveson (New York, 1989), pp. 63–64, 252–53, 156; Mary Fulbrook, *The Divided Nation* (Oxford, 1991), pp. 34, 57; W. Michalka and G. Neidhart, eds., *Die ungeliebte Republik* (Munich, 1980), p. 118; V. Berghahn, *Modern Germany* (Cambridge, 1996), p. 100; Harold James, "Economic Reasons for the Collapse of the

Weimar Republic," in Ian Kershaw, ed., *Weimar: Why did German Democracy Fail?* (London, 1990), chap. 1.

3. For example, Chancellor Brüning's deliberate "hardship and hunger" policy in quest of an end to reparations.
4. Ian Kershaw, *Hitler, 1889–1936: Hubris* (New York, 1999), pp. 8–16, 20–24, 37–38, 40–41.
5. *Hitler's Table Talk, 1941–44: His Private Conversations*, trans. N. Cameron et al. (London, 1973), 10/28/41, p. 97. Also known as the "Bormann-Notes," after Reichsminister Martin Bormann, who approved, corrected, and preserved in 1,054 typed pages informal accounts of Hitler's table talk, as written down by appointed note-takers.
6. Kershaw, *Hitler, 1889–1936*, pp. 42–43, 48–49. Later, as führer, Hitler financed the Bayreuth Festival with hundreds of thousands of deutsche marks, there entertained by, and very much at ease with, Winifred Wagner and the Wagner clan. Albert Speer, *Inside the Third Reich: Memoirs*, trans. Richard and Clara Winston (New York, 1970), pp. 149–50; *Table Talk*, 10/28/41, p. 97.
7. "The dog [Blondi] probably occupied the most important role in Hitler's private life; he meant more to his master than the Führer's closest associates." In addition to Blondi, he counted only Eva Braun as a loyal friend. Speer, *Inside the Third Reich*, pp. 300–302.
8. Kershaw, *Hitler: 1889–1936*, pp. 31–33, 36, 55–56, 58–59, 64.
9. Biographer Alan Bullock calls him "the greatest demagogue in history." *Hitler: A Study in Tyranny* (New York, 1962), pp. 25–27, 34–37, 68.
10. Ian Kershaw, *The Hitler Myth: Image and Reality in the Third Reich* (Oxford, 1987), p. 22.
11. On the latter, compare the Hohenstaufen Fredericks in chap. 2.
12. Although he seldom mentioned them by name in his table talk. *Table Talk*, 10/25/41, p. 89; ibid., 3/7/42, p. 358.
13. Contrary to Bullock, who roots Hitler's already expressive anti-Semitism in personal self-doubt. Bullock, *Hitler*, pp. 40–44; Kershaw, *Hitler: 1889–1936*, pp. 34–35.
14. Cf. Kershaw, *Hitler: 1889–1936*, pp. 81, 87, 89–90.
15. Ian Kershaw, "Hitler: 'Master in the Third Reich' or 'Weak Dictator'?" in Kershaw, ed., *The Nazi Dictatorship* (London, 2000), pp. 69–92.
16. Bullock, *Hitler*, pp. 50–51, 53, 55; Kershaw, *Hitler: 1889–1936*, pp. 92, 96–97.

17. On these interim councils and the so-called *Räterrepublik*, see chap. 9.
18. Kershaw, *Hitler: 1889–1936*, pp. 105, 109–17.
19. Ibid., 117–24.
20. Adolf Hitler, *Mein Kampf*, ed. John Chamberlain et al. (New York, 1940), pp. 5ff.
21. Bullock, *Hitler*, pp. 64–70, 76; Schulze, *Germany*, pp. 231–32; Adolf Hitler, *Mein Kampf*, ed. John Chamberlain et al. (New York, 1940), pp. 3–4; Kershaw, *Hitler*, pp. 105, 137, 144–45, 147. On Röhm's homosexuality and the purging of the storm troopers (SA), Speer, *Inside the Third Reich*, pp. 51–53. On who voted Nazi, and why, during the 1920s, see Richard F. Hamilton, *Who Voted for Hitler?* (Princeton, 1982); Thomas Childers, *The Nazi Voter* (Chapel Hill, 1983); Thomas Childers, ed., *The Formation of the Nazi Constituency* (London, 1986).
22. Kershaw, *Hitler: 1889–1936*, pp. 157, 169, 170, 184–85.
23. Speer, *Inside the Third Reich*, p. 101. Four other intimates were Röhm, Julius Streicher, Hermann Esser, and Christian Weber, all accomplished agitators and propagandists of the revolutionary 1920s. On Hitler's travels with Eckhart: *Table Talk*, pp. 211–19; Mosse, *The Crisis of German Ideology*, pp. 296–97.
24. See chap. 7.
25. Bullock, *Hitler*, pp. 82–83; Kershaw, *Hitler: 1889–1936*, 187–88.
26. Kershaw, *Hitler: 1889–1936*, p. 191.
27. On the devastating effects of inflation and reparations: Gerald Feldman, *The Great Disorder: Politics, Economics, and Society in the German Inflation, 1914–1924* (New York, 1993); Marc Trachtenberg, *Reparation in World Politics: France and European Economic Diplomacy, 1916–1923* (New York, 1980).
28. Fulbrook, *The Divided Nation*, pp. 34–35; Raff, *A History of Germany*, pp. 245–47.
29. Although four out of five reparation marks were now borrowed, mainly from American banks, payments were secured and put on a predictable schedule. See chap. 9.
30. Richard Bessel, "Germany from War to Dictatorship," in Fulbrook, *German History Since 1800*, pp. 248–49; Fulbrook, *The Divided Nation*, pp. 35–38; Schulze, *Germany*, pp. 210–12, 215–16.
31. Bullock, *Hitler*, pp. 107–8, 112–13; Kershaw, *Hitler: 1889–1936*, pp. 210–11.

32. Cited by Bullock, *Hitler*, pp. 116–17; Kershaw, *Hitler: 1889–1936*, pp. 212–219.
33. Kershaw stresses Hitler's success at changing history by uncannily evading logical or prescribed consequences; yet, in the end, he believes the larger sociopolitical-economic "context" had more to do with his success than "personality." Kershaw, *Hitler: 1889–1936*, p. 238, passim. For the intentionalist vs. functionalist interpretation of Hitler, that is, the degree to which Hitler was in charge and the degree to which he was swept along, see Tim Mason, "Intention and Explanation: A Current Controversy About the interpretation of National Socialism," in Mason, *Nazism, Fascism, and the Working Class* (Cambridge, 1995), pp. 212–30.
34. Kershaw, *Hitler: 1889–1936*, pp. 261–62.
35. "Don't believe that I'll issue a decree forbidding the navy to eat meat. Supposing the prohibition of meat had been an article of faith for National Socialism, it's certain our movement wouldn't have succeeded." *Table Talk*, 1/22/42, p. 230. "The battle between a repeating rifle and a rabbit—which has made no progress for three thousand years—is too unequal. If Mr. So-and-so were to outrun the rabbit, I'd take off my hat to him." *Table Talk*, 10/20/41, p. 94.
36. Bullock, *Hitler*, pp. 113, 120–21, 126–28 132; Kershaw, *Hitler: 1889–1936*, pp. 224, 231, 242–43, 257, 261, 271; Peter Fritzsche, *Germans into Nazis* (Cambridge, Mass. 1998), p. 187.
37. Bessel, "Germany from War to Dictatorship," p. 249; Bullock, *Hitler*, p. 132.
38. Bullock, *Hitler*, p. 143; Peukert, *Weimar Republic*, pp. 107–24.
39. Bullock, *Hitler*, pp. 132, 150–53, 179.
40. Schulze, *Germany*, pp. 237–38.
41. Kershaw, *Hitler: 1889–1936*, pp. 324–25, 333–34; Schulze has them gaining 130 seats, *Germany*, p. 233.
42. William S. Allen, *The Nazi Seizure of Power: The Experience of a Single German Town, 1930–1935* (Chicago, 1965), p. ix. Writing in the early 1960s when the wounds of war were still open and accurate information neither free nor safe, Allen fictionalized both the town ("Thalburg" instead of Northeim, using the latter first in the revised edition of 1984) and the names of the principal characters as a condition of the latter's cooperation.
43. Ibid., pp. 3–34, 272–81.
44. On the creation of this illusion, Kershaw, *The 'Hitler Myth,'* chap. 2.

45. Hindenburg's "habits of thinking and feeling are in revolt against all you represent." *Table Talk*, 1/18/42, p. 222; Bullock, *Hitler*, pp. 183, 187.
46. Bullock, *Hitler*, pp. 183, 190–91.
47. Hindenburg privately asked Hitler to conduct his campaign against the government in a "chivalrous" fashion. Bullock, *Hitler*, pp. 222–23; Kershaw, *Hitler: 1889–1936*, pp. 370–71, 373.
48. Bullock, *Hitler*, pp. 196–99, 201; Kershaw, *Hitler: 1889–1936*, p. 363; Berghahn, *Modern Germany*, p. 119.
49. Black-shirted bodyguards, their uniforms ghoulishly decorated with death's-head badges.
50. Peukert, *Weimar Republic*, p. 256; Fritzsche, *Germans into Nazis*, p. 157.
51. Bullock, *Hitler*, pp. 210, 220; Kershaw, *Hitler: 1889–1936*, pp. 365–67, 373–74; Craig, *Germany, 1866–1945*, p. 562–64.
52. Bullock, *Hitler*, pp. 226–27.
53. Kershaw, *Hitler: 1889–1936*, pp. 371, 394–95.
54. On Schleicher's plottings, Berghahn, *Modern Germany*, pp. 115–28; Kershaw, *Hitler: 1889–1936*, pp. 395–96, 399.
55. Bullock, *Hitler*, pp. 238–39, 244; Kershaw, *Hitler: 1889–1936*, pp. 419–421; Schulze, *Germany*, p. 243.
56. See Alaric, Athaulf, and Clovis, chaps. 1 and 2.
57. Kershaw, *Hitler: 1889–1936*, p. 434.
58. Ibid., p. 459.
59. Ibid., pp. 466–68.
60. Joachim C. Fest, *Hitler*, trans. Richard and Clara Winston (New York, 1974), pp. 397–98; Kershaw, *Hitler: 1889–1936*, pp. 456–60, 469–70. On Steel Helmet integration into the National Socialist Party, Allen, *The Nazi Seizure of Power*, pp. 205–6.
61. Hitler, *Mein Kampf*, pp. 395–99; *Table Talk*, pp. 7–11.
62. Kershaw, *Hitler: 1889–1936*, pp. 474–75, 478.
63. Ibid., pp. 145–48, 478–79, 482, 490, 494.
64. Among the dead were Schleicher; Major General Ferdinand Bredow, a close Schleicher associate; Hitler rival Gregor Strasser; and Hitler's buddy Röhm, who declined the "courtesy" offer of a suicide's death.
65. Fest, *Hitler*, pp. 470–74; Kershaw, *Hitler: 1889–1936*, pp. 499–504, 517–19. On internal military discussion and plotting against German invasion of its neighbors in the summers of 1938 and 1939, see Theodore Hamerow, *On the Road to the Wolf's Lair: German Resistance to Hitler* (Cambridge, Mass., 1999), pp. 239, 249, 254.

66. *Table Talk*, 7/5/41, p. 3; 7/11–12/41, p. 6; 8/11/41, p. 23; 9/17–18/41, pp. 33–34; 9/23/41, p. 38; 9/25/41, p. 40; 10/13/41, p. 55. Cf. Robert Proctor, *Racial Hygiene: Medicine Under the Nazis* (Cambridge, Mass., 1988), pp. 177–94.
67. *Table Talk*, 1/5–6/42, p. 182; John Keegan, *The Second World War* (London, 1990).
68. Donald Kagan, *On the Origins of War* (New York, 1995); Schulze, *Germany*, pp. 245–70.
69. Nipperdey, *Germany from Napoleon*, pp. 217–21; cf. Vick, *Defining Germany*, pp. 211–212.
70. Nipperdey, *Germany from Napoleon*, pp. 221–22.
71. Blackbourn, *Nineteenth Century*, pp. 287–88; William Carr, "Nazi Policy Against the Jews," in Bessel, ed., *Life in the Third Reich*, p. 70; Gall, *Bismarck*, pp. 70–72, passim.
72. See Martin Luther, chap. 3.
73. David Blackbourn, "Catholics, the Centre Party and Anti-Semitism," *Populists and Patricians: Essays in Modern German History*, (London, 1987), pp. 168–87. Majority Protestants could be as hard on minority Catholics as on minority Jews, but Catholics, too, had their own, less virulent anti-Semitism.
74. On the radicalization of Nazi plans to exterminate the Jews and the evolution of the Final Solution, see the documents collected in Jeremy Noakes and Geoffrey Pridham, eds., *Nazism 1919–1945: A Documentary Reader*, 3rd. ed. (Exeter, England, 1983), pp. 107–35.
75. Schulze, *Germany*, pp. 270–75. On the Goldhagen argument, see Evans, "Anti-Semitism: Ordinary Germans and the 'Longest Hatred,'" in *Rereading Germany History*, pp. 149–77; Fritz Stern, "The Goldhagen Controversy: One Nation, One People, One Theory?" *Foreign Affairs* 75 (1996): pp. 128–38; Ian Kershaw, *The Nazi Dictatorship: Problems and Perspectives* (New York, 2000), pp. 251–62.
76. Raff, *A History of Germany*, p. 227; *Table Talk*, intro., p. xxxiii.
77. Ian Buruma, "Depravity Was Contagious," review of Ian Kershaw, *Hitler 1936–45: Nemesis*, *New York Times Book Review*, 12/10/00, p. 13. Raul Hilberg, *The Destruction of the European Jews* (New York, 1985). On what the Allies knew or did not know about the concentration camps, see Richard Breitman, *Official Secrets: What the Nazis Planned, What the British and the Americans Knew* (New York, 1998), esp. chaps. 8–11, esp. pp. 231–32.
78. *Table Talk*, 9/14–15/41, pp. 29–30; Blackbourn, *Long Nineteenth Cen-*

tury, pp. 437–39; Bullock, *Hitler*, pp. 700–03; Evans, "Anti-Semitism," in *Rereading German History*, pp. 150–55, 160, 162, 165–66.

79. *Table Talk*, 10/18/41, p. 75; Noakes and Pridham, *Nazism*, pp. 1097–98.
80. Bullock, *Hitler*, pp. 407, 410–11; Kershaw, *Hitler: 1889–1936*, pp. 249, 275, 288–90.
81. *Table Talk*, 10/10/41, p. 51; 12/14/41, p. 146.
82. *Table Talk*, 12/1–2/41, pp. 140–41; 12/13/41, pp. 142–43. He calls this "a solution to the religious problem."
83. According to Baldur von Schirach, who led what would become the Hitler Youth, "'the destruction of Christianity was explicitly recognized as a purpose of the National Socialist movement' from the beginning, though 'considerations of expedience made it impossible' . . . until it had consolidated power." Joe Sharkey, "The Case Against the Nazis: How Hitler's Forces Planned to Destroy German Christianity," *New York Times*, 1/13/01, sect. 4, p. 7; Robert L. Bartley, "Christians, Jews, and Wotan," *Wall Street Journal*, 3/25/02, p. A19.
84. *Table Talk*, 10/21/41, pp. 76–78.
85. Sharkey, "The Case Against the Nazis." The documents of the Nuremberg Project spelling out Nazi plans to destroy German Christianity are available on the Web site of the *Rutgers Journal of Law and Religion* (www.cam-law.rutgers.ed/publications/law-religion). Ibid.
86. Speer, *Inside the Third Reich*, pp. 95–96.
87. Michael Balfour, *Withstanding Hitler in Germany 1933–45* (London, 1988), p. 17.
88. On German Catholics and Hitler: John S. Conway, *The Nazi Persecution of the Churches, 1933–45* (New York, 1968); E. C. Helmreich, *The German Churches Under Hitler* (Detroit, 1979); Günther Levy, *The Catholic Church and Nazi Germany* (New York, 1964), and L. D. Walker, *Hitler Youth and Catholic Youth, 1933–36* (Washington, D.C., 1979). On the euthanasia program, Jeremy Noakes, "Social Outcasts in the Third Reich," in Richard Bessel, ed., *Life in the Third Reich* (Oxford, 1987), p. 88; Proctor, *Racial Hygiene*.
89. Balfour, *Withstanding Hitler*, pp. 38–39.
90. The Barmen Declaration. Craig, *The Germans*, pp. 96–98; Mary Fulbrook, *The Divided Nation*, pp. 80–81; Doris Bergen, *Twisted Cross: The German Christian Movement in the Third Reich* (Chapel Hill, 1996).

91. *Table Talk*, 10/10/41, p. 51
92. Ibid., p. xxxiii, 10/24/41, p. 83.
93. "The dogma of Christianity gets worn away [by] the advances of science . . . [in whose light] the myths gradually crumble. . . . When the majority know that the stars are . . . worlds, perhaps inhabited like ours, then the Christian doctrine [of creation and its other myths] will be convicted of absurdity." Ibid., 10/14/41, pp. 59–60.
94. Ibid., H. R. Trevor-Roper's introduction, pp. xxvi–xvii.
95. Ibid., 10/21/41, pp. 78–79.
96. Ibid., cited by Trevor-Roper, introduction to ibid., p. xxvi.
97. Bullock, *Hitler*, p. 144. "A man with no credentials for running a sophisticated state machine." Kershaw, *Hitler: 1889–1936*, p. 423.
98. "The Nazi phenomenon was not a hyperventilated expression of German values. . . . Nazism was neither accidental nor unanimous." Fritzsche, *Germans into Nazis*, pp. 234–35.
99. This class consisted of "master craftsmen, professionals without academic qualifications, lower and intermediate employees . . . and officials (including elementary school teachers), and owners of small businesses." Balfour, *Withstanding Hitler*, p. 19
100. The astonishing high estimate is Sebastian Haffner's, *Anmerkungen zu Hitler* (Munich, 1978), cited by Fritzsche, *Germans into Nazis*, p. 255, n. 19. Kershaw strongly refutes: *The "Hitler Myth*," pp. 1, 83–104.
101. Fulbrook, *Divided Nation*, chap. 4; Balfour, *Withstanding Hitler*, chap. 3; Hamilton helpfully charts the percentages of Reichstag votes received by all parties from 1919 to 1933. *Who Voted for Hitler*, p. 476. See also Henry A. Turner, *German Big Business and the Rise of Hitler* (Oxford, 1985). On alternative youth cultures hostile to the Hitler Youth (prominently, the Edelweiss Pirates), see Peukert, *Inside Nazi Germany: Conformity and Opposition in Everyday Life*, trans. Richard Deveson (New Haven, 1987), pp. 145–64.
102. Kershaw, *Hitler: 1889–1936*, pp. 404, 407, 409.
103. Evans, "Whatever Became of the Sonderweg?" in *Rereading Germany History*, pp. 12–22. An important wedge for counterargument is David Blackbourn's review article, "The Discreet Charm of the German Bourgeoisie" (1981), in *Populists and Patricians*, pp. 67–83, elaborated more fully in Blackbourn and Eley, *The Particularities of German History*, pp. 253–60, 285.
104. Fritzsche, *Germans into Nazis*, pp. 163, 233. Invoking *Volksgemein-*

schaft, the Nazis denounced nonegalitarian aristocrats, bourgeois elites, capitalists, and Jews. Fritzsche speaks of a "national reassembly" and a "[shared] creative act of building a national community"—the Nazis "recognizing and enfranchising the people on the basis of what they did for the Volk, rather than who they were according to the scales of status." Ibid., pp. 178, 184, 192, 198, 201–02, 204, 208–09, 211, 228–31.

105. Cf. Fulbrook, *Divided Nation*, pp. 351–57. On the status of those values today, Müller, *Another Country*, pp. 1–20, 266–85.

106. Peuckert, *Weimar Republic*, pp. 94, 256; Schulze, *Germany*, pp. 182, 232–3; Mosse, *Crisis of German Idealism*, chap. 9.

11. The Composite German: Germany Since World War II

1. John Ardagh, *Germany and the Germans: The United Germany in the Mid-1990s* (New York, 1995), p. 23; Lothar Kettenacker, *Germany Since 1945* (Oxford, 1997), pp. 5–6, 35.
2. Mary Fulbrook, *The Two Germanies, 1945–1990: Problems of Interpretation* (Atlantic Highlands, N.J., 1992), pp. 1–3; Henry A. Turner, Jr., *The Two Germanies Since 1945* (New Haven, 1987), pp. 8–16.
3. Ardagh, *Germany and the Germans*, pp. 21–22, 371; Fulbrook, *Divided Nation*, pp. 131–33, 153; Kettenacker, *Germany Since 1945*, pp. 12–13.
4. For examples, Fulbrook, *Divided Nation*, pp. 135–36.
5. Ibid., pp. 146–47; Kettenacker, *Germany Since 1945*, pp. 17–18.
6. As Germans belatedly grieve the injustices they suffered and the sacrifices they made during and after WWII, their resentment has affected German-American relations. Richard Bernstein, "The Germans Who Toppled Communism Resent the U.S.," *New York Times* [*NYT*] 2/22/03, p. A7; Christopher Rhoads, "Revisiting History: Behind Iraq Stance in Germany: Flood of War Memories," *Wall Street Journal* [*WSJ*], 2/25/03, pp. A1, A8.
7. Fulbrook, *Divided Nation*; pp. 135–36, 140, 147–48, 150; Kettenacker, *Germany Since 1945*, pp. 17, 21.
8. Fulbrook, *Two Germanies*, p. 17.
9. Kettenacker, *Germany Since 1945*, pp. 29–32; Fulbrook, *Divided Nation*, pp. 157, 163–64.
10. Kettenacker, pp. 18–20, 50–51; Schulze, *Modern Germany*, p. 316.
11. Müller, *Another Country*, p. 22.

12. Fulbrook, *Two Germanies*, pp. 52–54; Kettenacker, *Germany Since 1945*, p. 1.
13. Ardagh, *Germany and the Germans*, pp. 104–6; Fulbrook, *The Divided Nation*, pp. 175–77, 181–85, 188–89; Fulbrook, *Two Germanies*, pp. 30–31.
14. Ardagh, *Germany and the Germans*, pp. 108–34.
15. "A strikingly large number of the conspirators belonged to the Old Prussian nobility." Fest, *Hitler*, p. 702. Fest finds scant participation in the resistance on the part of the left, representatives of the Weimar Republic, the lower middle class, businessmen, and workers. See also Ardagh, *Germany and the Germans*, pp. 171–81, esp. the interview with Prince Friedrich Karl of Hohenlohe-Waldenburg.
16. "On the whole [Germans were] no longer affected by class consciousness." Kettenacker, *Germany Since 1945*, p. 165.
17. "Internal democratization." Fulbrook, *Divided Germany*, p. 235.
18. Ardagh, *Germany and the Germans*, pp. 249–54.
19. Ibid., pp. 536–37; Fulbrook, *Divided Nation*, pp. 211, 282–86. Nobel Prize laureate Heinrich Böll, with Habermas and Grass a leading left-liberal, pleaded for mercy for Ulrike Meinhof. Müller, *Another Country*, p. 54. For the stories of Baader and Meinhof, see Julian Becker, *Hitler's Children* (London, 1977).
20. Fulbrook, *Divided Nation*, pp. 207–8; Kettenacker, *Germany Since 1945*, pp. 63–69, 74–75.
21. Ardagh, *Germany and the Germans*, pp. 273–80; Klaus J. Bade, "Exodus und Integration: Historische Perspektiven und aktuelle Probleme," in Paul Bockelet, ed., *Zu viele Fremde im Land? Aussiedler, Gastarbeiter, Asylanten* (Düsseldorf, 1990), pp. 9-20; also Bade, *Ausländer Aussiedler, Asyl in Bundesrepublik Deutschland* (Hannover 1994).
22. Roger Cohen, "Germany's Financial Heart Is Open, But Wary," *NYT* on the Web, 12/30/00.
23. Ardagh , *Germany and the Germans*, pp. 280–93; Kettenacker, *Germany Since 1945*, pp. 230–31; *Facts About Germany*, p. 16.
24. www.Einbürgerung.de.
25. Fulbrook, *Two Germanies*, pp. 18–19, 28–29.
26. Fulbrook believes that force was not everything. "The spaces for freedom of debate, the lack of ideological commitment, and the articulation of dissenting views"—the latter aided and abetted by the Protestant Church—played large roles; yet she also describes the

"main feature" of the GDR as the "effective imprisonment" of its population. Ibid., pp. 37, 40, 42–43.

27. Ibid., pp. 41, 65: "the only independent social institution in the GDR outside the . . . system."
28. See the prominent example of writer Christa Wolf in ibid., p. 68, and *Divided Nation*, pp. 293–94; Kettenacker, *Germany Since 1945*, pp. 169–70.
29. Fulbrook, *Divided Nation*, p. 272–73; *Two Germanies*, pp. 65, 69.
30. See chap. 3.
31. Fulbrook, *Two Germanies*, pp. 70–71.
32. Müller, *Another Country*, p. 55.
33. Ibid., pp. 48, 55, 137, 151. See Günther Grass below.
34. Fulbrook, *Two Germanies*, p. 86.
35. Fulbrook, *Divided Nation*, pp. 323, 327–28, 332–33; Ardagh, *Germany and the Germans*, p. 425.
36. On Kohl's own recollection of those events: "The Fall of the Wall: How Germany was United," *WSJ*, 1/9/99, p. A26.
37. Ardagh, *Germany and the Germans*, pp. 3, 5–7, 428–31; Fulbrook, *Divided Nation*, pp. 339–40.
38. See chap. 1.
39. Ardagh, *Germany and the Germans*, p. 218.
40. Christopher Brown, *Singing the Gospel: Lutheran Music and the Success of the Reformation in Joachimsthal* (Ph.D. diss., Harvard University, 2001).
41. Potter, *Most German of the Arts*, pp. 134, 201–2, 205, 225–26.
42. Kamenetsky, *The Brothers Grimm*, pp. 25–27.
43. Sheehan, *German History, 1770–1866*, pp. 547–50. Savigny was just one of numerous scholars driving the unprecedented historical scholarship of the age.
44. Wagner claimed that the piece "unbarred the sluices of the wrath of the entire European press." *My Life*, authorized translation (Bury St. Edmunds, 1994), pp. 564–66; Sheehan, *German History, 1770–1866*, pp. 837–39.
45. Potter, *Most German of the Arts*, p. 203; Anthony Tommasini, "A Cultural Disconnect on Wagner," *NYT*, 8/5/01, sect. 2, p. 27.
46. Potter, *Most German of the Arts*, pp. 134, 202, 205.
47. *Allgemeine Deutsche Biographie*, vol. 9, pp. 353–55.
48. James, *A German Identity*, pp. 15–24; Sheehan, *German History, 1770–1866*, pp. 545–54.

49. Goltz's term is "Organismus."
50. Bogumil Goltz, *Zur Geschichte und Charakteristik des deutschen Genius: Eine ethnographische Studie* (Berlin, 1964), pp. 1–13.
51. James, *A German Identity*, pp. 12–14.
52. On the intervening work of Heinrich Heine and the Young Germans, Sheehan, *German History, 1770–1866*, pp. 581–86.
53. Barraclough, *Origins of Modern Germany*, pp. 456, 461.
54. See Introduction.
55. Ibid., p. 456; Evans, "German Reunification in Historical Perspective," in *Rereading German History*, pp. 215–16.
56. *Facts About Germany*, pp. xix, 113–14, 138.
57. Evans, "German Reunification," pp. 215–18.
58. Barraclough, *Origins of Modern Germany*, p. 461.
59. Müller, *Another Country*, chap. 1; cf. Blackbourn and Eley, *The Peculiarities of German History*, p. 161.
60. "Anything to Fear?" *Time*, 3/26/90, pp. 32–47.
61. Ardagh, *Germany and the Germans*, p. 500.
62. For some ironical thoughts on this subject, cf. Peter Schneider, *The German Comedy* (New York, 1991), pp. 3–19; for the scholars, Noel D. Cary, "'Farewell Without Tears': Diplomats, Dissidents, and the Demise of East Germany [review article]," *Journal of Modern History* 73 (2001): 617–51.
63. Most state-owned industries had been privatized by mid-decade. Kettenacker, *Germany Since 1945*, pp. 213–14; Evans, "German Reunification in Historical Perspective," in *Rereading the German Past*, p. 214.
64. Ardagh, *Germany and the Germans*, p. 9.
65. Müller, *Another Country*, pp. 8–9, 10, 78.
66. Roger Cohen, "Schröder Aide Typifies New German Subtlety," *New York Times on the Web*, 12/29/98.
67. Müller, *Another Country*, chap. 3.
68. Ibid., pp. 16, 68–69.
69. *Ein Weites Feld* (1995) (English, *Too Far Afield*). James J. Sheehan, "The German Question: Günter Grass's Novel Compares the Events of 1989 With Those of 1871," *New York Times Book Review*, 11/5/00, sect. 7, p. 20. Müller portrays the older Grass as advocating "apocalyptic antiparliamentarianism reminiscent of the '60s," which the younger Grass had opposed. *Another Country*, pp. 64–66, 87–88.
70. Ardagh, *Germany and the Germans*, p. 575; Evans, "German Reunification in Historical Perspective," p. 222.

71. Evans documents "a general drive for a resumption of Germany's individual status as a great power." "Rebirth of the Right?" in *Rereading the German Past*, p. 227.
72. Cf. the criticism of rival Christian Democrat Wolfgang Schäuble, "How Germany Became Saddam's Favorite State," in *WSJ*, 9/19/02, p. A16.
73. *Schau ins Land* 11/5 (Nashville, Tenn., 1996), pp. 23–29.
74. Roger Cohen, "In Germany, Getting Together Is Hard to Do." *NYT*, 8/27/00, sect. 4, p. 6; Geoff Winestock, "Schröder, Sensing Opportunity, Initiates EU Debate," *WSJ*, 5/15/01, p. A23.
75. Edmund L. Andrews, "Germany's Consensus Economy at Risk of Unraveling," *NYT*, 11/26/99, p. C5; Michael Gove, "Don't Let Germans Buy Our Stock Market," *The Times* (London), 8/30/00, "Comment," p. 16; "Berlin Lacks Old Clout to Defend Germany Inc," *WSJ*, 11/24/99, p. A12.
76. Edmund L. Andrews, "Germans Offer Plan to Remake EU," *NYT*, 5/1/01, pp. A1, 3.
77. Winestock, "Schröder, Sensing Opportunity," *WSJ*, 5/15/01, p. A23; Cohen, "In Germany, Getting Together," *NYT*, 8/27/00, sect. 4, p. 6.
78. Peter Baldwin, *"The Historikerstreit": Die Dokumentation der Kontroverse um die Einzigartigkeit der nationalsozialistischen Judenvernichtung* (Boston, 1990); Kershaw, *The Nazi Dictatorship*, pp. 30–31, 231–32, 248–49; Evans, "Nipperdey's Nineteenth Century," in *Rereading German History*, pp. 29–31; Kettenacker, *Germany Since 1945*, pp. 168–69; "Ferment in the German Right," *NYT* editorial, 6/25/00, dismissing as "repugnant" Nolte's "arguments that the Holocaust was not unique and Germany's past not so abnormal," and denouncing the Deutschland Foundation for giving him the award.
79. On the contentiousness of this issue, also among Austrian Jews, see Roger Cohen, "Jewish Leaders Trade Barbs Over Austria's Nazi Legacy," *NYT*, 3/25/01, sect. 1, p. 6.
80. Roger Cohen, "A Haider in Their Future," *NYT Magazine*, 4/30/00, pp. 54–59, and "Even in Euroland, Money Isn't Everything," *NYT*, 9/17/00, p. 4; Donald G. McNeil, Jr., "Austrian Politician Sometimes Down But Never Out," *NYT*, 7/23/00, sect. 1, p. 3.
81. Reported, disapprovingly, in a *WSJ* editorial: "Buying Off Neo-Nazis," 4/24/01, p. A24.
82. Retired finance minister Theo Waigel, who played a key role in creating the euro that replaced the mark, was still receiving death

threats in the summer of 2001. C. Rohwedder and T. T. Th. Sims, "Don't Expect Germans to Offer Up Any Euro Paeans," *WSJ*, 8/14/01, p. A11; Neal Boudette, "It Takes More Than the Euro to Unite Europe," *WSJ*, 12/31/01, p. A4.

83. "Democracy has taken root so firmly, and is [today] so well safeguarded by the constitution, that any return to a totalitarian regime would be hard to imagine." Ardagh, *Germany and the Germans*, pp. 500, 505, 512.
84. Ibid., p. 499.
85. Steven Erlanger, "A Memory-Strewn Celebration of Germany's Jews," *NYT*, 11/10/01, p. A1.
86. Edmund L. Andrews, "Germany's Consensus Economy at Risk of Unraveling," *NYT*, 11/26/99, p. C1; David Wessel, Charles Rhoads, and William Boston, "Berlin Lacks Old Clout to Defend Germany, Inc." *WSJ*, 11/24/99, p. A1. The reference to "barbarians" was by Andreas Molitor in the newspaper *Die Zeit*, cited by Andrews.
87. Matthew Karnitschnig, "Why KirchGroup of Germany Failed to Spark a Rescue," *WSJ*, 4/11/02, pp. A1,11; M. Karnitschnig and Hans-Peter Siebenhaar, "Bertelsmann Mulls Stake in KirchPay TV Arm," *WSJ*, 4/18/02, p. A9.
88. "U.S. vs. Them: American Economy Offers a Model Others Both Envy and Fear," *WSJ*, 1/18/01, p. A1.
89. What Roger Cohen calls "the 'Americanization' of German memory, a fixation on the Holocaust that . . . excludes an abundantly rich cultural and political history and oversimplifies the twelve years of Nazism." Roger Cohen, "The Germans Want Their History Back," *NYT*, 9/12/99, sect. 4, p. 4.
90. Evans, "Anti-Semitism: Ordinary Germans and the 'Longest Hatred'," in *Rereading German History*, pp. 149–51; see also Fritz Stern, "The Goldhagen Controversy: One Nation, One People, One Theory?" *Foreign Affairs* (Nov./Dec. 1996), pp. 128–38; J. Hoberman, "When the Nazis Became Nudniks," *NYT*, 4/15/01, sect. 2, p. 13.
91. Holman W. Jenkins, Jr., "Nazi Slavery and the Politics of Business," *WSJ*, 12/29/99, p. A15; "Means of Atonement," *WSJ* editorial, 5/22/00, p. A38.
92. Barnaby J. Feder, "Lawsuit Says I.B.M. Aided the Nazis in Technology," *NYT*, 2/11/01, sect. 1, p. 47; see Edwin Black, *IBM and the Holocaust* (New York, 2001).

93. "Lawyers [who] know how to milk the spirit of the times [by] naming 'villains' and shuffling eye-popping sums around." Gabriel Schoenfeld, "The New Holocaust Profiteers," *WSJ*, 4/11/01, p. A18.
94. Jenkins, "Nazi Slavery and the Politics of Business," p. A15. Cf. Norman G. Finkelstein, *The Holocaust Industry: Reflections on the Exploitation of Jewish Suffering* (New York, 2000), chap. 2: "Hoaxers, Hucksters, and History." On the controversy within the American Jewish community, cf. Seth Lipsky, "The Strange Politics of Holocaust Restitution," *WSJ*, 9/13/00, p. A26.
95. Cf. Neal E. Boudette, "Seeking Reparation: A Holocaust Claim Cuts to the Heart of the New Germany," *WSJ*, 3/29/02, pp. A1, 8.
96. Ardagh, *Germany and the Germans*, pp. 541–42. "Realo" Greens, like Prime Minister Joschka Fischer, rather take a compromising stand, joining government in the pursuit of high environmental but not punishing utopian goals.
97. See chap. 7.
98. Roger Cohen, "Israel's Ties With Germany Elude U.S. Jews," *NYT*, 3/4/01, sect. 1, pp. 1, 10.
99. William Boston and Roger Thurow, "A Woman's Journey from Terrorism to Repentant Survivor," *WSJ*, 1/11/01, pp. A1, 8. On Luther's civic ethic, chap. 3.
100. Roger Cohen, "Sending Kosovars Home," *NYT*, 11/20/00, p. A10.
101. Roger Cohen, "German Official Pessimistic About Far-Right Violence," *NYT on the Web*, 8/26/00. For a more jaundiced view of Fischer and fellow radical French prime minister Lionel Jospin ("typical examples of the center left's habits of accommodation to the radical left"), see "Genoa Under Siege," *WSJ*, editorial, 7/20/01, p. A10.
102. Roger Cohen, "German Faults 'Silence' About Attacks on Immigrants," *NYT* on the Web, 8/1/00.
103. Cohen, "Sending Kosovars Home."
104. Christopher Rhoads, "Behind the Crisis in Germany, a Past That Is Crippling," *WSJ*, 12/6/02, pp. A1, A12.

Index